Gender, War, and Militarism

Gender, War, and Militarism

Feminist Perspectives

LAURA SJOBERG AND SANDRA VIA, EDITORS

Foreword by Cynthia Enloe

PRAEGER SECURITY INTERNATIONAL

PRAEGER

AN IMPRINT OF ABC-CLIO, LLC
Santa Barbara, California • Denver, Colorado • Oxford, England

Library of Congress Cataloging-in-Publication Data

Gender, war, and militarism : feminist perspectives / Laura Sjoberg and Sandra
Via, editors ; foreword by Cynthia Enloe.
    p. cm. — (Praeger security international)
  Includes bibliographical references and index.
   ISBN 978-0-313-39143-9 (alk. paper) — ISBN 978-0-313-39144-6 (ebook)
1. Sex role. 2. Women and the military. 3. Women in war. 4. Violence in
women. I. Sjoberg, Laura, 1979–   II. Via, Sandra.
  HQ1075.G46686   2010
  303.6'6—dc22   2010014499

ISBN: 978-0-313-39143-9
EISBN: 978-0-313-39144-6

14 13 12 11 10   1 2 3 4 5

This book is also available on the World Wide Web as an eBook.
Visit www.abc-clio.com for details.

Praeger
An Imprint of ABC-CLIO, LLC

ABC-CLIO, LLC
130 Cremona Drive, P.O. Box 1911
Santa Barbara, California 93116-1911

This book is printed on acid-free paper ∞

Manufactured in the United States of America

Copyright Acknowledgments

We thank the following:

The journal *Race, Class, and Gender* (the University of New Orleans) for permission for an edited reprint of "Thinking Through Intersectionality and War," initially published in that journal, Volume 14, No. 3–4, pp. 10–27.

The *Journal of International Cooperation Studies* (Kobe University) for permission for an edited reprint of "Confronting Militarization: Struggles for Peace and Security by Pacific Island Women," by Ronni Alexander, originally published in Volume 16, Issue 1 of that journal.

McGill-Queen's University Press for permission to print an edited and redacted excerpt of Chapter 7, "Fighting the Feminine," pp. 112–129 of *Women in Zones of Conflict: Power and Resistance in Israel*, by Tami Amanda Jacoby, originally published by that press in 2005.

Sage, the publishers of *Politics and Society*, for permission to reprint a shortened and edited version of "Variation in Sexual Violence during War," by Elisabeth Jean Wood, originally printed in Volume 34, Issue 3 of that journal.

The University of Minnesota Press, for permission to reprint sections of the Afterword, "Drag King Dreams Deferred," pages 200–209, of *Citizen, Invert, Queer: Lesbianism and War in Early Twentieth Century Britain* by Deborah Cohler, originally published by that press in 2010.

to the teachers who inspired us
and the students who push us

Contents

.

Foreword

"Feminist perspectives." It's so easy to say but so hard to create. Laura Sjoberg and Sandra Via have managed to bring together in this one volume an amazingly diverse collection of investigatory writers who do just that: they consciously fashion a feminist lens through which to dissect, explain, and critique—all three—the political workings of masculinities and femininities in war zones, in military institutions, and in militarized cultures in prewar, wartime, and post-war eras.

Adopting an explicitly feminist perspective is not the same as choosing to look at something from a gender perspective. Certainly there is substantial overlap, but they are not coterminous. Sometimes a lot of us describe our analytical exploratory approach as from a "gender perspective" because, we imagine, that sounds to many of our listeners and readers less frightening, less radical, less political than from a "feminist perspective." After all, we want to be heard, we want to be taken seriously, so we don't want our potential listeners and readers to run in the other direction (or to avoid our conference panels, or never assign our articles, or deem us unworthy for tenure, or…). Substituting "gender" for "feminist" doesn't seem cowardly; it just seems prudent. And then, too, there are those occasions when we really are not aiming to fashion a feminist analysis. Creating a gender analysis can itself seem hard enough.

For gender, of course, is not always on everyone's mind. Nor is it something a lot of people want to consider. As these smart contributors show us, some of the most well-meaning people can forget about the daily workings of masculinity and femininity. Getting journalists, legislators, drill sergeants, human rights activists, and our academic colleagues to take seriously the constructing, sustaining, and challenging ideas about and standards for what it means to be "manly" and what behavior fits into the tight shoe of "real womanhood" is no mean feat.

"Gender" today is inserted into scores of states' and international agencies' mandates. Gender data should be collected, data should be disaggregated by gender, projects should be designed with gender impacts in mind, and programmatic evaluations should be gender explicit. Nonetheless, all of these formal insertions—each of which has taken surprising amounts of concerted effort by alliances of outsiders and insiders to get into even the small print—has not succeeded as yet to transform the consciousnesses of most people, chiefly, but not only men, who are supposed to be following these mandates. And we won't be able to adequately explain that gap between printed page and actual practice until we ask feminist questions.

Thus, as challenging as it still is to get gender taken seriously, the subtitle that Laura Sjoberg and Sandra Via have chosen for this valuable collection is not "gendered perspectives," but "feminist perspectives."

Thanks to the strenuous sleuthing of researchers such as those whose work we can read here, there has grown up an Andean range's worth of evidence that these gendered politics matter, that they shape policy makers' assumptions and aspirations, that they determine whose security it deemed salient and whose is shrugged off, and that they bolt the doors to the participation of some while laying out the welcoming mat to the participation of others.

That is, what makes these *chapters feminist is* that each author here is conscious of—and wants us to become aware of—the political stakes in, and implications of, ideas about manliness and femininity. And paying close attention to politics means keeping our eyes on power. To craft only a gender analysis *without* an accompanying (informing) feminist analysis is to turn away from the workings of power. Who gains from this hierarchy of masculinities in a given constellation of militarized organizations? Who loses if this stigma is attached to a woman reporting rape in that conflict? Who has a vested interest in treating women as naïve in that peace negotiation? Who gains a new sense of public confidence if "security" is redefined to include freedom from domestic violence? What sorts of rewards, threats, persuasion, or coercion have to be wielded to keep certain men in line and to keep most women silent? What strategies have some women effectively used to tip the balance of gendered power during wartime?

The answers here are not presumed. They are pursued. That means each of these researchers have had to place questions about power on their own agenda. A feminist perspective doesn't come naturally. It is arrived at, often by initially trying out other, more conventionally accepted perspectives and finding them wanting. These researchers have found those nonfeminist perspectives to leave too much in the shadows, to leave too much unexplained. That explanatory deficit is one of the chief motivators for starting to ask explicitly feminist questions in one's investigations.

Most notably, researchers such as those who have created this valuable volume have come to the shared conclusion that to adopt anything less than a consciously feminist perspective risks underestimating the amount and the varieties of power that it takes to prepare for militarized conflict, to wage and sustain militarized conflict, and to pick up the pieces in aftermath of violent conflict in such a way that leaves the militaristic culture undisturbed. As wide ranging as are the sites chosen by these contributing investigators, all of their examinations are fueled by an unwillingness to take that costly intellectual risk.

Cynthia Enloe

Acknowledgments

The genesis of this volume was at a wonderful conference hosted at the University of Pennsylvania with the same title as the book, "Gender, War, and Militarism." The conference, held October 25 and 26, 2007, was sponsored by the University of Pennsylvania's Alice Paul Center for Research on Women, Gender, and Sexuality and Penn's Women's Studies Program. Without the support of the Alice Paul Center and the Women's Studies Program at University of Pennsylvania, as well as other conference sponsors (the SAS Conference Fund, the Middle East Center, the Annenberg School, Greenfield Intercultural Center, the African Studies Center, the Penn Women's Center, the English Department, the LGBT Center, the Political Science Department, the History and Sociology Department, the Anthropology Department, Gloria Allred, and Andrea C. Roberts), this book would not exist. Shannon Lundeen, the Associate Director of the Alice Paul Center; Demie Kurz, the Co-Director of the Women's Studies Program and the Alice Paul Center; and Rita Barnard, the Faculty Director of the Women's Studies Program and the Alice Paul Center, each were integral in the initial intellectual formulations of this project. Conference participants who did not ultimately write chapters for the book, including Marie Gottschalk, Caren Kaplan, Catherine Lutz, Jennifer Terry, Inderpal Grewal, Firoozeh Kashani-Sabet, Nadje Al-Ali, Raka Ray, Ayako Kano, Elizabeth Hillman, Heather Sharkey, Julie Mostov, Ritty Lukose, David Eng, Dyan Mazurana, Katherine Sender, Victoria Bernal, David Kazanjian, Ariane Brunet, Dasa Duhacek, and Charlotte Bunch, are present in this volume in that their questions, comments, and discussion strengthened the chapters ultimately included in the volume.

We were able to do the work for this project because of the financial, institutional, and creative support of the Political Science Department at Virginia Polytechnic Institute and State University, the Women and Public Policy Program at the Kennedy School of Government at Harvard University, the Institute for Research on Women and Gender at the University of Michigan, and the Political Science Department at the University of Florida. We have enjoyed working with Steve Catalano and the team at Praeger Security International. A number of people have been careful readers and advisers over the course of this project, including (but certainly not limited to) the contributors: V. Spike Peterson, Stephanie Anderson, Sandra Via, Denise Horn, Ronni Alexander, Tami Jacoby, Susan Shepler, Sondra Hale, Liz Kelly, Elisabeth Jean Wood, Megan Gerecke, Catia Confortini, Gwyn Kirk, Sigal Ben-Porath, R. Charli Carpenter, and Deborah Cohler. We also appreciate the input of several colleagues, including Caron Gentry, Megan McKenzie, Julie Mertus, and several anonymous reviewers, as this project came to fruition. Ruchan Kaya had the unenviable task of struggling with the bibliography, for which we are grateful. Finally, one of Laura's undergraduate students, Justin Fisch, read the entire manuscript beginning to end in the 48 hours before its submission.

Sandra would first like to thank her coeditor and dissertation cochair, Laura Sjoberg, for providing continual guidance and support throughout the editing and dissertation process. While taking me under her wing, Laura graciously included me in this wonderful project and has been instrumental in my intellectual evolution. I currently have two professional homes: Virginia Tech and Ferrum College. At Virginia Tech, I have found guidance and advice, both as a student and as a scholar, from the faculty in the Department of Political Science, especially Tim Luke and Karen Hult, who have been beacons of inspiration through my academic and professional career. Ferrum College was my first intellectual home, and I am now privileged to be able to teach alongside the many professors who influenced my scholarly pursuits. In particular, I would never have moved forward with my career in academia if not for Frederic Torimiro, my mentor and now colleague.

Personally, I would like to thank my family for their continual love and support. They have endured my long and sometimes arduous journey to achieve my academic and professional goals. Several of my friends and colleagues have served as a sounding board for my excitement and at times frustration while working on this book and my dissertation—especially Sabrina Tribbett, Corrine Browell, Courtney Thomas, Martin Saavedra, Kerri-Anne Crawford, and Sarah Solari.

Laura would like to thank her coeditor and first official PhD student, Sandra Via, for the intellectual exchanges that went into this project and the fun we had along the way. Professionally, I have benefited greatly from the intellectual and professional support of a number of communities I have come to find indispensable: the Feminist Theory and Gender Studies section of the International Studies Association, the Western and North-eastern Regional Organizations of the International Studies Association, the Women's Caucus for International Studies, Women in Conflict Studies, and the Boston Consortium for Gender, Security, and Human Rights. For the first time in my book acknowledgments, there's not an outside employer that provided a hiding space from my real job at which I finished the book. Perhaps that's because I have finally found an institutional home that *is* my comfort zone/hiding space: the Political Science Department (and Women's Studies Program) at the University of Florida, particularly with the International Relations faculty: Badredine Aarfi, Sammy Barkin, Leann Brown, (Dean) Paul D'Anieri, Aida Hozic, Ana Margheritis, Richard Nolan, and Ido Oren. I am extremely lucky to have them as colleagues.

Personally, I am energized by a network of friendships and support stronger than anyone deserves, and sustained the final effort to complete this book in large part because of the support of several friends (old and new) who helped me relocate my scholarly voice—especially Amy Eckert, Lisa Burke, Jen Heeg Maruska, Caron Gentry, and Lloyd Taylor. Last, but certainly not least, each of my Chihuahuas displayed a different brand of militarism as I worked on this book: Max played the aggressive sentry, biting all who would come between me, him, and the laptop; Gizmo was all bark (and Chihuahua-mohawk) and no bite, but it was a fierce bark; and April was, as always, the model of silent but firm command.

Those of you who have read more than one of my books (thank you, by the way) know that my acknowledgments usually end with a negative experience that reminded me of my inspiration to do work in this field. This one happened at a job interview last year. I had given my talk about the gendered representations of women who commit wartime sex crimes and was fielding questions about my previous work on portrayals of women's violence and my next book project. Several members of the audience asked questions I get fairly frequently: "Do you think women's violence is a different problem from men's violence?" (no), "What do I think about individual agency in global politics?" (relational autonomy), "Have you done the empirical research for the new book yet?" (no then, and still no). And then comes the question I am still reeling over: "Is gender really a social construction, or is your belief that gender is a social construction just your way, as a woman, of compensating for the fact that women are biologically weaker than men?" While I resisted the urge to let the questioner know that I was pretty sure I was not the one who was compensating, the very existence (if not social acceptability) of the question provides a reminder that the work of feminist scholars is far from done.

Introduction

Laura Sjoberg and Sandra Via

During World War II, the United States' success in driving the Japanese out of Baguio, the mountainous summertime capital of the Philippines, was credited to the indigenous Igorot women led by "a wizened old lady," Aning Andao (Gray 1945). With Aning, "pretty young girls and a few pregnant matrons" went "where the bulldozers have not gone and the trucks cannot go," hauling supplies through gunfire, where "men dropped their loads and scattered; the women, undisturbed, plodded on in a long single file to the front" (Gray 1945).

Ayat Akras was a Palestinian political journalist who had lost two family friends in the conflict between Palestine and Israel (Victor 2003). One "was killed by Israeli soldiers while he was planting a bomb" (Rubin 2002, 16), and "the second was a child playing with Legos in his home" (Sjoberg and Gentry 2007, 80; Victor 2003, 206). Ayat promised that she was going to "fight instead of the sleeping Arab armies who are watching Palestinian girls fighting alone" right before martyring herself in a Jerusalem supermarket, killing 2 and injuring 29, in March of 2002 (Patkin 2004).

In April 1918, the *New York Times* announced Mrs. Lindley Z. Murray's establishment of the National Tennis Women's War Relief Association, established for women to play charity tennis matches around the United States to fund "maintaining feminine physicians as workers in France" ("Women Plan" 1918).

Etsumi Tarihori, "a gray-haired, frail-looking woman" in Okinawa "spends bone-chilling January nights in a sleeping bag on a sidewalk outside the entrance to the U.S. consulate" (Allen 2003). She engages in "a round-the-clock protest" of the U.S. war in Iraq and has led the Okinawan women's peace movement for years. As David Allen relates, "she's been there every Friday for 76 weeks as a protest against the U.S. military presence on Okinawa," inspired by an incident when a U.S. soldier raped a Japanese woman (Allen 2003).

Sgt. Steve William Lisette Peterson, a member of Britain's elite 16 Air Assault Brigade, "ran away from the Army in a desperate attempt to come to terms with his homosexuality" because "he feared being dismissed, and the reaction of his fellow soldiers if he told them about his sexuality" ("Gay Soldier" 2007). His commanding officers assured journalists that, since he told his fellow soldiers about his homosexuality, "there has been no reaction against him whatsoever," but Sgt. Peterson, aware of the many anti-gay policies and hate crimes in militaries around the world, had reason to be afraid ("Gay Soldier" 2007).

Tabitha, now 18, "runs a group for former girl soldiers, knitting and performing plays about their military lives" (McFerran 2007). She was 11 years old when she was abducted by the Sudanese People's Liberation Army (SPLA) with her older sister. Tabitha was beaten "uncountable" times, and her sister was forced to be a "wife" of an SPLA officer and was impregnated (McFerran 2007). Tabitha and her sister Anna learned to do as they were told, "or the consequences would be terrible" (McFerran 2007). Since they have been free of the SPLA, Tabitha reports that "for the former girl soldiers, any hope of a 'normal' life is problematic. After their time in the army, they are often considered unfeminine and aggressive, making them poor prospects as wives" (McFerran 2007). Tabitha runs a group for former girl soldiers because their needs as women are often more complicated than the needs addressed in the supposedly gender-neutral disarmament, demobilization, and reintegration (DDR) process.

Houston, Texas, resident Sybil Roberts had a nephew serving in the U.S. military in the Persian Gulf as it ejected Iraq from Kuwait in 1991. Sybil was "so angered by antiwar protesters at her door carrying petitions that she wrapped the columns on the porch of her...rowhouse with yellow satin, and planted a sign in her lawn that read 'we support our troops' on one side and 'down with protesting' on the other" (Stanley 1991). She argued that it was unpatriotic for women to protest against wars other women's sons were risking their lives to fight.

In 1998, amid intensifying Lebanese assaults on the Israel Defense Force's (IDF) Paamonit observation post coinciding with personnel cuts by the IDF, Gal, an Israeli woman soldier, was left to keep watch over southern Lebanon and northern Israel (Levinson 1998). Gal expressed worry about her own morale and that of her fellow soldiers in the face of increasing death tolls, explaining that "nobody wants to die and nobody wants to fight" (Levinson 1998).

Aning, Ayat, Lindley, Etsumi, Steve, Tabitha, Anna, Sybil, and Gal lived in different times, in different parts of the world, and through different conflicts. They also played different roles in those conflicts. Some were peace activists, like the better-known women at Greenham Common (Junor and Howse 1995) or of the Women's International League for Peace and Freedom (Bussey 1965). Others supported war efforts from home, much like the American World War II icon Rosie the Riveter (Colman 1998). Others provided logistical support and health care in battle-torn areas, comparable to Clara Barton and the Red Cross (Barton 1898). Still others were active participants—soldiers (Addis, Russo, and Sebesta 1994), members of rebel groups (Luciak 2001), or terrorists (Sjoberg and Gentry 2007).

What these nine people share—across time, place, culture, religion, and sex—is that they lived in (different) worlds where gendered militarism pervades social and political life. While gender relations and conflict in global politics have changed dramatically over the past century, war-making still relies on gendered constructions and images of the state, state militaries, and their role in the international system. These gendered ideologies and images, as well as heavily skewed national budgets devoted to military expenditures, make militarism a stronger and stronger force in global politics and everyday life.

GENDER

The conventional wisdom is that sex is a biological phenomenon—some people are biologically men and other people are biologically women.[1] Gender is assumed to be directly related to, and map onto, sex—men are masculine and women are feminine. Feminists, however "have questioned the conventional assumption that gender differences (and subordination) are rooted in biological differences between women and men" (Sjoberg 2006a, 32). Instead, feminists have argued that gender is social characteristics only *presumed* to be related to perceived membership in the biological categories of male and female. Characteristics traditionally associated with masculinity include strength, protection, rationality, aggression, public life, domination, and leadership. On the other hand, weakness, vulnerability, emotion, passivity, privacy, submission, and care have been traditionally associated with femininity.

The distinction between traits associated with masculinity and traits associated with femininity is not a value-neutral one. Instead, characteristics associated with masculinity are valued over characteristics associated with femininity in social and political life. Manliness is prized whereas femininity is undesirable. As such, to "*feminize* something or someone is to directly subordinate that person, political entity, or idea, because values perceived as feminine are lower on the social hierarchy than values perceived as neutral or masculine" (Sjoberg 2006a, 34). As Catherine MacKinnon (1993) has argued, "feminization is something that can happen to anyone. It is only that we assume it is natural to happen to people identified as women."

Even though gender is divisible into masculinities and femininities (definable as stereotypes, behavioral norms, expectations, and rules assigned to men and women), it does not follow that gender-based expectations for human behavior are constant across time and place. Instead, the content of gender categories changes over time, place, culture, religion, and a host of other factors. While "the exact content of genders shifts with various and shifting socio-political contexts, gender subordination (defined as the subordination of femininities to masculinities) remains a constant feature of social and political life across time and space" (Sjoberg and Gentry 2007, 6, citing Risman 2005). Social classification and treatment based on perceived membership in a gender class is called *gendering*. In global politics, gendering does not remain constant in content or result, but always involves assumed traits not on the basis of an individual's characteristics but instead on assumed group characteristics (Skapoulli 2004).

Genders, then, are sets of discourses that shape, construct, and give meaning to social and political life. The distinction that gender(s) are a set of discourses rather than one discourse indicates that genders are experienced differently in different contexts and cultures. Still, the fact that genders are variable, discursive, and socially constructed does not make them or their social implications any less real. Instead, "people live gender and gendering across time, space, and culture" (Stoller and Nielsen 2005). In this interpretation, expectations of behavior based on gender are "both a product and producer of history" (Connell 1995, 81).

Gender-based categorizations and expectations are evident in a number of the brief stories discussed at the beginning of this introduction. Tabitha tells a story of the difficulty she and other former child soldiers had in reintegrating into Sudanese society, because their military experiences made people perceive them as aggressive and unfeminine where women were expected to be passive and innocent. Sgt Peterson, on the other hand, struggled with the possible consequences of his not measuring up to specific expectations about what a (military) man should be. Ayat Akras, on the other hand, in explaining her choice to engage in self-martyrdom implies that she would not have to do so if Palestinian and other Arab men were fulfilling their obligations as men to protect Palestinian societies. Each of these stories either asserts or implies a set of expected standards for behavior based on gender that is socially expected of people assumed to be men or women.

WAR

A number of scholars have recognized that gender-based expectations of human behavior have long been central to narratives justifying or explaining wars (e.g., Huston 1983). Jean Elshtain (1987) identified that war histories are often told in terms of brave, selfless, "just warrior" men defending or saving pure, innocent, naïve "beautiful soul" women. For example, the Trojan War is often told in terms of a just warrior (Odysseus) saving a kidnapped, innocent woman (Helen) from her aggressive, foreign captor (Paris). One of the largest and most important wars in Greek mythology was fought for and over an innocent woman. Helen was at once the justification for the war and the innocent who needed saving from it—the *casus belli* and a civilian.

Feminist scholars have identified similar gender-based stories in the justificatory narratives for the World War I (Elshtain 1987, 6), the Cold War (Enloe 1989), the First Gulf War (Enloe 1993), the conflict in the former Yugoslavia (Zalewski 1995), the conflict between Russia and Chechnya (Sjoberg and Gentry 2007), and the "war on terror" in Afghanistan (Stabile and Kumar 2005) and Iraq (Eisenstein 2004). As Cynthia Enloe commented about the First Gulf War, "the U.S. intervention in the Gulf would be harder to justify if there were no feminized victim" (1993, 166). This is a sentiment Krista Hunt echoed about the United States' 2001 invasion of Afghanistan (2002).

Both gender relations and war have changed since the mythical Trojan War, and even since feminist scholars recognized and defined the gender-stereotypical content of the just warrior and beautiful soul tropes in the 1980s. Mary Kaldor coined the term "new wars," arguing that warfare in the 21st century is distinct from past wars in its goals, fighting methods, and sources of financing. The "new wars," according to Kaldor, are about identity politics, fought with gruesome violence, and they are more decentralized than war in the era of world wars between state actors (Kaldor 2006, 6–10). They are, instead of purely interstate conflicts, "a mixture of war, organized crime, and massive violations of human rights. The actors are both global and local, public and private" (Kaldor 2006, 12).

At the same time wars have been changing, gender roles *in wars* have been changing. For example, women have always played some (generally unacknowledged) role in the making and fighting of wars, but women's representation in state militaries (Addis, Russo, and Sebestia 1994), guerilla groups (Luciak 2001), and terrorist organizations (Sjoberg and Gentry 2007; Alison 2009) has increased exponentially in recent years. Though they remain a minority in all of these organizations and are often prohibited from taking on certain roles of leadership or direct combat, women have been more active in the "new" wars of the 21st century than in any documented time throughout history.

At the same time women have been de facto integrated into war fighting in the post–Cold War era, attention to the impacts of armed conflict on women and girls has increased in the policy world. For example, United Nations Security Council Resolution 1325 mandates that women participate in the making and keeping of peace in the international arena. The adoption of such a policy[2] represents both symbolic and actual progress in redressing gender inequities around the world. Still, armed conflict rages around the world, and women are disproportionately affected by the making and fighting of wars.

It remains a puzzle to some scholars and policy makers why the situation of women around the world is not improving exponentially with their integration into war fighting and the proliferation of policies meant to protect them. Feminist scholars have argued that the disconnect between woman-friendly policies and results in women's lives is twofold. First, although women are being included in different areas of global politics with greater frequency, their needs *as women* often remain unconsidered and unaddressed. In other words, women are being integrated into a world that remains defined and shaped by men's interests and needs. Second, attempts to better the situation of women often do not pay attention to the gendered nature of the structures of government and economics that remain in place even when women are formally included.

In no area of global politics are these problems more evident than in the realm of armed conflict. More than 20 years ago, Betty Reardon (1985) identified the "war system," a cycle of violence that at once relies on and perpetuates the oppression of women. Many feminist scholars have observed the continuity of gender subordination in the realm of war and conflict. Women's needs *as women* are often not understood in international conflict. For example, for the first years of the United Nations sanctions regime on Iraq, Iraqi women had difficulty finding ways to buy prenatal vitamins and baby milk on the black market because they were not seen as basic needs and exempted from the embargo (Vickers 1993). The second point, the gendered nature of the structures that remain in place from before women's integration, is equally challenging. Cynthia Enloe pointed out that women's integration into state and other military groups does not change the gender basis of those groups' identities and expectations (2000). In other words, women who join war fighting and peacemaking do not do so in armies or negotiations that are suddenly gender neutral because they are willing to include women. Instead, they join groups whose terms, premises, and behavioral norms are already defined in terms of the masculine values that they have prized before the inclusion of women.

These gender-based difficulties about the nature and structure of war can also be found in the earlier stories. Tabitha needed to create a program to take care of the needs of former girl soldiers because the supposedly gender-neutral DDR process did not take account of the social challenges that women as women faced in reintegrating into normal social life. Sybil Roberts struggled with the question of whether women's gender roles affect how they could or should think about the First Gulf War.[3] The reporter who wrote about Etsumi Tarihori featured both her age and her gender in dramatizing her protests against the war in Iraq. Tarihori's involvement in protesting the war in Iraq was not directly gender related, but she'd become involved in the Okinawan peace movement because of a gender-based concern: rape committed by soldiers stationed in Okinawa.

MILITARISM

Though war is an essential condition of militarism—the apex, the climax, the peak experience, the point of all the investments, training, and preparation—militarism is much, much broader than war, comprising an underlying system of institutions, practices, values, and cultures. Militarism is the extension of war-related, war-preparatory, and war-based meanings and activities outside of "war proper" and into social and political life more generally. Peterson and Runyan (1999, 258) explain that "militarization refers to processes by which characteristically military practices are extended into the civilian arena—as when businesses become dependent on military contracts, clothing fashions celebrate military styles, or toys and games embody military activities." Peterson and Runyan's definition captures an important part of militarism, but a conceptual extension helps us see its pervasiveness. Instead of envisioning militarism as the extension of military practices into civilian life, it is possible to see it as the blurring or erasure of distinctions between war and peace, military and civilian.

Scholars cognizant of the impacts of war and militarism on women, like Betty Reardon who is cited earlier, have always argued that the artificial construction of boundaries between "war" (one day) and "not war" (the next day) do not represent the political realities or the humanitarian situations in conflict zones. Instead, as Chris Cuomo (1996, 31) has explained, war is best seen as a process or continuum rather than a discrete event. Where an event has a starting point and an ending point, militarism pervades societies (sometimes with more intensity and sometimes with less) before, during, and after the discrete event that the word "war" is usually used to describe. Because of this, "the spatial metaphors used to refer to war as a separate, bounded sphere indicate assumptions that war is a realm of human activity vastly removed from normal human life" (Cuomo 1996, 30).

Instead, many scholars have argued, war and militarization are a part of what has come to be normal human life. Militarism is pervasive in the political operations of states and the daily lives of people all around the world. As shown earlier, Ayat Akras grew up knowing only conflict between Israel and Palestine. Tabitha and Anna were abducted by a rebel fighting force before they were teenagers. Lindley Murray militarized exhibition tennis matches. Etsumi Tahihori's story is one of struggle with the impact of the presence of a foreign military base in her country. Sgt. Peterson's military career is the source of much of his anxiety about whether he can safely "come out" as a homosexual man or not. Gal sits, daily, alone with her gun, in a dangerous outpost looking over a volatile place in the conflict between Israel and Lebanon. Sybil Roberts feels the impact of militarization on her family—both as she embraces her nephew and supports the war for him.

Feminists have pointed out that this militarism that pervades global politics is not gender neutral, "natural or automatic" (Enloe 1993, 246). As Cynthia Enloe has explained, "militarization occurs because some people's fears are allowed to be heard, while other people's fears are trivialized and silenced" (1993, 246). Specifically, "the militarization of any nationalist movement occurs through the gendered workings of power" (Enloe 1993, 246). In the gendered process of militarization, "men are under constant pressure to prove their manhood by being tough, adversarial, and aggressive....In one highly legitimated and organized institution within most societies, men not only can, but—to be successful—*must* prove their masculinity" (Peterson and Runyan 1999, 118). This institution is the military, where the functioning of the military-industrial or military-civilian[4] complex needs men to be willing to kill and die on behalf of their state to prove their manhood *and* "women to behave *as the gender women*" (Enloe 1983, 212, emphasis added). In other words, "women must be properly subservient to meet the needs of militaries" (Peterson and Runyan 1999, 118).

The impacts of militarization on women's lives have been demonstrated in the lives of Korean camptown prostitutes (Moon 1998), immigrant domestic workers in Malaysia (Chin 1998), women soldiers in the First Gulf War (Enloe 1998), the U.S. military women accused of prison abuse at Abu Ghraib (Sjoberg 2007), the Sri Lankan tourism industry (Enloe 1989), and many other places around the world. Militarization is gendered in its aims (competitive power-over), its means (the military industrial complex), its language (of strength and domination), and its impacts (which disproportionately and negatively affect women).

A closer look at some of the brief stories that open this chapter show the intersection of gender, war, and militarism. Sgt. Peterson's concern about living up to ideal/typical images of (straight) militarized masculinity can be seen as intimately related to the gender relationships involved in war-justificatory narratives and the structured set of gender-role rules required to sustain militarism even in times where there are not immediate security threats to the nation housing the military in question. The undertones of the *Time* magazine journalist's report about Aning and her fellow Irogot women are all about gender and militarism. The descriptions of the "wizened old lady" with "pretty young girls and a few pregnant matrons" highlight the oddity of seeing women active in a war zone, even if they are doing tasks very similar to the work they would have been doing if a war were not being fought in their midst. Also, the author makes a point of highlighting that the women carried more, made more trips, and were less easily distracted than the men employed to transport goods to the troops in the mountains, implying at once that there was a deficit in militarized masculinity and that women were better at the "women's work" of moving supplies while men were better suited for the fighting going on at the top of the mountain. The battle of Baguio, according to Gray, required both men and women to win—but both needed to be fulfilling their traditional gender roles. In these stories, as in the situations analyzed throughout this book, gender, war, and militarism are inscribed on individuals' lives and on the larger picture of global politics and global conflict.

FEMINIST APPROACHES

Certainly, the term "feminism" has many meanings—at least as many meanings as it has claimants, speakers, and writers.[5] Just as there are many different women and many different femininities, there are many different feminisms. The contributors to this book do not always share the same definition of feminism or the same interpretation of gender. They do, however, share some epistemological and methodological commitments that make them "feminist approaches" and connect them for the purpose of this volume.

The first commitment these chapters share is some sense of the *function* if not the *content* of feminism. Spike Peterson (1999, 37) described a need for gender-based analysis: "if all experience is gendered, analysis of gender identities is an imperative starting point for the study of political identities and practice." The function of feminist theory, in this description, is to provide empirical information about how the world works that would not be available without using gender as a category of analysis. Feminists claim that we know more about global politics when we ask questions about women and gender. Sarah Brown (1988, 472) points out a second element of feminist scholarship: that it is "fundamentally a political act of commitment to understanding the world from the perspective of the socially subjugated." Putting these elements together, we can describe the function of feminism as "a political theory that coexists with and interacts with a political movement dedicated to eradicating the problems that women experience because of their sex" (Sjoberg 2006a, 43; Ruddick 1989, 234). The chapters in this book theorize about politics and politicize theory.

The second commitment these chapters share is a way of asking questions. Feminist scholars in International Relations (IR) have often described their commonalities in terms of looking through gendered lenses. Jill Steans details:

To look at the world through gender lenses is to focus on gender as a particular kind of power relation, or to trace out the ways in which gender is central to understanding international processes. Gender lenses also focus on the everyday experiences of women as *women* and highlight the consequences of their unequal social position. (Steans 1998, 5)

Lenses serve as filters "to foreground some things and background others" in political theory and political life (Peterson and Runyan 1999, 1).

These chapters share foregrounding concerns that come from gendered personal experiences of people who live gender, war, and militarism intermeshed with gender-aware readings of state- and system-level problems in global politics.

Finally, the feminist approaches in this volume share an understanding that the gendered system of war and militarism that the authors study individually and collectively is, though it is pervasive and far-reaching, ultimately fungible. Many of the disciplines the writers in this volume are rooted in describe this sort of theoretical perspective differently. In political science, our disciplinary home, Robert Cox (1986) laid out the distinction between problem solving and critical theory. Problem-solving theory studies the world *as it is* without asking questions about the normative content of that world or its potential for change. Critical theory, on the other hand, engages in the dual task of considering what is wrong with the world *and acting* to correct those wrongs. In those terms, the feminist project is critical theory: the feminist approaches in this book look at the intersections of gender, war, and militarism with a normatively critical eye, looking for possible alternatives that are better for the individuals they study and the global political arena as a whole.

GENDER, WAR, AND MILITARISM: FEMINIST APPROACHES

The feminist approaches in this volume look at two interconnected issues in the complex matrix of gender, war, and militarism: the impacts of war and militarism on people (especially but not limited to women) and the gendered construction of war and militarism, linked to systems of power and inequality based on race, class, nation, and so on.

Generally, investigating and assessing the impacts of war and militarism on women reveals that women are disproportionately affected by almost every aspect of the "war system" (Reardon 1985). Always masculinist endeavors, war and militarism have significant, distinctive, and heart-wrenching effects on women. Women are the majority of civilian casualties of war, before, during, and after the conflict. They are the primary targets of those who use rape and forced pregnancy as weapons of war. They make up the majority of refugees displaced from homes, farms, and sources of livelihood. Women also experience hardship and discrimination as members of state militaries and insurgent groups, which often replicate and exaggerate social inequalities.

Examining the gendered construction of war and militarism includes explorations of how militarism requires and produces gender inequality; how militarism generates gendered roles, ideologies, and expectations in times of war and conflict; the ways media outlets deploy gender in reporting and generating support for war; and the gendered elements of post-conflict reconstruction. These analyses show that gender is a linchpin not only of how war and militarism affect people but also of the very existence of the war system.

Seventeen chapters in five sections focus on gender, war, and militarism, varying "hot spots" of recent or current conflict: Bosnia, El Salvador, Iraq, Israel, Sierra Leone, Sudan, the Pacific Islands, the European Union (EU), and the United States. These analyses reveal that, although it takes different forms, gendering is a constant feature of 21st-century militarism.

The book opens with Section I, "Gender, Militarization, and Security," which features chapters exploring the conceptual relationships between gender, war, and militarism. V. Spike Peterson demonstrates that "thinking through intersectionality" allows us to see that militarism in the 21st century as intimately related to a presumption of heteronormative hypermasculinity, where not only women but minorities and other men who do not meet idealized images of the just warrior are devalorized through feminization. Stephanie Anderson explores the salience of feminization at the state level, as her chapter explains the EU's need to build a (redundant and ineffectual) military structure in terms of attempting to shed a feminized (and therefore devalorized) image as a soft power in international politics. In Chapter 3, Sandra Via explores the interplay of economic globalization and globalized militarisms, showing that the neoliberal ideology that permeates many of the processes of globalization reifies gendered ideas about war and militarism.

With these conceptual frameworks laid out, Section II turns to examining how gendered understandings of war and militarism are deployed in times of conflict. Denise Horn, in her chapter, "Boots and Bedsheets: Constructing the Military Support System in a Time of War," explores past and current strategies used by the U.S. military to inculcate loyalty among military spouses as a concerted strategy of indoctrination and control to maintain troop loyalty in the field. Studying intersections of gender(ed) violence, militarization, and resistance worlds away in a conflict in the pacific island of Bougainville, Ronni Alexander demonstrates that militarization has been used as a tool for the cultural governance of identity and maintenance of gender stratification. Tami Jacoby's Chapter 6 begins by looking at how women are affected by and react to militarism and then turns to women's participation in the structures of militarized violence. Jacoby explores the battle in Israel for women's "right to fight," which has become a key issue in advocacy for women's legal equality of opportunity there. Building on a tradition of feminist theory that analyzes "full citizenship" as connected to the image of a citizen-warrior willing to take up arms for his (or, in this case, her) state, Jacoby weaves a complicated web of feminist theory, women's peace activism, and intransigent conflict to analyze arguments for women's right to fight in the Israeli defense force. The women (and girls) in Susan Shepler's chapter, on the other hand, need to define what life is like after fighting for soldiers, some of whom fought willingly, many more of whom were abducted or forced into military

service. The tale Shepler tells of sex, violence, discrimination, and heart-
ache for girls associated with the fighting forces in Sierra Leone shows the
complexity and intricacy of the interweavings of gender, war, and militarism in conflict situations.

Section III moves from the deployment of gender in times of conflict to
analyses of a gender-specific weapon of war: rape. As the authors of this
section explain, wartime rape is something that happens almost exclusively to people of the female sex, and exclusively to people feminized by
their enemies. Sondra Hale tells of rape as at once a cultural identifier, an
erasure of cultural difference, and a tool of cultural destruction in the ethnocidal conflicts in Darfur and the Nuba Mountains in Sudan. Chapters
by Elisabeth Jean Wood and Megan Gerecke look to explain motivations
for and variations in wartime rape over different conflicts and different
times. Inspired by the World War II rape narrative *A Woman in Berlin,* Liz
Kelly argues for a continuum approach to sexual violence and war, where,
instead of separating (normal) rape and wartime rape, war and peace,
scholars and legal experts could look at a continuum of sexual violence
transposed onto a continuum of global conflict to see the links between
gender, war, and militarism in daily life and "high" politics.[6]

Section IV then moves from what happens in war to what happens in
the aftermath of war when war is seen as an event. These three chapters
show both the essential continuity of war and post-war militarism, as well
as some of the unique challenges of the processes of reconstruction, reconciliation, and peacemaking for women. In Chapter 12, Catia Confortini
examines the Women's International League for Peace and Freedom and its
efforts to address and transform the issue of disarmament into an ongoing
women's peace movement. In Gwyn Kirk's chapter, aptly titled "When Is
War Over?," the author explores women's stories of healing and rebuilding after the war in El Salvador to critically question the inherited notion
of the war as an event with a clean start and ending and to show the disproportionate effects of the conflict (before, during, and after) on women.
Sigal Ben-Porath looks through gendered lenses at the process and meaning of post-conflict forgiveness, reconciliation, and trust-building.

The fifth and final section, "Texts and Contexts for Gender, War, and
Militarism," analyses texts surrounding gender, war, and militarism for
what they tell us about the "real world" of war and the gendered portrayals of that world. In Chapter 15, R. Charli Carpenter demonstrates
that Bosnian "war babies" are represented in gendered ways in the global
print media. She recognizes three tropes in these stories: of the rapes as
part of an ethnic/nationalist conflict, of the raped women as victims of
childbirth, and of the babies as the product of an uncivilized culture in
need of neo-imperial humanitarian intervention. Examining a different set of texts a world away, Laura Sjoberg's Chapter 16 finds gendered
framings of idealized militarized masculinities and femininities in the U.S.
military in media presentations of the "hero stories" of four soldiers who

fought the "war on terror" in Afghanistan or Iraq. In Chapter 17, Deborah Cohler finds another set of narratives, where female masculinity, gay sex, and gay identities shaped and were shaped by the discourses of war, fear, and nationalist identity on the United States "homefront" in the "war on terror." Together, the chapters in the fifth section show the inseparability of representation and reality in the complex webs of gender, war, and militarism in the 21st century.

The volume concludes with reflections on what these accounts of gender, war, and militarism from five continents, numerous different contexts, and all stages of the war process tell us about the gendered nature of war and militarism amid "new wars" with "new" women fighters, transposed on age-old gender stereotypes and subordinations.

NOTES

1. This too is oversimplified, given that many people are neither classifiable as biologically male nor biologically female, but instead as transgendered, intersex, and so on.

2. And its replication around the world, in policies in the EU, the World Bank, the International Monetary fund, and the U.S. government.

3. Replicating the question of the gender gap, where scholars have observed that women throughout 20th-century warfare were more opposed to making and fighting wars than men were, though the "gender gap" narrowed as the century closed.

4. The military-industrial or military-civilian complex militarizes those who are not in uniform—civilians. The military-industrial complex organizes an economy and the production of goods around defense weapons, while also centralizing the occupations of civilians, such as engineers and scientists, around a corporate culture of defense (Peterson and Runyan 1999; Enloe 2007).

5. In common International Relations (IR) parlance alone, there's liberal feminist IR, constructivist feminist IR, critical feminist IR, postcolonial feminist IR, poststructuralist feminist IR, and postmodern feminist IR (Tickner and Sjoberg 2006).

6. High politics refers to the traditional sites of power in global politics, such as state governments and international organizations, as opposed to the "low" politics of everyday life with which most feminist work is concerned. Many of the chapters in this book serve as critiques of the continued interest in this dichotomy in IR and Security Studies.

PART I

Gender, Militarization, and Security

CHAPTER 1

Gendered Identities, Ideologies, and Practices in the Context of War and Militarism

V. Spike Peterson

In a recent article, Avtar Brah and Ann Phoenix (2004, 75) argue that "the need for understanding complexities posed by intersections of different axis of differentiation is as pressing today as it has always been." Exploring intersectionality in contexts of violence brings these complexities into sharp relief, in particular, when we consider "women" and marginalized masculinities in military organizations where heteronormative *hypermasculinity* is presumed. My chapter attempts to merge insights from feminist, queer, post-colonial, and critical race theories to "think through intersectionality" and apply the insights gained to problematics of militarization and war.[1]

I do so by presenting a discussion of intersectionality to make a case for understanding "feminization as devalorization." This entails a corollary privileging of masculinization that is paradigmatic in militarism and war. To forestall misunderstanding: I am *not* arguing for the primacy of "women's oppression" or the reduction of class and race to sex/gender relations. Rather than analyzing how different forms of subjection are produced, I am exploring how institutionalized hierarchies are *naturalized* by feminization and thus are effectively depoliticized. I understand this as one among a number of critical insights that can advance our analytical grasp of, and political responses to, *intersecting* oppressions of race/ethnicity, gender, class, and sexualities.

INTERSECTIONALITY AND FEMINIZATION AS DEVALORIZATION

For a variety of reasons elaborated elsewhere (Peterson 2005), I find the theory/practice emerging from feminist and critical race scholarship particularly fruitful for analyzing intersectionality. On the one hand, feminisms have transdisciplinary and complex analytical resources for investigating and theorizing about identity, difference, and structural hierarchies. On the other hand, differences among women have forced feminists (too often reluctantly and always uncomfortably) to reflect critically on the meaning of feminism, operations of power among women, the politics of representation, and the dangers of overgeneralizing. As one consequence, feminist scholarship has contributed to a richer understanding of analytics and politics, or theory and practice, as interdependent.

Key to this development is understanding gender as both an empirical and an analytical category. The former refers to the embodied and ostensibly biological binary of male–female sex difference. Understood empirically, gender can be deployed as a variable to investigate, for example, how women and men are differently affected by, and differently participate in, political and economic practices. This is the more familiar use of gender in contemporary research, especially in the social sciences. Analytical gender is less familiar; it refers to the signifying system of masculine–feminine differentiations that constitutes a governing code. The claim here is that gender pervades language and culture, systemically shaping not only who we are but also how we think and what we do. As historically constituted, the dichotomy of gender codes masculine qualities as oppositional to and more highly valued than feminine qualities. Understanding gender analytically then generates a crucial and transformative feminist insight: the (symbolic, discursive) *cultural* privileging of that which is identified with masculinity is key to naturalizing the (symbolic, discursive, cultural, corporeal, material, economic) *power* relations that constitute multiple forms of subjection. This knowledge allows for more adequately theorizing, and hence politicizing, intersectionality.

More specifically, feminist research documents the contingent and historical "normalization" of gender as a systemic code valorizing that which is characterized and privileged as masculine (reason, agency, control, objectivity, etc.) at the expense of that which is stigmatized as feminine (emotion, passivity, uncertainty, subjectivity, etc.). Two points are key. First, gender is relational, so that *privileging who and what is masculinized is inextricable from devaluing who and what is feminized.* Recognizing the interdependence of masculinity and femininity—one "requires" the other—provides particular analytical leverage. It displaces the prevailing tendency to think gender is primarily about women, insisting instead that gender necessarily and invariably involves masculinity as much as femininity. Similarly, it reminds us that gender is systemic, so that manifestations of gender are less individual "choices" than effects of institutionalized codes, norms, and rules. Second, the *privileging of masculinity does not privilege all men or only men*. The claim is rather that gender—with its lauded masculinity and denigrated femininity—pervades language and culture and devalorizes *all* feminized statuses. The more an individual or a social category is feminized, the more likely (not invariably) that its devaluation is assumed, or presumed to be "explained." In short, diverse hierarchies are linked and ideologically "naturalized" by *feminizing* those who are subordinated. I understand this insight as key both to advancing intersectional analysis and "bridging" the cultural (symbolic, discursive) versus economic (material, structural) divide that continues to handicap social theory.

The insight involves several interactive moves. In one sense, casting the subordinated as feminine devalorizes not only the empirical gender category of women but also sexually, racially, culturally, and economically marginalized men (e.g., "lazy migrants," "primitive natives," "effeminate gays"). Underpinning this claim is the observation that although structural hierarchies vary by reference to the "difference" emphasized and the modalities of power involved, they typically share a common feature: the denigration of feminized qualities attributed to those who are subordinated (lacking reason, agency, control, etc.). Invoking the "natural" inferiority of the feminine plays a powerful, though not exhaustive, role in legitimating these hierarchies.

In a second sense, and understanding gender analytically, not only subjects (women and marginalized men) but also concepts, desires, tastes, styles, "ways of knowing," cultural expressions (art, music), roles, practices, work, nature, and so on can be feminized—with the effect of reducing their legitimacy, status, and value. Importantly, this devalorization is simultaneously ideological (discursive, cultural) *and* material (structural, economic). Consider how what is considered women's work—whether done by women or marginalized men—is typically underpaid, or frequently not paid at all; and we hardly notice, in part because the depreciation of feminized activities is so taken for granted. This devalorization normalizes—with the effect of legitimating—the marginalization, subordination, and exploitation of feminized practices and persons.

Oppressions differ, as do attempts to explain and/or justify them. As Wendy Brown (1997, 86–87) states, "not simply the content but the modalities of power producing gender, race, or caste are specific to each production," even though "these powers of subject formation are not separable in the subject itself." Because oppressions take various structural forms, feminization is not the only "normalizing" ideology in operation. What distinguishes feminization and renders it so ideologically powerful is the unique extent to which it invokes a deeply internalized and naturalized binary—the essentialized concept of sex difference—which is then available to naturalize diverse forms of structural oppression.

This warrants clarification. Even as sex and gender are increasingly ambiguous to some, most people most of the time take a categorical, essentialized distinction between male and female completely for granted: as biologically given, reproductively necessary, and psychosocially obvious. Yet constructionists argue not only that sex difference itself is *produced*—through contingent, historical practices and institutionalizations—but also that sex difference as an essentialized binary and masculinism as a system of asymmetrical power are *co-constituted*. In other words, the deeply sedimented concept of sex difference and historically institutionalized practices of gender hierarchy are mutually constituted. As one effect, the naturalness of sex difference is generalized to the naturalness of masculine (not necessarily male) privilege, so that both aspects come to be taken-for-granted givens of social life. Common sense becomes a two-pronged justification of hierarchy. On the one hand, subordinated individuals or groups are devalorized by feminization; depictions range from lack of capacity and being weak or irrational to being offensive or posing a danger. On the other hand, responding appropriately to such individuals or groups requires masculinized practices; these range from patronizing and protectionist behaviors to disciplinary measures and violent coercion. In short, not only are the subordinated devalorized by feminization, but the qualities they supposedly lack are typically just what the dominating (masculinized) group has to offer, or is compelled to practice. This conveniently justifies both the necessity of rule and who should rule.

The common sense of privileging the masculine and devaluing the feminine is culturally and collectively internalized to such an extent that we are all variously complicit in its reproduction. And it is also implicitly and explicitly manipulated to reproduce inequalities as if this were natural and inevitable, thus making critique and resistance difficult. In short, devalorizing the feminine *produces even as it obscures* vast inequalities of power, authority, and resource distribution. Exposing how this power operates must be one objective of a critical political agenda.

I argue that the *transformative* potential of feminist critique lies in exposing and subverting *all* hierarchies that rely on denigration of "the feminine" to normalize and depoliticize subjection. I am not arguing that gender hierarchy is the "primary" oppression overshadowing race or class or sexuality. The point is rather that gender hierarchy and its elevation of "masculinity" is a historically contingent *structural* feature of social relations, that the subordination of women is not reducible to other structural oppressions (or vice versa), and that the dichotomy of gender underpins—as the denigration of the feminine naturalizes—hierarchies of gender, class, race, sexualities, and geopolitical "difference."

Because forms of subjection differ structurally, systematic and comparative analyses of race class, gender, and sexuality require attention to "different histories, different mechanisms and sites of power, different discursive formations, different regulatory schemes" (Brown 1997, 86). In this chapter, however, my focus is less on the production of subjection than on the exposure of the political work that collective and internalized gender coding does across multiple forms of subjection. I am not presuming that sexist oppression is the most salient or powerful hierarchy in any particular context; I *am* arguing that investigating feminization as devalorization allows a broader understanding of how oppressions are naturalized and provides us with greater analytical/political leverage. Although this is only one among a number of critical insights to be expanded and applied,[2] I consider it a particularly productive vantage point, especially in relation to militarization and war.

INTERSECTIONALITY IN MILITARIZATION AND WARS

In a recent volume, Hunt and Rygiel (2006b, 3) develop the concept of "(en)gendering" war to "disrupt and make visible the masculinized, militarized, racialized, sexualized, and classed dynamics through which war operates." They argue that official war stories do political work: they camouflage interests, agendas, and politics that underpin war for the purpose of legitimating and gaining support for militarization. A crucial aspect of their effectiveness is the extent to which they depend on gendered ideologies (masculinization and feminization) that are naturalized and therefore go unnoticed (2006, 5). By going unnoticed ideologies are depoliticized, even as the identities and practices they mobilize profoundly affect politics. In the remainder of the chapter I explore how feminization accomplishes typically unnoticed political work in war stories.

The most familiar theme in war stories involves constructing the enemy as "other": to distinguish "us" from "them," render others in some sense inferior, and thereby justify war's violence against "them." The specifics of othering vary by history and context but invariably involve some form of objectification so that "they" become objects to which norms of respect and non-violation need not be extended. Historical othering ranges from early Greeks characterizing Persians as effeminate to Christians casting nonbelievers as immoral to Europeans depicting "natives" as uncivilized. Thinking through how othering occurs in nationalist, colonial, and contemporary war stories reveals gendered identity investments and ideologies in operation.

Critics of European imperialism have produced a wealth of research documenting the manipulation of ideologies to justify colonial wars and obscure their racist, economic, and heteronormative dynamics.[3] What surfaces repeatedly are characterizations of the colonized as feminine: weak, passive, irrational, disorderly, unpredictable, lacking self-control, and economically and politically incompetent. European power wielders (not only men or all men) could then justify military interventions by casting themselves in favorable masculinist terms: as uniquely rational, sexually and morally respectable, and more advanced economically and politically. In colonial wars and geopolitical maneuvering, "civilization" became a code word for European superiority. Through this lens, military interventions were perhaps a regrettable but nonetheless a necessary component of "enlightening" and "civilizing" primitive, unruly (feminized) "others." As

Eisenstein (2004, 75) observes, although they extolled the virtues of reason as a progressive force, Europeans positioned rationality "against savagery (natives), emotionality (women), and sexuality (racialized others)."

At the same time—and complicating simplistic models of gender—the development of European nationalism and normalization of bourgeois respectability produced an idealized model of femininity: pure, dutiful, and maternal. This superficial valorization of femininity is contradicted by the practices it invoked. Romanticizing the maternal feminine did less to empower women than render them perpetual dependents. Feminine virtue and morality were best ensured by confining these qualities—and (bourgeois) women—to a private sphere of domesticity and assigning men the public-sphere responsibility of defending and protecting feminized dependents. Rather than empowering European women, the idealization of bourgeois (heteronormative) femininity became a tool for disempowering non-European men. The patronizing and protectionist logic of bourgeois norms provided imperial governments with a moral, and rational, justification for militarized colonization. In this war story, the barbarity of "other" men was proven by their (allegedly) oppressive treatment of women, and this demanded the rescue of victimized females by honorable, civilized men. In short, the protection of idealized femininity (to paraphrase Spivak's [1987] apt analysis) justified wars by white men to save brown women from brown men. The crusading rhetoric and protectionist logic obscured colonial government agendas, and it resurfaces with particular vengeance and new complexities in contemporary militarism and war.[4]

The U.S.–led "war on terror" exemplifies how identity investments, ideological commitments, and militarized practices interact. Some argue that George W. Bush's forceful response to the 9/11 bombings involved not only his outrage and claim to military leadership but also his desire to establish a hypermasculine image of himself *and* the United States. It is well-known that Bush had personal reasons for enhancing his militarist (manly) identity. He had avoided serving in Vietnam, was invested in the image of being a "guy's guy," and arguably hoped to redeem his father's failure to oust Saddam in the First Gulf War. For many Americans, the identity and power of the United States had been *feminized* by its defeat in Vietnam, made more humiliating by losing to a people stereotyped as ethnically/racially inferior. Feminization anxiety was also fueled by the increasing visibility of women in politics and the workplace and the growing strength of LGBT (lesbian, gay, bisexual, and transgender) political movements.

A yearning to remasculinize the nation (Jeffords 1989) was already present and readily tapped by Bush and his advisers as the nation responded to 9/11 and its spectacular demonstration of U.S. vulnerability to penetration by foreign men. The war story the Bush administration immediately cultivated featured fanatical terrorists inexplicably committed to destroying freedom, democracy, and (implicitly Western) civilization by any means. Enemies this irrational and unpredictable could only be defeated by drawing an absolute line between good and evil and adopting the strongest possible measures to eliminate those deemed evil. Feminization operates here to construct enemies as so absolutely different from "us" that the only viable strategy is their annihilation.

Those who were fearful, were skeptical, or actively opposed Bush's strategies were rendered unequivocally suspect—unpatriotic, anti-American, naively (irrationally) out of touch, or quite simply unmanly (lacking the guts to do what must be done). In this instance, feminization operates to deny absolutely the rationality of dissenters or any cogent reasons for critique. Dissenters are simply and irredeemably discredited: unwilling to stand up for their country, ungratefully abandoning the United States and freeloading on its military power, and/or failing to grasp real-world politics. Those seeking debate and diplomacy are feminized—cast as behaving like cowardly women *and* undermining U.S. interests by wimping out of military action. In effect, dissidents become a less stark but ultimately an equally threatening enemy: "If you're not with us, you're against us." And as enemies, those who are against us lose any claim to inclusion, respect, or (apparently) rights.

Investments in gendered identities and commitments to masculinist ideologies mattered for initiating the "war on terror," and they also matter within processes of militarization. Militaries, of course, are quintessential sites of hypermasculinity. Success in war is presumed to demand a constellation of qualities long considered the exclusive province of men: superior physical strength, incomparable male bonding, heroic risk taking, extremes of violence, and readiness to sacrifice one's life for the cause. Historically, military service afforded decisive proof of manhood and constituted a claim to citizenship. The identities and ideals of military service continue to inform recruitment and enlistment, with the increasingly crucial addition of economic incentives. Masculinist qualities remain key to military life but are complicated in today's services by a variety of differences among men (by ethnicity, race, religion, class, skills) and by the inclusion of women.

Within militaries, multiple masculinities are differently mobilized in pursuit of warring objectives.[5] More physically powerful and hypermasculine men are valued but subordinated to orders from above; commanding officers, with their presumed leadership competence, enjoy higher prestige and less ambivalent valorization. Increasing reliance on advanced technologies prompts new masculinities. While desk jobs that distance soldiers from the battle front were previously feminized, computer specialists and high-tech operators today are increasingly valorized (Blanchard 2003). If we consider the education and training required for these positions, classed and raced dimensions of masculinities come into view. Indeed, the techno-war paradigm of the U.S. military presents a new version of Western superiority: high-tech sophistication, efficiency, and awesome power.

Intersectional analysis is particularly complicated by the increasing numbers of women in military service, who face conflicting expectations and manipulations of their femininity, masculinity, and sexuality.[6] The effects of women's inclusion are variously interpreted, and there are no easy conclusions. Some analysts argue that women's presence humanizes and democratizes militaries—perhaps even rendering them less masculinist. Others are less optimistic. Given traditional expectations of virile, aggressive hypermasculinity, militaries are treacherous places for anyone who is feminized. Women especially—but not exclusively—are at risk. However much female soldiers struggle to prove and sustain their identification as sufficiently masculine, institutionalized patterns of male supremacy and sexual violence undermine their efforts. Lack of structural equality (and respect) between men and women in everyday life, enduring stereotypes of female dependence and physical inferiority, the embodiment of sex difference (menstruation, pregnancy), and the objectification of women as sexual targets interact to pose multiple threats to military women.[7] These are in addition to the dangers they face as soldiers in war zones.

Whether or not the presence of women humanizes militaries, the presumed femininity of women soldiers (contradicting the masculinism demanded of them) is variously manipulated in support of military objectives. The U.S.–led Operation Iraqi Freedom provides stunning examples of how the femininity, masculinity, and sexuality of female soldiers can be mobilized. The images from these war stories are familiar, but the gender, racial, and geopolitical politics underpinning them have largely gone unnoticed in public discourse.

For instance, soon after the invasion of Iraq, the March 2003 capture of U.S. Army Private Jessica Lynch and her subsequent rescue was a major media event. While initial reports praised her soldiering in the face of enemy fire, these were quickly overshadowed by feminizing her plight: a white woman supposedly subject to rape by Arab men *had* to be spectacularly rescued. The story worked to reproduce the virtue and vulnerability of (white) womanhood, the demonization of Iraqi men, and the heroic efforts of U.S. Special Forces to "save" her from presumed abuse. Equally important, the story also served Bush's military agenda by diverting attention from the increasingly visible Iraqi resistance, the flaws in U.S. policy and preparedness, and the larger questions these raised.

When accounts of abuse, rape, and torture of prisoners in the Abu Ghraib prison surfaced in late 2003, European and American audiences especially were shocked by the photos that were broadcast worldwide. There was the shock of viewing graphic abuse and the shame of coalition ("civilized") soldiers as perpetrators. But most disturbing were photos of American *women* torturing Arab *men*. The official war story blamed "a few bad apples," thus avoiding more critical interrogation of behaviors cultivated by militarism, valorized masculinism, and deteriorating security conditions in Iraq. Blaming the few was apparently persuasive to many in the United States, where identification as the "good guys" carries deep emotional investments and encourages collective amnesia about U.S. racism and military atrocities.

The initial outrage and political furor were quickly eclipsed by the (Western) media's focus not on the implications of torture and the reality of failing military policies but on the sensational photos. These were an easier story to "sell" and could serve multiple purposes. Several points warrant our notice. Fascination with the photos derived from many sources, variously generating repulsion and attraction. The pictures recalled images of Nazi concentration camps for some, and white voyeurism at racial lynchings for others. Even as they depicted abuse, the sexualized poses also eroticized domination. Goldstein (in Brittain 2006) observes that viewing a pyramid of exposed buttocks invited homoerotic arousal, whereas the presence of a grinning woman allayed any homosexual anxiety about that arousal.

As critiques of U.S. policies and calls for Secretary of Defense Donald Rumsfield's resignation intensified, the media focus shifted. At least 1,600 photos were made available for Congressional screening. Presumably there were more numerous images of men abusing men, yet these were displaced by a few photos featuring Lynndie England—a (white) woman—sexually humiliating (brown) men. England quickly became the focal point of condemnation. Details of England's personal life (early divorce, out-of-wedlock pregnancy, romance with an accused wife beater) effectively constructed her as a very "improper" woman who appeared to revel in doing "improper" things (Brittain 2006, 88).

For critics of the United States, the Abu Ghraib photos, and especially those of England, confirmed the moral hypocrisy of American righteousness. The United States—not alone but most blatantly—was prosecuting a deadly war in the absence of (rational?) foresight and planning, and on the basis of faulty intelligence that was increasingly exposed as willful misrepresentations. It was snubbing its nose at (civilized?) international law and human rights conventions, while claiming moral superiority and a crusading protectionist commitment to freedom and democracy. And the arrogance displayed in the photos was demoralizing to all who identified with the Islamic faith and/or sympathized with embattled Iraqis. The damage to U.S. credibility and national interests—including the security of its soldiers and the safety of its homeland—was inestimable. Some feared, others hoped, that the scandal of Abu Ghraib would bring down the Bush administration and prompt a reassessment of the war in Iraq. Instead, Bush staunchly defended Rumsfeld, the war raged on, and the President was reelected in November.

Without denying the enormous complexity of how this transpired, I want to insist that we notice the media's complicity and what the official war stories obscured. The most telling point is the timing of these stories and hence their political effects. The shift to sensationalist Abu Ghraib abuse photos and their feminized depravity diverted attention from the implications of the U.S. government's expanding detention activities, engaging in torture, and disregarding international conventions. Pornographic images of a bad girl did the political work of sidelining the issue of rights and suppressing debate about the war's objectives and operational practices. A second point is how the gendered and racialized messages in the images camouflaged neo-imperialist interests. Casting England as the ultimate bad apple positioned *her* as the problem, rather than the predominately male power wielders and the policies of the U.S. government. England and a very few others paid with demotions and prison sentences while Bush and his regime escaped blame and accountability. Spoiled femininity took the rap for imperial masculinity.

We might also notice how casting England as the depraved figure of femininity avoided all interrogation of privileged (white) masculinity and its arguably depraved history of violence. The most obvious examples include racial lynchings, torture and death of detainees, rape as a weapon of war, fire bombings, nuclear weapons, environmental warfare, use of land mines, and the indiscriminate maiming and killing of civilians. In addition, the England story completely diverted attention from the violence cultivated within militaries by hypermasculinist norms—violence that is practiced not only against external enemies but against all who are feminized, including servicewomen themselves. Major media rarely turn their notice to the repetitive incidents of sexual harassment, rape, and other forms of violence against women (and gays) in U.S. military organizations. These incidents are now extensively documented, though the accused are rarely prosecuted and—like detention and torture practices—even more rarely punished.

Finally, and in spite of the incalculable damage done to individual lives and America's reputation by the abuses at Abu Ghraib, the official war stories focused attention in ways that still managed to serve an imperialist agenda: "The images of Arab men being broken, subdued, shamed and disciplined by a white woman allow for the realization of the 'American dream' of the total demasculinization and humiliation of Arab men" (Brittain 2006, 89), assuring the American public that "they are still on 'top' in terms of their ability to inflict sexual humiliation and violence on the Iraqi enemy" (Brittain 2006, 91).

INTERSECTIONALITIES OF MASCULINISM, MILITARISM, AND IMPERIALISM

To conclude, I review how gender identities, ideologies, and institutionalized practices interact to normalize domination and mobilize violent practices.

No one escapes gender socialization and its historically sedimented norms of heterosexism. We cannot help but be invested in identities that our culture deems appropriate, necessary, and worthy of esteem. While we are not locked into unchanging or monological scripts, following paths of least resistance is easier than not conforming—much less actively criticizing "the way things are." Because the naturalized "given" of binary sex difference is coded into gender identities and ideologies, it gives the status quo inordinate power to obstruct critique and transformation.

Females are cast as, and socialized into, subjectivities and roles that feature dependence, accommodation, lack of personal autonomy and power, and implied consent to male domination. The effects of conformity seem to invite ideologies of protection, if not contempt. Women who defy the stereotypes are deemed suspect, social problems, and unnatural (African American "matriarchs," "anti-family" career women, "man-hating" feminists, "depraved" torturers).

Males are no less—and in important respects, more abusively—socialized into subjectivities and roles that feature aggression, being in control (emotionally, physically, politically, economically), and denying anxiety, ambivalence, and vulnerability. Conforming to gender expectations costs men—and women and societies—dearly. As "compensation," men are accorded a sense of entitlement: to autonomy, power, and sexual access. Objectified and subordinate "others" may require protection but are also "at the disposal" of their superiors. This is the central dilemma constituted by gendering: the specific qualities of (weak, agentless) femininity are seen to demand a corollary exercise of (powerful, entitled) masculinity.

Not surprisingly, most men attempt to comply, often at high personal cost. Because the edifice of masculinity is a mythic construction, the pressure to "prove" one's manhood is relentless. However much individual males struggle to sustain their identification as sufficiently masculine, it is perpetually subject to challenge. One can be "unmanned" (feminized) by any evidence, or worse yet, simply the accusation of "gayness," weakness, or lack of control. Potential failure, and the despised vulnerability it invokes, is ever present. This is true for all masculinities, no matter race or class.

This relentless pressure is particularly acute on the stage of political and military power. The stakes are high, especially in the context of impending or ongoing war. Leaders and soldiers respond accordingly, with displays of hypermasculinism: President Bush "must" prove himself and U.S. invincibility, civilized nations "must" assert cultural superiority, soldiers "must" torture to secure intelligence, suspect others "must" be detained, civilians "must" be patriotic, critics "must" be silenced, deeper questions "must" be postponed.

Official war stories not only camouflage the agenda of power wielders during war; they also obscure the reproduction of hierarchies in everyday life. Their tacit (and sometimes explicit) manipulation of gender coding does the political work of normalizing, hence, depoliticizing how gender operates to perpetuate inequalities and the violence that attends them. The core dilemma of gender plays throughout: constructing women and feminized others in ways that demand masculinized identities and action. This is so taken for granted that alternative—to say nothing of structurally "equal"—arrangements are rendered unthinkable. In the "war on terror," gender coding reproduces feminized others who must be protected, controlled, detained, or eliminated by masculinized agents of ruling states. Like advocates of neoliberal capitalism are forever telling us: there is no alternative. The systemic effects constitute a tragic drama of global proportions: hypermasculinized identity investments, arrogant ideological claims, and excessive—arguably depraved—military practices.

Critics of imperialism have exposed how the idealization of Western femininity has been manipulated to justify Western wars to "save" "other" women. Understanding feminization as devalorization affords an additional insight: that marginalized men more generally are subject to this crusading and protectionist logic—in colonial wars to "modernize" gender relations, nationalist wars to promote idealized families, invasions to "liberate" oppressed groups, wars on terror to eliminate the (perceived) irrational religious, wars on poverty that demoralize the (racialized) underclass, and battles against HIV/AIDS that demonize gay men.

In sum, official war stories not only camouflage political agendas but also suppress critical thinking about *institutionalized* racism, sexism, classism, and homophobia. By obscuring the reciprocal constitution of valorized masculinity and vilified femininity, these stories avoid critique of gender itself, with the effect of reproducing multiple forms of subjection and violence. My thinking through intersectionality tells a different story. It too is limited by its perspective, commitments, erasures, and excessive generalizations. My story casts emotional commitments, cultural productions, and material practices as mutually constitutive. It foregrounds investments in gendered identities and gender ideologies not to privilege them but to explore how militarism and war making depend on them. I do not claim that mine is the superior story, though I believe it is an urgent one. I do claim that gender matters, and especially for "thinking through" militarism and war. More pointedly, I am arguing that we can neither adequately analyze violence, nor effectively advance intersectional analyses, if we ignore how feminization devalorizes.

NOTES

1. The problematic of intersectionality divides feminists, primarily (I believe) because of different conceptualizations of the term. Recent attempts to clarify the debates and advance analytical strategies include Brah and Phoenix (2004), McCall (2004), Knapp (2005), Phoenix and Pattynama (2006), and Klinger and Knapp (2008). I also note here that no single model of militaries, war, rationality, race,

gender, class, sexuality, national culture, or state apparatus can be adequate to the multiple and complex forms these terms conflate. For reasons of space and the analytical focus of my chapter, I deploy generalizations throughout that I recognize warrant much closer attention and complication. Similarly, in this chapter I note the neglect of agency and resistance and political economic dimensions of war. Finally, at the risk of reproducing "northern" theory (Connell 2006), I adopt a U.S.–European vantage point to critically think through militarism and the "war on terror."

2. For example, Gimenez (2001) argues for the vantage point of class in analyzing structural hierarchies.

3. Key works include Said (1979, 1993), Spivak (1987), Chatterjee (1989), Stoler (1991), and McClintock (1995).

4. While cultural generalizations of enemy groups or nations typically feminized them, European notions of ethnic/racial hierarchies permitted selective valorization of men identified with "martial races" and "warrior" cultures. Without conceding any sense of their military superiority, imperial governments selectively allied with soldiers of particular cultural identities to advance colonial interests. The British, for example, recruited Nepali Gurkhas to fight their wars, and now recruit Fijian men. In today's "war on terror," the United States selectively allies with ethnically and religiously differentiated groups—without exception extremely masculinist—that best serve their (short-term?) military objectives, with little attention to the hierarchies—especially of gender and sexuality—these exacerbate.

5. Models of masculinity are continually reworked to "fit" changing contexts and politics. Relatively new masculinities germane to this chapter but not developed here include peacekeeping forces (Whitworth 2004), masculinities due to privatizing security forces (currently exceeding the number of U.S. soldiers in Iraq), the caricature of "terrorist men," and constructions of "the new man" in Western contexts (in touch with his emotions, unthreatened by women's equality, engaged in parenting).

6. Jeffreys (2007, 21) details the impossibility of women's equality and the multiple threats women face within militaries. For example, the only violent crime more frequent inside than outside of the military is rape.

7. Feminist critiques of protectionism include Stiehm (1982), Brown (1992), and Young (2003).

CHAPTER 2

From "Soft" Power to "Hard" Power: The Gendered Militarization of the European Union

Stephanie Anderson

Nicole Gnesotto, head of the European Union's (EU) Institute of Security Studies, asked: "Why, after 50 years without any military role, are the European member states now collectively engaged in constructing a Union defence policy?" (Gnesotto 2004, 12) Heretofore, the EU took pride in being a civilian power. The EU faces no outside military threats. Why develop a defense identity now?

Using discursive analysis, this chapter argues that the answer is image. Like a knight saving a damsel in distress, the United States, whether in World War I, World War II, or the Cold War, has come to Europe's rescue. The EU, with its focus on economics, cooperation, and communication, has appeared helpless on the world stage where force was needed. As a result, the EU is depicted as the "woman" in its relationship with the United States; Europe is passive and dependent, a soft power. In an attempt to demonstrate to the world that Europe has now "come of age," the EU is pursuing a military identity to showcase its power and to "assert its identity on the international scene."[1] The EU must be viewed as America's equal and not its lapdog. The stakes are high: otherwise the EU could appear to the world and its own citizens as impotent.

To substantiate its assertions, this chapter first questions the necessity of an EU security and defense policy. Not only are there no territorial threats to continental Europe but the EU's Common Foreign and Security Policy (CFSP) and its more muscular sibling, the European Security and Defense Policy (ESDP), provide no such protection. The next section addresses the role of security and defense in identity building. Politicians' statements, news reports, and even political cartoons demonstrate a great concern with Europe's image in the world. The EU's military ambitions are a direct result of the EU trying to look tough so as to be taken seriously as an international actor. However, the emphasis on the military belies a gendered understanding of international relations and citizenship.

NATO AND EXTERNAL THREATS

Why change the EU into another security organization? Of the 27 EU member states, 21 are members of the Atlantic Alliance.[2] Europe faces no external threats. The United Kingdom (UK) Ministry of Defence stated categorically that it sees no emerging threats and, in fact, will stop producing tanks.[3] The German Defense Ministry has briefed its officials that Russia could not attack Europe even if it wanted to.[4] The EU's 2003 Security Strategy (ESS) opens with the statement: "Europe has never been so prosperous, so secure, nor so free." The ESS lists the key threats to Europe today: terrorism, the proliferation of weapons of mass destruction, regional conflicts, state failure, and organized crime.[5] With the possible exception of regional conflicts, the ESS lists no traditional security threats. Why, then, does the EU need a security dimension?

To further complicate matters, the six EU member states that are not members of the North Atlantic Treaty Organization (NATO)[6] identify themselves as neutral, yet they support the ESDP. Why does participation in the ESDP not compromise their neutrality? Additionally, the EU member states vary significantly in size (ranging from Germany to Malta), military power, and inclination to get involved in world crises. With such disparate abilities and interests, why would they seek to work collectively in the security arena? Considering how strapped European governments are for cash to keep their generous pension schemes afloat for their aging citizenry, why channel money toward an EU security dimension?

Nevertheless, starting with the implementation of the Maastricht Treaty in 1993, the EU has actively pursued a security policy. To show the seriousness of this endeavor, the EU has taken measures to consolidate its defense industry, has stopped reducing member states' spending on defense, and has made firm commitments to a multinational rapid reaction force. Even Ireland has promised to contribute, saying that its participation will not dilute its neutrality ("Irish Troops" 2000). Why?

Sten Rynning (2003a) characterized the development as puzzling for three reasons. First, NATO continues to have tremendous military advantages over the EU. Second, a European pillar could have been developed within NATO; there was no need for it to be developed within the EU per se, and "finally, because the usual suspects, the French, simply cannot have masterminded the EU development single-handedly" (Rynning 2003b, 53–54). All the member states must have some reason to support the creation of a foreign, security, and defense policy for the EU: What is that reason?

THE EU AS A CIVILIAN POWER

The EU has long been characterized as a civilian power. In the 1970s, François Duchêne, a key adviser to Jean Monnet, argued that the European Community (EC) had successfully replaced military power relationships in Europe (for example, between France and Germany) with economic ties, thereby becoming "the first of the world's civilian centres of power" (Duchêne 1972, 43). Many academics continue to characterize the EU as unique precisely because it relies on economic and cultural power for its influence abroad, and not on military arm-twisting (Hill 1990, 54)

Many EU politicians have embraced this characterization of the EU as a soft, civilian power as a way of distinguishing Europe from the more militaristic United States. The 2005 Club de Madrid conference, which brought together world leaders, including United Nations (UN) Secretary-General Kofi Annan, Afghan President Hamid Karzai, and various heads of government or state, as well as about 180 experts from 50 countries, concluded that military power had limited usefulness. The consensus was that "a 'soft' power approach based on engagement, economic development, assimilating and integrating immigrants into host nations," was best (McCullough 2005). With regard to the U.S. military first, hard power approach toward terrorism, and its accompanying general disregard for multilateral, cooperative solutions, Hubert Védrine, then the French Foreign Minister, asked: "Should we reduce all the world's problems solely to the battle against terrorism? Must this be waged solely by military means, ignoring the deep-seated causes and roots? That is what would be too simplistic, dangerous and ineffectual" (French Foreign Ministry Web site 2002).

"Soft" and "hard" are adjectives international relations theorists use to define power derived from economics or cultural influence as opposed to power derived from the barrel of a gun.[7] The EU has identified with its "soft" power status:

"Soft power" is another aspect which should not be underestimated. In many parts of the world, the EU is seen as a model of peaceful cooperation as well as political and economic development. Combined with our commitment to multilateralism and international law, this provides us with credibility when it comes to promoting stability and democracy abroad. (Scharioth 2005)

A good example of the EU's use of soft power is its instigation of the Barcelona process or the Euro-Mediterranean Partnership. By encouraging democratic reforms, a free-trade zone, and a venue to discuss peaceful resolutions to different conflicts, the EU is engaging the Muslim countries of the Mediterranean in fruitful dialogue. Despite the efforts, the results have been disappointing: to the embarrassment of the EU, a majority of the Muslim nations' leaders did not bother to attend the meeting (McLean 2005, A9).

EUROPEAN SECURITY AND GENDERED IDENTITY

Such is the problem of being a soft power: it commands little respect. Instead, the EU is often characterized as a passive foreign policy actor, mired in bureaucracy. A pawn during the Cold War, Europe is seen as dependent on the United States for its protection, with little ability to impact international affairs.

One key objective consistently overlooked in analyses of ESDP is its importance to the EU's identity-building project that is so essential to further integration. According to Javier Solana, High Representative of the CFSP, understanding the CFSP/ESDP requires going beyond traditional concepts of states defending their material or security interests or of changes in the structure of the international system:

These "realist" and "structuralist" accounts miss out on one crucial factor. And that is the impact of identity on foreign policy. For what you do on the international stage is surely also a function of your identity—of how you define yourself and the values you seek to promote abroad. (Solana 2007)

As Theo Sommer explained, "Such military body-building does not in any way amount to a 'militarisation' of the European Union, as some critics have it. It is a matter of self-esteem" (Gnesotto 2004, 253). French President Jacques Chirac put it more bluntly: "There is no Europe if it does not have the capacity to defend itself" (Tagliabue 2003, 3).

The classifications of hard and soft powers have associations with gender stereotypes. Hard powers are described in masculine terms, and soft powers in feminine terms. The United States is often characterized as active, independent, autonomous, hard-nosed, powerful, and militaristic—all masculine qualities. By contrast, the EU is seen as passive, dependent, vacillating, weak, and civilian in nature—all feminine qualities.

Although this imagery is often beneath the surface, it is also sometimes explicit. Robert Kagan (2002), alluding to the famous book on relationship advice (Gray 1992), argued that America was "from Mars" and Europe "from Venus." Like men, Kagan (2002) characterized the United States as more violent with "Americans generally favor[ing] policies of coercion rather than persuasion, emphasizing punitive sanctions over inducements to better behavior, the stick over the carrot." Being very powerful, the United States could work alone.

Being weaker, Kagan (2002) characterized Europeans as "generally favor[ing] peaceful responses to problems, preferring negotiation, diplomacy, and persuasion to coercion. They are quicker to appeal to international law, international conventions, and international opinion to adjudicate disputes. They try to use commercial and economic ties to bind nations together." In other words, like women, Europeans place a higher value on communication, cooperation, and consensus. As Michael

O'Hanlon explained, these dichotomies spilled over into analysis of defense policies:

The conventional wisdom among defence analysts holds that in US-European relations there is a neat division of labour: the US "cooks dinner," dominating the war-fighting effort, before the Europeans step in to "do the dishes," consolidating successful battlefield outcomes through peacekeeping. Some defence experts argue that this division of labour plays not only to America's strengths, but to those of Europe as well, since European soldiers are arguably better at peacekeeping than US forces. (O'Hanlon 2004, 41–42)

Many Europeans rankle at the idea of cleaning up after the American war machine, which relegates Europe to second-class status as a nurturing soft power. Liora Sion's study of Dutch peacekeeping units confirms links between military (especially combat) activities and masculinity: many in the units were unwilling to abandon the combat-oriented self-image for a peacemaking tasks (Sion 2006, 471).

Europeans recognize their weaknesses in this area. In a speech, Chris Patten (2004) admitted "while we clearly pull our weight in the exercise of 'soft power' (development assistance and so on), it is difficult to argue the same for the harder sort." NATO General Secretary George Robertson called the EU a military pygmy (Harding 2003). Later, he changed his mind adding "I'm quite prepared to say I made a mistake when I called Europe a military pygmy. In fact, it's not. It's a giant, but it's a flabby giant with no muscle and unable to do anything when trouble comes upon it" (Harding 2003).

This characterization of Europe as a soft power affects its relationship with the United States. Stanley Sloan and Heiko Borchert (2003) asserted, "Europe's hard power deficit undermines the gravitas of its diplomacy, particularly in dealing with its superpower U.S. ally." Relations between the United States and the EU have often been depicted as unequal, with Europe subordinate and dominated by America. For example, UK prime minister Tony Blair was often accused of being U.S. President George W. Bush's "lapdog" ("50% See" 2002); after his speech to the U.S. Congress, French President Nicolas Sarkozy was called a "poodle" ("Bush's New" 2007).

Among political cartoonists, in international affairs, the EU is often represented as insignificant, weak, or a woman. Political cartoonists from all over Europe, such as Karsten Schley, Olle Johansson, and Christo Komarnitski, often depict Europe as being very weak (for example flies bothering Iran) or as a woman to be wooed or at the mercy of stronger powers such as the United States and Russia (see Figure 2.1 and Figure 2.2).

As the EU celebrated its 50th anniversary, the cover of the *Economist* compared it to a 50-year-old woman, horrified at her appearance, using the image of an aging Marianne (the symbol of France) looking in the

Figure 2.1
Bush Courting Europe. © Copyright 2005 Olle Johansson—All Rights Reserved.
Politicalcartoons.com

Figure 2.2
Happy Birthday Europe. © Copyright 2007 Christo Komarnitski—All Rights Reserved. Politicalcartoons.com

mirror. In other words, the EU was portrayed not only as weak and powerless but also as past her prime and no longer desirable.

In media and policy discourses, too, the EU is depicted as a weak woman,
the soft power, the immature, weak almost-state that is subordinate to the
United States and has little influence on hard politics. Although the ESDP
will likely have no power to defend Europe, its symbolic power could be
significant if it counters the EU's negative, feminized image.

THE EU'S RELIANCE ON GENDERED CONCEPTS OF POWER AND SECURITY

One goal of the ESDP is to make Europe equal to America, not its feminine counterpart. The Europeans have sought and continue to seek equality with the United States. Politicians state this very clearly; European
Commission President José Manuel Barroso has said that the United States
needs to treat the EU as an equal partner (Sciolino 2005). As one official in
Solana's office explained, "it's a Union defined by the money and defense,
not the regulation of hairdressers."[8] To play with the "big boys," to be seen
as powerful, the EU needs to have military power.

However, using the military to make the EU appear more muscular is
inherently gendered as a premise for three reasons. First, it likens modernization to puberty and equates maturity with military might. Second,
it privileges masculine conceptions of security, that is, the state is made
more secure by channeling resources into the military. Third, it privileges
masculine conceptions of citizenship. Considering that the EU has been
dominated by a "reign of old men," it is not surprising that male issues of
impotency also dominate ("Charlemange" 2008).

Modernization Equals a Military

Ilya Prizel explained, "Foreign policy, with its role as either the protector or the anchor of national identity, provides the political elite with a
ready tool for mass mobilization and cohesion" (Prizel 1998, 19). With an
artificial entity such as the EU, many argue that such pride is a necessary
tool to encourage cohesiveness (Waever 1995).

A common sight in the developing world and communist countries is
the military parade, where tanks and weaponry march down the capital's thoroughfare and throngs come to watch. The idea is to demonstrate the country's power to the world, and thereby create a feeling of
pride among the people. Although such parades have lost their cache
in the developed world, they have reappeared in the EU. In his first
oversight of the Bastille Day celebrations, French President Sarkozy sat
in the back of a military vehicle leading military contingents from all
27 EU countries down the Champs Elysées. He explained, "It's Europe's
party.... It was a parade of armies but it is peace that we want to celebrate" (Kubosova 2007).

A military parade is an opportunity to show off European prowess: a modern military denotes a powerful, modern international actor (Eyre and Suchman 1996). Catherine V. Scott agreed, writing: "Modernization is the triumph of penetration, identity, and legitimacy, and the subordination of tradition, nature and the 'feminine'" (Scott 1995, 39).

This modernization and militarization is likened to political maturity. Whereas before the EU was not fully developed, the ESDP and its accompanying military might means the EU has come of age and is able to let off shots. Academics and policy makers alike argued that the EU must "grow up" if it was to become an equal to the United States (Bahr 2002). Peter van Ham (2004) argued that Europe's new security strategy was a sign of the EU maturity as it moved the EU beyond the realm of soft power allowing it to "get real" in a reference to realpolitik and hard power politics. In a clear reference to one's "coming of age" and losing one's virginity, the *Financial Times* remarked "the new strategy document [the ESS] completes the loss of innocence from a time, only a decade ago, when the EU was no more than a regional civilian power, symbolised by its dispatch of unarmed observers dressed in papal white at the start of the Yugoslav conflict" ("America's Deputy" 2003, 6). In fact, the language of "coming of age" appears frequently in academic and policy discourses about the EDSP.[9]

Male Conceptions of Security

Scott notes that the source of nationalism is often in the need to protect men from humiliation by foreigners (1995, 11). In this view, one of the basic measures of a state is its ability to protect its people. Europe has not been able to defend itself. American cemeteries in Belgium, France, Luxembourg, the Netherlands, Italy, and the UK, along with 294 U.S. military installations on the continent provide constant reminders of this fact (BBC News 2005).

Europeans have not been masters of their own territory. American intervention decided the outcomes of World War I and World War II. During the Cold War, Europeans were divided and placed in the shadows of the superpowers. In the past, they were not the protectors: the United States was and is through NATO. Now, the EU can be looked to as a de jure provider of security, although not de facto. The ESDP provides control over "European" space.

Significantly, although the ESDP is geared toward crisis management, it is sold to the public as a way to defend Europe. The Greek Defense Minister Ioannis Papandoniou (2003, 16) said: "To us, the crucial issue is not just to promote European security and defense; we need to send the Greek people the message that, through the bolstering of ESDP (European Security and Defense Policy), from now on they can rely on Europe too for their safety. This message we can convey today, now that the EU goal has been achieved, namely, the operation of the European task force." Two years later, European Commission President José Manuel Barroso (2005) had the same message: "The citizens expect that European actions will contribute to their individual security."

The ESDP is key to a vision of getting rid of feelings of powerlessness and vulnerability. As a result, despite significant reductions in defense spending,[10] the EU is full of statements that it no longer needs to rely on the United States. At a defense conference in Sälen, Sweden, Gustav Hägglund, the EU's military chief, argued that Europe should bear its own defense burden because it was uncertain whether the United States would continue to have the resources or political will to defend Europe (Kirk 2004).

Masculine Conceptions of Citizenship

This conception of masculine protection of a specific territory also corresponds to the EU's *mission civilisatrice*, that is, the exporting of the EU model in order to "save" the rest of the world. As Javier Solana explained in a speech, "CFSP is about Europe making a difference in international politics. It is about the EU being able to project *its values and its interests— the core of its political identity*—effectively beyond its own borders" (Solana 2000). Therefore, the EU must prepare to send soldiers abroad to protect the interests of Europe and the world.

The Member States in the Laeken Presidency conclusions gave the EU an immense mandate:

The role it has to play is that of a power resolutely doing battle against all violence, all terror, and all fanaticism, but which also does not turn a blind eye to the world's heartrending injustices.[11]

The words chosen by the leaders of the EU member states are significant: "The role it has to play." Two meanings are possible: (1) that the EU is play acting, or (2) that the EU actually has to be a superman, or, perhaps in this case, a super-state. Both meanings are problematic, and neither has anything to do with actual defense. The EU is to show its people that it is in a constant battle against evil defined as "all violence, all terror, all fanaticism" and even worldwide injustice.[12]

Embracing the idea of chivalry, the rhetoric of the EU frames it as seeking to protect people everywhere and to export European values to the rest of the world. These discourses may be a bit reminiscent of colonialism, although with a nicer face. As Iris Marion Young (2005, 18) describes the mind-set of this masculine protector: "The world out there is heartless and uncivilized, and the movements and the motives of the men in it are unpredictable and difficult to discern. The protector must therefore take all precautions against these threats, remain watchful and suspicious, and be ready to fight and sacrifice for the safety of his loved ones." This conception has ramifications for those left at home: "The feminine woman, rather, on this construction, adores her protector and happily defers to his judgment in return for the promise of security he offers. She looks up to him with gratitude for his manliness and admiration for his willingness to face the dangers of the world for her sake" (Young 2005, 18).

In other words, the men become the better, more important citizens in the role of both protector and ambassador. The soldiers in EU Battlegroups, nearly all male, are deployed to uphold EU values. As Luc Frieden, Luxembourg President-in-office of the Council explained, "European soldiers in the world are like our visiting card" ("UE/Defence" 2005). Therefore, the Council adopted standards of behavior to be applied to all categories of personnel involved in ESDP operations. Any violation of human rights is to be reported, and all are to respect the ethnic, religious, and cultural diversity of the local population. Drug use and sexual exploitation are forbidden: "It is a code of conduct so that EU soldiers are worthy representatives of the EU in difficult missions throughout the world" ("UE/Defence" 2005). In pursuit of this goal, the EU created a European Security and Defence College with the goal of forging a European security culture and fostering a common understanding of the ESDP for civilian and military staff of the Member States and European institutions ("NATO Web site" 2005).

In this conceptualization, (male) Europeans are willing to die for their beliefs. In a response to the question "who will die for Europe," German Foreign Minister Joschka Fisher replied, "European soldiers are facing danger in Afghanistan, Bosnia and Kosovo... They are there as members of national contingents, but they are serving a wider interest—Europe's. There is a soul,... [t]here is a spirit. And people die for Europe, and have died" (Berstein 2005).

Women are almost universally underrepresented in combat (Goldstein 2001), and the EU is no exception. Even in the Nordic countries, a region renowned for its equal treatment of the sexes, 95 percent of those participating in the Nordic Battlegroup are men (Kronsell 2008). Like many other EU militaries, the Nordic Battlegroup's recruitment materials focus almost entirely on men and male imagery (Kronsell 2008). As nonparticipants, women become subordinate citizens.[13]

CONCLUSIONS: SEARCHING FOR MR. EUROPE

By 2008, through the ESDP, the EU has initiated almost 20 different missions. Many have received very favorable press, for example, in the Congo:

A great deal is riding on French, British and German troops who now stand guard outside the UN headquarters in Bunia or drive bulldozers, extending its airport. This is the first truly European army since the time of Charlemagne—King of the

Franks and Emperor of the Holy Roman Empire—twelve-hundred years ago. True, it is no standing army—rather a coalition of the willing, as the phrase goes. But there on the streets of this dilapidated Congolese town are the first stirrings of a force that could, in time provide the European Union with the kind of military that might end America's status as the only superpower. (Plaut 2003)

In this interpretation, the ESDP is a cure-all: with it, the EU is tough and capable, able to assert its influence on the world stage as the equal to the United States. The ESDP allows the Europeans to escape their role as lapdog or maid forced to clean up after the U.S. war machine; the ESDP challenges the U.S. position as superpower. However, the EU is using masculine conceptions of power and security.

If the ESDP has militarized the EU, as Ian Manners (2006, 189) suggests, then the EU has privileged violence for problem-solving, and in doing so has marginalized women, because, as Cynthia Enloe (2004, 154) explained, "Militarism legitimizes masculinized men as protectors, as actors, and rational strategists."

Margot Wallstrom, Vice-President and most senior woman in the European Commission, has derided the EU as a "reign of old men" (Küchler 2008). The EU is searching for "Mr. Europe"—that is new leaders to take on the positions of EU foreign policy chief and presidents for both the European Commission and the European Council (Küchler 2008). The problem, according to Wallstrom, is that "old men choose old men, as always" (Küchler 2008). Without female perspectives for balance, the men continue to define security in terms of military investments ("Charlemange" 2008).

A writer for *Economist* agrees with Wallstrom that the EU is dominated by men and characterized by "camp-forming, bribery, and bullying. Its summits are like meetings of some ghastly men's club" ("Charlemange" 2008). Perhaps it is not surprising that EU leaders are concerned with looking impotent and see the military as the solution.

NOTES

1. Treaty of European Union (1993), Title I:B.

2. The 21 EU states that are members of the Atlantic Alliance are Belgium, Bulgaria, Czech Republic, Denmark, Estonia, France, Germany, Greece, Hungary, Italy, Latvia, Lithuania, Luxembourg, Netherlands, Poland, Portugal, Romania, Slovakia, Slovenia, Spain, and the United Kingdom.

3. *The Future Strategic Context for Defence* (2001) assumes at paragraph 64: "No conventional military threats to the UK are likely to emerge over the period to 2030. The UK has recently indicated that the present generation of main battle tank will be its last." In Michael Alexander and Timothy Garden, "The Arithmetic of Defence Policy," 509, footnote 1.

4. Interview with diplomat in the German Permanent Representation to the European Union, Brussels, Belgium, December 7, 2005. The diplomat requested to remain anonymous.

5. The Secure Europe in a Better World: European Security Strategy was adopted at the European Council in Brussels on December 12, 2003.

6. The six EU countries that are not members of NATO are Austria, Cyprus, Finland, Ireland, Malta, and Sweden.

7. For more on hard versus soft power, see Brooks and Wohlforth (2005), Nye (2004), Pape (2005), and Paul (2005).

8. Official of the General Secretariat of the Council of Ministers, interview by author, December 7, 2005. The official requested to remain anonymous.

9. See Rynning (2003b), Rose (2000), Kupchan (2002), Valasek (2004), Islam (2003), Fischer (2000), and Bujon de l'Estang (1996, 1998).

10. All countries that have been both EU and NATO members since 1986 have significantly reduced their defense spending since the end of the Cold War. See NATO Web site (2005). Only 11 countries have been members of both organizations since 1986: France, Germany, Italy, Belgium, Luxembourg, the Netherlands, the United Kingdom, Greece, Spain, Portugal and Denmark. Although many other countries joined NATO during the 1990s, the same countries did not join the EU until 2004.

11. European Council Presidency Conclusions, Laeken, December 14–15, 2001, Annex I.

12. Ibid.

13. For analysis of the gendered nature of the soldier-citizen dichotomy, see Sjoberg (2006a, 2006b), Gardam (1993), and Stiehm (1983).

CHAPTER 3

Gender, Militarism, and Globalization: Soldiers for Hire and Hegemonic Masculinity

Sandra Via

In the study of gender, war, and militarism, the increasing globalization of politics, in theory and in practice, cannot be ignored. The gendered nature of militarism has been recognized in soldier training (Goldstein 2001), states' understandings of the relationship between citizenship and military service (Elshtain 1987), stories of war criminals (Sjoberg and Gentry 2007), and stories of war heroes (Sjoberg, chapter 16, this volume). This chapter is interested in exploring those dynamics as they relate to globalization and the changing nature of militarism. As such, it uses as a starting point feminist work that frames gendered militarism in terms of the idealized or hegemonic masculinity in a given state or at a given time. Building on this analysis, this chapter argues that the atemporal and globalizing forces in current politics hybridize hegemonic masculinities, creating dissonance and conflicts between gendered militarisms. It examines the interplay of economic globalization and globalized militarisms in contemporary international and intrastate conflicts, pointing out the complex evolution of the relationships between gender, war, and militarism in an increasingly globalized world. It examines the neoliberal ideology that permeates many of the processes of political globalization, and the ways in which those processes reify the dominance of certain ideas about gender and conflict.

In these explorations, this chapter focuses on a particular aspect of militarism: the rise of private military corporations (PMCs), particularly the private security giant formerly known as Blackwater (first, Blackwater USA, then Blackwater World, now Xe). Focusing on Blackwater's role as a contractor for the U.S. military and the Iraqi government in the ongoing conflict in Iraq and for the U.S. government in New Orleans, this chapter argues that, at the height of its involvement in Iraq, Blackwater and its contractors epitomized the hegemonic masculinities found in gendered militarisms, and their operations relied on the subordination of a feminized, racialized other. The chapter explores how Blackwater's operations were based in hypermasculine ideas about security, both in Iraq and in New Orleans. It concludes by tracing the company's purposeful change of face from its cowboy masculinity identity as "Blackwater" to its emphasis on a protective masculinity in its new identity as "Xe."

MILITARISM AND HEGEMONIC MASCULINITY

Feminists have identified the realm of international security as being dominated by masculine values and norms (Tickner 2001; Sjoberg 2009). Particularly, in the international security realm, values associated with masculinities (e.g., strength, rationality, autonomy) are prized over values associated with femininities (weakness, emotion, interdependence) (Tickner 1992). Within this dichotomy, there is a power hierarchy between different masculinities and different femininities such that an ideal-typical masculinity sits on top of a gendered hierarchy of traits in the international arena (Connell 1995; Hooper 2001). Feminist scholars have identified this ideal-typical masculinity as "hegemonic masculinity" (Connell 1995). Hegemonic masculinity refers to certain masculine norms and values that have become dominant in specific institutions of social control and remain in those institutions to maintain patriarchal social and political orders (Kronsell 2005, 281; Tickner 1992, 6). The dominance of hegemonic masculinity in international security is related to but not reliant on the overrepresentation of men in positions of political and defense leadership (Pettman 1996). Masculinities are prized in political and military leadership, even when that leadership is performed by women.

The dominance of hegemonic masculinity relies on its opposition to and competition with subordinated masculinities and femininities. Hegemonic masculinities at once promote a particular organization of the political order and reinforce unequal relationships between men and women in order to promote the legitimation of masculine authority (Tickner 1992, 6). Charlotte Hooper explains, "as masculinity is the valued term, it can be argued that femininity is merely a residual category, a foil or Other for masculinity to define itself against" (Hooper 2001, 43). Values associated with masculinity are prized *only insomuch as they are superior to* values associated with femininity (Hooper 2001, 43). A man's (or anyone's) claim to masculinity, therefore, is a positional claim in opposition to a feminine other that society has constructed to be the lesser of the two binaries. Without the existence of an individual or group that can be labeled as the weaker party, masculine social norms would be without content.

Masculine social norms in international politics are particularly evident in militarized institutions, which are structured around gendered, hierarchical relationships both within the institutions and in their accomplishment of their missions (Tickner 1992). The term "militarization" is used to denote when "militaristic values (e.g., a belief in hierarchy, obedience, and the use of force)" are adopted by states, organizations, individuals, corporations, and so on (Enloe 2007, 4). Feminists have associated militarism, masculinity, and wartime hero narratives, arguing that militaristic behavior is a path by which men and masculine states can prove their masculinity (Huston 1983, 271; Sjoberg 2006b). Idealized masculinities for soldiers throughout history have included characteristics associated with aggression, bravery, courage, service, precision, and protection (Hooper 2001, 81). Idealized militarized masculinities are social, but they are also physical, where militaries emphasize the soldiers' physical strength, particularly upper body strength, by means of training exercises and certain areas of specialization within militaries (i.e., the Navy SEALS, Army Rangers).

Many militaristic cultures emphasize the physical and social traits of a soldier in opposition to femininity. These accounts emphasize the importance of physical and upper body strength, framing soldiering in opposition to women's "natural" lack of upper body strength and other physical capabilities (Miller 1998). If "men" are physically capable of soldiering and physical incapacity to soldier is feminized, then both the "sex" (male/female) and "gender" (masculine/feminine) compositions of militaries are overdetermined. Other characteristics associated with masculinity and valued by the process of militarization (such as stoicism and rationality) also masculinize militarism. Ultimately, soldiering is related to and inseparable from masculinity, where masculinity is proved by soldiering, which is reliant on preexisting (assumed) masculinity.

The conceptual and actual interdependence of masculinity and soldiering does not mean women are excluded from the practice or profession of soldiering. As feminists have noted, women are increasingly both professional and recruited soldiers (Enloe 2004; Sasson-Levy 2003). Still, women do not enter militaries that are suddenly degendered or gender-neutral because of their presence (Enloe 2000; Sjoberg 2007). Instead, like their male counterparts, many women soldiers are being asked to prove their masculinity in terms of physical prowess and military-favored social characteristics (Cohn 2000). At the same time, military recruiting ads that feature women show a double standard, where women are required to exhibit the capabilities and traits associated with masculinity while maintaining feminine appearance (including high heels, makeup, and jewelry) (Brown 2006). As several female soldiers have described, they are expected to emulate (and even exceed) masculine gender characteristics, and challenged not to show any of the perceived weaknesses associated with femininity, all while walking a gender-role tightrope where they do not deconstruct the gender dichotomies on which sociopolitical relationships are founded.

Many militaries remain gendered not only in the personality characteristics they select for but also in the experiences of women who are a
part of those organizations. Many military organizations exclude women
from combat roles (Kornblum 1984; Horrigan 1992). Many militaries have
high levels of sexual violence perpetrated by male soldiers against female
soldiers and other implicit and explicit sexually discriminatory policies
(Morris 1996). Other military organizations construct soldiering in opposition to militarized feminized roles, such as military wives (Enloe 1990;
Horn, chapter 4, this volume) and civilians (Elshtain 1987; Kinsella 2005;
Sjoberg 2006a). The role of military wife involves a willingness to relocate quickly and frequently, self-sufficiency to raise children and take care
of the home when the soldier is sent on a tour of duty, support for male
troops and other military wives, and service as motivation for the soldier
to fight well and return home safely. In these militarized feminine roles,
women must act and perform as (stereotypical) women (Enloe 1990). Cynthia Enloe documents the extent to which women, "acting as women," are
essential to the success of a military.

A large part of the gendered roles in and around militarization can be
accounted for by understanding the centrality of hero narratives to both
soldiering and citizenship. In these narratives, the heroic warrior defends
the feminized other for the good of self, family, and country (Huston 1983;
Elshtain 1987; Young 2003). In this social structure, men are not only honored as citizen-warriors but are also bound to fight when called upon
(Goldstein 2001), while women serve as biological and social reproducers
of the nation generally and soldiers specifically (Yuval-Davis 1987).

GLOBALIZING GENDERED MILITARISMS
AND PRIVATE MILITARY COMPANY

Although globalization is a highly contested concept, scholars agree
that it is a phenomenon neither purely economic nor purely cultural,
but instead shows the interdependence of economic and cultural forces
in global politics (Freeman 2001, 1007–9). Moreover, "it is effected both
through large powerful actors and institutions as well as by 'small-scale'
individuals engaged in a complex of activities that are both embedded
within and at the same time transforming practices of global capitalism"
(Freeman 2001, 1008). From whatever origin, globalization has become a
transnational phenomenon. Cynthia Enloe describes this transnational
phenomenon as process, defining globalization as "the step-by-step process by which anything—a movie industry, vegetable production, law
enforcement, banking, the nursing profession, higher education, an individual's own sense of movement—becomes more interdependent and
coordinated across national borders (Enloe 2007, 3). In other words, globalization is the growing economic and cultural interconnectedness of
labor, communication, and the means of production.

Much of the literature sees this growing global interdependence and interconnectedness as gender-neutral, but feminist scholars have pointed out a number of ways in which it is possible to see globalization as inherently gendered. For example, J. K. Gibson-Graham contends that the language of globalization is formulated through a masculine script through which "virgin" markets are "penetrated" by the globalizing forces of commodification, corporatization, and privatization (Gibson-Graham 1994; Freeman 2001, 1014). Corporations, typically from the West, inject previously untapped markets with new ideals, cultural values, and beliefs. Local cultural values are subordinated and replaced by values dominated by consumer culture. Some aspects of local culture are co-opted and commodified by private corporations, which are then marketed abroad. Some newly "penetrated" markets resist the subordination of their cultural values, but others accept the values of a dominating commodified culture by embracing the privatization of previously public goods or the merger of corporate, political, and social values.

The shift to the private sector also alters the traditional public/private gender dichotomy that has pervaded society. Among the many dichotomized gender values in global social and political life is the public/private divide, where public life (politics) is associated with masculinity and private life (the home and family) is associated with femininity (Peterson and Runyan 1999, 104). Despite the traditional association of women and femininity with the private sector, women are not associated with the rising power of the (global economic) private sector, which is characterized as highly masculine and dominated by corporate and private interests. Instead, women are relegated to the (global economic) public sector, which has been feminized and is becoming more subservient to the private sector, especially as governments continue to shift away from public and social goods in favor of privatized goods and individual responsibility. Although essentialized gender roles are being "reversed" in this economic organization, gendered power dynamics remain intact. As a result, elements of masculinity are co-opted in the new perception of the private and public spheres as a means of legitimizing the authority of the private sphere and delegitimizing (through feminization) the public sphere (Hooper 2001, 155).

An important part of the gendered story of globalization is its association with neoliberalism. Neoliberalism is a "theory of political economic practices that proposes that human well-being can best be advanced by liberating individual entrepreneurial freedoms and skills within an institutional framework characterized by strong private property rights, free markets, and free trade (Harvey 2005, 2). To perpetuate a neoliberal agenda, states will set up "military, defence, police, and legal structures and functions to secure private property rights," which is often accomplished through force (Harvey 2005, 2). Furthermore, neoliberalism promotes a reduction in the public sector and the elimination of social solidarity, which also results in a decrease in public spending on welfare programs, public goods, and even defense and police services. Because states are then no longer able to provide these services, this suggests that the public sector is too feminine or too soft; thus, the private sector must perform the tasks and provide the services that the feminized state can no longer provide for its citizens (Peterson and Runyan 1999, 104).

However, neoliberalism is also accompanied with the rhetoric of fear and danger, which allows for the neoconservative right to emphasize the importance of the militarization of the state (Harvey 2005). As the world becomes more globalized, the threat of terrorism internationally and domestically has come to dominate many discourses of national security. In response to non-state threats and the globalized nature of military technology and competition, states have been militarizing socially (in terms of garnering support) and actually (by hiring PMCs) outside the traditional confines of state militaries.

It is important to note (though it may initially seem counterintuitive) that most militarization occurs and most militarized people are outside the confines of militaries as they are traditionally understood (Enloe 2005). Militarization can be found in cans of Campbell's Soup (Enloe 1983), in police forces, in schools, in popular culture, and in a number of other common places in social and political life (Enloe 2005).

The social and political pervasiveness of militarization can also be seen in the recent privatization of militarism and security services, where providing private military services has become an extremely lucrative enterprise for many retired military and intelligence personnel all over the world.[1] Competition for superiority in the production of military technology spurred by globalization, the reduced size of standing militaries, and the increased perception that current security threats (especially those coming from terrorism) are unique and require unique strategic and tactical responses have created a market for PMC services in international and intrastate security. Many governments now find it necessary to coordinate their police actions and security abroad via security contractors, such as Xe (formerly Blackwater), DynCorp, and Triple Canopy.[2] On a number of occasions, governments have found it to be more cost-efficient to contract their security needs to private security firms than to create the military resources to meet changing needs (Clark 2007, M18). The use of private security contractors eliminates or reduces the need for national governments to obligate their citizens and/or allies to service, instead leaning toward the use of a truly volunteer private army (Scahill 2007, 4). More than 60 PMCs and private security firms hold contracts with governments around the world at the time of the writing of this chapter (Eckert 2009).

SOLDIERS FOR HIRE: RISE OF BLACKWATER USA

The use of private security companies is not a new phenomenon in international security. The U.S. government contracted with military contractors during the Cold War, and the number of military contractors rose after the Vietnam War. After the events of September 11, 2001, Donald Rumsfeld (then secretary of defense) invited Blackwater to join the "war on terror" and offered it the State Department's Worldwide Personal Protective Service contract, which gives the contracting organization the responsibility of protecting U.S. diplomats, Congressional Convoys in war-torn regions, and even high-ranking military officials (Clark 2007, M18).[3]

Erik Prince, a former Navy SEAL, founded Blackwater USA in 1997. Prince created Blackwater as a private military training camp "to fulfill the anticipated demand for government outsourcing" (Clark 2007, M18). The corporation employed people with numerous skill sets, ranging from snipers, weapons specialists, demolition experts, drivers, and those with medical or flight training. However, Clark reported that, in 2007, 2,300 of Blackwater's operatives were former soldiers (Clark 2007, M18). Operatives who are employed by the corporation are trained and tested in its camps (now located in North Carolina, California, and Illinois) under combat conditions, along with traditional military personnel whose training is outsourced. A number of reports give accounts that training in Blackwater's facilities has consisted of simulated convoys that are fired upon with live ammunition and fire-range training (Leigh 2004). In addition, those who attend Blackwater's training campus can take courses in varying proficiencies of pistol, pistol/carbine, and rifle shooting; self-defense (one is specifically offered to women); counterterrorism driving; K-9 units; and hostage negotiation to name a few (Blackwater Worldwide 2008).

Blackwater USA (especially during its 2007 transition to Blackwater Worldwide and its 2009 transition to Xe Services) managed its public image carefully, choosing to portray its corporate identity in terms of a given set of values and characteristics that the corporate leadership saw as key to successfully obtaining and executing military contracts. In Blackwater's initial instantiations (as Blackwater USA and Blackwater Worldwide), the corporation's public presentation associated it very closely with values traditionally understood as masculine.

The Blackwater USA and Blackwater World Web sites (now no longer online) depicted rotating pictures of men with weapons in combat training situations, which show the trainees and employees in positions that emphasize bravery, daring, and technical skill. A number of images portrayed the Blackwater men as protectors, even at their own physical peril. The dominant Blackwater imagery emphasized adventure, and what Charlotte Hooper identified as "frontier" masculinity, where technology, science, business, and exploration are integrated in soldiering missions, extending imagery of the Wild West and cowboys (Hooper 2001, 160). In the old Blackwater Web sites, (though the company employed women) only men are pictured as trainees and contractors. As Paul Higate notes, "there are few if any arenas that demonstrate the 'potent...connections between violence, power, and sex...in the post 9/11 'manly moment' as explicitly as those that concern the largely unregulated privatization of force" (Higate 2009, 4; Eisenstein 2007, 161). Paul Higate identifies the hypermasculinity inherent in Blackwater's self-identification as "self-fetishization" of identities that can be described as "gladiatorial" and "exaggeration of the embodied masculine self" (2009, 5). Higate notes that Blackwater effectively combined a particularly rogue sort of militarized masculinity with what he characterizes as a "warrior diaspora"—(male) fighters without a state military to fight for, who "adhere to a brutish Hobbesian rather than kinder Lockean worldview" (Higate 2009, 7). Blackwater recruited "professional operatives," "mavericks," and "cowboys," emphasizing the language of masculinity in each recruiting campaign. Blackwater's professionals often came from, worked in, and worked for the United States, though it marketed its security "services to foreign governments and corporations through an off-shore affiliate, Greystone Ltd." in Barbados (Scahill 2007, 4). The Greystone application asks applicants to indicate their proficiency in the use of various weapons including, "AK-47 rifle, Glock 19, M-16 series rifle, carbine rifle, machine gun, mortar and shoulder-fired weapons" (Scahill 2007, 4). Moreover, the application indicates that the types of applicants sought include "Sniper, Marksman, Door Gunner, Explosive Ordinance, Counter Assault Team" (Scahill 2007, 4).

COWBOY MERCENARIES: BLACKWATER
USA IN IRAQ

The primary role of Blackwater contractors in Iraq was to provide security to diplomats and government officials (the protected) in the region. The protected is an individual who is "at ease in the public sphere" (Enloe 2005, 61). These individuals are often female, but when they are not, they are feminized, framed as requiring a protector to protect their physical (and often personal) integrity. Much like traditional soldiers, then, Blackwater operatives were asked to serve as the protectors of civilians (Eckert 2009).

Blackwater's performance of these fairly traditional military tasks, however, has been the subject of substantial scrutiny. Questions of what (if any) laws govern private military corporations (Walker and Whyte 2005), of what moral standards should apply to these organizations (Eckert 2009), and if there are standards of accountability for PMC soldiers who commit war crimes (Leander 2005). Blackwater has been accused of producing unnecessary civilian casualties, engaging in wanton violence, using illegal interrogation tactics (Mazzetti and Risen 2009).

Many reports of Blackwater's conduct in Iraq have scrutinized Blackwater operatives for their reckless behavior. "Blackwater…has gained a reputation among Iraqis and even among American military personnel serving in Iraq as a company that flaunts an aggressive, quick-draw image that leads its security personnel to take excessively violent actions to protect the people they are paid to guard" (Broder and Risen 2007).

One American official noted, "you can find any number of people, particularly in uniform, who will tell you that they do see Blackwater as a company that promotes a much more aggressive response" (Broder and Risen 2007). Another U.S. military official told *Washington Post* reporters, "They maneuver around town very aggressively, they've got weapons pointed at people, they cut people off" (Raghavan, Partlow, and DeYoung 2007, A01).

The rough-and-tumble behavior of Blackwater guards and contractors emulates that of popular culture exemplars of hegemonic masculinity. In Iraq, Blackwater's antics and overzealous tendency to shoot first, and ask questions later has triggered the image of a cowboy in the West.[4] The cowboy representing the man's man who is able to solve a dispute or protect the innocent with the slightest quiver of the hand. It also provokes the image of frontier warfare in which the cowboy fights against the savage Indian (Connell 1995, 185). Higate explains that, among Blackwater operatives in Iraq, "weaponry and defensive equipment are consciously and meticulously co-opted into presentation of self in ways that engage a particular aspect of warrior identity" (2009, 9).

PROTECTING THE "HOMEFRONT": BLACKWATER IN NEW ORLEANS

The U.S. government also retained the services of Blackwater USA to "join the hurricane relief effort" in New Orleans (Scahill 2005, 1). In 2004, Hurricane Katrina left the city of New Orleans underwater and its residents in shambles. As a result, the federal government turned to Blackwater USA and other private security companies to "help maintain order" in the city, prompting the first deployment of private security contractors in the United States (Merle 2006, A01).[5] Blackwater guards (approximately 150 Blackwater operatives) were the first to arrive in New Orleans (Clark 2007, M18). According to a number of accounts, the presence of Blackwater USA in New Orleans transformed one of the "most relaxed and easy-going" cities in American in to a militarized war zone where troops "in full battle gear spread out into the chaos" (Wilson 2005; Scahill 2005).

In New Orleans, Blackwater contractors roamed the streets, acting as police personnel, protecting the homes of the rich and government institutions, securing neighborhoods, and "confronting criminals" (Scahill 2005). In New Orleans, Blackwater men carried automatic weapons and handguns and wore flak jackets containing extra rounds of ammunition (Scahill 2005). Licensed to carry these weapons by the state of Louisiana, these men made their weapons visible to those around them specifically as a means of intimidation. Jamie Wilson, a reporter for *The Guardian*, interviewed David Reagan, commander of Blackwater's operation in New Orleans. When asked if Reagan and his men had crossed paths with many looters in the city, Reagan responded that "the sight of his heavily armed men—a pump action shotgun was propped against near to where he was standing—was enough to put most people off" (Wilson 2005). Scahill provides a detailed description of the presence of Blackwater troops:

Some patrolled the streets in SUVs with tinted windows and the Blackwater logo splashed on the back; others sped around the French Quarter in an unmarked car with no license plates. They congregated on the corner of St. James and Bourbon in front of a bar called 711, where Blackwater was establishing a makeshift headquarters. From the balcony above the bar, several Blackwater guys cleared out what had apparently been someone's apartment. They threw mattresses, clothes, shoes and other household items from the balcony to the street below. They draped an American flag from the balcony's railing. (Scahill 2005, 2)

Although the Blackwater guards did not drive down streets allegedly shooting indiscriminately at "threatening cars" or at suspicious individuals as they did in Iraq, they did still engage in gun battles on the streets. Clark writes that a Blackwater unit engaged in a firefight with black gang members that left civilians wounded (Clark 2007, M18).[6] The behavior of Blackwater operatives was described in the media as "vigilantism," and their organization was characterized as "paramilitary," but Blackwater leaders emphasized that their role in domestic law enforcement in New Orleans was not unique (Scahill 2005). Referring to their mode of operation in New Orleans, a Blackwater employee explained, "this is a trend. You are going to see a lot more guys like us in these situations" (Scahill 2005, 4).

XE: THE "NEW" "FACE" OF BLACKWATER

A visit to www.blackwaterusa.com will now get redirected to www.ustraining.com, because "Blackwater" is now "Xe Services," and its "Blackwater Lodge and Training Center" is now "U.S. Training Center." The company, which made headlines for shooting and killing 17 civilians in Iraq in 2007, declared in February 2009 that it was changing its name, and its image with it. In announcing the name change, Anne Tyrrell, a spokeswoman for the company, explained that "the idea is to define the company as what it is today and not what it used to be" (Hedgpeth 2009). Observers linked this to the perception that the company's masculinity had gone rogue:

RJ Hillhouse, a national security expert and author of the blog called The Spy Who Billed Me, said the company is "obviously trying to distance itself from their image as reckless cowboys that's etched into the world's mind from the September shooting. With a new name, "there are a lot of people who probably won't connect the dots," she said. "In a year or two, people won't remember that's Blackwater." (Hedgpeth 2009)

Unlike the old Blackwater advertisements, the new U.S. Training Center and Xe Web sites have a softer image. The U.S. Training Center Web site, while maintaining some pictures of gun-range training, has no direct combat pictures. The rolling image on the front page includes women trainees, several rescue scenarios, several class-like group shots, and trainees working with a dog. The motto "training today to meet the challenges of tomorrow" is followed, on the testimonials page, not with private military operatives but with the thanks of police officers, sheriffs, Drug Enforcement Administration (DEA) agents, and members of the U.S. military. The Xe Services Web site is now divided into four parts, emphasizing training, travel, technology, and human resources. Other than a small U.S. Training Center icon at the bottom of the first page, there is little indication that Xe, "where excellence is standard," is a military/security corporation at all.

Recent news developments suggest that this change of face for Blackwater is just that: in late 2009, Xe Services was linked to attacks in Pakistan (Mackey 2009), bribery in Iraq (Tran 2009), and gunrunning (Mazzetti and Risen 2009). Still, the stark change in the company's intended public image is important, not least because it shows a change in the gendered characteristics the company links to its identity. Whereas Blackwater's early public presentations emphasized aggressiveness, independence, stealth, strength, glory, and vigilantism, the public face of Xe emphasizes patriotism, efficiency, discipline, management, protection, and organization.

In gender terms, though, this shift is not one from displaying characteristics associated with masculinity to displaying characteristics associated with femininity. Instead, it shows a shift between one image of masculinity and another. A number of feminist scholars have documented that the militarized masculinity in the United States in the immediate aftermath of 9/11 can be characterized as "hypermasculine," or favoring some of the more extreme characteristics associated with masculinity (Heeg Maruska 2010). On the other hand, Steve Niva noted that, in the immediate post–Cold War era, the United States' militarized masculinity could be described as "tough but tender," a theme repeated in the military heroism stories in the "war on terror" (Niva 1998; Sjoberg, chapter 16, this volume). The image shift from "Blackwater" to "Xe" can be seen as a shift from a hypermasculine, "cowboy" masculinity as hegemonic to a disciplined, subdued, rational masculinity as hegemonic in this corporation's public images and discourses.

CONCLUSION

Feminists have long studied the gendered nature of war and militarism generally (Enloe 1990; Tickner 1992). Although it would be an exaggeration to say that the rise of PMCs presents a unique case of militarized masculinity, it is important to study the gendered nature of PMCs alongside and in comparison to the gendered nature of state militaries. This chapter provides only a glimpse into one of those private security firms and its operatives—Blackwater turned Xe. This chapter's brief analysis demonstrated the hypermasculine image of Blackwater in Iraq and New Orleans, and chronicled the shift to a more "tough but tender" public image of Xe. A more thorough feminist examination of PMCs is needed, especially as these companies appear to be backing out of the public eye while maintaining deep involvement in international conflicts. As this brief investigation notes, it is important to understand PMCs not just as gendered organizations but also as gendered organizations whose composition and public persona changes with the changing societal hegemonic masculinity.

NOTES

1. *The New Zealand Herald* contends that private military companies are becoming the fastest-growing industry in the global economy, noting that the sector is worth around $120 billion (in U.S. dollars) annually (Howden and Doyle 2007).

2. These are the three primary private security companies with contractors in Iraq.

3. General David Petraeus has indicated that he has been guarded by private security guards, including Blackwater operatives, rather than U.S. military soldiers (Scahill 2007).

4. Representative Jan Schakowsky (D-IL) referred to Blackwater contractors as "cowboy guys" who lack regard for the "rules of the game" (Broder and Risen 2007).

5. The U.S. government is now considering hiring private security contractors (Blackwater is one of the primary companies vying for a contract) to monitor the U.S. border (Scahill 2007, 4).

6. Clark does not provide any details about the events that lead to the gun battle.

PART II

Deployment of Gender and Sexuality in Times of Conflict

CHAPTER 4

Boots and Bedsheets: Constructing the Military Support System in a Time of War

Denise M. Horn

Sitting on the beach at Fort Macon, North Carolina, at the northernmost tip of Emerald Isle, you witness the most mundane of holiday activities. Toddlers run haphazardly across the sand. Young mothers do their best to keep hats on babies, suntan lotion on young children, and dogs on leashes. The fathers roughhouse in the water, big playmates tossing children into the surf.

But these are different families. The young mothers look unusually tired, stressed. The children cling a little too tightly; they refer to their father for comfort and their mother for discipline. The fathers are young, fit, and muscular, and try too hard to make the children laugh. A closer look shows that most of these men have the close-cropped hair that marks them as military men, and in this part of North Carolina, they are probably Marines, stationed just an hour south at the world's largest concentration of Marines and Naval personnel, Camp Lejeune and its satellite bases, near Jacksonville.[1] They are enjoying their holidays having just returned from Iraq and are awaiting their turn to head off to war or new orders to another duty station.

Driving down NC Highway 24 away from the beach and toward the base, you see everywhere evidence of militarization and hyperpatriotism. The highway has been christened "Freedom Way." American flags flap in the wind from every building. Cars sport Marine Corps stickers and yellow "support our troops" ribbons. Then you see the long chain-link fence that demarcates military housing from the civilian highway that leads to the base. This fence tells the story of the families: you know from this fence if the troops are away, if they've just left, or if they're on their way home.

When the troops are on their way out, toward the ships or planes that will transport them to war, the fence is covered with homemade signs—usually made from white bed sheets—telling them how much they are loved, how much they will be missed, and how strong and valiant they are. While the troops are away, the fence remains empty, save for a few faded sheets flapping in the wind. When they are bound home, however, the fence once again blooms with the rowdy-colored laundry. These are happy signs that loved ones are returning home alive and babies have been born in the interim. The signs proclaim that their brave Marines are heroes.

But the real story is how the modern military family becomes the bearer of these nationalist tendencies, and how national interests are reflected in the individual pressures placed on these families. As Cynthia Enloe has reminded us for the past 20 years or more, the process of nationalistic support is inextricably linked with the process of militarization, and women play an integral role within this process.

Nationalism and its attendant support for government policies abroad is relatively easy to promote when foreign policies are popular, when a common enemy is readily available, or when the national community feels threatened from forces abroad, whether physically, economically, or culturally. Mueller (1970, 1973) traced the effects of the "rally 'round the flag" phenomenon, sparking an extensive literature on the subject. Jervis (1976) has described the phenomenon of creating external enemies.

But given the difficulties the Bush administration faced in garnering public support for its arguably misguided policies in the Middle East, maintaining morale among the troops and their families is a crucial task. Keeping military families happy is not simply a question of keeping the home fires burning—it is a question of maintaining the military's core support system in the face of growing opposition to government policies. In short, the administration and the military must keep those sheets flapping in the wind if it wants to keep boots on the ground.

KEEPING MORALE UP WHEN THE NUMBERS ARE DOWN

In August 2006, President George W. Bush's approval ratings were at a historic low, and continued to drop to historic lows by 2008. A statement offered by the administration in 2006 placed support for the troops as the pivotal—and finally, the only—reason for war:

In A Time Of War, We Have A Responsibility To Show That Whatever Our Political Differences At Home, Our Nation Is United And Determined To Prevail. We have a responsibility to the men and women in uniform who deserve to know that support will be with them in good days and bad. We will settle for nothing less than complete victory. *Support for the mission in Iraq should not be a partisan matter. Some of our finest men and women have given their lives in freedom's cause, and we will not waver, or weaken, or back down from the cause they served.* (White House 2006; emphasis added)

Lives lost as a justification for future loss of life has been an ongoing theme since the war began. This rhetorical strategy has underpinned the administration's efforts to shore up support, placing dissent as the highest form of disloyalty. The effect of fighting a war with an all-volunteer force, however, is that this kind of rhetoric is made all the more necessary—the war has not touched most civilians' personal lives in any significant way (aside from those with friends and family involved in the war), meaning that sympathy and loyalty must be derived for those who are suffering the consequences of the war. Military men and women are then cast as selfless heroes, and their families as unwavering patriots.

The purpose of this chapter is to explore past and current strategies used by the U.S. military to inculcate loyalty among military spouses. I focus mainly upon the United States Marine Corps (USMC), which has exceptionally high recruitment and retention rates (compared with the other services), but which, historically, has also lagged behind in terms of support for military dependents. I offer that a concerted strategy of indoctrination and control through family (dependent) policies is used by the military as a means of maintaining troop loyalty in the field. Although the military has made efforts to improve dependents' benefits since the 1970s, the current "war on terror" and the U.S. wars in Iraq and Afghanistan have taken precedence over these efforts.

THE RELATIONSHIP BETWEEN STATE INTERESTS AND FAMILY READINESS

When Marines know everything is fine on the home front, it makes it easier for them to perform their best while away. Family readiness enhances unit and individual performance.
    —U.S. Marine Corps Brigadier General Kenneth Glueck (2001)

Inasmuch as military policies reflect national interests and priorities, the types of policies created to encourage a supportive "homefront" also reflect these priorities. "State interests" are constructed through iteration— policies beget policies, which, in turn, beget behavior. I argue here that the construction of national interest occurs on a variety of levels—the elite, the public, and the private. An analysis of military family policies reveals the interdependent nature of these levels and the effects: elite policy makers identify vital interests, public campaigns are engineered to garner support of resulting policies, and individuals' lives and attitudes are affected through these campaigns.

A feminist analysis of the process of deriving "national interest" shows that there is a relationship between the formation of the national interest and questions of gender and power. This is an important point when considering military "family readiness" policies because these policies are themselves based on gendered notions of family responsibilities. Further, family readiness policies address the military family's unique role as the foundational support of the national interest's defense.

The "national interest," particularly in terms of "national *security* interests," is generally conceived as representative of *all* within the state, presupposing a "good" that could exist for all, irrespective of cultural and societal hierarchies and norms. In this way, the "national interest" elides differences within society, particularly gender stratifications.

Although state interests may be socialized by the norms of the international community, as Martha Finnemore (1996) contends, there is a process of domestic socialization at work as well. More specifically, the reification of the state and state interests in much mainstream international relations literature ignores the power relations *within* states, which are translated *beyond* state boundaries. That is, state interests are formed through a process of mutually reinforcing hierarchical power structures both domestically and internationally.

Gendered power relations are not only obscured by the concept of the "national interest," but they are also replicated in relations between states in "their" pursuit of these interests. According to Zalewski (1995, 344), "gendered power hierarchies" refer to the way in which perceived differences between men and women have been "reified into a hierarchical opposition which positions the male subject as the standard or norm and which both naturalizes women's subordination and obliterates the political significance of the private sphere." As Pettman (1996) has shown, these hierarchies are evident in the gendered international political economy within the processes of globalization and the international sexual division of labor.[2] In the case presented here, military spouses represent a site of contestation, creation, and reification of the national interest as embedded within the military family structure.

IN THE NATIONAL INTEREST: MEN ON THE "WARFRONT," WOMEN IN THE KITCHEN

The structural effects that produce a concept of the national interest also reproduce gendered power relations and privilege a masculine state ideal.[3] As Joan Scott (1987, 1067) has argued, gender "is a primary way of signifying relationships of power." Gender is delineated by four elements: symbols, normative interpretations of these symbols, politics, and subjective identity. Because the national interest, and its defense, is heavily laden with the symbols of masculine power, we might also argue that these elements are replicated on the international level as gendered relationships of power that have become solidified in the rhetorical conception of the national interest. This is not to say that we should encourage debates about aggressive men and passive women, but rather, as Tickner argues, we should strive "to better understand unequal social hierarchies, including gender hierarchies, which contribute to conflict, inequality, and oppression" (1999, 11).

This discussion is not one of biology, but of the idealized gender categories that structure the lives of citizens within states and inform their conceptions of what the state interest is and how it is to be defended. Enloe (2000, 238), for example, points to the need to reinforce an idealized masculinity within the military and its overseas missions. When the military is faced with less than masculine missions, such as peacekeeping, the rhetoric surrounding national interest changes subtly, yet that rhetoric remains overtly masculinized. Many of the debates surrounding the United States and North Atlantic Treaty Organization's (NATO) 1995 bombing in Bosnia, for example, explicitly reiterated that the military mission is to fight wars, not to keep the peace, especially where peacekeeping (that is, not being able to attack, only defend) might lead to military casualties. The subsequent NATO "peacekeeping" mission in Serbia was highly militarized and resembled traditional warfare more than prior United Nations peacekeeping missions. Although the use of ground troops in 1995 was considered a last resort, the use of destructive bombing raids not only allowed NATO to flex its military might but also allowed the Western powers (particularly the United States) to speak of peacekeeping as a distinctly masculine endeavor (Zalewski 1995; Enloe 1993, 2000; Brown 2001).

Likewise, the wars in Afghanistan and Iraq have been framed in terms of protection of the U.S. homeland and the oppressed peoples of Afghanistan and Iraq, who needed to be liberated. The images from the Iraq war serve to further masculinize the war, whether the images portray an emasculated Saddam Hussein emerging from his "spider hole" or the images from Abu Ghraib prison revealing Private Lynndie England's shockingly unfeminine behavior. As Charlotte Hooper has suggested, there is a cultural need to masculinize international politics, which is based not only on a masculine/feminine dichotomy, but also on multiple hierarchies of masculinity, whereby the ideal masculinity may change as the conditions of society change; it remains, however, an ideal that is usually artificial and unattainable (Connell 1987; Enloe 1993; Hooper 1998).

To further explore the structural effects of gendered power hierarchies in relations between states, I argue that we must look at the ways in which "national interests" are constructed and defended domestically. Western military and security institutions offer one such view of the Western masculine/feminine stereotypes that pervade society (Cohn 1987). As far as national security issues are concerned, we can imagine this dichotomy in terms of a "homefront"/"warfront" distinction, which is replicated not only within the military hierarchy but within military families as well. The "homefront" represents feminized characteristics, yet it is obviously implicated in the "warfront"; without the support of the "homefront," the "warfront" could not exist. This necessitates socialization toward acceptance of certain war-front values within the "homefront."[4]

The structural effects of this dichotomy have some important consequences. First, the masculine/feminine political socialization process creates a situation of double jeopardy for women: the first being the virtual disenfranchisement of women within foreign policy institutions, and the second being a relegation of "women's issues," such as peace and personal security, to the realm of "soft issues." War and "state security" (in the form of military and economic power) are the "high politics," the "real" masculine issues. Tickner (1999, 8) notes, "Associations of women with peace, idealism, and impracticality have long served to disempower women and keep them in their place, which is out of the 'real world' of international politics." The role of the military spouse in the modern age is indicative of this dichotomization. Military spouses (read: wives) are socialized to accept their role as caretaker and peacemaker, and further socialized to accept that these issues are secondary issues, a footnote to the "national security interest."

Further, physically fighting (and dying) for a national interest is perceived as masculine, whereas it is the proper sphere of women to sacrifice within the home to defend those interests. Gender exclusion from combat, for example, continues to be based on essentialist ideas of women and men (although, as the military notes, the distinction between combat and non-combat positions is becoming increasingly blurred as the "war on terror" and the war in Iraq continue). Although the justifications for exclusion tend to be based on biological assumptions (women are too weak; men and women cannot work together because of the possible disruption of sexual attraction), several feminists point out that underlying gender biases are also at work (Murphy 1996, 523).

We can demonstrate, through the use of the military to achieve foreign policy goals, that the state has a clear conception of what means are necessary to protect any future threat to state interests, and that these means must necessarily be defined as male and not female in order to satisfy the structural conditions that reify masculinity (Zalewski and Parpart 1998). The battlefield must be clearly delineated from the "homefront," in that the battlefield must reflect the need to protect a greater good (the imagined state[5]) and the "homefront" must act to serve and reinforce the needs of the fighting force in battle. The national interest is thus served through an elaborate home-front support system, which is marked by a "natural" gendered division of labor.[6] Harrison and Laliberté note,

Like other gendered organizations, the military community takes for granted the naturalness of the patriarchal notion of a masculine-feminine polarity, or the idea that men and women are fundamentally different. Relatively few members of this community question the patriarchal dichotomy between "tough warrior" men and supportive "dependent" women.... The military uses its socially constructed polarity between masculine and feminine in order to use masculinity as the cementing principle which unites "real" military men in order to distinguish them from non-masculine men and women. (Harrison and Laliberté 1997, 36)

The naturalness of this relationship, however, is completely constructed and, as such, must be continually negotiated to maintain the support structure. This is accomplished through a variety of ways, such as military marriage policies, domestic abuse policies, and emerging family readiness policies.

THE MILITARY FAMILY AS SITE OF FOREIGN POLICY PRIORITIES

Support of military dependents has fluctuated with the needs of the military and demands of the national interest. For example, the 1942 Servicemen's Dependents Allowance Act provided a way in which military men could (voluntarily) provide monetary allowances to their wives during wartime, to be matched by the federal government. When the war ended, however, the allowance was rescinded as the military attempted to return to a single man's army. In the 1950s, during the Korean War, the benefits were again extended to military dependents, and foreign marriage policies were relaxed (e.g., 1950 Dependents Assistance Act, 1956 Dependents' Medical Care Act). A required allotment to families on the "homefront," however, was not established until the late 1970s, after the establishment of the all-volunteer force in 1973. Even today, many wives face the hardship of attempting to raise a family on very little income and often little emotional support from husbands who have been stationed abroad.[7] Current policies are attempting to correct these issues, as I will explain later, but military families (particularly junior enlisted families) continue to face economic hardships and poor support.

Military wives also face discrimination within the civilian communities in which they live; indeed, military families often continue to be viewed as transients and troublemakers in these communities, which, ironically, greatly depend upon the revenue brought by military installations. In response to the hostile perception of the military by civilian communities, from the late 1950s until the early 1980s the military published pamphlets instructing wives how to behave properly. These pamphlets reinforced the idea that it was the wives' duty to care for the "homefront" so that their husbands could do their job on the "warfront" more effectively (Alt and Stone 1991, 115).

In addition to outside views of military families, the community of spouses within the military represents an important factor in military wives' socialization. The pressure on wives to keep up appearances and behave appropriately has taken less formalized means as military wives' Web sites, chat rooms, and blogs have proliferated. Numerous postings excoriate the "sluts" who cheat on their husbands while they are deployed (for example, the "husband's away, let's play!" personal ads are common in the *Jacksonville Daily News* when the troops are deployed). In response to an article posted on one Web site that described the "shenanigans" of military wives while their husbands were deployed, a military wife describes silence on these issues as an affront to military readiness and loyalty (Gowans 2007).

Older wives counsel young wives to stay tough for their Marines, to not complain or bring them down when they call. Young women are admonished to maintain OPSEC (Operations Security) to protect the troops: there should be no mention of where, when, or how long troops are away for fear of terrorist attack and monitoring of troop movement, the assumption being that the enemy monitors all military-related Web sites and chat rooms. As one article entitled "How to get the most out of being a military spouse" advised: "Be a quality person...Nurture your marriage" (Livermore 2007).

A more formalized system of social support was then created on many bases (but not all): for instance, drug and alcohol treatment centers, domestic violence shelters, and child care centers have been instituted.[8] In the Marine Corps, while troops must answer to the commanding officer (CO), the CO's wife has traditionally acted as an organizing force for the wives of the unit. She is the "key volunteer" (terminology that has recently replaced the more gender-specific term "key wife") and is responsible for organizing various committees and functions designed to maintain social order among the wives. Among her main roles, however, the key wife is charged with maintaining unit cohesion through performing an informal disciplinary role among the wives, including encouraging appropriate behavior. Acting "appropriately" means accepting particular gender roles, such as caring for the children, keeping house, and supporting husbands in their roles as military men. Military wives (particularly officers' wives) are encouraged to volunteer wherever possible on base and in support of military social needs. The military values the reinforcement of wives' roles as components of a military social unit because the social unit also acts as a censor and help ensure that no wife behaves inappropriately while the husbands are away.

Keeping a happy home, however, does not necessarily mean military wives are protected from the violence with which their husbands live on a daily basis (Lehr 1999). In the military, especially among the enlisted ranks, there is an inordinately high degree of alcoholism, family violence, divorce, and poverty (Lehr 1999, 124). Domestic abuse in military families has been historically endemic; a more effectively concerted military response to the problem, however, did not develop until 2005, when a memo issued by the Department of Defense (DOD) created more centralized family advocacy programs on bases around the country. These policies were a response to Congressional demands for accountability after a well-publicized 1998 murder where a soldier killed his wife. The DOD addressed Congress's concerns at that point, but after the subsequent invasions of Afghanistan and Iraq attention to the issue appeared to take a backseat to the more pressing need to retain troops for the "warfront" (Alvarez and Sontag 2008).

INSTITUTIONAL CHANGES AND THE "WAR ON TERROR"

> A time of war is a time of sacrifice, and a heavy burden falls on our military families. They miss you and they worry about you. By standing behind you, they are standing up for America—the families are standing for America. And America appreciates the service and the sacrifice of the military families.
>
> —President George. W. Bush[9]

Since the military services became all volunteer in 1973, the government has been forced to make military service more attractive to prospective soldiers *and* their families. Between 1979 and 1982, Harrison and Laliberté (1997, 41) note, the Navy, Marine Corps, Air Force, and Coast Guard "caught up with the American Army" by creating their own family support programs, with the goal of co-opting military wives: "Virtually all military family research since 1970 has therefore posed the implicit or explicit question: How can the military encourage wives to develop positive attitudes toward military life?" The efforts of military wives, feminists, and key Congresspersons (particularly Rep. Patricia Schroeder), resulted in the Military Family Act of 1985, which provided for day care, employment services for spouses, alcohol abuse counseling, and couple's counseling. Schroeder was also instrumental in passing the Uniformed Services Former Spouses' Protection Act (USFSPA) of 1982, which was designed to protect women who divorced their military husbands, granting them up to half of their former husbands' military pensions as alimony, depending on the number of years they were married.[10]

The "war on terror" and concurrent need to recruit and retain more troops has meant that the military has been forced to pay more attention to the needs and demands of military spouses. Employment and education have become the touchstones of current policy. Recent statements from the White House, including the 2008 State of the Union Address, have made the explicit link between maintaining troop morale through maintaining the well-being of military spouses.[11] As a result, new policies have been developed to increase family readiness through addressing Quality of Life (QOL) issues such as employment and child care.

In 2007, a new, formalized position was created on several Marine bases: Family Readiness Officer. This is a civilian position, reporting to the Unit Commander, charged with providing "command outreach, support and assistance to the unit's military personnel and their families and assist Marines in their responsibility to attain and maintain personal and family readiness"[12] This is a significant development for the Marine Corps in that this more formalized approach to family readiness indicates a growing awareness of the importance of creating a more inclusiveness and transparent environment for military families. It also means, of course, that a more institutionalized approach to controlling and maintaining family loyalty to the military and the national interest is also being constructed.

President Bush's call for providing greater employment support has resulted in a new pilot program on several bases. Jobs and education benefits are now at the center of family readiness at these lab sites (Camp Lejeune is one of these). Spouses are given preferential treatment in hiring on bases, and new offices provide information and support in career development in local industries off base.[13] Further, military members are now permitted to transfer their unused GI Bill education benefits to their civilian spouse. All of these new programs specifically target junior enlisted and junior officers, and especially their young spouses.

More support is also being developed for those families affected directly by the "war on terror." In November 2005, the Marine Corps created the Combat Operational Stress Control "to ensure that all Marines and family members who bear the invisible wounds caused by stress receive the best help possible, and that they are afforded the same respect given to the physically injured."[14] As reports of troops suffering from post-traumatic stress disorder have increased (despite DOD denials), the military is moving to address the attendant issues, including family violence and depression. These programs are in their infancy, and it remains to be seen how effective this approach will be.

CONCLUSION

The result of these ongoing improvements, however, is a strengthening of the "homefront"/"warfront" dichotomy. This dichotomy is reflected in the language of readiness, in which the military must be constantly prepared for battle. Indeed, advocates for military wives have discovered that the most effective way to achieve these improvements is to demonstrate that happier wives would, in fact, improve readiness. Even before the current "war on terror" began, a 1999 report from the DOD's Office of Family Policy emphasized the relationship between family readiness and military preparedness.[15]

Managing these changes, however, does not mean the mission of the military will change, nor does it mean deployments and separations will become less frequent. Many of the new programs developed to support military wives are geared toward accepting increasing hardships, rather than addressing the root of family problems. Although it is recognized that military spouses will not perform well if there are problems at home, this recognition does not seem to extend to questioning the basis upon which those problems are founded.

Many of the wives of retired military personnel with whom I have spoken acknowledge that there is a coercive nature to the more structured socialization. That the military recognizes the importance of happy wives and families is laudable; however, several wives commented that there *is* something ominous about the socialization processes involved. To what extent should the government be involved in the personal lives of its military personnel? What happens to those wives who dissent, and how does the husband's responsibility for his wife's behavior reinforce the socialization system? What if she chooses her happiness and that of her family over the demands of the military machine? And, more importantly here, what would these choices mean for the national interest as it is currently conceived by the state?

Even with the military's new concern for the well-being of the family unit, it is a family unit closely monitored and circumscribed by the watchful gaze of a masculinized war machine. Below the surface of the military's family programs is the constant awareness that the military is designed to fight wars, not provide social welfare programs. I have argued that, rather than approaching the subject of state interests from a purely international level, we must also explore the relationship between power and masculinity within families, within state institutions, *and* between states.

Perhaps the proliferation of voices on the international agenda will also begin to reframe the mission of the military such that its homeland support springs from more popular agreement on the state's interest. This would entail a new appreciation of what constitutes a "threat" to the state, particularly in a globalized world where issues of human rights, poverty, and environmental degradation play an increasingly salient role in state security. The "homefront"/"warfront" dichotomy, then, may fall away as state security is equated with the fundamentally interconnected nature of human security. However, given the continuing reliance on the rhetoric of security, which posits an external enemy forever encroaching on American freedoms, liberties, and lifestyles, this appears unlikely. In that case, it also seems unlikely that the socialization of military dependents as a vital support structure of the military will change in the foreseeable future. Indeed, as the war has dragged on and the country has largely disavowed its support for the war's continuance, families in places such as Camp Lejeune continue to hang their bedsheets along Freedom Way, wishing their brave warriors luck and Godspeed, and professing undying loyalty to God, country, and the U.S. Marine Corps.

NOTES

1. Camp Lejeune is home to a number of Marine commands and a Naval Hospital. The base is about 250 square miles, and has about 45,000 active duty service

members. Together with satellite facilities, Lejeune makes up the largest concentration of U.S. Marines and U.S. Navy sailors in the world (see www.lejeune.usmc.mil).

2. See also Fernandes (2000).

3. See Leela Fernandes's outstanding study of gender and class in the Calcutta jute mills, *Producing Workers* (1997). She argues that gender is a *structural* force, which "produces and negotiates patterns within social and cultural life" (11).

4. Enloe also uses the image of the "homefront"/"warfront" dichotomy. See Enloe (1989, 2000).

5. See Benedict Anderson (1983).

6. This issue is complicated by the growing numbers of military women with civilian husbands and military men married to military women. However, these numbers remain fairly small. The Department of Defense reports that women make up 14 percent of the military population; of that number, 20 percent of female service members are in joint-service marriages (meaning their husbands are also military), in contrast to only 4 percent of male service members in joint-service marriages (see http://www.militaryhomefront.dod.mil/).

7. A 1995 Associated Press article in the *Wilmington Star-News* (Wilmington, NC), for example, reported, "While food stamp use is relatively low among military families, demand for the Women, Infants, and Children program is so high that there's an office at Fort Bragg" (see "Military Families Rely on Welfare," http://www.wral.com/news/local/story/142724/).

8. For a more in-depth look at the military's more formalized attempts to deal with military families and their needs, see Albano (1994).

9. President George W. Bush in address to Idaho National Guard Families, Nampa, Idaho, August 24, 2005, accessed at: http://www.whitehouse.gov/news/releases/2005/08/20050824.html. Accessed 13 March 2008.

10. It should be noted that the USFSPA continues to be met with much resistance within the military community; however, at the time of its creation, the USFSPA was touted as a great development in the protection of military wives' rights as former partners in a military household.

11. Accessed at http://www.whitehouse.gov/news/releases/2008/01/20080128–13.html. Accessed 13 March 2008.

12. "NAF Vacancy Announcement: Family Readiness Officer" Marine Corps Community Services Human Resources Division, Camp Lejeune, NC, October 21, 2007.

13. See, for example the DOD's MilitaryHOMEFRONT Web site (http://www.militaryhomefront.dod.mil/), which offers career development assistance and other quality of life tools.

14. See http://www.usmc-mccs.org/cosc/?sid = fl. Accessed 10 March 2008.

15. From the Military Family Resource Center, formerly at http://mfrc.calib.com/pubs.htm.

CHAPTER 5

Confronting Militarization: Intersections of Gender(ed) Violence, Militarization, and Resistance in the Pacific

Ronni Alexander

Gender(ed) violence, and resistance to it, is everywhere, including the islands of the Pacific. In spite of their reputation as paradise, colonization and militarization have made the Pacific Island countries and territories a part of the complex culture of violence that envelops our world. The objective of the present chapter is to begin to look at the intersection of militarization, gender(ed) violence, and resistance in the gendered and militarized spaces in the Pacific Islands region. It will explore how current cultural governance, which emphasizes gender (in this case generally meaning women), both creates spaces for resistance to violence and recreates the militarized culture of violence in the region. To do this, it will introduce a brief case study of the Bougainville Crisis in Papua New Guinea. Using this case, it will suggest that in order to be transformative, resistance must address not only gender and gender(ed) violence but also militarism/militarization and demilitarization.

COLONIZATION AND MILITARIZATION IN THE PACIFIC ISLAND REGION

The Pacific Ocean covers approximately one-third of the globe, and many of its island countries encompass more water than land. With the exception of Tonga, the Pacific islands dotting the ocean surface were all colonized, and most achieved independence in the 1970s. In a few cases, such as that of the British in Fiji or the Japanese in Micronesia, colonization went hand in hand with plantations and labor migration, bringing profits to the colonizers, changing island demographics, and incorporating the islands into the world economy. Some island countries, such as Papua New Guinea, are still dependent on mineral exploitation today. For the most part, however, from the perspective of the colonizers, the value of the Pacific Islands lay not so much in the exploitation of the land resources so much as in the access they provided to ocean spaces and resources. The strategic importance of marine and deep sea spaces to the extra-regional powers remains significant today, even after decolonization.

The colonization and militarization of Pacific spaces has not been limited to physical spaces but has also created militarized cultures, identities, and bodies. Military coercion has become embodied through the intergenerational effects of nuclear and/or toxic contamination on Pacific peoples, their forced migration/relocation due to the contamination of their living spaces, and the Amerasian and other children of mixed background living near military bases. It is also visible in the Pacific Islanders serving overseas in peacekeeping forces, those working for private security companies in Iraq, and the families those soldiers are supporting through wages and sometimes through death.[1]

CULTURAL GOVERNANCE AND THE MANAGEMENT OF IDENTITY

Colonized spaces are controlled not only through military coercion and economic regulation but also through the creation and management of identity. Colonization creates new and often artificial borders; after independence, post-colonial states take over the attempt to align territorial and cultural boundaries. The creation and maintenance of gendered identities plays an important role in this cultural governance, which often seeks legitimacy in militarism and capitalist modernity.

Cultural governance creates and destroys identities, both personal and collective. Colonization created the Pacific, an entity composed of islands in a far sea, dry surfaces far from power centers. In the binary worldview of the West, the Pacific Islands were neither Orient nor Occident. Not only was the mission of "civilizing" the "savage" Islander a powerful tool in the colonization process, but even today, Pacific Islanders are neither East nor West, but "other."

Armed conflict is one place where the priorities of cultural governance, militarization, and militarized spaces are visible. Conflicts bring military activities and create military economies, but military and militarized cultures remain, even after the conflict is over. Violence, particularly gender violence, is one example. Often resistance to this violence seeks to be transformational, aiming at alternative cultural production, but much of it actually serves to promote hegemonic militarism and militarization.

MILITARIZATION AS A TOOL FOR
CULTURAL GOVERNANCE

When societies and institutions commit themselves and their resources to the waging of war they are engaging in militarism (Reardon 1985). Militarism and militarization happen in all countries, but militarism is a hegemonic project that is "constituted through systematic power relationships that privilege certain ways of knowing, being and acting and that give voice to only certain people's experiences and agendas" (Nayak and Suchland 2006, 469).

Militarization is a powerful tool of cultural governance, and it uses gender to further its goals. The archetype of women as mothers, wives, and caregivers commits women to bearing and raising sons to send off to war to fight for their nation. When caregiving institutions are militarized, the people who work in them (largely women) are serving military aims, even if they do not consciously support them.

Cultural governance and militarization also work to define gender violence, as they marginalize women in general and certain women in particular, thereby legitimizing some forms of gender violence but not necessarily others. Laura Kaplan (1994) explains the relationship between privileged masculinity and militarization with what she calls "patriarchal militarism." One aspect of patriarchal militarism is that it encourages men to create images of women as "devalued others" and then use those images as a "model for training and inspiring masculine warriors to devalue and distance themselves from enemies" (L. Kaplan 1994, 124). The devalued images of women used by the military encourage gender violence, often so much so that it is disguised or made invisible. Patriarchal militarism uses dual images of male and female, masculine and feminine to enhance male violence at the expense of women. In that both men and women play the roles based on this gender opposition, they are part of this process.

CONFLICT AND GENDER VIOLENCE

In the Pacific, as elsewhere, militarization and militarized mentalities often constitute a form of structural violence that is gendered and is not only violent in and of itself but also, under certain circumstances, results in direct violence. Quite frequently, this takes the form of gender violence, most often directed against women by men. Gender violence is "a systematic, institutionalized and/or programmatic violence (sexual, physical, psychological) that operates through the constructs of gender" (Nayak and Suchland 2006, 469).

In the Pacific, conflict and gender violence are at least in part a legacy of colonial rule that institutionalized male privilege through systems for control over social and economic resources such as land and social position, as well as by recreating and reinforcing gendered roles. Colonization and cultural governance also created ethnic tensions as different ethnic and/or tribal groups were brought together, often in ways that suited the needs of the colonizers, and later those of local elites, rather than the colonized. The pyramid of colonization privileged white over nonwhite, male over female, and some ethnicities over others, generally ensuring white men a secure spot on top and relegating indigenous women to the bottom. Similarly, modern cultural governance metes out legitimacy to some more than others, privileging men over women and giving transgendered people virtually no place all.

Pacific women identify the following as the major causes of conflict in the region:

Increasingly unequal access to land, paid employment and economic resources, particularly when inequality is based on ethnicity; centralisation of resources and services; lack of involvement in decision-making and authority; a weakening of traditional methods of dispute resolution; and the growth of a "Rambo" culture of violence and guns among young unemployed men. (Thomas 2005, 157)

Local violence is manifested not only in an increase in armed conflict but also in direct violence by armed youth gangs or increasing domestic violence. It is also visible as structural/cultural violence in such forms as gender and ethnic discrimination, lack of access to social resources for women and particular ethnic groups, and discriminatory legislation. The outbreak of armed conflict in the region, the use of peacekeepers to contain that conflict, and participation by Pacific Island forces in international peacekeeping have helped to spread the culture of violence within the islands, reaching more and more people and causing more and more pain.

CASE STUDY: THE BOUGAINVILLE CRISIS

One thing the army did was to make men strip and commit anal sex with each other at gunpoint. People were afraid of the gun and would do these things to avoid being shot. (Sirivi and Havani 2004, 64)
Violence is glamorous masculinity in Melanesia. (Macintyre 2000, 42)

Bougainville Island, together with neighboring Buka Island and several small atolls, forms one of the 19 provinces of Papua New Guinea (PNG). When PNG attained independence in 1975, Bougainville likewise declared independence, but it lasted only one day. Although Bougainville is geographically and ethnically closer to the Solomon Islands than to PNG, the presence of the Panguna Copper Mine in central Bougainville ensured that independence would come at a high price, if at all. The mine, at the time of its opening in 1972, was the largest open-pit mine in the world. It was run by Bougainville Copper Limited (BCL), a subsidiary of the British-Australian mining giant Rio Tinto Zinc/Conzinc Riotinto of Australia (which later merged to form Rio Tinto), and a minority share (20 percent) was held in the name of the PNG government.

During the 1970s and 1980s, the mine was PNG's main source of foreign exchange, and it served as the backbone of the PNG economy. Labor for the mine was provided in part by workers from other parts of PNG who were ethnically different from the Bougainvilleans. The mine not only had disastrous environmental effects but also far-reaching social implications, including dissatisfaction with the amount of compensation provided to landowners. These warning signs went largely unheeded by the PNG government.

In 1989, a former mine employee, Francis Ona, changed things. "Claiming to speak on behalf of all Bougainvilleans affected by the huge copper mine that BCL had dug through his ancestral lands, Ona had formed the 'New Panguna Landowners Association' and delivered an ultimatum to the company: pay up 10 billion kina (A$14.7 billion {1989 value}) in compensation for the impact of the mine, or else" (O'Callaghan 2002). The "or else" won the day, and a campaign was launched to sabotage BCL and ultimately the national government. Explosives were stolen from the mine, arson attacks were waged against strategic locations, and then, "to the dismay of the miners and the surprise of everyone, the massive power pylons supporting the feeder lines along the mine-access road began to fall, their supports expertly blown away by one of the first of Ona's recruits; a bright, young, Australian-trained lieutenant from the Papua New Guinea Defence Force, Sam Kauona had joined the 'holy war'. It had been a long time coming" (O'Callaghan 2002).

For the next 10 years, Bougainville saw the longest and bloodiest clash in the Pacific since the end of World War II (Garasu and Boge 2004). By its conclusion, between 15,000 and 20,000 people had lost their lives. Women, traditional custodians of the land in Bougainville, were torn from their land and subjected to all manner of violence not only by the official parties to the conflict but also by groups of young men who used the chaos to their own advantage, engaging in rape, assault, and murder. The blockade of Bougainville Island instigated by the PNG government with Australian assistance deprived local communities of medical and other supplies, seriously affecting not only the wounded but also the reproductive health and rights of women and their children. Many of the stories of the conflict told by women describe their struggle to find medicine or medical relief for their children and the pain and hardship of being pregnant and giving birth in the bush while on the run.

Bougainvilleans traditionally live by gardening, hunting, and fishing. In physical appearance, they tend to be darker-skinned than people from the PNG mainland. Most language and cultural groups are matrilineal, giving women an important role in family and the clan. In particular, it is the woman's line that determines inheritance and use of land. Women are thus powerful, although they seldom raise their voices directly in the public arena but instead use a male relative. Because of their strong connection with the land, women are often referred to as "Mothers of the land," a term that has been used frequently in describing the role played by women during and after the conflict.

Society is built around land, of which the women are the traditional custodians. The development of the mine disrupted the social fabric not only through the presence of ethnically and culturally different workers but also through destruction of the land and forced relocation. Moreover, the PNG Constitution only provides compensation for the surface of the land, giving complete ownership of everything else to the PNG government. Compensation for use by the mine was made once and only once (if at all); there was no renegotiation. It was this loss—the loss of land not just to one generation but to all the generations to come and all those that had been— that hit the people of Bougainville the hardest" (O'Callaghan 2002).

The mine was closed in May 1989, and in June, the PNG government declared a state of emergency in Bougainville and the Papua New Guinea Defence Forces (PNGDF) were sent to quell the violence. Occupation and violence by the PNGDF served only to make things worse. By the early part of 1990, the Bougainville Revolutionary Army (BRA) had gained control of the closed mine, airstrips, roads, and other strategic locations. Violence at the hands of the PNGDF was rampant, and after a ceasefire in March 1990 was declared, the PNGDF left the island. They returned, however, by force. A blockade, enforced with patrol boats donated by Australia, halted almost all air and sea transport with the exception of the sea border with the Solomon Islands. The blockade prevented the arrival of emergency medical and food supplies, as well as emergency evacuations, and eventually led to more deaths than the fighting itself. Ona declared independence for Bougainville on May 17, 1990, and a free-for-all of violence began. In the absence of traditional and/or modern cultural restraints, murder, rape, and robbery in the name of the "war" became everyday occurrences. Local Resistance forces, armed and supplied by the PNGDF, sprang up in communities, adding a new party to the conflict. Thousands fled into the bush in an effort to avoid the violence.

In 1997, after the fall of the PNG prime minister, Sir Julius Chan, peace negotiations began in earnest with the help of New Zealand. In 2000, the peace agreement was finalized, and in May and June 2005, elections for the first autonomous Bougainville government were held.

The war had an impact on all women and men on Bougainville, both in terms of their everyday lives and in terms of their communities. The lives of women in government-controlled areas were regulated by the curfew and other measures, and their access to food, medicine, and other necessities was limited. Women could not go daily to their gardens because of the restrictions and fear of violence. The breakdown of services affected women's reproductive health because of shortages of human and material resources, including medicine. Interruption of the supply of sanitary protection made it difficult for women to leave their homes during menstruation.

Militarization and the presence of weapons brought sexual violence to Bougainville for the first time. Power, rather than being in the hands of chiefs, was in the hands of young men because they had guns. Women were raped and tortured, often in front of their husbands and children (Hakena 2005, 162). Women in care centers were subject to sexual abuse by PNGDF and resistance force soldiers and were often required to pay for necessities with sexual acts.

For women in the BRA-controlled areas, however, the situation was even more difficult. They had to endure attacks by the PNGDF and the resistance, the blockade prevented access to basic necessities and medical care, and those who fled into the bush had to plant new gardens and build shelters to live in. Women in the government-controlled areas suffered from sexual violence and harassment from the government and resistance forces, but women in the BRA areas experienced violence and rape from all three factions (Garasu 2002).

Life in the bush was hard, but it enabled some people to put their skills and creativity to work. For example, they figured out how to make what they called "blockade soap" from cocoa pods, run their cars and trucks on coconut oil, and store the hydroelectric power they generated from mountain streams in used car batteries. Women supporters of the BRA became "mamas" for the men when they came to the villages, and in exchange for feeding and caring for them, the men brought smuggled supplies in or smuggled sick children out to the Solomon Islands for treatment (Havini 2004, 70).

In terms of community and women's organizing, before the conflict, there were two women's organizations on Bougainville. In the 1960s, the Churches' Women's Organization held programs for self-reliance in the villages and the Northern Solomons Provincial Council of Women was active in the 1970s and 1980s. The latter was trying to form a network of women's organizations when the conflict began, putting an end to its efforts (Garasu 2002).

The "divide and conquer" strategy of the PNGDF and Resistance Forces made networking difficult, and peace groups had to begin work within their own communities in isolation from one another. Women formed church and other groups to provide aid to one another and their children. Sometimes women used their traditional role as peacemaker to go into the bush and bring their sons back from fighting. High-status women served as go-betweens to help negotiate peace, and in some parts of the island, women went into the jungle to negotiate with the BRA. Through activities such as prayer meetings, reconciliation marches, peace marches, and petitions, women were able to influence the peace negotiations, particularly as some of the women's groups used contacts in Australia and New Zealand to bring in international support. For example, in 1991, efforts by local women resulted in the declaration of a Peace Area by the Selau people, disarming the local BRA and getting the resistance to agree to stay out of the area. Peace marches led by women in 1993 and 1994 led to peace negotiations, and in 1995 women from both sides sent delegations to the Beijing Women's Conference. The Bougainville Inter-Church Women's Forum, established in 1995, attempted to bridge the gaps between women of different denominations and helped to organize a Women's Peace Forum for 700 people later that year. The following year, another forum attracted participation from women from both sides of the conflict.

The Bougainville Women for Peace and Freedom[2] was a group of BRA and Bougainville interim government supporters who worked for peace and unity from the BRA side. From that perspective, the hardship of daily life led women to begin to organize themselves, forming family, church, and nondenominational groups to feed orphans and widows and to generally help each other and those in need. By 1996, some of these groups had come together to form the Bougainville Community Based Integrated Humanitarian Program. They established their headquarters in the Solomon Islands, run by Bougainville refugees, and part of their work entailed establishing blockade-breaking access to Bougainville and ferrying supplies donated by nongovernmental organizations in other countries (Havini 2004, 71). This network was in place by the time of the first serious peace negotiations in 1997, and it helped to get women a place in the negotiation process.

As stated earlier, in Bougainville, one traditional gender role for women is that of peacemaking. Although women were no doubt very much involved in the peacemaking process, the perception of the extent of that participation varies. Although women were present and active in the official negotiations, it was a struggle to be heard. In spite of general acknowledgement of the importance of women's initiatives, actual negotiations and decisions were carried out by men (Garasu 2002). Political participation by women in post-conflict Bougainville is minimal. Only 6 of 106 people initially appointed to the Bougainville People's Congress were women, and the Bougainville Interim Provincial Government had only four women. The Bougainvillean delegation to the 2001 talks on autonomy, referendum, and arms disposal had only two women. The Autonomous Bougainville Government has three seats (out of 33 elected seats) reserved for women in the House of Representatives.[3]

In general, media and other coverage of the role of women in the Bougainville conflict tends to be self-congratulatory, with a few reservations regarding the future. Macintyre (2000, 43) for example, says that in post-conflict Bougainville, the reality of women in reconstruction is that "women's organizations are heavily dependent on outside funding, and that, in projects aimed at reconstruction and development, men are the major decision makers and beneficiaries."

The Leitana Nehan Women's Development Agency, founded in 1992 and recipient of the first UNIFEM Millennium Peace Prize in 2001, is one of the women's organizations working for peace and reconciliation. Leitana recognized that the violence experienced by women during and after the crisis did not arise solely as a result of the conflict but rather was related to violence that existed in peacetime, too. Moreover, the group recognizes "a strong connection between violence against women and militarization of Bougainville society" (Hakena 2005, 165). As a result, the agency is currently working with entire communities, including men, youth, and ex-combatants. This work is based on a belief that gender mainstreaming needs to be improved and strengthened. This need is demonstrated by the fact that when Leitana began to work on arms disposal, the agency was told "bluntly that arms control was not a women's issue" (Hakena 2005, 168–69).

The success of women in peacemaking in Bougainville was through use of their traditional gender roles as women, combined with an acknowledgment from outside that women are important in reconstruction and rehabilitation. In other words, women used their gender in a form of cultural governance to promote peace. A feminist analysis of this use of traditional women's roles would conclude that it limits the opportunities for peacemaking. However, an antimilitarist approach to peace "insists that traditional images of masculinity and femininity reinforce both militarism and sexism," as it fails to challenge the ways these roles contribute to the continuation of patriarchy and militarism (Burguirees 1990, 6). Hence, efforts for peacemaking might in fact be successful, but only in so far as women stay within the general confines of established gender roles. Unless the conceptions of masculinity and femininity that sustain systems and structures of domination and oppression are changed, post-conflict society will return to pre-conflict modes of gender expression and domination. Perhaps what we are seeing in Bougainville today is a version of continued oppression due to the inability to totally dismantle and rebuild traditional gender and power relations after the war ended.

CONCLUSION

This chapter has attempted to look at the intersection of cultural governance, militarization, and gender(ed) violence using the example of the Bougainville Crisis. All conflicts, including the case discussed here, have at least two sides, and in order for the conflict to continue, it is essential that both sides continue to view each other in a negative way, as the "enemy" or at least "other." Cultural governance imposes these "we/they" distinctions on people, often in contradiction to their personal preferences and identities. In their gender(ed) role as "women," many Bougainvilleans were important participants in the peace process, but they were given relatively little notice or credit for their work. Moreover, "peace" is not necessarily accompanied by demilitarization or with new roles for women. Here it is suggested that traditional roles of women as "peacemakers" and gender initiatives that fail to recognize the gender(ed) and structural violence upon which they are predicated can be of limited use over the long term in truly involving women in the processes of governance and peace building. These processes must redefine the terms of cultural governance, making gender(ed) violence visible, and engaging in demilitarization.

In the Bougainville Crisis, women used their gender identity as a starting point for their opposition to violence and militarization. Women on both sides of the conflict recognized the importance of unity in ending the fighting, and they used their traditional role as peacemakers to call for unity among the warring parties and pave the way for official peace talks. Women first arranged for discussions among Bougainvilleans only, without participation from PNG, New Zealand, Australia, or other outside parties. These discussions paved the way for the official peace talks. In demanding and finding unity, the Bougainville women were able to transcend their allegiance to one side or the other in order to re-create and re-embody themselves as Bougainvilleans. Unity would have been impossible without a rejection of militarization and military means to problem solving.

What is less clear is the extent to which unity and the rejection of militarization in a particular situation leads to a more generalized stance in opposition to structural violence and ultimately to nonviolent work for peace. Without such an analysis, the success of women's efforts in such situations may in fact lead to perpetuation of factors underlying the violence in the first place, giving temporary relief without providing a long-term solution. Gender mainstreaming seeks to address this issue by increasing the participation of women and focusing on their needs. In theory, these measures seek to address both "gender violence" and "gendered violence," but in practice, the conflation of gender with women has kept attention on the former to the detriment of the latter. This chapter has shown that work to overcome gender(ed) violence must include efforts to address militarization in all its forms, including racism and patriarchy. This involves recognition of various forms of difference and acknowledgment that we are both similar to, and different from, our friends and our enemies. Efforts to resist cultural governance and create alternatives must include such work if they are to be truly transformational. Focusing on women, or gender, or even unity is not enough.

NOTES

1. In 2005, about 1,000 Fijians were said to be working as private security contractors in Iraq, and another 2,000 former Fijian soldiers were working for the British army. See, for example, Inter Press Service News Agency Web site (2006). By the end of 2006, 13 Fijians had been killed. The number of military personnel from American Samoa killed in Iraq on a per capita basis is almost 13.5 times the U.S. national average.

2. The Bougainville Women for Peace and Freedom (BWPF) is an organization that developed a human rights program in the formerly blockaded areas of Bougainville. Their meetings for women also attracted large crowds of men and chiefs. During the war, BWPF members recorded human rights abuses, often risking their lives to send their information to Sydney. These lists have been recognized by both the Bougainville interim government and the BWPF, even though they contained information of abuses committed and suffered by all sides in the conflict. See "Backgrounder on Bougainville Women for Peace and Freedom," 2008. Available at: http://www.converge.org.nz/pma/bouwom.htm.

3. See the Pacific Islands Governance Portal Web site for more details: http://www.governance.usp.ac.fj/top-menu-29/countries-and-territories-175/bougainville-png-195/?no_cache=1.

CHAPTER 6

Fighting in the Feminine: The Dilemmas of Combat Women in Israel

Tami Amanda Jacoby

The struggle for equal opportunity of women in Israel is inextricably linked to the campaign for women's "right to fight." In Israel, the central role of the military, on account of the persistent state of belligerence in the region, has positioned the Israeli Defense Forces (IDF) as one of the most influential institutions in Israeli foreign policy making and in Israeli society. For this reason, and the fact that Israeli women undergo compulsory conscription, the Israeli military has been a primary target for women's struggles for advancement, promotion, and equality with men. The logical conclusion of this struggle would undoubtedly be the equal opportunity for women to bear and use arms, fight wars alongside men, and engage in bloody combat with enemy forces. This has problematic implications for feminist theory and women's peace activism in Israel that are considered against the background of the campaign for women in combat in Israel.

The "woman warrior" or female combatant has presented a peculiar figure for feminist theory that has yet to be subjected to comprehensive examination. Sharon Macdonald notes that bellicose women, with the few exceptional historical figures such as the Amazons, Joan of Arc, and Elizabeth I, continue to represent uncharted territory in the study of feminism and international conflict largely because of hegemonic representations of women's natural affinity with pacifism (Mcdonald 1988, 1). The feminist peace ethic based on symbols of motherhood, caregiving, and female morality has dominated in accounts of women and international relations (Chodorow 1978; Gilligan 1982; Ruddick 1989; Reardon 1993). However, history has demonstrated that women have occupied many diverse positions in conflict zones as military soldiers, combatants, guerrilla fighters, terrorists, and so on. Women do not necessarily abstain from support for militaristic policies and thus do not necessarily reside within the Western feminist norm.

Since the entry of women into combat positions has formally dismantled the last preserve of male privilege in the modern world, feminists have increasingly debated the gendered significance of women's role in warfare. Proponents of the "right to fight" suggest that women's liberation and attainment of full civic rights depend on their equal representation in all domains, and that to occupy leadership positions, women must be present everywhere crucial decisions about war are made. This perspective is defined by feminist realism or liberal feminism, and it is represented in Israel by the Israel Women's Network (IWN; a lobby and advocacy group for women in Israel) and the Parliamentary Committee on the Status of Women (in the Israeli *Knesset*). By struggling for the "right to fight," these organizations promote full participation of women in practices of war, although one of their main concerns is to monitor the circumstances of women's inclusion in male-dominated domains in ways that promote gender equality.

The underlying motivations for women's struggles for the right to fight are diverse and, at times, contradictory. For example, some female soldiers are motivated by their loyalty and willingness to serve the nation in times of crisis without any attempt to construct a gender consciousness. However, other female fighters are explicitly motivated by considerations of gender equality. For example, some women perceive the military as a potentially transformative realm, holding out the promise of a better life and the opportunity to overcome the restricted domains available to women in civil society and the home. This argument is made by female soldiers struggling to "empower themselves both physically and emotionally" (Yuval-Davis 1997, 102). Whatever the underlying reason for women's struggle for the right to fight, their contribution to and role in feminist agendas has been vigorously debated.

Critics of the right to fight are skeptical about whether women's participation in combat has implications for equality. Some argue that female combatants simply replicate the image of the male soldier, as women train and master traditional war-fighting strategies and modes of behavior—just like men—and, in a sense, strive to become masculine. A woman in the Israeli military described the pressure on women to replicate male behavior:

For a woman, being a "good soldier" essentially means pretending to be a man. In my commanding course, we were repeatedly told that we were the toughest and best of the women soldiers—supposedly self-evident, given that we would be among the lucky few to work with "real soldiers" (men). But I was warned not to raise my voice when speaking to soldiers, as it would go up in pitch and would sound "like a girl"—as if my soldiers would suddenly discover that I was female after all, and their respect for me would vanish. (Jacoby 2005, 114)

This so-called equality in the military can inadvertently be counterproductive for women if it does not challenge patriarchal norms and does not allow women to "be themselves" so to speak. Women's equality in the military may even be achieved at the expense of a transformative-oriented agenda for women because "token women" are often used as a way to argue that the problem of feminism has already been resolved. As a former woman soldier in Israel noted, "opportunities to join combat and combat support units does not necessarily translate into equality for women or an appreciation of what women traditionally have to offer."[1] Consequently, there is no reason to reconsider the dominant forms of patriarchal authority and power that render women marginal and subordinate. As Rebecca Grant argues, combat renders the experience of women soldiers an "ambiguous model for reform," (1991, 93) because it merely reproduces the masculine givens of militaristic systems that restrict and repress many other women and devalue modes of behavior associated with femininity.

Others suggest that women's entrance into the military does not necessarily eradicate the informal barriers women face. For example, the high rate of sexual harassment in the military has become a serious issue as women enter into more military domains in mixed-gender units. Sexual harassment seriously affects women's self-esteem and confidence and thus strips their professional achievements of meaningful value. On the other hand, in many military units, women continue to be trained separately from men. This division legitimizes women's occupation of positions that reflect traditional female domains, such as providing moral support, serving coffee, and taking care of the soldiers (Yuval-Davis 1997, 101). The personal success of female soldiers does not necessarily eradicate the gendered structures, both formal and informal, that continue to characterize the imposition of sexual difference in the military and in society at large. Therefore, the gendered significance and experience of women in combat is contradictory and provides only limited insight for purposes of a feminist agenda.

In Israel, compulsory conscription ensures that all women (with the exception of women who are pregnant, who are married, or who claim a religious lifestyle) become soldiers. However, since the 1948 War of Independence (and until recently), Israeli women were excluded from combat duty. For this reason, the struggle for the right to fight (or women in combat) is a crucial dimension of the struggle for gender equality in Israel. The first instances of women's campaign for the right to fight in Israel occurred during the 1970s. A period of parliamentary activity took place after the devastating 1973 war. During her term in the Israeli *Knesset*, Marcia Freedman, a veteran of the Israeli feminist movement, campaigned vigorously on issues of gender equity. Her efforts, along with increased public debate about the gender division of labor in the post-war period, and the military's willingness to fully utilize the available womanpower for future military operations, led to a gradual broadening of the professions of women in the Israeli military. For example, in 1978, women were authorized to instruct male soldiers in combat courses such as tank and artillery, and to occupy other jobs traditionally reserved for men.

Since the 1970s, efforts to promote a more comprehensive inclusion of women in the Israeli military have used both the mainstreaming and independence strategies, and campaigns have been waged from inside and outside the military establishment. Parliamentary activity has been a crucial component of this struggle. In 2000, the Israeli *Knesset* approved an amendment to the Defense Service Law, initiated by MK Naomi Chazan from the Meretz Party, which officially opened all military professions to women, including combat. The amendment to the Defense Service Law made possible the service of women in the police force; the border police (e.g., paramilitary border police in combat positions, border patrols, and post inspectors along the Israeli–Egyptian border); anti-aircraft units; and all land-based units, such as the armored corps, artillery, engineering, and infantry. Women went from instructing men in these courses to being fully prepared to engage in battle themselves. Since the summer of 2001, female recruits have become integrated in the anti–chemical warfare and routine security maintenance units along the Jordanian and Egyptian borders.

Restructuring efforts have also been initiated within the military. These changes have been designed to promote greater efficiency, although they also encourage gender equality and opportunities for women to reach a broader range of positions in all services and units with an emphasis on promotion to higher ranks. Former chief women's corps officers Orit Adato and Israela Oron were heavily involved in seeking changes to military policy and attitudes toward women from within the system. After the completion of a comprehensive research project aimed at evaluating the tasks and goals of the Women's Corps, a major reorganizational process was initiated in 1997 in relation to the system of women's service. The basic motivation for these changes was to improve the management of issues unique to women's service in the IDF by upgrading the level responsible for these issues to Women's Corps officers at the command and corps levels.[2] The reconstituted mission of the Women's Corps involves consulting with the General Staff on ways to achieve the full potential of women soldiers in the IDF by integrating the needs of the army with the individual abilities and qualifications of the female conscripts. As well, the Women's Corps is directed to manage issues specific to women's service, which include, but are not limited to, sexual discrimination and harassment, inequality in promotion, non-egalitarian directives, and gynecological issues.

On August 1, 2001, the Women's Army Corps was dismantled and replaced by Chen, a body headed by the Advisor for Women's Affairs to the IDF Chief of Staff. From then on, Chen became incorporated into the General Staff and ceased acting as an independent unit. The policy of the IDF Chief of the General Staff toward women was expressed in terms of five major objectives. First, the service of women would be based on the principles of partnership and equality. Second, the duration of women's service in identical roles would be adjusted to that of men's service. Third, the service of women would be broadened to include the variety of possible roles. Fourth, the placement of female petty officers would take place in operational units and central roles. And finally, the appointment of female senior officers would be conducted according to their quality and not their service course.[3] The equal service time of male and female conscripts is a significant change that counters efforts since the early 1990s to curtail the time of women's service. The service time of women recruits was reduced from 24 to 21 months as part of a larger program designed to cut military expenditures. However, the campaign for gender equality in the military has ensured that women recruited for combat units serve 30 months and do reserve duty until the age of 38 years (previously 24).

Women's right to fight in Israel has relied heavily on the judicial system, the courts, the Supreme Court in particular, and prominent lobby groups. A primary target for judicial activity has been the Israeli air force (Chel Avir), one of the fundamental pillars of Israel's defense strategy. In 1994, Alice Miller, a native South African, immigrated to Israel and applied to train with the air force as a pilot. Despite the fact that she was an experienced aeronautical engineer and held a civil pilot's license, she was rejected automatically on the grounds that women were not allowed to serve in combat units.

Miller submitted a precedent-setting appeal to the Israeli Supreme Court under the representation of two key lobby groups, the IWN and the Association for Civil Rights in Israel. The IWN was established in 1984 as a nonprofit and voluntary organization that advocates for women's rights in Israel in government, law, education, the workplace, and the private sphere. The IWN operates through a variety of legal and legislative activities, empowerment and leadership training programs, and consciousness-raising and education. It represents a group of nonpartisan women from different political perspectives, religious affiliations, and ethnic backgrounds united toward the objective of raising the status of women in Israeli society. The Association for Civil Rights in Israel has campaigned since 1972 for Israel's commitment to civil liberties and human rights through litigation, education, counseling, and public outreach.

With the aid of these two groups, the Supreme Court ruled in 1995 that Miller could participate in the course. Although she did not pass the pilot's admission procedures, which includes a written and physical exam and an interview, her case opened the doors for subsequent women to pursue a career in the Israeli air force with the amendment of the Defense Service Law in 1995. Since then, more than 100 women conscripts enlisted in the pilot's training course. Of the three female graduates to date, all were trained as navigators capable of operating the highly sophisticated navigational systems on F-16 and Phantom jet fighters. On June 29, 2001,

Lt. Roni Zuckerman became the fourth woman to complete the Israeli Air Force's pilot course and the first to reach the status of fighter pilot (Shuman 2001b).

A similar campaign for women's integration has taken place in the Israeli navy. The navy is widely regarded as the military branch most hesitant about integrating women into its ranks, particularly on account of the tight living quarters, lengthy periods of time spent at sea, and ramifications of mixed-gender relations onboard fighting ships. Recently, however, the Israel Navy opened its prestigious Naval Officers Course to women. A slow integration process has begun, but there is still a long way to go.

Finally, one of the most controversial achievements in the campaign for women in combat in Israel has been the ability of women to enter enemy territory. Israel is surrounded by Arab states, which all at one point since 1948 have been at war with Israel. For the first time, the IDF—in consultation with the Air Force and the Human Resources Branch—decided to allow women to cross into enemy territory while on military missions. This decision was directed specifically at airborne female physicians. However, one woman campaigned for a key negotiating position on the international monitoring committee in Israel's "security zone" in southern Lebanon (before Israeli withdrawal on May 24, 2000) to address violations of agreements reached between Israeli and the Hizbullah (Party of God) in 1996. Having graduated from law school before conscription, Lt. Gabby Blum was suited to the job, although because of the necessity of entering enemy territory, she had to campaign vigorously. "There was a lot of hesitation about agreeing to send me. It took a lot [to convince] the other commanders. No one was questioning my ability as a woman or as a lawyer to do the job; the problem was the location" (Prusher 1998). The traditional rationale behind the prohibition of women in combat in Israel is related to the issue of female casualties. The most serious factor in this regard is the anticipated devastating effect on national morale should a woman be captured by the enemy. Indeed, when Hani Abramov, a new female recruit to the border police unit, was shot and seriously wounded by Palestinian gunfire on a patrol in July 2001, questions were raised about the protection of women serving on active fronts (Shuman 2001a). This type of tragedy reaches to the very heart of a society that regards women as representing its cultural values and the responsibility for social reproduction. The desire to protect women stands as a basic pillar of Jewish national self-determination in Israel.

In recent years, women entering combatant corps have slowly contributed to the coed environment of the Israeli military. Corporal Odelia, from Zichron Y'akov joined the ranks of an Engineering Corps Company on August 19, 2002, to use her specialization in chemical and biological warfare to disinfect a chemically and biologically poisoned area. Commenting on the increase in coed training and specialization in the Israeli military, Lieutenant Dudi, commander of the coed company states "The number of women wanting to enlist in combatant Corps is increasing. Every four months, at least ten women join the Corp. There are many women who are willing to give so much, they prove time and time again that they are just as good as anyone else."[4] Tamar, another female soldier who serves along-side male soldiers agrees that "participating in training with men allows women to prove they are equally capable, both physically and psychologi-cally, of getting the job done."[5]

Despite the gains made by individual women soldiers and the restruc-turing efforts either initiated by the military or enforced by the Supreme Court, informal barriers nevertheless continue to restrict women's equal inclusion in military service. First, the military has been gradually mov-ing toward a system of selective service in order to deal with a surplus of conscript-age citizens. There has been strong bipartisan support (from both the far Left and the religious Right) for eliminating this surplus by canceling women's conscription altogether.[6] This sentiment was not sup-ported by the mainstream, however.

Another major issue has been the incorporation of high-technology information and weapons systems into the IDF (Cohen, Eisenstadt, and Bacevich 1998). Despite the fact that such systems operate without the upper body muscular strength that is necessary for more conventional weapons, patriarchal attitudes continue to envisage women as the reserve army of unskilled labor in the military and thus a group incapable of such sophisticated and highly skilled tasks. These attitudes originate within the military itself. For example, in his statement to the *Knesset* Commit-tee on the Status of Women, Brigadier General Gil Regev articulated the patriarchal sentiment in the military that "the air force cannot cope with large numbers of female soldiers." To reinforce the view that women are not as capable as men he asked, "Do you know what it takes to fly an F-16?" (Dewitte 1998). Major General Dan Halutz, commander-in-chief of the Israeli Air Force, made a similar statement with reference to women in the air force, confining women to their reproductive roles, he claims,

It is clear that women have the talent and abilities, but psychologically and bio-logically we have to see if they meet IAF demands. Let's assume, in an utopian situation, that 50 per cent of the airforce was women. Statistically, we can't allow ourselves to get to a situation where some of our commanders and pilots are grounded because they are pregnant. (Shuman 2001b)

Intense opposition continues to characterize the military culture in Israel with its reluctance to see women serving in combat. The integration of women confronts stereotypical and chauvinistic attitudes such as the no-tion that women's presence would obstruct the camaraderie and battle readiness of male soldiers. Women's integration would also necessitate major structural changes to institute gender-sensitive training and selec-tion processes, which require time, effort, and financial resources.

As women enter more military professions, a direct dilemma for female conscripts has been that of sexual harassment. Israel has developed one of the most comprehensive and progressive legal frameworks in the world for dealing with and investigating cases of sexual harassment. In March 1998, the *Knesset* passed the Sexual Harassment Prevention Law, the result of collaboration between Dr. Orit Kamir from the Hebrew University of Jerusalem, legal adviser Rachel Benziman of the IWN, and the Israeli Ministry of Justice. This legislation defines sexual harassment in the broadest terms, covering acts and insinuations ranging from obscenities toward women, sexual insults and innuendo, sexual objectification, and indecent proposals.[7] In addition to this law, the *Knesset* Committee on the Status of Women developed new guidelines on sexual harassment in areas of employment, business, academia, and consumer relationships. In cases involving minors or patients, or if the harasser is in a position of authority over the victim, the conduct is prohibited even if consensual. Not only does this law define sexual harassment as criminal activity, but it also provides clear channels through which women can file complaints, allows civil suits for damages, and makes employers responsible for preventing sexual harassment in the workplace.

By way of comparison to other areas of the labor force and society targeted by this law, sexual harassment in the military has been a key area of concern. According to Dafna Izraeli, "the Israeli military is a hothouse for exploitative sexual relationships. It has been common for pretty young female soldiers to become 'trophies' of the commanders" (Motro 2000). Carmela Menashe, military correspondent for the Voice of Israel, has described the fighting culture in the IDF as one of "rampant licentiousness" in which male warriors represent an aura of potency and thus a corresponding "sense of entitlement" (Beyer 2001). The atmosphere of permissive license in the military is related to the structure of authority in which young female soldiers normally serve under an older man of higher rank who has enormous control over his subordinates.

Although Chief of Staff Shaul Mofaz declared a policy of zero tolerance in 1998, it is not surprising that the highest number of complaints of sexual harassment has been filed in the Ministry of Defense. In 1997, for example, 280 women soldiers filed complaints of sexual harassment, an increase of 20 percent from the previous year. The number of complaints increased after the new legislation, and the IDF received an average of one complaint per day in 1999 (Beyer 2001). In 1998 and 1999, 54 officers and noncommissioned officers were discharged from the military as a result of sexual harassment charges. Others found guilty either by a disciplinary officer or a military court were subject to demotion and even jail time.

A number of high-profile cases have raised the issue of sexual harassment in the military to the top of the public agenda. For example, former defense and transportation minister, and retired Israeli Defense Forces General Yitzhak Mordechai, was charged with three counts of sexual assault and one count of harassment. Once considered a likely candidate for future Prime Minister of Israel, Mordechai was accused of indecently assaulting a female officer under his command when he was a leading general in 1992. Also, a female Likud party activist complained that Mordechai sexually harassed her when he was the country's defense minister in 1996. Although under Israeli law, Mordechai faced a maximum sentence of 10 years, on April 30, 2001, he ultimately received an 18-month suspended sentence by the Jerusalem Magistrate Court for indecent assault of two women and an acquittal in relation to the third woman. Public protestors considered Mordechai's light sentence an outrage, but it was at least partly a result of the court's consideration of his decorated military career ("Anglos spearhead" 2001). The positive role military experience can play, even in a criminal court case, demonstrates the prestige in Israeli society attributed to combat at the expense of women's rights.

Although the Mordechai trial prompted an angry public reaction, it also succeeded in raising political awareness of the issue of sexual harassment in Israeli society. Sexual assault crisis centers in Israel received 15,000 complaints in 2000, nearly double the 8,000 cases reported in 1999, as women "drew courage about challenging what had once been accepted practice in the workplace and in the army, which has been accused of tolerating abuses of young women soldiers by generals and senior officers" (Goldenberg 2001). The media attention generated by the Mordechai case was followed by an equally heated public debate over the promotion of Brigadier General Nir Galili to Major General after being accused by a young female recruit of engaging in intimate sexual relations with her while acting as commander of her base. The Israeli High Court of Justice ultimately blocked the promotion. Currently, new recruits—both male and female—participate in a program of empowerment and awareness to counteract harassment in the military, including a course specifying how to file a complaint.

One of the major remaining dilemmas for women's right to fight in Israel is the intangible social pressure in Israeli culture, which dissuades women from pursuing a military career in the first place. Women's lack of interest in investing in a military career can result from the perceived or real incongruence between military and familial responsibilities, and the more subtle pressures from friends and family against such a combination. Women interested in raising a family are more restrained by men as a result of the time component of women's reproduction systems. For example, as stated, women who are married or pregnant are exempt from the military, and the military pays for abortions for women who do become pregnant during their service. The absence of space for parenting in the military makes it difficult to combine service with child care. Upon completion of service, soldiers are recalled to reserve duty at least one month a year, men to the age of 51 and single women to the age of 24 (now 38 for women in combat). This difference in reserve duty promotes

the traditional family by ensuring that women are available for childrear-
ing while men are called to duty. These boundaries coincide uneasily with
recent gains made by women in their right to fight, and critics argue that
they maintain a diminished status for women in the IDF.

Another, more pronounced, area of opposition to women in combat
derives from the religious sector in Israel. Since the founding of the State of
Israel, religious parties in the government coalition have continuously and
vehemently opposed women's conscription on moral grounds. Since the
1970s, men who identify with the national-religious camp have served
the IDF in a special framework, the Yeshivot Hesder, in which military
training is alternated with religious study over a period of 4 to 5 years. In
developing this program, the military has sought to cater to the special
needs of this category of conscripts in terms, for example, of Sabbath and
dietary restrictions. However, the March 2000 law sponsoring the integration of women in combat has raised serious questions about the ramifications of women's military service for that of religious men.

The two major concerns, as expressed by members of the National Religious Party and rabbis from the religious-Zionist military schools and
pre-military yeshivot (religious study schools), are that mixed-gender
combat units involving men and women intermingling physically in close
quarters would violate the halachic (Jewish law) principles of n'gia (physical contact among the sexes) and norms of modesty (tsniut) in relation to
dress and codes of behavior (Prince-Gibson 2001). The Orthodox religious
community in Israel is concerned that close contact with women, especially secular women, would expose their religious men to moral influences that contradict those of their own closed community and way of life
in which men and women do not touch outside of marriage and during
days described as impure by the female menstrual cycle. This sentiment
against mixed service was expressed by the Sephardi Chief Rabbi of Israel,
Eliahu Bakshi-Doron, who made a psak-halacha (public halachic ruling)
ordering hesder students to refuse military service altogether if their rabbis
could not confirm that their standards of modesty in the military would
be upheld ("Gender Skirmishes" 2001).

Although Israeli women in combat do not tend to describe their efforts
in feminist language, religious opposition to women in combat forces the
issue of feminism. Orthodox pronouncements against women in combat
do not refer only to the practical issues involved in daily contact, but they
also relate to broader principles in Israeli society involving the nature of
the Jewish family and the role played by the Orthodox establishment in
formulating codes of conduct for men and women in the state. The resolution of the issue of women and religious men in the IDF will depend on
how the relationship between religion and statehood in Israel develops
in the future and the extent to which women and the Orthodox establishment can reconcile their different goals. Thus far, the formal campaign for women in combat in Israel has been successful insofar as the

administrative barriers to women's entrance into combat units have been removed. In the early years of the 21st century, Israeli women are slowly pervading all areas of the Israeli military after successfully completing their training courses.

However, informal barriers such as religious opposition, cultural norms, discrimination, and sexual harassment continue to plague women's advancement in combat corps. The resolution of informal barriers will depend on the capacity of women to control the conditions of their own inclusion and promote gender issues and women's rights within the framework of their military service.

NOTES

1. Personal interview with Tamar, former Israeli soldier, Jerusalem, July 16, 1998.

2. For more information, see Israel Women's Network Web site at http://www.iwn.org.il.

3. Accessed at the Israel Defense Forces (IDF) Web site: http://www.idf.il/resources/ppt/yohalan_eng.PPT.

4. Accessed at the Israeli Defense Forces spokesperson's unit: http://www.idf.il/newsite/english/1124–5.stm.

5. Personal interview with Revital, Jerusalem, July 25, 1997.

6. "In Uniform: Social Encroachments," Israel Yearbook and Almanac 1996, accessed at http://www.iyba.co.il/96/soldiers.htm.

7. See the description of sexual harassment law on the Israel Women's Network Web site: http://www.iwn.org/law/#employ.

CHAPTER 7

Post-war Trajectories for Girls Associated with the Fighting Forces in Sierra Leone

Susan Shepler

The 10-year-long civil war in Sierra Leone is well known in the West for three things: blood diamonds, amputations, and child soldiers. Of course, the conflict is much deeper than that, and a range of theories about political, economic, and social causes underpin the outbreak and long duration of the conflict. In particular, the war has been explained by various analysts as, in part, a crisis of youth (Richards 1995, 1996; Abdullah et al. 1997; Fanthorpe 2001; Abdullah 2002; Keen 2003, 2005). But usually when these analysts talk about youth in Africa or about child soldiers they are talking about young men. We still do not know enough about the participation of young women in the war in Sierra Leone or about their possibilities for reintegration into post-war society (Fithen and Richards 2005; Coulter 2008).

By some estimates, girls make up a third of the population of children abducted by the rebel groups in Sierra Leone. The key point is that girls (and women) affiliated with the fighting forces in Sierra Leone have a different set of scripts to draw on and different possible trajectories of identity to follow in their post-war remaking. In particular, girls face an explicitly moral discourse about their participation in the war. In this chapter, I will focus on girls' post-war trajectories more than on describing how they became involved in fighting or what they did during the war. Recruitment and participation of girls have been addressed in numerous human rights reports, though more could be done to understand the cultural underpinnings of girls' recruitment. More importantly, now that the war has come to a close, it is impossible to conduct ethnographic interviews with girls except in the register of memory, but the issues of post-war reintegration are ongoing. First, I will give a brief introduction to the war; second, I will define the set of girls I will be discussing; and third, through some ethnographic examples, I will talk about some of the ways girl ex-combatants' post-war reintegration is different from that of boys. I will conclude with a brief discussion of some of the problems with reintegration programs promoted by UNICEF and others, and how they grow directly out of the issues I discuss.

THE WAR IN BRIEF

The course of the war (1991–2002) has been very confusing for outsiders and insiders alike, characterized by shifting alliances, coups and counter-coups, and different international actors at different stages. I will not go into the timeline here, but the main fighting factions were the Revolutionary United Front (RUF) or "the rebels"; the Sierra Leone Army (SLA), which at certain points was allied with the rebels (these renegades were sometimes called "sobels"—soldiers by day, rebels by night); the locally organized Civil Defense Forces (CDF) or "Kamajohs" who grew out of traditional secret societies and became known for their use of magic and medicine; and the international peacekeeping forces, first the mainly Nigerian West African regional force ECOMOG (Economic Community of West African States Monitoring Group) and then the United Nations (UN) forces UNAMSIL (United Nations Mission in Sierra Leone).

Many explanations for the war in Sierra Leone have been put forth from many different quarters, but the "crisis of youth" explanation, perhaps most famously put forward by Paul Richards, will most concern us here. He argues convincingly in *Fighting for the Rain Forest* (1996) that participation of young men and boys in the rebel movement can best be understood against a backdrop of political and economic exclusion of youth in Sierra Leone in the years of one-party rule before the outbreak of the war. The 1997 report by Conciliation Resources points out that Paul Richards's book focused exclusively on boys (Conciliation Resources 1997). The report goes on to note that, "the deleterious effects of Sierra Leone's deteriorating services and resources were not unique to boys. On the contrary, girls are more vulnerable to hard economic times." It seems an obvious step to extend the analysis to the political and economic exclusion of girls and young women.

Peace was officially declared in January 2002, and a relatively successful national election was held in May 2002 and again in August 2007. People are now turning to the pressing issues of post-war reconstruction. Refugees and Internally Displaced Persons (IDPs) have mostly returned to their places of origin, and houses and roads are undergoing repair. But more than just the physical world must be rebuilt. In Sierra Leone today there are serious ongoing struggles about the shape of post-war society, what changes might be wrought to prevent war from erupting again, and in particular about the provision of benefits for ex-combatants.

This work on girl soldiers is a part of broader research on youth and war in Sierra Leone. I spent a total of 18 months doing ethnographic fieldwork around the country, working in interim care centers for recently demo-bilized child ex-combatants, and doing ethnographic fieldwork in some of the villages and towns where child ex-combatants were reintegrating. I met with the young people and their families, communities, teachers, social workers, and so on. I also tracked public perceptions to see to what extent the general populace seemed willing to forgive these children and accept them back into society. My work took me all around the country, and I investigated different experiences by region, ethnic group, fighting faction, and gender.

THE POPULATION OF GIRL SOLDIERS

Defining girls' roles in the conflict in Sierra Leone is difficult, and even the terminology is controversial. Some identify the girls as "girl soldiers" and others prefer the label "girls associated with fighting forces." Some worry that identifying girls as soldiers hides both the level of involuntariness of their participation and their often nonmilitary roles, and others think the classification of girls as only "associated with fighting forces" denies both their agency in their actions and the fact that many girls did play combat roles. Following UNICEF's Capetown Principles terminology:

"Child soldier" in this document means any person under 18 years of age who is part of any kind of regular or irregular armed force or armed group in any capac-ity, including but not limited to cooks, porters, messengers, and those accompany-ing such groups, other than purely as family members. It includes girls recruited for sexual purposes and forced marriage. It does not, therefore, only refer to a child who is carrying or has carried arms. (UNICEF 1997, 1)

In the case of Sierra Leone, girls were associated mostly with the RUF and some with the SLA (especially the AFRC—the Armed Forces Revo-lutionary Council—who seized power after an alliance with the RUF in 1997), but not in general with the CDF.[1] There are different patterns of association: some were abducted, some joined for protection, some seem to have joined at their parents urging, and some seem to have joined more or less willingly. There are different patterns of experience: many were raped and used for sex, though some report forming relationships with particular commanders who protected them from other combatants. Some were domestics, cooking, cleaning, and so on. Some became fighters, and some even respected commanders (Bah 1997; National Forum for Human Rights 2001; Mansaray 2000; Coulter 2006). Some of the boy soldiers

I interviewed told me that some young women who were the wives of commanders had great power and hardly had to work because they had legions of young boys to work for them (Coulter agrees, and Utas [2005] notes the same phenomenon in neighboring Liberia).

To try to ground the notion of girl soldier in Sierra Leone, I will recount the story of one girl I met in May 2001 during my research. I will call her Aminata.[2] She lives in a very small village near the capital. Her father is the headman of the village. In early 1999, the rebels and the SLA were driven out of Freetown after a six-week occupation. During their retreat, they stopped in small villages along the way to loot and destroy, sending a message to the population using classic terror tactics. The people of Aminata's village lived under rebel control for several months, afraid to leave, working for the rebels harvesting their own crops. Aminata was raped early in the occupation. At that time, she was about 14 years old. Her father decided that it would be in her best interest to give Aminata to a woman collaborator, Mammy Haja, who traveled with the rebels, selling them drugs and supplies they could not loot. Aminata told me the story this way:

She said "Pa, I want your child. Why don't you give her to me now before another man goes and holds her." So, then the Pa said, OK, I will tell her mother. . . . Because at that time, they had already held *all* my fellow girls. Men held them all and carried them away to Blama. So my mother said OK, before rebels come hold me and carry me away, let him leave me with the woman. . . . He left me in the woman's hands. But at that time, when I was with the woman, I wasn't with any man again. I was in the woman's hands.

Aminata's father told me that he assumed the separation would not be for long. As the rebels moved on, Mammy Haja went along and took Aminata with her. They also took all of the young boys and young men to train. The adults of the village were heartbroken, not knowing when they would see their children again. During this time, Aminata was often sent into Freetown to buy drugs—mostly a crude form of heroin and some cocaine—to bring back to the fighters.

She knew if she tried to escape she would be found out and possibly even killed. Eventually, her family was able to secure her release, and now she is attending secondary school with her fellow ex-combatant children. She says those days are hard to forget. She still sees some of her former captors, men who have been retrained as members of the national army, manning checkpoints near her village. She never went through a formal demobilization program, so she is not eligible for the benefits nongovernmental organizations (NGOs) offer other child ex-combatants. In fact, of the approximately 20 young people in her village who were abducted, only three are eligible for benefits.

Aminata's story is interesting for many reasons. First, there are the issues of abduction and sexual abuse that are familiar in stories of female child soldiers. But in this case, she was not exactly abducted. Rather, her father turned her over willingly in an effort to protect her. She never carried a gun but played a supporting role. She was not living with a rebel commander but moved along with the rebels, with someone who saw herself as an adoptive mother. Her main concern now is how to get registered somehow to get some of the benefits she sees others getting.

Hard data on girl soldiers in Sierra Leone are notoriously hard to come by. Conciliation Resources (1997) estimated that 10,000 women were associated with the RUF. McKay and Mazurana (2004, 92) estimate that 35 percent of all fighters were children and that 25 percent of these were girls. Save the Children UK (2005) claims that as many as 40 percent of child soldiers were girls. Despite these high numbers, the percentage of girls in formal demobilization programs was about 8 percent compared to boys (hence the difficulty in collecting reliable data on the population of girl soldiers) (Brooks 2005, 16). Most of what we know about girls associated with the fighting forces who did not go through a formal demobilization (most of them) is through interviews with random individuals.[3]

Girl soldiers are often mentioned as a priority in UN documents. The Capetown Principles (Conciliation Resources 1997) state that "particular attention should be paid to the special needs of girls and special responses should be developed to this end." The 1998 report by Olara Otunno, the Special Representative of the Secretary General for Children and Armed Conflict, discusses the situation in Sierra Leone at great length; however, he makes no mention of the need for special programs for girls in Sierra Leone. In the section on "Promoting research on thematic issues," Otunno (1998) concludes that more research is needed on sexual abuse and violence against girls and young women. He also concludes that more research is needed on the role of local value systems, especially local values favoring child protection, the status of such values, and ways in which they can be reinforced. In particular, he recommends finding ways to support the Sande and Poro initiation societies that girls and boys, respectively, join to become social adults, but he is not clear on the form such support would take.

The fact is, there are few programs for girl soldiers and little is known about them. In Sierra Leone, some girls went through the formal system, showing up in interim care centers, but their number was small, and they were not well served. Brooks (2005) reports that as the girl combatants moved into the interim care centers and the reintegration phase, there was a lack of attention to the need for separate and gender-specific services for girls. He concludes that programming was shaped by the profile of beneficiaries, who tended to be male adolescents.

This is not to say that nothing was attempted for girls. I know of several programs in Sierra Leone, for example the Conforti Centre in the east end of Freetown. The center was designed for young mothers who hope to return to their communities. It provides a form of extended interim care to ensure the protection and development of their infants, time for mediation with the families and skills building for the young women to sustain them in their futures. In addition, the Forum for African Women Educationalists has several programs to assist girl ex-combatants with education.

To be fair, partly in response to concerns about girls in Sierra Leone, there has been new interest in this topic in the past several years, and gender mainstreaming in DDR (disarmament, demobilization, and reintegration) for adults and children is a new topic of interest for those planning responses to today's African conflicts. McKay and Mazurana (2004) have done some important comparative work on girl soldiers. Although child soldiers exist around the world, a focus just on Africa reveals that in Angola, Mozambique, Uganda, and Liberia there is a similar pattern of low rates of formal demobilization among girls (Mazurana et al. 2002, 119). A number of possible explanations have been put forward for this state of affairs, but clearly to design better programs it is necessary to understand the problems of girls' reintegration. I claim that in Sierra Leone girls' reintegration is different from boys', and it is explicitly gendered.

REINTEGRATION OF GIRLS

My main point in this section is that the problems of war-affected girls are different from the problems of war-affected boys, and yet reintegration programs tend to be one-size-fits-all, to the detriment of girls. There are many fewer programs for girls, and they do not serve the population of girls affected by war. There are, of course, also boys who are spontaneous reintegrators, but the issue is much more widespread for girls. Why don't these programs attract the people they are designed to help? The answer can be found by understanding the set of cultural possibilities for girls. It is important to recognize the fact that both their participation and reintegration happen in specifically gendered ways, and that any hope of understanding their situation requires a sociocultural approach.

In their struggle to be accepted back into their communities, boys use what I have called discourses of abdicated responsibility: "I was on drugs," "I was abducted," "It wasn't my choice," and so on.[4] Interestingly, I have found that the discourse "I am just an innocent child" is *not* as important in Sierra Leone as it is to a Western audience. On the other hand, I rarely heard girls making use of the same discourses of abdicated responsibility as boys. Though, in practice, they often had very similar situations— they were abducted just as the boys were—there is some degree to which sexual activity, even rape, is perceived to be their own fault, or at least something that cannot easily be undone.[5] My research shows that in many cases it is easier for a boy to be accepted after amputating the hands of villagers than it is for a girl to be accepted after being the victim of rape. As Mansaray (2000, 143) notes, "For some women, life will never be the same;

while men can move on, remarry and start new families, women victims of rape have no such chance. Although they are victims, their lives are forever marred by the social stigma associated with rape."

What this means is that girls use different scripts about their reintegration. It means they are more likely to slink home anonymously (with their pregnancy or their baby) and try to keep the whole thing quiet. Their strategy is secrecy and hope for eventual marriage. This is true partially because of the culture of girls going away to get married, and families will often collaborate in secrecy to keep a girl marriageable. Bledsoe (1990), writing about Mende girls' marriage strategies, talks about women and marriage as currency for patron/client hierarchies. She says, "since young women bear valued children and provide most subsistence and household labor, giving them in marriage has long comprised the cornerstone of families' efforts to create obligations toward both potential patrons and clients" (Bledsoe 1990, 292). For these reasons, in general, girls are more likely to be informal reintegrators or "spontaneous reintegrators."

Some girls ended up with their demobilized commanders in DDR camps[6] as "camp followers" rather than demobilizing on their own. Some analysts speculate that the control the fighter lost by giving up his arms was compensated for by keeping as many children as possible under his control in the camp. Girls were kept under particular control and represented a presence among "camp followers" that contrasted sharply with their absence in interim care centers (Brooks 2005).

Another reason girls may choose not to enter formal reintegration programs is that the primary long-term benefit offered by formal reintegration programs is help with schooling. Most girls in Sierra Leone don't go to school (especially those who may have missed years of potential schooling while "in the bush"). Formal programs simply don't offer the sort of help many girls feel they need to achieve what they want or feel pressured to earn: respectability and marriage potential.

There are skills training programs in soap making and gara dying, but there are many critiques of such programs: the explosion of similar skills training programs around the country means that people with those skills will easily exceed demand, and production of these products requires an investment in raw materials that may be difficult. Of course, similar problems have been noted with skills training programs for boys, but again, we come up against the notion of different social trajectories for boys and girls because of the traditional sexual division of labor in Sierra Leone. It is easier to imagine an ex-combatant boy, trained for example as a tailor and possibly provided with a sewing machine, making a new identity as a local tailor. It is rare to see a woman who can support herself solely through such individual industry.

Young mothers are especially vulnerable; their babies are sometimes perceived as the "rebels" of tomorrow.[7] Some are rejected by their communities;

others leave ashamed of their failure to fulfill the roles expected of them. One outcome is a proliferation in the number of commercial sex workers in the cities; another is their return to their commanders in the bush. Interestingly, some agencies are addressing the problem of child mothers by, in some cases, encouraging girls to marry their former commanders and captors. People generally realize this is a delicate position, but the point is that culturally marriage somehow solves the problem of reintegration for girls in a way unavailable to boys. No one would suggest that boys formalize their relationship to their erstwhile captors.

However, there is discussion of trying to get former rebel boys and girls to marry each other. The staff of a child protection NGO that ran an interim care center and other alternative care facilities for child ex-combatants were very proud of the fact that two of their hardest cases—a boy and a girl, formerly fighters with the RUF—had been married by the priest who ran the program and were now trying to make it on their own. I heard this strategy echoed by ordinary members of the public. In a debate with a young Sierra Leonean lawyer I knew, I asked whether it seemed fair to him that "rebel girls" were less easily accepted into society than "rebel boys." He agreed that it was not fair, but that it was unavoidable. "I wouldn't want one of those girls marrying into my family," he explained. He suggested the solution that the rebel boys and girls should be married to each other; then there would be no stigma. This strategy is not only suggested for ex-combatants, but the National Forum for Human Rights (2001, 12) reports that "in some parts of the country, perpetrators of rape are encouraged to marry the victim."

On a more positive note, there are some changes for girls and women in Sierra Leone. The Search for Common Ground Report on human rights in Sierra Leone (Abdalla et al. 2002) found that many Sierra Leoneans are, perhaps surprisingly, talking about the positive effects of the war. They say things such as "there's a new awareness. We can never go back again." In particular, several informants mentioned that there is a new appreciation in Sierra Leone of the role of women. This came about from women's struggles to support themselves and their families in displacement.

In particular, some teen mothers do return and are accepted by their families and communities. I met the mother of a teenage girl abducted by rebels who told me proudly that she had accepted her girl back, that she was raising her daughter's baby as her own, and that after several years of disruption in her schooling, her daughter was now at the top of her class. This population of girls is changing some of the old rules that say that once a girl gives birth, she can never attend school again.[8] Although I have talked a lot about the unequal impact of a moral discourse, and the traditional expectation that girls should just get married, one of the unexpected results of the war is that the practices and ideologies surrounding youth and gender in Sierra Leone are changing to some degree in response to this population of war-affected girls.

GENDER INEQUALITY AS STRUCTURAL VIOLENCE

Although there have been some small changes, the power relations inherent in the patriarchal and gerentocratic system in Sierra Leone were not produced by the war, and to a large degree they exist unaltered after the war. I believe it is imperative to draw the connection between gender inequality as structural violence and the more spectacular exceptional violence of war. As the UN Development Fund for Women (UNIFEM) says, "The extreme violence that women suffer during conflict does not arise solely out of the conditions of war; it is directly related to the violence that exists in women's lives during peacetime" (Rehn and Sirfleaf 2002, 13). Others have noted continuities between the atrocities of the prewar era and the atrocities of the civil war era (Ferme 1998; Richards 1996), but it is also possible to draw that connection forward into the post-war period.

Drawing such a connection starts with the well-publicized February 2002 study by the Office of the UN High Commissioner for Refugees (UNHCR) and Save the Children UK in which displaced and refugee children told investigators that aid workers and some security forces extracted sexual favors in exchange for food and other services (Save the Children UK, 2002). This was widely reported in the Western media as the sex-for-food scandal. There was shock in the Western media, and Kofi Annan demanded follow-up actions, but no Sierra Leoneans I know were surprised to hear of it.

I was on a big public lorry, traveling to Freetown from up country. We stopped at one of the many checkpoints along to way for the driver, through his apprentice, to give the police a little something. Two ECO-MOG soldiers carrying guns approached the driver for a lift for a fellow soldier and his girlfriend. What could the driver do but comply, and the two new passengers hung on near the doorway. The girl couldn't have been more than 13, and she was dressed skimpily and giggling. The soldier shouted and waved to his colleagues along the way. My fellow passengers started commenting on this sorry state of affairs in a way that the girl could understand but the man could not. She just smiled back at them. When the two came down from the vehicle, the passengers erupted in critique: "What is wrong with our youth today? Why do they live such useless lives? Why don't they value education?" However, there was no criticism of the ECOMOG soldier.

It was reported in the Child Protection Committee meetings organized by the Ministry of Social Welfare, Gender and Children's Affairs that there was a problem with young girls hanging around outside UNAMSIL camps up country in hopes of connecting with some rich UN peacekeeper, or at least of trading local produce for UN food supplies. The UNAMSIL representative at the meeting denied that this was happening, but the Sierra Leoneans did not seem surprised. "What can we do?" one asked. "Most times it is the girl's parents who have sent her there."

There is a continuity here that must not be ignored. The problems of girls in Sierra Leone did not start and stop with the war, and understanding their "reintegration" requires understanding the situation of young women in Sierra Leone. What does it mean to be "reintegrated" into a system of such inequity? How does one define a successful reintegration: a return to the status quo? Or is there room for another model?

CONCLUSIONS

When most people talk about "youth" in Africa they usually mean young men. And the discussion about post-war reintegration—the national debate about what to do with these young men—rarely spreads to discussions about the girls. They are for the most part simply not on the nation's agenda. Humanitarians working for reintegration of child soldiers admit that girls are falling through the cracks of their interventions. I believe they are missing a great deal by applying a normative framework, seeing these girls always as passive victims, and by not seeing the range of possible desirable outcomes that the girls themselves see. As Burman says about Western conceptions of children affected by war, "If the price of innocence is passivity, then the cost of resourcefully dealing with conditions of distress and deprivation is to be pathologised" (1994, 244). We gain a lot by close attention to how the girls are maneuvering through the system and how girls understand their ambivalent agency—what choices, if any, they see for themselves.

I argue that ethnography makes some things clear that are missing to the humanitarians who tend to see all the girls as victims. The humanitarian agencies use a model that works like this: While children were captive, they were passive victims. Now that they are demobilized, they are choosing what they want to be, getting training, and doing something forward looking. There is an assumption for all child ex-combatants that they go from one type of space to another: *there* they had no agency and were not learning anything; *here* they have agency and are doing something better for their future. The assumption is of a clear break. In many ways in practice, the break is not that clear. Children are dealing with some of the same daily struggles. There is still structural and symbolic violence in their everyday lives. There are continuities that are ignored by the humanitarian viewpoint.

In her article on Western fantasies of childhood and the iconography of emergencies, Burman (1994, 248) concludes: "the commitment to ... Northern models of childhood pathologises children and helps to promote dynamics of relating towards emergencies and disasters that reiterate prevailing power relations." I would like to end on a somewhat provocative note in this era of the triumph of truth and reconciliation commissions. I believe one challenge for humanitarian agencies is to find a way to help girls rebuild their lives while working *within* the culture of secrecy.

Usually, when policy analysts talk about the need for culturally appropriate solutions to post-war reconciliation, they are looking for some kind of silver bullet, for example, a community cleansing ceremony that can be funded and performed. Understanding the day-to-day practices of forgiveness and reconciliation requires a much more nuanced understanding of culture. Because the current outreach efforts aren't working, perhaps the only way forward is to figure out how to work within a framework of secrecy *without* complicity in violence, structural and otherwise.

NOTES

1. McKay and Mazurana disagree with me about the presence of women in the CDF. However, I have asked several experts on the CDF, and they agree that women were involved in ceremonial initiation activities but not in combat.

2. The names of all informants in this chapter are pseudonyms.

3. One exception to this is Coulter's evaluation of the "girls left behind" project of UNICEF, where she went out of her way to interview beneficiaries and nonbeneficiaries of the program about their challenges; another is Megan McKenzie's 2006 interviews of women combatants about the DDR process, published in MacKenzie (2009).

4. Utas (2005) describes the same phenomenon in Liberia, but calls it "victimcy."

5. Burman (1994, 241) notes that key areas that threaten to blur the heavily invested boundary between childhood and adulthood include children's knowledge (especially sexual knowledge) and activity (especially political, economic and violent activity).

6. DDR camps were set up for demobilizing adult ex-combatants to, in part, provide counseling on life in post-war Sierra Leone.

7. A recent chapter by Baldi and MacKenzie (2007) looks in more detail at the problems of the children born as a result of sexual violence in Sierra Leone.

8. Bledsoe (1990) cites a Sierra Leonean secondary school teacher who says, "The schools in Sierra Leone do not generally admit girls who have given birth: mothers. She is not considered a school girl again."

PART III

Sexual Violence in War and Conflict

CHAPTER 8

Rape as a Marker and Eraser of Difference: Darfur and the Nuba Mountains (Sudan)

Sondra Hale

Like many other ethnic conflicts in the contemporary era, conflicts in Sudan have been marked by oversimplifications of the religious and ethnic makeup of the fighting parties. The Sudanese civil war was often framed as a fight between the "Arab Muslim" North and the "African Christian/animist" South, ignoring the unrepresentativeness and fluid nature of these categories and the existence of culturally and religiously diverse regions in the East and West of Sudan. In reality, these conflicts are much more complicated than they are often portrayed. For example, in the Nuba Mountains in Western Sudan, adherents to various religions have historically shared not only towns and territories but also homes and families. In Darfur, the "Arabs" are indigenous, black, and African, and often cannot be racially distinguished from the "indigenous" people they are portrayed as attacking for racial reasons.

Despite these real-life divergences from the inherited notion that the Sudanese conflicts are between Arabs and black Africans, this discourse is perpetuated in the international arena. These stories have become self-fulfilling prophecies in the Darfur region, where animosity has now become rigidified around the political labels assigned to Arabs and Africans. People are increasingly behaving according to their place in this constructed racial dichotomy. Citizens are becoming racialized in relation to each other and, partially as a result of that racialization, the conflict has become sexualized. In winning international support, Darfur leaders of particular ethnic groups, usually more settled agriculturalists, have learned to characterize themselves as the African victims of an Arab regime (de Waal 2004a; Aidi 2005, 40–56).

In this chapter, I use gender, race, and culture as lenses to read aspects of genocide in Sudan and genocide more generally. In this analysis, I explore the causes and reasons for the high volume of perpetration of gender-based (mainly sexual) violence in the Darfur region in Western Sudan and in the Nuba Mountains in West-Central Sudan (de Waal 2004; Aidi 2005).

Using evidence from years of ethnographic fieldwork in Sudan, from my recent interviews (in 2002, 2003, and 2004) with Nuba women, and from knowledge and impressions of the Darfur crisis gleaned from an early visit to Darfur and from firsthand reportage, I argue that the uses of women's bodies to symbolize the culture is a way for the men to maintain their power, exalting women's bodies in ways that beg the protecting of women's bodies and the products of those bodies. In times of crises, women's bodies, at some point, lose that symbolic role and become material. In these crises, such as the prolonged war in the Nuba Mountains and the current conflict in Darfur, women are logical targets for the enemy.

I also argue that the rapes occur in the Nuba and Darfur areas not just because men target women for revenge, power, and booty; men are raping *specific* women, that is, members of a particular group. The defiling of women's bodies becomes both symbolic and material/physical, and the culture itself, through the bodies of women, becomes defaced and deracinated. The body, the village, and the ethnic group are left violated. The raping of women of Darfur and of the Nuba Mountains reflects, simultaneously, both *erasures* and *markings*. Rape is an erasure of identity and a marker of identity.

DEFINING GENOCIDE

Within the broader realm of international human rights, perhaps, the most extreme form of the violation of human rights—genocide—is the most difficult to define and to prove. And within this area of human rights, it is not clear just how sexual violence fits into the pattern of genocide. Feminist scholars have, over the past 20 years, been trying to demonstrate the conceptual links between gender subordination, sexual violence, and genocide. Wartime rape is an experience "which is almost exclusively reserved for biological women, and...an act of feminization wherever perpetrated" (Sjoberg 2006a, 11). Spike Peterson and Anne Sisson Runyan point out that there are a number of different types of institutionalized wartime rapes—recreational, national security, and genocidal (1999, 127). Judith Gardam has explained that "wartime rape is never truly individual, but an integral part of the system ensuring the maintenance of the subordination of women" (1993, 363–64). This is all the more salient in instances where rape and genocide are paired. Women (and children) suffer in particular ways from crisis situations such as civil war, famine, and attempted genocide or ethnocide, but until very recently, this phenomenon has been deemphasized in law and scholarship. It is these particular ways, manifested horribly in Sudan, that this chapter explores.

I argue that the intersection of gender and culture in genocidal rape can explain more about sexual violence in genocide than previous gender-based analyses. Specifically, I argue that the particular suffering of women in genocide must be read through culture. One cannot stress enough the significant and strategic positioning of women within culture. As we know, women are often thought of as the site of culture (Yuval-Davis 1997).

I argue that genocide and genocidal rape need to be reconceptualized in terms of culture. Many experts argue that we should rely on a very tight technical definition that implies intent by the State to eliminate, physically, a particular group of people, an action based on the fact that those people belong to a particular ethnic, cultural, racial, or religious group. However, in many cases of genocide that we have witnessed, intent by the state is very difficult to discover and to prove, not the least problem being the definition of what and who are or are not acting on behalf of the State, for example, in the case of the existence of out-of-control militias or apparatuses of the State that are not under the tight control of the central government, or where the government can disavow them when it is expedient to do so.

An example of this sort of definition is the one in the Convention on Genocide, approved by the United Nations on December 9, 1948, which defines genocide as:

any of the following acts committed with intent to destroy, in whole or in part, a national, ethnical, racial or religious groups, as such: (a) Killing members of the group; (b) Causing serious bodily or mental harm to members of the group; (c) Deliberately inflicting on the group conditions of life calculated to bring about its physical destruction in whole or in part; (d) Imposing measures intended to prevent births within the group; (e) Forcibly transferring children of the group to another group. (Kuper 1981, 19)

Although I am arguing that we still retain the 1948 United Nations (UN) Genocide Convention's definition of "genocide," I propose broadening the scope of the concept beyond physical (eliminating a people) and even biological (restricting births), to include cultural genocide. Instead of diluting the concept, expansion may serve to clarify and, therefore, to give more utility to the general concept of genocide.

What was originally included and ultimately omitted from the final version of the Convention is cultural genocide, that is, "destruction of the specific character of the persecuted 'group' by forced transfer of children, forced exile, prohibition of the use of the national language, destruction of books, documents, monuments, and objects of historical, artistic or religious value" (Kuper 1981).

However, even broadening the concept of "genocide" to include "eth-nocide" is inadequate in aiding interpretations of the particular ways in which women are affected in some of these areas, including Sudan, often with the intent or de facto effect of ethnocide (e.g., enslaving women, rape, forced marriage). Therefore, I argue that (1) foregrounding atrocities and aggressions against Sudanese women may enhance our theoretical and political abilities to analyze genocide, in general; and (2) focusing on the Nuba Mountain and Darfur groups gives us the broadest range of behaviors on which to develop a theory of cultural genocide or ethnocide by which we can elaborate for the rest of Sudan and beyond.

SUDAN AND CULTURAL GENOCIDE

Sudan, an invention of colonialism,[1] exhibits staggering social, cultural, religious, and economic diversity, with nearly 600 ethnic groups and 110 separate languages. A familiar story is that the Anglo-Egyptian admin-istration divided the country into two main spheres—the North and the South. The North was ruled indirectly through traditional Islamic leader-ship. Islam was allowed to flourish, and Christian missionaries were kept under tight control. The South, on the other hand, was ruled directly and as much by Christian missionaries as by Anglo-Egyptian officials. Mean-while, what is not such a familiar story is that Eastern Sudan (mainly Beja and Hedendowa) and Western and West-Central Sudan (namely Darfur and the Nuba Mountains) were left to languish and have since been embroiled in major conflicts with the central Islamist military gov-ernment that has been in power since 1989. That does not mean these areas were left alone, however. The British alienated land in the Nuba Mountains and moved people around to control that land. Darfur has been a constant site of political incursion since Sudanese independence (Johnson 2003).

The Nuba Mountains is an area roughly 40 miles by 90 miles in West-Central Sudan, which is inhabited by about 50 ethnic groups and has been the site of substantial conflict between the government of Sudan and a number of antigovernment militarized groups in recent decades. Though the conflict is lesser known than the one in Darfur, it has been in many ways equally horrifying.

During this conflict, virtually every act that has been discussed in the theoretical and popular literature as falling under the rubric of "genocide" has been witnessed and testified to, even if these have not always been carried out simultaneously. In fact, the African Rights group used the term "genocide by *attrition*" (African Rights 1995, 331) to describe the relent-less and exhaustive assaults against citizen groups, some of which were directly sanctioned by the State and others of which were an indirect result of state actions. During these genocidal acts, women have been targeted as a way to destroy the culture and society.

Darfur, about the size of Texas, had a total population of around six million before the genocidal conflict began. Most of the population has been affected by the conflict, which has complicated historical and economic roots that are often obscured by racialized portrayals in global politics and global media. In Darfur, 1.8 million people have been internally displaced, 200,000 have fled to neighboring Chad, and well over 70,000 have died.[2] During this conflict, there has been an intense and focused targeting of women as a pathway to the destruction of culture and society, which, I argue, can be identified as "gendercide."

GENDER, RACE, CULTURE, AND GENOCIDE

In my empirical research in Sudan, I have observed paradoxes in the victimization of women and in the role women play in conflict narratives. The paradox in the victimization of women is that women are highly visible as victims in times of war or crisis, and yet the violence against women in times of war is often obscured and normalized. The paradox in the role women play in conflict narratives is that they are often exalted as markers of culture but play an equally important (if opposite) role in discourses about cultural erosion or collapse.

Catherine MacKinnon, in associating rape and genocide in the Bosnian case, argued that:

Human rights have not been women's rights—not in theory or in reality, not legally or socially, nor domestically or internationally. Rights that human beings have by virtue of being human have not been rights to which women have had access, nor have violations of women as such been part of the definition of the violation of the human as such on which human rights law has traditionally been predicated. (MacKinnon 1994, 5)

MacKinnon asserts that in genocide through war, "mass rape is a tool, a tactic, a policy, a plan, a strategy, as well as a practice." As a result, "in the West, the sexual atrocities have been discussed largely as rape or as genocide, not as what they are, which is rape as genocide" (MacKinnon 1994, 9). What is significant to MacKinnon is not that this (the Bosnian, or Nuba, or Darfur cases) is the kind of aggression men routinely perpetrate against women. To her, this obscures the fact that these rapes (performed during genocidal war) "are being done by *some* men against *certain* women for *specific* reasons" (MacKinnon 1994, 10; emphases mine). This, I would add, we could clearly call "gendercide."

The situation in Sudan is even more complicated than MacKinnon's formulation, which takes culture, inscribed onto women's bodies, as a given. If what is different about a culture, that is, how a culture distinguishes itself from others, is seen by members of that culture (usually male members, with the complicity of some women) to reside in the bodies of women, then violating the bodies of women becomes a violation of that culture. And, in the case of Darfur, where bodily differences between those classified as Africans and those classified as Arabs may be subtle, rape can be simultaneously an erasure of difference and a marker of difference. That is, when a man rapes a woman, he is distinguishing himself as a man raping a woman. In ethnocide cases, he is marking difference by raping the woman of the other. But by raping her, he is committing one of a series of acts to annihilate difference, that is, culture, while perhaps augmenting his own. Evidence for this interpretation can be seen in both the Nuba and Darfur conflicts.

THE NUBA

The Nuba have been subjected to the following elements of genocide, cultural genocide, and ethnocide: murder; massacre; rape; detention and torture; abduction and disappearance; dislocation; incarceration and isolation; assault on religion (even on their brand or type of Islam); loss of place names, monuments, and other markers of culture; the changing of their names; removal or disruption of subsistence livelihood; land alienation; forced circumcision of males and females; women forced to marry outside the group; a purge of the educated among them; loss of language and religion; destruction of homes, property, and animals; massacres such as the one carried out in 1991; slavery; harassment and intimidation; separation from one's family (especially men and women have been separated in the peace camps); the withholding of food or the manipulation of food distribution (and resultant famines); missionizing, reeducating, or reindoctrinating; and many other negative strategies. It is not hard to see the centrality of women in these processes.[3]

Women of the Nuba Mountains have also been subjected to gender-specific violence, particularly rape. Rape functions in this situation in a number of ways: (1) as a kind of ethnic cleansing; that is, it is used as a way to eliminate a despised group; (2) to humiliate and demoralize the opposition; (3) to reproduce a different group of Nuba, that is, a group without a clear ethnic identification, what we term deracination; (4) to break down the social fabric of the society; (5) to undermine the moral canons of the society; and (6) to bring half of the population into submission. At the same time the act of humiliating the women of one's enemy serves as a morale booster for the state armies and militias.

DARFUR

The people of Darfur have experienced a number of processes that would seem to be elements of the annihilation of group difference, the most effective of which seems to be gendercide. Among the acts to annihilate difference are murder; massacre; rape; detention and torture; abduction and disappearance; dislocation; incarceration and isolation; the loss of place names, monuments, and other markers of culture; the removal or disruption of subsistence livelihood; land alienation; a purge of the educated among them; destruction of homes, property, and animals; slavery; harassment and intimidation; the separation from one's family; the withholding of food or the manipulation of food distribution; and many other negative strategies. As in the Nuba case, it is not hard to see the centrality of women in these processes.

As in the Nuba Mountains, the people of Darfur have been the targets of gender-specific violence, including sexual violence and genocidal rape. The conflict in Darfur, however, demonstrates clearly that gender-based violence in ethnic conflict is not only about gender but also about culture.

Mass rape, as we witnessed in Bosnia and are now seeing in Darfur, is more specific than men being aggressive with women, targeting them because they are weaker than men, or unarmed, or left behind in the villages. They are targeted because of what they represent in the culture and the ways in which they represent the culture itself, the ways in which the culture resides in women's bodies. Therefore, if annihilating difference, which is part of what we are seeing in Darfur, is the intent, then annihilating women's dignity and rights through a violation of her body is the same as annihilating the culture.

Rape is usually seen as an appropriation of the woman's body. I argue, instead, that rape is a cultural marker, an act that creates a racial or ethnic difference where one did not exist before, except perhaps in name. In Darfur it is a marking of territory, a branding. But it is also an exposure of difference. To put it another way, differences are created or invented through rape. The process of deracination through rape is an attempt to annihilate difference, not to make you just like me, but rather to erase what you have been. This makes deracination very different from forced assimilation. Unlike forced assimilation, it is a way of marking. One leaves one's mark. The raped person is marked. The former person is erased. The group is deracinated by one.

The matter is further complicated when the conflict situation is so clearly racialized in the act of attempted deracination, for example, when a Janjaweed man says to a woman whom he has raped, "This is to make a whiter baby."[4] Yet it is even more complicated when he is as dark-skinned as she is.

Although the Darfur crisis is Muslim against Muslim and African against African, the central government in its Arabo-centered ideology has invented it otherwise, and the world press has obliged. Whether or not genealogies are putative, the Janjaweed are invented as "Arab" and act as such; whereas the Fur, Zaghawa, and Masalit are treated as "African." This is a creation of the last phase of this conflict, with the militia acting in their role as enforcers, like the armed cowboys of the American western range trying to drive the farmers off the land so the cowboys' cattle can graze and roam. That the conflict has taken on a racial dimension (when differences are very subtle and oftentimes nonexistent) only serves to intensify the violence against women.

Women have been subjected to individual and gang rapes, to torture, and to other forms of sexual violence. Rape has been used for humiliation by raping women in front of their husbands, relatives, or the wider community. Abductions and sexual slavery have also been rampant. Rapes and abductions have been frequent in Internally Displaced Persons settlements, sometimes carried out by the Janjaweed, who often attack these camps, or by government security forces.

CONCLUSION: RAPE AND THE EROTICS OF VIOLENCE

Long ago feminist scholars dismissed the idea that rape was erotic, or even sexual, and while I agree with that notion, one cannot now refute imperial (with attendant militias) attempts to sexualize violence. Most of the rapes in Darfur and the Nuba Mountains have been carried out by militaries or paramilitaries. This sexualization of violence serves a number of purposes, as I have argued, not the least of which is the demolition of particular ethnic groups.

The sexualization of violence in the long-lasting Sudanese civil war (north against south) and the Darfur and Nuba conflicts demonstrates first that wartime sexual violence against women is not only *about women and gender* but also *about race and culture,* and cannot be understood without both analytical concepts. Second, the racialization of a conflict, or the perpetration of ethnocide or cultural genocide, serves to intensify wartime violence against women, particularly sexual violence. This intensification is caused by the identification of women as symbols of culture, and the identification of a culture's strength or weakness with the ability to protect its women.

Third, and more complexly, the intensification of sexual violence against women in ethnic conflict has multiple meanings. It means, as we have come to understand through the work of many feminist scholars, that the culture is being attacked through the symbol of its strength—its women. But it can also be seen, as this chapter has argued, as both a marker and erasure of difference. Genocidal rape marks difference by attacking the "other," but it also erases it by destroying or attacking the ethnic purity of the "other" through forced pregnancy. Sexual violence against women in ethnocide, then, both identifies and destroys the otherness of the victim. Fourth, the otherness that sexual violence in war marks and erases is itself often a cultural construct. As the introduction to this chapter pointed out, the framing of the Sudanese civil war (the recently ended conflict between northern versus southern Sudan) as one of Arabs against blacks and Muslims against Christians is oversimplified if not without basis in history.

Likewise, the framing of the struggle in Darfur as Arabs against Africans is oversimplified. Still, and finally, it is important to note that the construction of the otherness marked on and erased from women's bodies in ethnic conflict does not make it any less real, or the humanitarian consequences for women any less devastating. Instead, using gender, race, and culture as lenses to read genocide, we can see the complexity of constructed race and gender roles culturally inscribed on women's bodies as a source of the prevalence of sexual violence in ethnic conflict, in Darfur, in the Nuba Mountains, and around the world.

NOTES

1. This is to say that the borders of Sudan as a political entity were not drawn by the Sudanese people or their government, or a group including those people and their relevant neighbors. Instead, they were drawn by imperial Britain with the input of British-colonized Egypt, without extensive consultation with the people who would be grouped in the Sudanese state.

2. This is a conservative estimate; some have placed the death toll at around 300,000. For an in-depth discussion, see Hagan, Rymond-Richmond, and Parker (2005).

3. Through my interviews with Nuba women in Kampala, Uganda, in 2002 and in Khartoum/Omdurman, Sudan, in 2003 and again in 2004, I was able to see the particular ways women were the focus of the government and of Arab militias in breaking down the family, deracinating through various means such as forced marriage outside the group, creating cultural confusion through forced relocation, and depleting the morale of the entire group by sexually humiliating women.

4. Personal interview material collected by the author between 2001 and 2004.

CHAPTER 9

The Everyday/Everynightness[1] of Rape: Is it Different in War?

Liz Kelly

Much is to be learned about rape (inside and outside of "war") from an extraordinary contemporaneous account covering 63 days at the end of World War II (Anonymous 2005). The anonymous female journalist challenges us to think carefully about not only how we define rape but also what it means to women and how they manage physically and emotionally in the aftermath, including the complexity of their silences. *A Woman in Berlin* contains haunting accounts of the horror and trauma of rape by the Russian army, but also of the patriarchal bargains many women made as the need for preservation of self and others came to the fore. As news of German defeats outside Berlin seeps through, women begin making nervous jokes about what they may face next. Sexual violence is spoken of, but implicitly, recognized as a threat to everyone, and some young women are hidden in roofs and crawl spaces and some choose to pass as men.

Our diarist describes the first days of the Russian army's occupation of Berlin as "unbridled raping sprees," with individuals and groups of men taking sex whenever and wherever they feel like it. Understanding the male protection racket, many women try to adapt it to this chaotic context—making alliances with individual men, preferably officers and/or men feared by others—trading sexual access for food and a semblance of protection. On one hand, the book is an account of the unrelenting unwanted sex visited on the women of Berlin—rape not as weapon of war, but women as the spoils of war. On the other hand, the book, and the experiences of the women it documents, graphically illustrates the conundrum of victimization. This memoir honors how women negotiate the limited space for action available to them, while never shirking from describing the daily brutality. The challenge for feminists is to construct theory with such complexities and nuance.

As a feminist who has worked on violence against women for three decades, what remained with me from the narrative was the variations—in what happens to women, how they attempt to manage marauding men and relations with others, and how they construct meaning. Some young and older women are saved, others suffer and are even sacrificed, many cope as best they can, and others are killed, seriously injured, and/or lose their minds. Military men are not presented as a rapacious gang—some are brutal and animalistic, others operate only in groups, and a few are presented as seeking female company and never using physical force. Then there are the German men in Berlin who have to deal with defeat, dishonor, and being unmanned. That these variations exist does not detract from the coercive context, a militarized gender order, but they do demand that we pay attention to the ways in which human beings use their space for action, requiring more complex explorations in theory and research not just of masculinities but also of men's actions and motivations (see, for example, Coy, Horvath, and Kelly 2007, on men who pay for sex).

This chapter sets out to do just that. Combining empirical evidence and feminist analytical frameworks, it argues for a continuum approach to "wartime rape" and "rape" more generally, looking at the benefits of connecting work on sexual violence across contexts and the payoffs for the shared feminist project of challenging the presumption of firm boundaries between war and peace.

SEXUAL VIOLENCE IN THE FEMINIST PROJECT

Many histories of 20th-century feminism regard rape and sexual violence as a key organizing issue, which it undoubtedly was during the 1970s. Heady combinations of activist protest, passionate polemic, and more considered research and commentary led governments to embark on reforms of statute and procedural responses to rape and sexual assault. These changes gathered momentum in the 1980s and early 1990s, informed by critical legal commentary and rigorous research on the process of reporting rape and conducting rape trials (see Kelly 2002). Some aspects of the reform process were common—for example removing unique evidential requirements, such as the corroboration rule (Temkin 2002)—others, including how rape was defined, varied across jurisdictions. A shared ambition among reformers, however, was to increase reporting and confidence in the criminal justice system. In addition, feminist and critical legal theorists were also committed to the removal of explicit and implicit gender bias in the letter and practice of law. Implicit in these efforts was recognition that sexual violence was underreported and that legal cases faced discriminatory barriers to achieving just outcomes. Research findings confirmed both, and prevalence studies on violence against women demonstrated that sexual violence was less likely to come to the attention of state agencies and officials (Johnson, 1996).

The 1990s, however, was the decade of domestic violence, and rape was only recognized in the context of conflict. Here a parallel process of awareness raising and reform was undertaken at the international level. The recognition of rape as a war crime, and in certain contexts as a form of genocide, are the most widely recognized achievements, but arguably, the definition of rape as "sex in coercive circumstances"[2] and making sexual history and character evidence irrelevant are as significant in international jurisprudence (Bedont and Hall-Martinez 1999). As with the reforms at national levels, the intent was to challenge impunity, enhance access to justice, and challenge narrow understandings of sexual violence.

A key question for this chapter, therefore, is how effective these strategies have been. I offer some reflections through an examination of how rape is named, defined, and understood and the process of attrition. In the process I raise some questions about feminist and international agency rhetoric with respect to rape in the context of war.

THEORIZING COERCIVE SEX

A basic issue in any context is what counts as rape or sexual violence. Feminist research and activism have had considerable success in extending narrow legal framings, through establishing comparable harms across forms of assault and relationships with perpetrators. At the same time, the media—and to an extent women's advocacy groups—have drawn on the extremes, emphasizing the paradigmatic elements of rape, including its traumatic impacts, as a strategy for change (Gavey 2005). This pattern is also evident with respect to conflict, with the emphasis on the mass rapes, those taking place in public and those that were part of deliberate actions with nationalist and militarist motivations. Outside of conflict, we know that most rapes take place in the complexity of everyday interactions between women and men, and that women frequently struggle to name their experiences of unwanted sex rape. Feminist researchers have approached this conundrum in several ways: when doing qualitative research I allocated incidents to categories that reflected women's definitions, crafting a continuum between pressurized and coerced sex and rape. Others using quantitative data have applied legal definitions to behavioral descriptions, labeling as rape events women have not yet named as such. Neither is right; both are valid approaches to a contested and complex terrain.

In the early feminist texts, while rape is seen as one form of social control of women, rapists are still implicitly understood as strangers with deviant sexuality. The presumed relatively rare events were connected, by some, to more mundane "petty rapes" (Greer 1971), but the journey from this point to asking foundational questions about the construction of heterosexuality and masculinity spanned two decades and encompassed key texts and argumentative engagements within and without women's movements. One of the earliest moves, however, was in the opposite direction—with strong efforts, especially in North America, to redefine rape as a crime of violence rather than sex; this claim was intended to refocus attention away from female victims and onto the actions of male perpetrators.[3] Catherine MacKinnon (2001) subsequently, and succinctly, notes that to define rape as a crime of violence is to avoid asking what the harms of "sex as usual" are for women. The concept of sexual violence as a continuum (Kelly 1987) provided one route for theorizing connections between taken for granted sexual pressure and coercion and criminalized violations. Social research provided both new information and confirmation of these shifts (Hamner and Saunders 1984; Russell 1984), especially by documenting that most sexual violence is committed by men known to women and girls, men who are part of their everyday lives and whose very normality challenged clinical constructions of sex offenders.

For almost two decades currents of thinking and representation have been pulling in different directions: some feminist analysis has continued to locate sexual violence (and rape in particular) within understandings of heteronormativity; others have focused on specific contexts, such as conflict, alongside a resurgence in more traditional criminological and psychological constructions of sex offenders and sexual offenses as representing a break with social norms. Within feminist theory the victimhood/agency debate constitutes a new fault line, and the more thoughtful engagements explore intersections between the two (see, for example, Kelly, Burton, and Regan 1996; Lamb 1999) that are rarely acknowledged. As social scientists were exploring these complex questions about how we become women and men and how we "do" gender, feminist activism—at least in much of the West—declined. Simultaneously, and not unconnected, popular culture returned to more comforting binary positions, preferring to otherize sex offenders—through the rehabilitation of the term "pedophile" (Cowburn and Dominelli 2001; Kelly 1996) and use of the term "date rape" as a shorthand through which to suggest that incidents of unwanted sex are not really rapes at all (McColgan 1996)—in response to the feminist challenge that had implicated fathers, partners, pastors, and friends as common sex offenders. In some senses the rape war trope fitted this revision, and many commentaries located sexual aggression in the enemy and the rules of war, rather than analyzing how gender orders and gender relations are miltarized. I argue in the remainder of this chapter that the perceived distinction between everyday/everynight[4] rape and wartime rape ignores both the sexual nature of rape in war and the harms and symbolic meanings of all rapes.

IS RAPE IN WAR DIFFERENT?

This section revisits arguments used to distinguish rape in war. Some scholars have argued that rape is in war is more silenced. Sexual crime carries shame and stigma in all contexts, but it is accentuated in *some* conflict situations by the deliberate manipulation of ethnic divisions. Here, to speak out brings shame to the social group not just the individual woman. However, the power of this framing is precisely that these meanings already exist and silence women. At the same time, at some points in conflict situations women may be encouraged to speak out, to expose the inhumanity of the enemy, and reenergize nationalist sentiment. Invariably this injunction to speak out is reversed by governments as political rather than military resolution to the conflict takes the fore. Sexual violence is never entirely silenced in any context, and some women and girls always choose to voice their complaints; so here we need to ask who authorizes pain to be spoken and recognized. When and for what purpose and why do women respond?

Another argument made about wartime rape is that the risk of victimization is heightened. The threat of rape acting as a limitation on women's freedom has been a recurring theme in feminist thought, empirically bolstered by data on the fear of crime and women's use of public space (Gordon and Riger 1991). The sense and actuality of risk is contextual, and although all women may be raped, the distribution of risk is not equal across age and other social divisions or contexts. As Elisabeth Wood (2006) has argued, there is considerable variation across conflicts.

Third, it has been argued that wartime rape can be distinguished by the failure to vigorously investigate and prosecute rape and uphold women's right to sexual autonomy. Although failure to recognize and punish wartime rape is evident, this relies on a presumption that, outside conflict, rape is dealt with in a more rigorous and effective manner. That marital rape is not criminalized in much of the globe is just one indicator of the extent to which women's sexual autonomy is not recognized, let alone protected, in law and life.

The fourth argument used to separate wartime rape is that, despite much international concern, there is a failure to provide basic services for victims. This failure represents a continuity across war and peacetime, and there has been limited development of resources for sexual violence services over the past two decades. At least one researcher (Ward 2002) notes that in some countries sexual violence services may be established in a post-conflict context.

BUSINESS AS USUAL

> Men, in part, rape because they can—anything that increases opportunity, access and impunity increases sexual assault. (MacKinnon 2006, 220)

Impunity is a core theme in human rights thinking, initially focused on the ways in which states protect themselves from being held to account for violations of human rights. Calls to end impunity, therefore, have been calls to recognize violations and provide redress. There are parallels with both the feminist project of naming violence against women and the claim that men use violence because they can, and calling men to account is a necessary strategy if violence against women is to be addressed and stemmed.

Impunity formed a central plank of lobbying for rape in conflict to be addressed into international law, focused most intently on recognition of mass rape as a crime against humanity. Feminists have been effective in changing international law and the International Criminal Court (ICC), and specific tribunals are required to investigate and end impunity under the Rome Statutes. They are tasked to focus on the most responsible and worst crimes, and local states are responsible for the rest. Who can be a victim and what counts as rape has been and remains contested, and feminist readings are being reworked. The "impunity gap" is yet to be bridged, and feminists are divided as to whether there have been any gains in terms of the rights and treatment of victims in international law (MacKinnon 2006).

Most commentaries on the ICC and tribunals note that the jurisprudence is good, but the implementation is weak (see, for example, MacKinnon 2006) and plagued by poor investigation, limited resources, and a perception that rape cases are hard to prove.

So how far can progress be said to have taken place at the national level? After a flurry of work in the late 1970s and early 1980s, very few social scientists have devoted their research careers to sexual violence, and even fewer have asked whether the widespread changes to statute and procedure have achieved the anticipated goals of increasing reporting and removing gender bias in legal processes. Feminists and lawyers alike presumed that disconnecting rape from morality, widening its definition, and removing the unique evidential requirements would increase reporting, prosecutions, and convictions.

Rape continues to be the most underreported crime, much more so than intimate partner violence (Kelly 2002), and the decision to not report is connected to fears of disbelief or blame, distrust of the criminal justice process, and divided loyalty where the perpetrator is a intimate/family member/friend.

Exploring the attrition process—the proportion of reported rapes that fall out of legal processes before there is a prosecution or conviction—has been a strong theme in research by the Child and Woman Abuse Studies Unit for more than a decade. Indeed, it was in 1997 that we first traced the process in England and Wales, finding year on year increases in reporting, limited movement in prosecutions, and a virtually static number of convictions; the conviction rate had fallen from one in three reported rape cases in 1977 to less than one in ten in 1997. These trends continued, and the conviction rate reached an all-time low of 1 in 20 in 2005 (Kelly, Lovett, and Regan 2005).

We have subsequently investigated attrition at the more micro level in England and Wales (Kelly, Lovett, and Regan 2005) and contributed to a wider debate about attrition and justice (HMCPSI 2007). Earlier work looking at attrition across Europe (Regan and Kelly 2003) revealed a conundrum: the achievement of formal gender equality in the Nordic countries appears to have had minimal impact on violence against women in general (Kelly 2005) or the attrition rate in rape. This leads in several possible theoretical directions: that violence against women needs to be introduced as a key measure in equality indices, that it has a relative independence from other aspects of formal equality, or that it is a mechanism that some men use to resist changes in gender orders (Kelly 2005).

Most cases are lost at the earliest points: they are not reported at all; there is a failure to investigate properly; there is a dearth of appropriate support to enable victims to feel supported and protected in the process; or the cases is designated as weak evidentially, which is all too often a statement about the credibility of the woman. Many of the problematic issues identified by feminist legal scholars with respect to international law are also relevant at the national level. Prosecutors in national and intentional systems regard rape cases as difficult to prove.

Our attrition studies show that successive legal reforms, including a total overhaul of sexual offenses law in 2003, have failed to halt the increase in impunity. That no other European country can boast any substantial increases in reporting and prosecutions suggests that deeper social and cultural processes are at play (Regan and Kelly 2003). One is undoubtedly the paradoxical way in which feminist knowledge both informs reform processes and is simultaneously disavowed. Thus, despite an acceptance of the wider definition of rape in statute, and to some extent in public attitudes, a narrower meaning—what has been termed "real rape" continues to be reinscribed through the criminal justice system process and populist media: a process noted in early feminist scholarship (Gavey 2005). Here we have direct parallel with the international tribunal processes. We need to explore these overlaps, the continuities between contexts, in order to explicate what factors contribute to impunity across contexts.

The irony here is that many of the rapes publicized with respect to conflict, and certainly those prosecuted as genocidal rape, fit the real rape template. Here, as in peacetime, it is the unwanted sex, which sit on other parts of the continuum, that is not only more complex for women to name—as illustrated by *A Woman in Berlin*—and for legal systems to prosecute but that also represent the deeper challenge to gender orders. This is precisely why feminist jurisprudence is contested. It is not a failure to address sexual violence in war that is the fundamental issue, but that feminist challenges to male entitlement, wherever it is enacted, are a challenge business as usual.

In analyzing sexual violence as a continuum (Kelly 1987), I argued that between consensual sex and rape there is a considerable amount of unwanted and coerced sex. What preoccupies me now is how inclusive it is possible to make the legal concept of rape. How do we get the fact that most rapes are committed by known men to suffuse consciousness? How do we move away from the comforting notion of "date rape" to a more accurate understanding that takes its point of departure as the shifting terrains and content of gender relations in specific contexts. Predatory men do not have to hang around in parks or learn to break into apartments in order to identify potential women victims; they can go to the nearest bar or club and target the woman who looks unhappy, is isolated, and is drinking too much. That he may buy her a drink, engage in conversation, or even offer to see her home does not mean they were on a date. It means he is a skilled operator, one who sets traps that she falls for. Sexual violence is a continuum, some is out of the ordinary and unbearably brutal, much is banal and unbearably mundane; we need all of it in our sights.

One paradox that has received limited attention is the unintended consequence of the construction of rape as a heinous and intrinsically traumatizing event. While it may well be both, it also takes place in the messiness of everyday lives, which too few representations of it allow for. This both encourages many women to not define their experiences of forced sex as rape and ensures that expectations of damage and distress determine whether complainants will be accorded the status of victim. Again, *A Woman in Berlin* provides us with connections.

What does it mean rape? When I said the word for the first time aloud, Friday evening in the basement, it sent shivers down my spine. Now I can think it and write it with an untrembling hand, say it loud to get used to hearing it said. It sounds like the absolute worst, the end of everything—but it's not. (Anonymous 2005, 83)

Undertaking more open and detailed contextual explorations of the complex intersections between silence, shame, support, and trauma, especially the ways in which women do and do not provide space for recognition of harm, would add to a literature that has become overly psychological and individualized (Lamb 1999).

Analyzing the continuum and impunity could lead to a counsel of despair—that legal systems are incapable of understanding, and therefore adjudicating, on all but the most extreme forms of coerced heterosex and that despite our best efforts we are left with real rapes being prosecuted effectively whatever the context. Although there is considerable disappointment in our attempts to craft feminist legal reform, there are also some grounds for hope—cases are prosecuted now that could never have been previously, albeit that progress is halting and insufficient. Women and girls continue to report their rapists, to seek out justice, whatever the context

We need to fill not just the concept of rape, but also responses to it, with new and contemporary meanings, and to guard ourselves against presenting sexual violence in ways that disconnect it from the continuum of unwanted sex in women's lives.

It may only be now that we understand how huge a challenge it is to rethink what rape is and through this develop new understandings of how to approach, investigate, and prosecute it. We have yet to address our best energies to exploring potentials of investigative legal systems and what defining rape as sex in coercive circumstances might offer.

One contribution to this process must include transcending the victim/agency opposition that has bedeviled contemporary theory and critique. A useful place to start would be the voices of women who reflect upon their experiences of sexual violence. Susan Brison (2002), in a moving account of how rape changed her, including how as a philosopher she theorizes the self, challenges simplistic constructions of rape victims in ways that offer a route out of at least one paradox—while victimization constitutes a denial of certain forms of agency, dealing with it and the aftermath necessitates regaining it.

> I develop and defend a view of the self as fundamentally relational—capable of being undone by violence, but also of being remade in connection with others…[the] tension between living to tell and telling to live, that is between getting (and keeping) the story right in order to bear witness and being able to rewrite the story in ways that enable the survivor to go on with her life. (Brinson 2002, xi, xii)

CONCLUSION

Rape and sexual violence are fault lines in gender orders that, when examined, offer insights, and I have drawn on women's accounts and research data across contexts to suggest that there may be more continuities than differences in rape inside and outside war. I conclude that calls to increase support services, improve access to justice, and challenge impunity are common across the contexts of war and peace. If justice and redress are absent when there is no militarized conflict, it cannot be created in its aftermath, no matter now creative and determined we are as academics and activists.

Linking the issues across contexts—alongside calls for procedural justice, access to recognition, support, and redress—might not only challenge impunity but also show ways to increase accountability of men, militaries, and states. So rather than, as Marsh and Ward (2006) do, calling for investment in sexual violence services in the context of post-conflict and humanitarian disasters, feminist and UN agencies should make common cause and demand that the highest quality support and responses are available to women and girls wherever they live, whatever the circumstances.

A close reading of *A Woman in Berlin* demands that we extend the rape as genocide construct of sexual violence in war to recognize the more mundane, and in some conflicts more extensive, everyday/everynight rapes women endure. Within gender orders, militarized or not, we need to be mindful of the continuum of sexual violence: only by guarding against a focus on only the most dramatic examples can we ensure that we are not—however unintentionally—reinforcing notions of "real rape" that continue to play a significant part in reproducing impunity.

NOTES

1. Following Dorothy Smith (1987), indicating the temporal and experienced regularity of trauma.

2. This wording was the definition of rape used in the Akayesu case in the International Court Tribunal for Rwanda in 1998: ICTR-96-4-T.

3. Subsequent research and theorization has illuminated sexual assaults suffered by men and boys, and the occasional involvement of women as perpetrators. This chapter focuses on the paradigmatic and most common pattern—female victimization and male perpetration.

4. I am drawing here on the work of Dorothy Smith (1987).

CHAPTER 10

Sexual Violence during War: Toward an Understanding of Variation

Elisabeth Jean Wood

Sexual violence occurs in all wars, though the extent varies dramatically. During the conflict in Bosnia-Herzegovina, the sexual abuse of Bosnian Muslim women by Bosnian Serb forces was so systematic and widespread that it constituted a crime against humanity under international law. In Rwanda, the widespread rape of Tutsi women was a form of genocide, according to the International Criminal Tribunal for Rwanda. Yet sexual violence in some conflicts is remarkably limited despite other violence against civilians. Even in some cases of ethnic conflict, sexual violence is limited; the conflicts in Israel/Palestine and Sri Lanka are examples. Some armed groups, such as the Salvadoran and Sri Lankan insurgencies, appear to effectively prohibit their combatants from engaging in sexual violence against civilians.

The form of sexual violence varies as well. In some conflicts, it takes the form of sexual slavery; in others, state agents engage in sexualized torture of persons suspected of collaborating with insurgents; in others, combatants target women of particular groups during ethnic or political cleansing; in still others, individuals engage in sexual violence opportunistically; and in some conflicts, all or nearly all forms of sexual violence occur. In some wars, women belonging to particular groups are targeted; in others, the attacks are much less discriminate. In some wars, only females are targeted; in others, males are as well. Some acts of wartime sexual violence are committed by individuals; many are committed by groups. Some acts occur in private settings; many are public, in front of family or community members.

In some settings, wartime sexual violence appears to magnify existing cultural practices; in others, patterns of sexual violence appear to be innovations. In some conflicts, the pattern of sexual violence is symmetric, with all parties to the war engaging in sexual violence to roughly the same extent. In other conflicts, it is very asymmetric as one armed group does not respond in kind to sexual violence by the other party. Sexual violence often increases over the course of the conflict; in some conflicts, it decreases.

Sexual violence varies in extent and form among civil wars and interstate wars, among ethnic and nonethnic wars, and among secessionist conflicts (Wood 2006). Despite the challenges to gathering data on this sensitive topic, the variation does not appear to be a product of inadequately reported violence: there are well-documented cases at the low end and the high end of the spectrum of sexual violence. Recognizing the variation in the frequency and form of wartime sexual violence has important policy implications. In particular, if there are armed groups that do not engage in sexual violence despite other forms of violence against civilians, then rape is not inevitable in war as is sometimes claimed, and we have stronger grounds for holding responsible those armed groups that do engage in sexual violence. Understanding the determinants of the variation in sexual violence may help those United Nations (UN) officials; members of nongovernmental organizations; and government, military, and insurgent leaders who seek to limit sexual violence and other violations of the laws of war.

In accordance with recent international law, by rape I mean the penetration of the anus or vagina with any object or body part or of any body part of the victim or perpetrator's body with a sexual organ, by force or by threat of force or coercion, or by taking advantage of a coercive environment, or against a person incapable of giving genuine consent (ICC 2000, Article 8[2] [e] [vi]-1). Thus, rape can occur against men as well as women. Sexual violence is a broader category that includes rape, nonpenetrating sexual assault, mutilation, sexual slavery, enforced prostitution, enforced sterilization, and forced pregnancy. (Sexual violence differs from the broader category of gender violence in that the latter includes violence that occurs because of the victim's gender without necessarily including sexual contact.)

Focusing on sexual violence against civilians by combatants, I first summarize patterns of variation in form and extent across several war settings. In particular, I document the absence of sexual violence in some conflicts and on the part of some groups. I then assess whether the causal mechanisms identified in the literature (often implicitly) explain the variation. In the conclusion, I sketch an analytical framework for the study of sexual violence as part of armed groups' repertoires of violence and suggest avenues of research that should contribute to scholarly understanding of sexual and other forms of violence.

SELECTED CASES CONTRASTING HIGH, LOW, AND ASYMMETRIC PREVALENCE OF SEXUAL VIOLENCE

In this section, I describe the pattern of sexual violence in several wars, including interstate and civil wars, ethnic and nonethnic conflicts, and wars in which sexual violence was very prevalent and wars where it was not.

World War II

As the Soviet army moved westward into German territory in early 1945, large numbers of women were raped (Naimark 1995). Although women of various ethnicities were raped in the course of looting of villages and cities, German women were particularly targeted. As the Soviet army occupied Berlin in late April and early May 1945, thousands of women and girls were raped, often by several men in sequence, often in front of family or neighborhood, sometimes on more than one occasion (Beevor 2002). Soldiers sometimes detained a girl or woman for some days in her home or elsewhere and subjected her to repeated rape. Sexual violence gradually subsided as occupation authorities realized the harm being done to the Soviet post-war political project and gradually instituted stronger rules against fraternization in general and rape in particular.

The sexual violence by Soviet troops appeared to be an exercise in collective punishment and perhaps the taking of victor's spoils. Did the Soviet troops engage in such widespread sexual violence in retaliation for sexual violence by German troops? Sexual violence by German troops occupying Eastern Europe appears to have been widespread in some areas, according to recent research in newly available archives (Burds 2009). According to Wendy Jo Gertjejanssen (2004), German soldiers raped girls and women of various ethnicities, including Jews, despite regulations against sexual relations with non-German women.[1] Much sexual violence appears to have taken the form of forced prostitution, as many girls and women were forced to serve in military brothels in cities and field camps. Although some volunteered to serve in the brothels as a way to survive in the dire circumstances of the occupation, others were forced to serve under threat of death or internment. German military authorities also organized brothels in labor and concentration camps, which were visited by favored prisoners. Some girls and women were forced to serve in these brothels; others, when offered the choice of internment or service in the brothels, chose the latter. The scale of sexual violence in the concentration and labor camps (aside from the sexual humiliation of forced undressing and the violence against homosexuals, which often took the form of medical experiments) appears to have been limited, as the number of women in the brothels appears to have been a small fraction of the number interned in the camps.

Massive sexual violence also occurred in the Pacific theater. The "rape of Nanjing," the widespread violence by Japanese soldiers in the environs of the Chinese city of Nanjing for eight weeks beginning December 13, 1937, included extensive sexual violence. According to Iris Chang (1997), 20,000 to 80,000 women and girls were raped and then executed; that is, 8 to 32 percent of the approximately 250,000 female civilians present in the city at the time of the takeover. Among them were prepubescent girls, pregnant and elderly women, and Buddhist nuns; most were summarily executed afterward. Sexual violence in Nanjing also included various forms of sexual abuse of men, including rape, the forcing of men to have intercourse with family members or the dead, and the forcing of celibate men to have intercourse.

One result of the negative international publicity in the wake of the violence in Nanjing was the widespread implementation of the "comfort women" system of military-organized and controlled brothels that accompanied Japanese forces (Goldstein 2001, 367). According to a 1993 study by the Japanese government that included a review of wartime archives and interviews with military personnel and former "comfort women," more than 200,000 women from across East and Southeast Asia were recruited by force and deception to serve as on-call prostitutes subject to immediate violence if they resisted. In establishing the "comfort stations," Japanese officials sought "to prevent anti-Japanese sentiments from fermenting [*sic*] as a result of rapes and other unlawful acts by Japanese military personnel against local residents in the areas occupied by the then Japanese military, the need to prevent loss of troop strength by venereal and other diseases, and the need to prevent espionage" (Japanese Cabinet Councillors' Office on External Affairs 1993, 14). Most of the comfort women were between 14 and 18 years old, and most were Korean.

Bosnia-Herzegovina

Sexual slavery was also a prominent form of sexual violence in the conflict in the former Yugoslavia in the early 1990s. According to a European Union investigation, approximately 20,000 girls and women suffered rape in 1992 in Bosnia-Herzegovina alone, many of them while held in detention facilities of various types (Goldstein 2001, 363; Enloe 2000, 140). The most authoritative investigation of sexual violence in the former Yugoslavia was carried out by a UN commission, which found that the "vast majority of the victims are Bosnian Muslims and the great majority of the alleged perpetrators are Bosnian Serbs" (UNSC 1994, Annex IX.I.C). The commission identified several distinct patterns of sexual violence, including against men. Among the characteristics stressed by the commission were an emphasis on shame and humiliation (many assaults occurred in front of family or in public), the targeting of young girls and virgins along with educated and prominent female community members, and sexual assault with objects. The commission concluded that while some cases were the result of the actions of individuals or small groups acting without orders, "many more cases seem to be part of an overall pattern. These patterns strongly suggest that a systematic rape and sexual assault policy exists, but this remains to be proved" (UNSC 1994, Annex IX Conclusions). Although not explicitly stated in the report, the inference is clear that the commission believed it probable that rape was part of the systematic ethnic cleansing on the part of the Bosnian Serb forces. Direct evidence that Bosnian Serb and possibly Serbian forces planned a campaign of sexual violence as part of the ethnic cleansing of Serbian areas of the former Yugoslavia is lacking, but it may emerge as the various trials at the International Criminal Tribunal for the former Yugoslavia continue.

Sierra Leone

Sexual violence during the war in Sierra Leone, in contrast to Bosnia-Herzegovina, did not involve explicit ethnic targeting. According to the Truth and Reconciliation Commission of Sierra Leone (TRC), sexual violence was carried out "indiscriminately on women of all ages, of every ethnic group and from all social classes" (TRC [Sierra Leone] 2004, chapter 3b, par. 282). The commission found that "all of the armed factions, in particular the RUF and the Armed Forces Revolutionary Council, embarked on a systematic and deliberate strategy to rape women and girls, especially those between the ages of ten and 18 years of age, with the intention of sowing terror amongst the population, violating women and girls and breaking down every norm and custom of traditional society" (TRC [Sierra Leone] 2004, par. 298). The commission noted that some armed groups targeted young women and girls presumed to be virgins as well as those girls and women associated with other armed groups. The violence was also extremely brutal (Human Rights Watch 2003). Gang rapes often took the form of very young victims enduring rape, with rebel combatants lining up to take turns. Many of those who suffered sexual assault did so on multiple occasions. A particular form of sexual violence in Sierra Leone was the detention of girls and women, often for long periods of time, as slaves serving and sexually servicing a rebel camp or a particular rebel. The commission did not analyze patterns of sexual violence in detail and therefore makes a less compelling case for sexual violence as a systematic strategy than that advanced by the commission for the former Yugoslavia, which laid out specific patterns not easily accounted for except by such a strategy.

Other cases in which sexual violence appears to be very prevalent include the present conflict in Darfur, Sudan, where rape occurs frequently in the context of the campaign by militias and government forces to punish villages thought to be associated with rebel groups (Amnesty International 2004). During the genocide in Rwanda, some Tutsi girls and women (and, in much fewer numbers, Hutu women thought to support Tutsis) suffered rape and mutilation before their execution. Estimates of the prevalence of sexual violence in Rwanda vary widely but appear to merit inclusion in the high prevalence category (African Rights 1995; Human Rights Watch 1996; Sharlach 1999).

Given the high prevalence of sexual violence in these very different conflicts, one might conclude that sexual violence inevitably accompanies war. However, the following cases in which the incidence of sexual violence is remarkably low or sharply asymmetric compared with the preceding cases demonstrate that such a conclusion is incorrect.

Israel/Palestine

In the Israeli–Palestinian conflict, also an ethnic conflict characterized by the increasing separation of ethnically defined populations, sexual violence appears to be extremely limited. Although the forced movement of Palestinians out of some areas in 1948 was accompanied by a few documented cases of rape (Morris 2004), at present neither Israelis nor Palestinians carry out sexual assaults despite the killing of Israeli civilians by Palestinian groups and the killing of Palestinian civilians by Israeli security forces (Wood 2006). It could be the case that the intensive international monitoring of the conflict deters the practice of sexual violence, but both sides do not appear much deterred in their other practices despite their frequent condemnation by international actors.

Sri Lanka

Like Bosnia-Herzegovina, Sri Lanka is also a case of a secessionist ethnic conflict, but in Sri Lanka the level of sexual violence appears to be significantly less and is also highly asymmetric. When it does occur, it has generally been wielded by government forces against women associated with the insurgency. Police, soldiers, or security forces occasionally subject displaced Tamil women and girls to various forms of sexual assault, including gang rape and rape with foreign objects, after their arrest or detention at checkpoints, sometimes on the grounds that they or family members are suspected members of the Tamil insurgency (Amnesty International 1999). Various human rights groups report that sexual torture by police and security forces against male and female political and criminal detainees occurs frequently. Of particular interest is the relative absence of sexual violence against civilians by the Tamil insurgent group, despite their inflicting frequent civilian casualties during attacks on non-Tamil villages, assassinating political and military leaders, and their forcing non-Tamil populations to leave areas of their control, as in 1990 when 90,000 Muslims were forced to leave the Jaffna Peninsula on extremely short notice (Wood 2009). Despite the frequent recruitment by force of girls as combatants, the group does not appear to engage in sexual abuse within its own ranks (Human Rights Watch 2004).

El Salvador

Sexual violence during the civil war in El Salvador, a nonethnic conflict pitting a leftist insurgency against an authoritarian government, was
one-sided and very low in comparison to Bosnia-Herzegovina and Sierra
Leone. Government soldiers and security forces occasionally engaged in
sexual violence, including gang and multiple rapes, against some suspected insurgent supporters (including some men) detained in both official
and secret detention sites. Government forces carried out sexual violence
while on operations early in the war; for example, some of the nearly 1,000
people killed by the Salvadoran military at El Mozote in 1981 were raped
(Danner 1994). The final report of the UN-sponsored Truth Commission
mentions only one incident of rape, carried out by government forces in
a village in eastern El Salvador in 1981. However, the unpublished annex
to the commission's report discussed sexual violence in more detail; all
incidents were reported to have been carried out by state forces or agents
(Truth Commission for El Salvador 1993, Anexos. Vol. II, 8–10, 15). No
incidents of sexual violence were attributed to the insurgent force. Sexual
violence in the Salvadoran conflict was thus asymmetric, distinctly low
compared to other cases, and declined over the years of the war.

The type of war (at the broadest level) does not explain the variation
even among these few cases. Sexual violence varies in prevalence and form
among civil wars and interstate wars, among ethnic and nonethnic wars,
among genocides and ethnic-cleansing cases, and among secessionist conflicts. Nor does the prevalence of sexual violence simply reflect the intensity of conflict: the prevalence of sexual violence in Bosnia-Herzegovina
was remarkably high compared with the frequency of lethal violence, but
it is disproportionately low in Israel/Palestine and sharply asymmetric in
El Salvador and Sri Lanka.

Before continuing, however, a preemptive concern must be addressed.
Perhaps the variation described here is merely an artifact of inadequate
knowledge about the empirical patterns present in each case. The reported
variation may reflect different intensities of domestic and international
monitoring of conflicts rather than different prevalence rates; violence in
some regions appears to garner more international attention than in others. But variation in sexual violence is sufficiently well documented across
enough wars and armed groups to suggest that it is real and not solely an
artifact of bias in reporting and observation or a reflection of variation in
peacetime levels (Wood 2006).

EXPLAINING VARIATION IN WARTIME
SEXUAL VIOLENCE

Several causal mechanisms that might explain the observed variation
appear (often only implicitly) in the literature on sexual violence during

war. In this section I assess whether these mechanisms in fact do so. Candidate explanations for the variation also come from the recent literature on mechanisms of collective violence (for a more detailed discussion, see Wood 2006 and 2008).

Opportunity

One hypothesis, often implicit, is that the oft-observed increase in sexual violence during war reflects increased opportunity. Institutions of social control are often weaker in war, particularly when young combatants fight far from their home; communities are scattered to distinct areas; norms of respect for elders are undermined by new sources of authority, such as guns; and armed groups loot kitchens for supplies. This approach implies that the pattern of sexual violence should mirror those of other forms of violence (because opportunity to loot and rape is also opportunity to kill), that combatants should not target civilians of a particular ethnicity (unless opportunity depends directly on ethnicity), and that sexual violence should be higher on the part of groups that loot provisions.

Some studies weakly confirm these implications. Neil Mitchell and Tali Gluch (2004) found that prevalence of sexual violence was significantly correlated with the presence of war. However, their finding was based on data for only one year and relied on a crude coding of limited human rights sources, principally U.S. State Department human rights reports. Madeline Morris (1996) found that the rates of rape by male U.S. military personnel in World War II were three to four times higher than the rate by male civilians of the same age. (In contrast, military rates during peacetime were significantly lower than civilian rates.) Sexual violence in some conflicts does appear to vary with other forms of violence, the frequency increasing and decreasing in the same patterns across time and space.

More generally, however, variation in opportunity does not account for the observed variation in sexual violence. Many armed actors target particular groups in patterns not explained by opportunity; in both Bosnia-Herzegovina and Rwanda, perpetrators had roughly equal access to civilians of various ethnicities yet targeted particular ones. The Salvadoran insurgency depended closely on residents of contested areas for supplies but did not engage in systematic rape of civilians. And sexual violence does not always vary with other forms of violence; the Sri Lankan and Colombian insurgencies appear to strictly limit sexual violence but engage in other forms of violence against civilians.

Incentives

A distinct approach argues that wartime experience increases individual incentives to engage in sexual violence. There are several versions of this argument.[2] Some scholars interpret wartime increases in sexual violence to the breakdown of patriarchal institutions during war (Brown-miller 1975; Enloe 1983). Arguments based on patriarchal social relations imply that sexual violence should be more prevalent in wars in which traditional gender norms are more disrupted. But in many civil wars, gender roles become less polarized because village hierarchies break down as the population disperses and women take on tasks normally carried out by men. It does not appear to be the case that sexual violence is higher when traditional norms are more disrupted. Contrary to the patriarchal thesis, in some conflicts patriarchal relations are so disrupted that there are significant numbers of female combatants in insurgent factions. Rather than the predicted high rates of sexual violence, rates appear to have been very low in two such cases: the insurgencies in Sri Lanka and El Salvador. And women sometimes participate in sexual violence as in Rwanda, where women sometimes incited men to rape, and in the sexual humiliation of men detained by U.S. forces in Iraq, Guantánamo, and Afghanistan. Nor does the argument account for the targeting of enemy civilians (Skjels-baek 2001).

A second argument that does account for such targeting is that of revenge: combatants target enemy civilians with violence in revenge for the violence suffered by their community. However, why revenge takes the form of sexual rather than other kinds of violence is usually not explained. Sexual violence is sometimes said to occur in retaliation for sexual violence previously suffered (or rumored to suffer) by co-ethnics, but as our cases showed, some armed groups do not respond in kind to sexual violence.

The militarized masculinity approach (Morris 1996; Goldstein 2001) does account for the targeting of enemy women and men, and with specifically sexual violence. To persuade men to fight and endure the hardships of war, societies develop members willing to stand fast under fire, usually via the development of sharp distinctions between genders: to become men, boys must become warriors. Leaders persuade soldiers that to be a real man is to assert a militaristic masculinity, and the result is that soldiers represent domination of the enemy in highly gendered terms and use specifically sexual violence against enemy populations. Moreover, bonding among members of the small unit—the loyalty that enables warriors to fight under the terrifying conditions of war—also takes gendered forms, reinforcing the militaristic masculinity of training.

Wartime memoirs from some conflicts (for example, memoirs by U.S. soldiers who served in Vietnam) offer anecdotal support for this approach. Particular types of small-unit bonding, such as joint visits to brothels, may play a role in the frequent occurrence of gang rapes in wartime. However, if this approach is to explain variation in wartime sexual violence, armies should promote different notions of masculinity, and armies that emphasize more militaristic notions of manhood would be responsible for higher levels of sexual violence. I am not aware of systematic comparisons of

military training, norms, and practices across state militaries; the variation in sexual violence among state militaries appears significantly greater
than the surprisingly limited variation in their training. Moreover, the
militaristic masculinity approach does not clearly specify what mechanism underlies its link to sexual violence, whether armies inculcate new
norms, provide incentives to reward compliance without internalization,
or recruit only those attracted to militaristic practices.

Sexual Violence as Instrumental for the Group

In the explanations based on increased opportunity and incentive, sexual violence occurred for reasons of individual gratification or as a by-
product of supposedly necessary training. In contrast, some armed groups
promote (or tolerate) sexual violence as an effective means toward group
goals. Although strategic sexual violence may not be explicitly ordered, it
is (at least) tolerated; if any punishment occurs it is symbolic and limited,
clearly for external consumption rather than deterrence. Such violence
appears to take two broad forms. The first is sexual torture and/or humiliation of persons detained by an armed group. The second is widespread
sexual violence as a form of terror or punishment targeted at a particular
group, which frequently takes the form of gang (and often public) rape,
usually over an extended period of time, most notoriously as part of some
campaigns of "ethnic cleansing," to force the movement of entire populations from particular regions claimed as the homeland, and as part of
some genocides.

The conditions for such instrumental promotion of sexual violence are
not well identified in the literature. Some authors suggest that particular cultural beliefs provide the relevant condition: where armed groups
understand sexual violence as a violation of the family's and community's
honor, they are likely to engage in sexual violence as a weapon of war
(Enloe 2000). However, this appears to predict significantly more sexual
violence than is in fact observed as such beliefs are present in many societies where massive sexual violence has not occurred, as in Sri Lanka,
El Salvador, and Colombia. Moreover, such broad notions of cultural
proclivity do not account for cases where one party to the war promotes
sexual violence while the other does not.

Sanctions against Sexual Violence

The effectiveness of an armed group's command-and-control structure
is particularly important for the effective prohibition of sexual violence.
An armed group's leadership may prohibit it for strategic, normative, or
practical reasons (Wood 2006). If an organization aspires to govern the
civilian population, leaders will probably attempt to restrain combatants'
engagement in sexual violence against those civilians (though perhaps

endorsing it against other civilian groups) for fear of undermining support for the coming revolution. Similarly, if an armed group is dependent on civilians, leaders will probably attempt to restrain sexual violence against those civilians.

Reasons for prohibiting sexual violence may reflect normative concerns and practical constraints. Members of a revolutionary group seeking to carry out a social revolution may see themselves as the disciplined bearers of a new, more just social order for all citizens; sexual violence may conflict with their self-image. A norm against sexual violence may take a distinct form; sexual violence across ethnic boundaries may be understood by leaders or combatants as polluting the instigator rather than humiliating the targeted individual and community. New social norms against the use of particular forms of violence and in favor of others may also be actively cultivated by an armed group as a matter of strategy or principle. The Salvadoran insurgency attempted to shape individual longings for revenge toward a more general aspiration for justice because revenge seeking by individuals would undermine insurgent discipline and obedience (Wood 2003). Despite systematic celebration of martyrdom in pursuit of victory, the insurgency did not endorse suicide missions and explicitly prohibited sexual violence. The Sri Lankan insurgency carries out suicide bombing and, arguably, shapes desires for revenge toward that end, yet does not engage in sexual violence toward civilians despite its practice of ethnic cleansing.

Dependence on international allies may also constrain sexual violence if those allies have normative concerns about such violence. Even if neither the armed group nor its sponsor is itself normatively concerned, it may seek to avoid criticism by international human rights organizations.

An army in which females are a high fraction of combatants may also be constrained in its use of sexual violence. This is suggested by the empirical pattern that female-intensive insurgencies in El Salvador, Sri Lanka, Peru, and Colombia appear to carry out less sexual violence. However, the mechanism is not clear, and these insurgencies share other characteristics, such as an unusual degree of internal discipline.

For the cases of promotion and prohibition of sexual violence, whether an armed group effectively enforces strategies decided on by the leadership depends on the group's internal discipline. The use of violence poses dilemmas to principals whose agents prefer a level or type of violence distinct from theirs (Mitchell and Gluch 2004). Many armies probably prohibit sexual violence yet do not in fact discipline soldiers who commit it. However, under some, possibly rare, conditions the prevalence of sexual violence may be low without relying on the hierarchical discipline of the armed group, namely when combatants themselves have internalized norms against sexual violence or if small units share such a norm and may therefore effectively enforce the norm.

CONCLUSION: A RESEARCH AGENDA

The literature on sexual violence during war has yet to provide an adequate explanation for its variation across wars, armed groups, and units. Although many authors have distinguished between opportunistic and strategic sexual violence, the empirical pattern of variation is wider, including wars where sexual violence is remarkably low on the part of one or more parties to the conflict. In the light of comparative analysis, we do not adequately understand the conditions under which armed groups provide effective sanctions against their combatants engaging in sexual violence or those under which groups effectively promote its strategic use. To conclude, I offer a theoretical framework and suggestions for further research on the patterns and sources of variation.[3]

In research on sexual violence, scholars should disaggregate our analysis to focus on distinct types of sexual violence (or combinations thereof) as the underlying mechanisms generating high or low prevalence may be different for each type. Major subtypes should include sexual torture (including of men), sexual slavery, sexual violence (particularly rape) in the context of ethnic or political cleansing (rape and displacement; rape and genocide), sexual violence (particularly rape) as collective punishment, and opportunistic rape. Some work has already been done along these lines (see Enloe 2000).

Whether or not an armed group engages in sexual violence in general and particular forms in particular should be understood as a question about the group's repertoire of violence, by which I mean the analogue for violence of Charles Tilly's (2004) notion of the repertoire of collective action. This broader concept suggests several avenues of research. While focusing on the variation in sexual violence, this chapter has also shown that the repertoire of violence varies across conflicts and armed groups, and may vary across units within a group. More specifically, the repertoire of a particular group may be constant over time and space, with the relative incidence of different forms of violence remaining approximately the same. In other cases, the repertoire may not be constant, as disappearances and executions rise and fall together but sexual violence remains constant. An obvious implication is that scholars should collect and code for all kinds of violence, not just lethal violence.

To understand the repertoire of violence, I suggest that armed groups (both state and non-state) should be approached as complex organizations that (in a particular setting, with more or less success) define opportunities, enforce specific norms, shape particular incentive structures, embrace some strategies and condemn others (see Wood 2009 for more on this theoretical framework). In focusing on why violence sometimes but not always takes sexual form, we should not assume that male combatants will rape given the opportunity; rather, the sexual aspect of violence should be explained, not presumed. This approach suggests a focus on four units of analysis and their interrelationships: the armed group leadership, its hierarchy, the small unit in which combatants have face-to-face relations, and the individual combatant.

Key to explaining the observed variation are the conditions under which armed groups, small units, and individuals develop sanctions and norms that effectively endorse or constrain combatants' engagement in sexual violence. The distinction between leaderships that endorse sexual violence as an effective form of terror against or punishment of a targeted group and those that do not is, of course, essential. Patterns of violence also depend, however, on whether the armed group provides effective incentives that promote sexual violence or sanctions that prohibit it. If there are no effective sanctions promoting or discouraging sexual violence (either because the group does not have an explicit policy or because there is no effective enforcement of that policy), the degree of sexual violence engaged in by combatants depends on whether the group has access to civilians (as when it loots kitchens and fields for food) or not, whether small units promote norms prohibiting or endorsing sexual violence, and whether individuals have such norms.

Norms and practices should not be assumed to be static; rather, they must be understood as evolving over the course of conflict. Individual combatants enter an armed group with (possibly heterogeneous) norms, preferences, and cultural practices concerning sexual violence. The initial socialization in their small unit; the brutalizing processes of witnessing, enduring, and wielding violence; and the pressure to conform to the evolving practices of their unit may reshape those norms, preferences, and practices in fundamental ways. The extent of opportunistic sexual violence depends on the absence of sanctions and norms (on the part of the armed group, the small unit, or the individual) that effectively prohibit it and on proximity to potential victims. Where individual and small-unit norms prohibit sexual violence, perhaps on the grounds that it is polluting to the perpetrator, sexual violence will not occur even if a unit has ready access to civilians and even if the armed group does not punish those who engage in it.

This approach suggests a number of hypotheses that might guide scholarly research (see also Wood 2006, 330–35). First, where armed groups depend on the provision of support (supplies, intelligence) from civilians and aspire to govern those civilians, they do not engage in sexual violence against those civilians if they have a reasonably effective command structure.

Second, where norms held by individual combatants and small units, either condemning or approving sexual violence, are the same and are also endorsed by the armed group's leadership, sexual violence by that group will be either very low or very high, respectively. Specifically, where armed groups reinforce cultural taboos against sexual contact with the potential target populations, sexual violence against that population will be low; in the absence of such taboos, where armed groups promote sexual violence, violence will be high.

Third, if an armed group prohibits sexual violence against a particular population, the less effective the military discipline of the group, the more likely combatants are to engage in sexual violence (unless they hold particularly strong norms against it). Thus, ill-disciplined militias, ill-trained armies of conscripts, poorly trained military police, and little-supervised service troops are more likely to engage in sexual violence than well-trained troops (in the absence of a policy promoting sexual violence). The challenge in conducting research on military discipline is of course to do so without the tautology of the kind that occurs when an absence of discipline is inferred from a pattern of violence against civilians.

This approach raises questions as well. To what extent is sexual violence accounted for by a breakdown in command-and-control structure and morale versus a change in norms on the part of combatants? What accounts for the emergence of an organizational structure strong enough to enforce strategic decisions by the leadership? How and why do small-unit norms evolve that enable sexual violence by its members? In what conditions does military victory, on the one hand, and military stalemate, on the other, contribute to sexual violence? To what extent do international norms and law constrain the practice of sexual violence? Why are men targeted in some settings but not in others? Democracies rarely engage in widespread rape but sometimes endorse limited sexual violence: what constrains democracies, and why do those constraints not prohibit all forms of sexual violence?

The ongoing brutality in Darfur reminds us that sexual violence remains a horrifying aspect of war, one that occasions great suffering on the part of civilians—particularly women and girls—trapped in conditions of insecurity and terror. Yet, rape is not inevitable in war, as this chapter's emphasis on negative and asymmetric cases has illustrated. Understanding the determinants of the variation in sexual violence may help those UN officials; members of nongovernmental organizations; and government, military, and insurgent leaders who seek to limit sexual violence and other violations of the laws of war.

NOTES

1. See also Friedman (2002, chapter 2). The German military treated rape of civilians by German soldiers on the eastern front much more leniently than on the western front, where military courts imposed significantly more severe punishment (Beck 2002).

2. See Wood (2006, 17–19) and Goldstein (2001) for consideration of biological versions.

3. For the author's specific suggestions concerning promising research directions, see Wood (2008, 346–48).

CHAPTER 11

Explaining Sexual Violence in Conflict Situations

Megan Gerecke

Theories of sexual violence are often derived from single case studies, and their applicability to other conflicts is rarely tested. Applying these theories comparatively has the potential to reveal gaps, overlaps, and silences within them. In this vein, this chapter applies two major theories of sexual violence to three well-documented conflicts—those of Bosnia and Herzegovina, Rwanda,[1] and Sierra Leone.

There are many explanations for sexual violence; however, in the policy community, theories relating to gender predominate. These theories focus on (1) gender inequality and identity and (2) gender and ethnicity. In the former explanation, wartime sexual violence is caused by gender inequalities and skewed gender norms, and in the latter, ethnic norms act upon such inequities and lead to sexual violence: women come to represent the honor of their community, and shaming them becomes a strategic rational act of war.

Two other important explanations of sexual violence are those of (3) opportunity and social breakdown and (4) military organization and structure. In the former, wartime sexual violence is driven by male desire and increased opportunity due to wartime changes in men's access to women, relative power, and impunity. The latter explanation highlights the variation in the practice of sexual violence between military groups and suggests that organizational and structural features make certain groups more prone to rape. The brief treatment of these theories here is not a judgment on their validity but instead a reflection of space constraints.

This chapter will begin by giving a brief description of the three conflicts and their patterns of sexual violence. It will continue with a description of the alternative theories before moving on to a more detailed application of the gender-based theories. It will conclude with a summary of the findings and possible policy applications.

BRIEF DESCRIPTION OF THE CONFLICTS

The conflict in Bosnia and Herzegovina began with the state's declaration of autonomy in March 1992 and ended in December 1995 with the Dayton Peace Accords. The conflict was divided along ethnic lines, initially with Croats and Muslims fighting Serbs. The alliance between the Croats and Muslims fell apart in April 1993. The Croats aligned with the Serbian army until March 1994. At this point, they signed the Washington Agreement, joined the Bosnian forces, and, with the help of the North Atlantic Treaty Organization (NATO), defeated the Serbs.

The Rwandan genocide followed the 1990–1993 civil war between the Rwandan Patriotic Front (RPF) and Rwandan government forces. The genocide began after Hutu President Juvénal Habyarimana was killed when his airplane was shot down in April 1994. The genocide lasted until July 1994 when the RPF defeated the Rwandan Army in the country's capital, Kigali. In the course of the war an estimated 750,000 Tutsis and moderate Hutus were killed. In addition to armed groups, Hutu civilians also played an important role in carrying out the genocide.

Sierra Leone's civil war began in March 1991, with the Revolutionary United Front's (RUF) raids on Freetown. Initially, the war was between the RUF and the Sierra Leone government and the Sierra Leone Army (SLA),[2] but after launching a coup in 1997, the Armed Forces Revolutionary Council (AFRC), a splinter faction of the SLA, made an alliance with the RUF. These groups united to fight the Sierra Leone government forces and the newly conglomerated (and quickly growing) ethnically organized Civil Defense Force militias. The Lomé Peace Accord was signed in July1999 and demobilization commenced. Unfortunately, Sierra Leone relapsed into war, and it was not until May 2001 that demobilization efforts recommenced. The war officially ended in January 2002, with the Declaration of the End of the War.

SEXUAL VIOLENCE IN THE CONFLICTS

Sexual violence[3] was widespread in all three conflicts. In Bosnia and Herzegovina, an estimated 13,000–50,000 women were raped, in Rwanda an estimated 250,000–500,000, and in Sierra Leone an estimated 250,000. Across the conflicts, the use of gang rape, public rape, violent rape, and rape as a spectacle was common. Sexual violence was predominately carried out by men, though in each conflict some women perpetrated sexual violence as well. Likewise, although sexual violence predominately targeted female victims, there were male victims in all cases. Across the cases, sexual violence was used asymmetrically, that is, some military groups practiced sexual violence at a much higher rate than others.

There are important differences between the three cases. Most of the sexual violence in Bosnia and Herzegovina was carried out in custodial settings (whether that be rape camps, prisons, or detention camps), whereas in Rwanda it was largely carried out by militias and civilians who had "turned Interahamwe," and in Sierra Leone it was largely carried out by two rebel groups: the RUF and AFRC. In its forms sexual violence differed across the cases; rape until impregnation was important in Bosnia and Herzegovina, rape murders and rape with intentional transmission of sexually transmitted diseases were important in Rwanda, and sexual slavery was important in Sierra Leone.

BRIEF DESCRIPTION OF ALTERNATIVE THEORIES OF SEXUAL VIOLENCE

Opportunity and Social Breakdown

Likely the simplest—or least sophisticated—explanation of wartime sexual violence is found in the theory that, given the opportunity, men naturally choose to engage in sexual violence. This concept prevails in many military structures with the idea of "boys being boys," though in academic discourse, authors implicitly call up the idea by suggesting that sexual violence is a reward that free agents seek (Mazurana et al. 2005; Butler, Gluch, and Mitchell 2007).[4] Some authors are more explicit and can go as far as suggesting that evolution has made the male sex as a whole biologically prone to raping (Gottschall 2004).

According to this theory, the breakdown of state and society during war reduces safeguards for women and social constraints on men, while also increasing men's access to women and their individual power. This is argued to increase opportunities to rape and explain the sharp rise in sexual violence (Cohen 2007, 6–7; Wood 2006, 321; Butler, Gluch, and Mitchell 2007, 669). Although social breakdown is easily credited as facilitating sexual violence, sexual violence in itself may be a means of social breakdown resulting in a questionable chicken-and-egg problem that draws attention to what comes first. As opposed to treating social breakdown as an independent variable, one must consider how and why it happens.

Despite the theory's drawbacks, it highlights the element of sexual desire in sexual violence; many wartime rapes involve erect penises, suggesting that desire warrants consideration in explaining rape. To truly discern the influence of desire, a large amount of individual-level data would be necessary; as of yet, such sources do not exist across the cases.[5]

Military Organization and Structure

Building on the literature on human rights violations during war, some scholars locate the cause of sexual violence within military groups' organization and structure. Groups are posited to be prone to sexual violence when they have faulty combatant selection mechanisms, poor compensation, and weak hierarchy and unit cohesion. Sexual violence is less likely when military groups

- have a high ratio of female combatants;
- have a normative image that is incompatible with the practice of sexual violence;
- are dependent on civilians for resources or recruits;
- believe it will strategically benefit them by reducing civilians' desire for revenge;
- are concerned with their combatants' health;
- are dependent on international allies; or
- want to avoid humanitarian and other international criticism.

When such situations arise, military groups will likely prohibit sexual violence. For such sanctions to be effective, the command must have adequate information and disciplinary capacity (Cohen 2007; Wood 2006; Butler, Gluch, and Mitchell 2007).

A cursory look at the cases suggests that women's involvement alone is not enough to limit sexual violence, given their high participation in the Rwandan and Sierra Leone conflicts. A well-established hierarchy and a willing and capable command may be important in ensuring their influence and the influence of norms.

APPLYING GENDER-BASED THEORIES OF SEXUAL VIOLENCE TO THE CONFLICTS

Gender Inequalities and Identity

The Theory

The idea of gender inequalities and identities driving violence hinges on the concept that there are concrete and ideational power divides between the genders, which can be used instrumentally against victims and their associated communities. Gender is a sociocultural category, rather than a biological one. Scholars who focus on gender characterize wartime sexual violence as an extension of the skewed gender identities and gender inequalities seen in peacetime. During conflict, militarized masculinity further polarizes gender roles and exacerbates patriarchy, leading to more abuse of power. Furthermore, men punish women with rape when they transgress gender roles due to the social turmoil of war.

Early feminists expected wartime sexual violence to target women. They implicitly assumed a connection between the female sex and female gender. Later feminist work has questioned this connection and suggested that gender is a preformed identity (one that you can "do" rather than "be"). Sexual violence becomes an exercise of power between unequal genders. Regardless of sex, perpetrator and victim (and their associated communities) are gendered into a powerful masculine role and a weak feminine role, respectively. In other words, sexual violence is not simply a performance of fixed genders but a gendering act (Skjelsbaek 2001). To take this one step further, Judith Butler introduces the concept of marked bodies (Butler 2003). People are physically marked—whether sexually or ethnically—and these "markings" take on social meanings and expectations, calling women and men to "perform" learned identities (Sharlach 1999). Butler's theory draws one's attention to how bodies' markings are targeted during sexual violence.

Applying the Theory to the Conflict

The nuanced approach to gender demands that the roles of perpetrator and victim are not cast by sex. Nonetheless, the weaker position of women helps explain their predominance among sexual violence victims seen in the three cases discussed here. Indeed, although there were male victims in each conflict, women were typically targeted, as seen in the staggering numbers of women raped listed earlier.[6]

Yet divergences from the general male-on-female pattern existed in all cases. Across the conflicts, women perpetrated some sexual violence, took an active part in general violence, and held positions of command. In Sierra Leone, for instance, women were involved in carrying out approximately a third of all rapes, either as perpetrators or observers (Cohen 2007, 23).[7] In both Rwanda and Sierra Leone, female participants were (reportedly) more violent and cruel than their male counterparts (Cohen 2007, 24; Denov and Gervais 2007, 896; Sharlach 1999, 387).

Also defying sex-based expectations, male victims of sexual abuse existed in all conflicts.[8] In Bosnia and Herzegovina, men were targeted with castration, circumcision, electric shocks to the scrotum, penis removal, and other forms of sexual mutilation (C. Carpenter 2006, 94).[9] In Sierra Leone, rape often targeted adolescent boys (C. Carpenter 2006, 95). In both countries, forced incest was common and can easily be seen as constituting a form of sexual violence against both parties, regardless of their position as penetrator or penetrated. These divergences from the general male-on-female pattern, although limited, reinforce the idea that sexual violence is not simply a performance of fixed genders but a gendering act. More attention is needed to determine how gender inequalities matter and the limitations on what they can explain. When do gender inequalities matter? Which gender identities and what types and levels of gender inequality facilitate sexual violence? Are there similarities in the substance of gender divides across cases of widespread sexual violence? Regrettably, inter-case comparison is rarely attempted in wartime sexual violence studies, and thus, our understanding of when and how gender imbalances matter is limited. The following paragraphs will attempt to compare gender inequalities and identities across the cases, using prewar data and providing global comparisons where possible.[10]

Measuring Gender Inequalities and Identities

Gender inequalities are typically measured across multiple spheres, with indicators highlighting political, economic, health, educational, and legal inequalities between sexes. Equality is typically measured along outcomes rather than opportunities or capabilities, as the latter are more difficult to quantify (for interesting work in this area, see Nussbaum 2000 and others). Sex, rather than gender, is typically used in quantitative comparisons.[11]

Figure 11.1 shows that there is significant variation in gender inequality in Bosnia and Herzegovina, Rwanda, and Sierra Leone. In all cases, women's formal political equality was diminished by low representation in government. Although this may seems like evidence of exceptional inequality, in actuality women in most countries suffer unequal political

Figure 11.1
Political participation and equality

	Bosnia and Herzegovina	Rwanda	Sierra Leone	Global Firsts and Averages
Female right to vote (at sovereignty)	✓	✓	✓	
Female right to stand for elections (at sovereignty)	✓	✓	✓	
First legislature of the present sovereign state	1900	1965	1962	
First female parliamentarian	1990	1981	1981[a]	1907
CEDAW[b] adoption	1993	1981	1988	1980
Female president or prime minister[c]		✓		3.7–6.4%
Female representation in parliament, 1990[d]	18.2%	17.1%	3.5%	10.3–14.8%

[a]First appointed in 1957.
[b]CEDAW = Convention on the Elimination of All Forms of Discrimination against Women.
[c]A. Uwilingiyimana (July 1993–April 1994); global figures are for 1985 and 1995, respectively.
[d]Lower house; global figures are for 1993 and 1988, respectively.
Compiled from: Inter-Parliamentary Union (2005a); UNESCO Institute for Statistics (2000); Walters and Gwen Mason (1994, 54); UN Division for the Advancement of Women (2007); Inter-Parliamentary Union (2005b).

outcomes despite enjoying formal political equality. In light of global comparison, female participation in parliament in Bosnia and Herzegovina and Rwanda was actually high in 1990, and the presence of a female head of state in Rwanda was extraordinary.[12] In each case, women were politically disadvantaged; however, it would be questionable to claim that this disadvantage was exceptional internationally.

Men were much more active economically than women in Sierra Leone and Bosnia and Herzegovina, whereas economic activity rates were nearly equal in Rwanda (see Figure 11.2). Economic inequality can occur after women are employed, as they may be sequestered to low-wage sectors or low-level positions. It is important to note that, across the cases, women were also responsible for domestic tasks, working a second shift after their regular jobs. Nonetheless, with the data available, it appears that women's economic equality varied significantly across the cases, with Rwanda appearing to be the most equal and Sierra Leone the least.

Looking at enrollment levels, one can see that educational equality differs significantly across the three cases (see Figure 11.3). Educational outcomes were most equal in Bosnia and Herzegovina, closely followed by Rwanda, and least equal in Sierra Leone. Female–male literacy ratios follow the same pattern at 100 percent, 98 percent, and 63 percent for Bosnia

Figure 11.2
Population by sex and sector (percent of economically active population), 1990

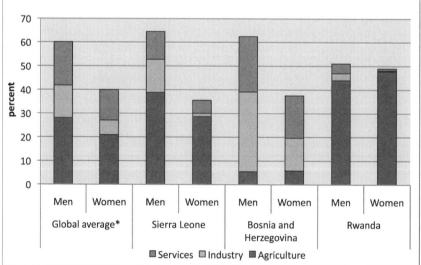

*179 countries.
Source: United Nations Statistics Division (1999), "Topic 3.8: Estimated Economically Active Population by Sex and Branch of Economic Activity."

Figure 11.3
Gross enrollment ratio by sex, 1990, primary and secondary students

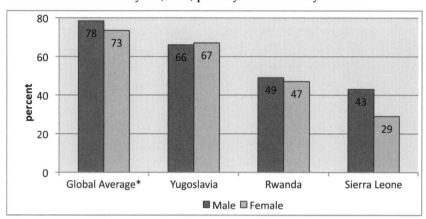

*166 countries.
Source: United Nations Statistics Division (1999), "Topic 2.7: Gross Enrollment Ratio by Level of Education and Sex."

and Herzegovina, Rwanda, and Sierra Leone respectively (UNESCO Institute for Statistics 2000).

Evidence on life expectancy and maternal mortality ratio suggest that sex inequalities in health were least pronounced in Bosnia and Herzegovina and most pronounced in Sierra Leone.[13] In 1990, Sierra Leone had the highest maternal mortality rate among the countries ranked by the United Nations (UN). Its rate of 18 maternal deaths per 1,000 live births was more than 4.5 times the global average. Rwanda trailed closely behind, with a figure of 13 deaths, more than tripling the global average. Fertility rates were much higher for Sierra Leone and Rwanda than Bosnia and Herzegovina, though this is in line with regional averages (see Figure 11.4)

Legally, all countries guaranteed formal sex equality and prohibited sex discrimination, yet there were important deviations from this ideal even within the laws themselves; this is evident in Rwanda and to a greater extent Sierra Leone (see Figure 11.5). Women in these countries were disadvantaged in laws relating to marriage, inheritance, reproduction, and autonomy within the family. In addition to general acceptance of the practices of sexual violence and domestic violence, gaps existed within all countries' legal frameworks (for instance, marital rape is not recognized). Unequal legal frameworks may explain the high rates of sexual violence, though the level of inequality varied across the cases Yugoslavian women were legally equal, but women in Sierra Leone were quite disadvantaged.[14]

In terms of gender identities and expected roles, all cases emphasize females' virginity, subservience, motherhood, and fertility. The high rates and acceptance of domestic and sexual violence bring into focus women's

Figure 11.4
Estimated and projected total fertility rate, 1970–2010

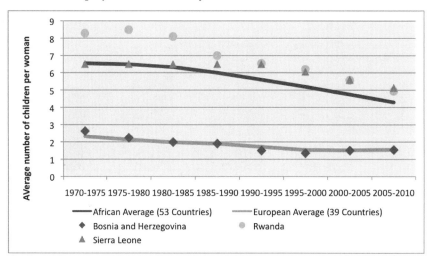

Compiled from: United Nations Statistics Division (1999), "Topic 4.4: Estimated and Projected Total fertility Rate."

subservient status. Each country had a patrilineal system in which custom favored men, who were expected to be strong and sexually virile. Despite similarities in ideals, different practices existed. Gender norms and identities appear the most restrictive in Sierra Leone and Rwanda and the least restrictive in Bosnia and Herzegovina—where, by contrast to the other two cases, we see a budding feminist movement and women with lower birth rates. Whether the common gender roles observed in the three cases are exceptional in a global comparison is unknown (though commonsense would say they are not); comparative study of pre-conflict norms, including cases with high and low levels of sexual violence, could cast more light on the influence these roles have.

Conclusions

Although all three cases show evidence of gender inequality, the content of such inequalities differs widely between conflicts. Women in Bosnia and Herzegovina were significantly better off in educational opportunities and outcomes, and women in Rwanda participated in the economy at a surprisingly high rate, especially in comparison with the global average.[15] Differences also existed in gender norms and identities, as outlined earlier. Women in Sierra Leone were consistently more disadvantaged than women in the other two cases. The variation between the cases casts doubt on the unequivocal assumption that gender inequality matters and demands further study on how and when it matters.[16]

Figure 11.5
Pre-conflict legal equality

	Bosnia and Herzegovina	Rwanda	Sierra Leone
Antidiscrimination law on the basis of sex*	✓	✓	✓
No caveats to antidiscrimination law	✓	Citizenship contingent on husband's nationality; head of household is officially male.	Discrimination permitted for personal law (e.g., marriage)
Equal right to divorce	✓	✓	Rights vary with applicable system of law
Equal right to inheritance	✓	Women ineligible to hold land	Unequal under all three systems of law; in customary law, a woman herself could be inherited.
Unrestricted right to abortion	✓	Only if women's physical or mental health is endangered	Only if women's physical health is endangered
Domestic violence illegal	✓	✓	Rights vary with applicable system of law; permitted under customary law
Extramarital sexual violence illegal	✓	✓	Punishment varies with age of victim
Marital sexual violence illegal	✗	✗	✗
Economic autonomy	✓	Women ineligible to hold land; husband's consent is needed for commercial activities and employment	Rights vary with applicable system of law; guaranteed property rights under general law

*Rwanda (1991 constitution, article 16), Sierra Leone (1991 constitution, Clause 8).

Gender and Ethnicity

The Theory

Explaining sexual violence during ethnic wars, scholars have looked at how gender imbalances intersect with ethnic identities to contribute to widespread sexual violence. Strict gender norms and inequalities allow for the instrumental use of sexual violence by ethnic groups. Misogynistic norms that reduce women to their chastity and reproductive capacities, and associate these qualities with personal and communal honor, provide a structure in which sexual violence is rational and strategically efficient. Inter-ethnic sexual violence becomes a way for perpetrators to assert their power over victims and, by extension, over their victims' ethnic group.[17] An attack on women represents both an attack on the community at large and the humiliation of men, as it highlights men's inability to protect their dependents. Although emphasis has been given to female victims, theorists also posit a flexible approach to gender as outlined earlier.

Applying the Theory to the Conflict

Ethnic divides played a central role in the violence in Rwanda and Bosnia and Herzegovina and constituted an interesting silence in the case of Sierra Leone. In Rwanda and Bosnia and Herzegovina, sexual violence followed ethnic lines in numbers and justification. Immediately preceding both conflicts there was a wave of propaganda linking gender and ethnicity in confrontational ways.[18] Tutsi women were portrayed as beautiful but immoral, untrustworthy, promiscuous, arrogant, and undignified (Bastick, Grimm, and Kunz 2007, 55). Women in Bosnia and Herzegovina were urged to return to the "ideals of hearth, home and land" and were undermined as bringing a "white plague" with low fertility rates (Cockburn 1998, 161). Propaganda and jokes commonly featured sexual violence, with the opposite ethnic group being targeted or victimized (Olujic 1998; Skjelsbaek 2001, 217).

Given that ethnic sexual violence will likely take the form of a gendering performance, one should observe spectacle-like qualities surrounding it. This could include unnecessary marking of bodies—particularly in sexual ways—and the use of media coverage and public settings. As expected, bodies were "marked" in both countries, whether it be through genital mutilation (commonly practiced on men in Bosnia and Herzegovina) or by desecrating corpses (e.g., stripping dead women and splaying their legs) (C. Carpenter 2006, 94; Sharlach 1999, 396). Genital mutilation targeting ethnicity was also reported as part of a larger pattern that attempted to remove typical Tutsi characteristics from women's bodies (Human Rights Watch 1996, 63).[19] In both cases, the use of media and crowds was also common, as was rape in front of family members (and occasionally forced rape among family members).

Overall, the patterns and forms of sexual violence observed fit the model given by theories of ethnicity and gender. As noted earlier, in both cases women were vulnerable to sexual violence because of the elevation of their motherly role and the importance placed on their virginity and chastity. The historic connection between ethnicity and gender, and its instrumental presentation immediately preceding the conflict, further substantiate this theory of gendered ethnic violence. Thus, within these archetypical cases, this thesis has unquestionable explanatory power. However, areas for further research still exist regarding the extent to which ethnicity modifies sexual violence, and whether ethnic conflict makes sexual violence more likely.

Areas to Consider Further: How Ethnic Modifies Ethnic Sexual Violence

How the adjective "ethnic" modifies sexual violence has been neglected in the literature on ethnicity and gender.[20] Although ethnic sexual violence obviously delineates the targeted victims, a close look at sexual violence in Sierra Leone reveals even non-ethnic sexual violence has similarities in its form and underlying cultural values.

Although historic animosities existed between the major ethnic groups in Sierra Leone, the war was not ethnic, nor was the sexual violence within it (TRC of Sierra Leone 2004, para. 282).[21] Military groups were made up of many ethnicities, and sexual violence often occurred between co-ethnics (Cohen 2007, 6). Women were targeted for being on the "other side" of the conflict, especially abducted "bush wives" of militants (TRC of Sierra Leone 2004, para. 291).

Despite ethnicity's marginal role in the conflict, important similarities exist in the cultural values and forms of sexual violence observed. As noted previously, there was a similar focus on females' virginity, subservience, motherhood, and fertility, which, by extension reflected on their associated networks and communities (Taylor 2003). Rape often took similar forms as well, becoming a spectacle in which gruesome violence and the unnecessary marking of bodies, sexually and otherwise, took place in public settings or using media coverage. Forced incest, public rape, and gang rape were common. Victims were forbidden from crying or showing emotion and family members were often forced to clap or laugh while relatives were being violated (TRC of Sierra Leone 2004, para. 250). For instance, nonsexual forms of violence included forcing victims to eat dismembered body parts of family members or breast-feed their beheaded children (TRC of Sierra Leone 2004, para. 250, 276–77). As already mentioned, women were left with marked bodies sexually (and otherwise).[22]

The main difference between ethnic and nonethnic sexual violence seems to lie in the statements of perpetrators. In Rwanda and Bosnia and Herzegovina, perpetrators made explicit references to ethnicity. In Rwanda, they made mention of Tutsi women's alleged pride and sexual desirability (Human Rights Watch 1996, 18).[23] In Bosnia and Herzegovina, perpetrators targeted their victim's reproductive capacity; for instance, Serbian perpetrators told victims they would have "Chetnik babies," Chetnik being an ethnic slur for Serbs (Niarchos 1995, 657). In contrast, Sierra Leonean women note perpetrators' silence on ethnicity; instead, perpetrators aimed to undermine traditional emotional responses and familial relations.

Despite different stated motives, the use of female honor and its tie to community does not appear to significantly change how sexual violence interacts with many forms of the body politic. Spectacle was used consistently. Forms of sexual violence thought to be specifically ethnic were observed: rape to impregnation was practiced (though in a much less systematic way than in Bosnia and Herzegovina), and rape murders were typical in Sierra Leone and Rwanda.[24] The forms of sexual violence that have been seen as typical of ethnic violence may actually be typical of conflicts that involve substantial civilian attacks. These preliminary results highlight the need for further study.

Areas to Consider Further: Ethnicity Predicting Sexual Violence?

In the literature, the cases in which gendered ethnic war does not erupt are rarely explored, and one has little understanding of the cultural conditions and gender norms necessary or sufficient to create an ethnic war with widespread sexual violence.[25] More study is needed of ethnic conflicts that do not have high levels of sexual violence. In the narratives of sexual violence in Rwanda and Bosnia and Herzegovina, the progression from underlying ethnic tensions and skewed gender relations to eventual widespread sexual violence is presented as a logical (if reprehensible process); the progression almost becomes teleological. This teleology needs to be reexamined. It is interesting to note that preliminary statistical analysis casts doubt on the importance of ethnic fractionalization in predicting sexual violence and suggests that the steps in this progression need to be reexamined.[26]

SUMMARY OF FINDINGS AND POLICY IMPLICATIONS

Findings on Theories

One of the weaknesses of theories of sexual violence is that they have often been derived from single case studies, and their applicability to other conflicts has not been widely tested. This study attempted to remedy this situation by testing gender-based theories using three well-documented cases.

Although many have assumed that gender inequality matters in determining wartime sexual violence, few have questioned how and when it matters; unfortunately, there is little comparative work testing the correlation between the levels and forms of gender inequality and wartime sexual violence. This study makes a preliminary attempt at filling this gap. It finds that although all three cases show evidence of gender inequality, the level and texture of such inequalities differ widely between conflicts.

Not every conflict has sexual violence on the widespread scale seen in these three cases. A more nuanced approach to gender could reveal the factors that matter within gender equality. This small *N*, comparative case study, obviously suffers from its limited sample, attenuating the validity of its conclusions; a larger study on the impact of gender inequality and identity would be extremely welcome.

As outlined in the cases of Rwanda and Bosnia and Herzegovina, the proposed interaction of ethnicity and gender successfully explains much of the dynamic observed. However, this study highlights two silences in the literature on ethnicity and gender. Although ethnic sexual violence obviously demarcates the targeted victims, it is unclear the extent to which the form of such violence is altered by ethnicity. Also underspecified are the conditions under which ethnic sexual violence is likely not to occur in ethnic conflicts; preliminary statistical data undermine the connection between ethnic conflict and sexual violence, and add further weight to the idea that widespread sexual violence has its own qualities that are unrelated to ethnicity. Comparison of ethnic conflicts with exhibiting varied in levels of sexual violence could help elucidate this connection.

Findings on Cases

Case studies of wartime sexual violence have suffered from a lack of cross-case comparison; thus obscuring alternative explanations. This study represents a small step forward to remedying this gap and suggests that further comparative work could be very fruitful.

Inter-case comparison casts doubts on the importance of gender inequality in facilitating sexual violence in Bosnia and Herzegovina. In actuality gender inequality in this country was quite limited in light of cross-case and global comparison. Interestingly, inter-case comparison highlights the similarities between Bosnia and Herzegovina's ethnic war and other nonethnic wars. Inter-case comparison casts doubts on the importance of gender inequality in facilitating sexual violence in Bosnia and Herzegovina. In actuality gender inequality in this country was quite limited in light of cross-case and global comparison. Interestingly, inter-case comparison highlights the similarities between Bosnia and Herzegovina's ethnic war and other nonethnic wars.

Policy Implications

This study reveals similarities in ethnic and nonethnic sexual violence, particularly in the use of spectacle to induce terror and break down communities. Nonetheless, ethnic and nonethnic sexual violence are treated differently within international law; for instance, the definition of forced pregnancy limited to cases that occur across ethnicity (TRC of Sierra Leone 2004, para. 185). As the ethnic conflicts in the former Yugoslavia and in

Rwanda set the precedent for international law on sexual violence, the ethnic influence on law is unsurprising. Yet given the observed similarities, it is not necessarily justified and—like the concept of genocidal rape—poses the danger of elevating one group's suffering above another's.

This study casts doubt on the impact of gender inequalities and identities in driving sexual violence. Though this unexpected finding definitely merits attention, it does not warrant the abandonment of gender-sensitivity programming, which, even if limited in its impact on sexual violence, has a greater normative value.

NOTES

1. This chapter will focus on the genocide rather than on the Rwandan civil war.

2. It is important to note that the lines between soldiers and rebels were blurred; the idea of sobels—soldiers by day, rebels by night—help explain the fluidity of alliances seen in the conflict.

3. To clarify, in this chapter, sexual violence includes but is not limited to rape and attempted rape (whether individual or gang; in public or private; in detention centers; or coupled with homicide, impregnation, or intentional transmission of sexually transmitted diseases), forced incest, torture and mutilation of genitals, sexual slavery, and forced contraception or abortion. In international law, rape is defined as the "penetration however slight of the vagina or anus by a penis, object or other body part, or of any other body part by a penis" (TRC of Sierra Leone 2004, para. 285).

4. Interestingly, a silence pervades the literature on the costs of sexual violence, both on an individual and a group basis. The threat of disease, emotional costs, and opportunity costs individuals face are rarely considered, nor are the costs of disease and increased civilian resentment on military groups' strategic interests (Cohen 2007, 9, 20–22).

5. Among the cases presented here, Sierra Leone has the best, wide-scale individual-level data as many surveys were carried out among former combatants and victims. This case would likely be the most fruitful in revealing the role of desire.

6. It should be noted that the barriers to reporting (such as shame and stigma) are much greater for men than for women, and men are often excluded from post-conflict initiatives to address sexual violence, which further reduces their incentive to report (Ward 2002, 16). In addition to sexual violence, men experience gender-based violence during war in other forms, such as the disproportionate numbers of men massacred, detained, and recruited (Carpenter 2006, 98)

7. In Rwanda, Hutu women in command positions ordered the deaths of Tutsi girls and observed their rapes, in addition to using rape as a reward for soldiers (Sharlach 1999, 392; Fletcher 2007, 38). In Bosnia and Herzegovina, although their involvement was less common, Serbian women helped co-ethnics sexually humiliate Muslim men, and in at least one instance took an active role in sexual violence by castrating a prisoner (UNSC 1994, 674).

8. Though it was least common in Rwanda (Sivakumaran 2007, 258).

9. Interestingly Carpenter notes that these cases were not prosecuted as rape but as torture and degrading treatment; thus, the men did not have access to the same wealth of resources of female rape victims (2006, 95)

10. Prewar data are chosen to reflect the trend in the literature and to ensure that the gender inequalities can be seen as an influence on the conflict, rather than a result of it.

11. While recognizing the difference between sex and gender, the fact that these two categories usually overlap justifies this exercise. The differences between sexes likely represent opposite ends of the feminine–masculine spectrum.

12. As a sympathetic Hutu, she was also the first victim of the genocide.

13. Infant mortality rate was excluded because data were lacking.

14. Admittedly unexplored in this text, across the three countries an environment of impunity and lack of enforcement weakened any legal guarantees. This exception calls for deeper study into which laws matter.

15. Using the global average as a baseline to measure gender inequalities is problematic. As noted previously every country in the world still has gender inequalities and appreciable levels of gendered sexual and domestic violence. Nonetheless, not every conflict sees sexual violence on the widespread scale seen in these three countries. For instance, the Israeli-Palestinian conflict experiences low levels of sexual violence despite entrenched patriarchy.

16. Though perhaps these misgivings on the importance of gender go too far. These data aim to reflect gender differences established over time; nonetheless, the instrumental use of gender in the short term may merit further attention.

17. See Skjelsbaek (2001) for a comprehensive overview of this school of thought and its scholars.

18. Historically, in both cases there were alternative interpretations and modalities of ethnicity and gender. The frequency of interethnic marriage in both countries suggests that women did not act under the sole purview of their ethnic groups and were not always associated with one ethnicity.

19. Sexual violence was not the only spectacular violence in Rwanda; spectacle was common in much of the violence of the Rwandan genocide. For instance, Fletcher (2007, 39) suggests that mass slaughters in public places (such as churches) forged an idea of a collective complicity—if not agency—in a group project.

20. This phrasing is inspired by Brubaker and Laitin's 1998 work on ethnic violence.

21. Interestingly, when the RUF first attacked Sierra Leone in 1991 it attempted to incite ethnic violence by targeting Fula, Madingo, and Lebanese traders (Global Security 2005). Ethnic violence, however, did not emerge.

22. The Sierra Leone war was notorious for its rampant amputations.

23. Examples given by Human Rights Watch (1996) include: "We want to see how sweet Tutsi women are"; "You Tutsi women think that you are too good for us"; "We want to see if a Tutsi woman is like a Hutu woman"; and "If there were peace, you would never accept me" (18).

24. The practice of raping women to death actually appears to have been more frequent in Sierra Leone; many women were left to bleed out after death or were brutally raped with sticks and weapons.

25. Hayden (2000) is exceptional in theorizing on the conditions under which ethnic conflict incites sexual violence. He suggests that when the goal of one group

is secession, sexual violence is used to partition people psychologically. Comparing ethnic conflict with and without the goal of partition, he substantiates this theory.

26. After a statistical analysis of the 35 civil wars between 1989 and 1999, Cohen (2007, 5) finds preliminary evidence that ethnic conflict does not predict mass rape. Similarly Butler, Gluch, and Mitchell (2007, 680) find that when one controls for the state strength (as seen in state control and hierarchy), ethnic fractionalization does not significantly predict levels of sexual violence.

PART IV

Gender, War, and Militarism in Disarmament and Post-Conflict Reconstruction

CHAPTER 12

Links between Women, Peace, and Disarmament: Snapshots from the WILPF

Catia Cecilia Confortini

In a nationally televised speech, Russian President Vladimir Putin argued that "the world is engaged in a new arms race," and claimed that, although "it is not our fault, because we did not start it," Russia will "always respond to the challenges of a new arms race by developing more hitech weaponry" (BBC News 2008a). Soon after, Australia's Prime Minister, Kevin Rudd, declared that his country "must be prepared to respond to an emerging arms race across the Asia-Pacific region. The Australian military would be built up to meet the challenge" (BBC 2008b). In early 2008, Andrew Downie observed that "increased defense spending by Venezuela, Brazil, and Ecuador, coupled with significant arms purchases by Chile and Colombia, may mark the start of an arms race in South America" (2008).

At such a time in global politics, the issue of disarmament is more salient in global politics than it has been since the height of the Cold War. This chapter explores the issue of disarmament as it has evolved in the women's peace movement, specifically in the discourses and policy recommendations of the Women's International League for Peace and Freedom (WILPF). Though women's peace movements have a wealth of information to share about the relationship between gender, war, and militarism and women's perceptions of that relationship, they have often been neglected in the academic study of gender issues in international security generally, and especially in studies of arms races.[1]

Since its inception, the WILPF has consistently favored total and universal disarmament and has supported the role of international organizations in bringing it about. For the WILPF, disarmament is inextricably linked to peace, insofar as the organization believes there can be no meaningful peace in an armed world. Peace for the WILPF has always meant both the absence of armed conflict and the achievement of some degree of social justice and human well-being. The existence of arms of all types has been considered an obstacle to the achievement of both. This consistency in policy, however, has rested atop different theoretical perceptions in the history of the WILPF, both about the specific relationship between women and war and global politics more generally.

As the WILPF wrestled with the question of whether women had a special relationship with, and/or obligation to promote, peace, the organization's understanding of what peace is and how it should be attained also evolved. Specifically, in the immediate post–World War II era, the WILPF emphasized both the power of laws and the political neutrality of science to argue for disarmament. As the WILPF's views evolved, the organization came to see the international arms race as structural rather than incidental, and came to question the political neutrality of science. These developments have created a WILPF that, today, remains in favor of disarmament but sees that specific problem and the general relationships between gender, war, and militarism very differently. These shifts have important implications not only for disarmament policies but also for the greater relationship between gender, war, and militarism.

WOMEN, WAR, AND MILITARISM IN THE WILPF

Coming out of the World War II and having fought alongside men against Nazism, many women in the WILPF doubted the necessity of a women's peace organization. Some, like Dutch member J. Repelaer van Driel, argued that not only had war shown women to be as bellicose as men (or as peaceful as men) but that maintaining a separate women's organization devoted to peace after women had attained the right to vote in almost all countries where the WILPF was represented, meant to perpetuate the status of women as inferior. Van Driel argued:

To pull out in groups to aspire to such vast plans as that of International Concord, women too easily "donnent prise aux homes" who raise their shoulders and judge those groups and their efforts as "really feminine", "sentimental" or "out of touch with reality", etc. without realizing, moreover, that they too try to hide their inferiority complex and their own failings in the achievement of universal peace. (Devons-nous dissoudre la L.I.F.P.L.?, J. Repelaer van Driel, 1946 Congress, SCPC Microfilm, reel 141.2, 127)

Mildred Scott Olmsted instead argued in favor of maintaining the WILPF, using maternalist rhetoric and depicting women as "by nature more concerned than men with the conservation of life and the creation of conditions under which children may grow up safely and happily" (Shall the W.I.L.P.F. continue or dissolve?, Mildred Scott Olmsted, 1946 Congress, SCPC Microfilm, reel 141.2, 126).

The WILPF Congress overwhelmingly voted to maintain the WILPF in 1946, but during the rest of the 1940s and continuing in the 1950s it rarely, if ever, entertained any discussion on the relationship between women and peace. While it worked on women's rights and equal representation at the United Nations (UN), for example, feminist-inspired reflections on disarmament, peace, and gender were notably absent from WILPF documents of the first two decades after the war. This absence partly reflected the lack of input from a feminist movement that in those years was rather dormant in much of the Western world (see Foster 1989, 32).

In the mid-1970s, however, the WILPF started to systematically address women's contribution to peace work and disarmament issues. Led by International President Kay Camp, the WILPF actively participated in the preparations for the first world conference on the status of women that took place in 1975. It also helped launch a series of disarmament campaigns that focused on women's role in disarmament and peace. Significantly, in 1975, the WILPF's International Executive Committee also called for WILPF Disarmament Year in 1976 and decided to undertake disarmament actions on International Women's Day of that same year. With these actions the WILPF was expressing its belief that women had the obligation to active political participation and a special interest in questions of peace. Thus, Swedish member Aja Selander, addressing the Conference of Women's Organizations on European Cooperation and Security, proclaimed:

Our task as European women is not only to work for equality and development. We should not hesitate to deal with all political questions that have impact on the future of mankind. (Conference of Women's Organizations on European Cooperation and Security, Aja Selander, 1973, Box 7 FD 7, 2nd Accession, 2)

In this new interpretation, not only did women possess a special obligation toward peace but they were also uniquely apt at peacework: "The discussions and 'negotiations' proved that women have ways of overcoming difficulties and reaching agreement, and that women show understanding and tolerance" (Meeting in Preparation for the World Congress for the International Women's Year, unsigned report, *Pax et Libertas,* December 1974, Box 162 FD 1, 2nd Accession, 22).

THE SHIFT FROM LIBERAL MODERNISM TO CRITICAL RETHOUGHT WITHIN THE WILPF'S APPROACH TO DISARMAMENT

The WILPF's early confidence in liberal laws and international institutions was underpinned by a specific gender ideology, which privileged a particular (liberal) conception of human nature and the international system grounded on masculinist notions of autonomy, freedom, and obligation. This, in turn, led the WILPF to underplay the role of economic and other structural constraints in shaping states' policies toward disarmament. As long as the women of the WILPF remained unquestioningly bound to the liberal internationalist tradition, they also reproduced the gendered assumptions of liberal political thought.

The WILPF's positions on disarmament in the immediate post-war years reflected the WILPF's belief in the power of law, rational thinking, and deliberation to bring about peace, both as absence of armed conflicts and as a degree of social justice. Starting at the first Congress after World War II and continuing through the mid-1960s, WILPF's members were convinced that laws and rational reasoning would lead to the elimination of the war system, and thus the elimination of states' weapon arsenals. In 1963, in a widely circulated background paper, the U.S. Section interpreted Jane Addams's thoughts as follows:

Jane Addams and the other founders of the Women's International League for Peace and Freedom were idealistic realists. They exemplified and preached reconciliation and compassion but they never assumed that the world community was ready wholly to substitute these for war as a method for settling international disputes, maintaining order, and promoting human welfare. Their political proposals envisaged, not love, but *law* as the substitute for war....According to their analysis, wars are caused by the fact that there is no other means to settle international disputes or bring about necessary changes in the international status quo and war can be prevented only by the creation of "an international government able to make the necessary political and economic changes." (The United Nations and World Law, 1963, Box 119 FD 7, 2nd Accession, 1)

The belief in logical reasoning, deliberation, and an international system of law went hand in hand with a distinctly modern belief in science and rationality. The WILPF of the two immediate post-war decades believed reason and science would ultimately show people and world leaders alike that there was no other way but disarmament, because the rational, reasonable, and scientifically proven way to avoid wars was to get rid of the instruments of war.

In 1946, Clara Ragaz, from the Swiss section, expressed her belief thus:

It is true that we have...a new ally which pleads in favor of our cause in a more effective and pressing manner than we could do. It is the atomic bomb.

With that I mean not only to say that the atomic bomb will pull even the indifferent out of their lethargy; fear is a bad advisor by itself and can lead to anything but reasonable conclusions. But it seems to me that the atomic bomb should show even to those most indifferent and to those most apathetic what war means, and make them understand that we are lost if we keep putting our trust in violence. (Discours d'Ouverture, Clara Ragaz, 1946 Congress, SCPC microfilm, reel 141.2, 17)

Reason thus could only lead to one conclusion: if the possible outcome of any war, small or big, was the resort to the atomic bomb, which carried with it the possibility of world annihilation, then people will realize that all wars, and all preparation to war, must be eliminated to avoid the likely consequences of the use of the atomic bomb. "Wars on a small scale, whether civil or international, carry within themselves the seeds of world war. A world war, even if begun with so-called conventional weapons, would almost certainly end as a nuclear war. We must neither begin such war deliberately, not slide into it accidently [*sic*]" (Statement on Policy, IEC Meeting, 1955, Box 3 FD 17, SCPC, 1).[2]

Because reason, not politics, guided science, the WILPF viewed science and technology with great optimism: it was through science and technology that humanity could be guided through to salvation.[3] When reporting her work at a World Health Organization (WHO)[4] meeting in Geneva in 1954, for example, Gertrude Baer was keenly aware of the dangers, contradictions, and political and nonpolitical problems raised by nuclear science and technology. She enumerated in great detail the possible public health consequences of radiation, the risks associated with the existence of nuclear reactors near inhabited locations, the dilemmas of safe disposal of nuclear waste, and other questions related to the use of nuclear energy for peaceful purposes. However, her report also made it clear that these were technical questions that the world scientific community could and would address and solve (Report of the Work of the WILPF with United Nations in Geneva, Gertrude Baer, IEC Meeting, 1955, Box 14 FD 3, SCPC, 1–8). Moreover, Baer was eager to see the WHO and other international bodies discuss questions related to the use of "nuclear energy for destructive purposes" from a "scientific" point of view:

[s]cientific discussion of the questions of radiation through atomic weapons, if put into the context of the many other aspects with which the [UN] Conference [for Peaceful Uses of Atomic Energy] is going to deal, may bring about a relaxation of the fear now obsession of vast populations.... We are convinced that a frank and open presentation would strengthen the confidence in those who organize and participate in, the Conference and lessen the profound anxiety of so many people around the globe. (Report of the Work of the WILPF with United Nations in Geneva, Gertrude Baer, IEC Meeting, 1955, Box 14 FD 3, SCPC, 9)

The WILPF shared with other peace movements of the time (Wittner 1993, 1997)[5] the sense that the system of security based on fear and power politics was obsolete and suicidal. On the other hand, the scientific endeavor, though corrupted by politics, was in itself extraordinary:

Modern scientific warfare has made it obvious that the concepts and doctrines of security hitherto existing have become utterly obsolete and that new measures are urgently required—measures as bold and unparalleled as the evil design of making the fantastic progress in science and technical skill serve wholesale diabolic destruction. (Baer's UN Report of 1956, 3)

By contrast, the 1970s saw the WILPF offer a radical reassessment of its position toward the relationship between women, disarmament and peace and with it of the role of power in international relations. Resolutions approved at WILPF's International Congress in 1974 indicted "an economic system based on production for profit rather than production for human needs" as ultimately responsible for the arms buildup and called for "fundamental economic change by non-violent means" as the only way to "eliminate war, racism, violence, repression and social injustice." Further, the WILPF strongly condemned nuclear power, "whether used for weaponry or peaceful purposes," as a threat to peace and asked for the cessation of nuclear arms testing and the use of nuclear energy for peaceful purposes. Finally it linked women's emancipation with "the achievement of peace and the relaxation of international tension" (WILPF, International Congress Resolutions, 1974, http://www.wilpf.int.ch/statements/1974.htm—accessed October 17, 2007).

These resolutions represented a switch in emphasis from a reliance on and faith in international law to a more sustained critique of the international economic system. They reflected an increased skepticism toward the rules of liberal democracy: with them the WILPF was also critiquing, or starting to doubt that principles of liberal democracy and democratic deliberation were in themselves sufficient to bring about peace in the context of unequal power relations, which were manifested in a world divided into "three political blocs and two economic blocs (rich countries and poor countries)" (On WILPF Aims and Purposes, Yvonne Sée, IEC, 1972, Box 2 FD 8, SCPC, 1). Moreover, the WILPF critiqued those elements of the international system that made impossible or negated, in the WILPF's views, human obligations to each other (including laws and agreements).

Developing an economic critique of the arms race went hand in hand with revisiting the WILPF's early support of the use of nuclear energy for peaceful purposes. This reversion of policies was made possible by an increasing skepticism toward the supposed "neutrality" of science. In fact, references to scientists and "experts" as the "saviors" of humanity disappear almost entirely from WILPF documents of the 1970s.

Though changes in the WILPF's thinking about disarmament began to manifest themselves more visibly in the 1960s, thanks to a more favorable international environment, there had been many occasions in which dissenting opinions had emerged in internal WILPF debates. In 1957, the Committee against Scientific Warfare, led by Gertrud Woker, proposed a resolution condemning "those who profit from the war industry" and asking that governments

in all circumstances, even in relation to the "peaceful uses of atomic energy", . . . consider the life and health of the peoples above the economic advantages and profit interests of a reactor industry which may develop without any such inhibitions. (Resolution of the WILPF Committee against Scientific Warfare, IEC, 1957, Box 26 FD 7, SCPC, 3)

It further advocated the exploration of alternative sources of energy, other than nuclear.[6] It is unclear from the existing records whether the proposal by Woker's committee actually became part of the International Executive Committee Resolutions of that year. However, it is indicative of the kinds of skeptical input that the WILPF was receiving from some executive members on the political economy of nuclear energy.

Individual (especially younger) WILPF members had participated in Women Strike for Peace since the early 1960s, and it was those younger members who were the most ardent critics of both the WILPF's methods and its ideological entrenchment in liberalism (see Foster 1989, 27–28). Participation in Women Strike for Peace was especially crucial: although the movement used maternalist rhetoric to call for disarmament (at least this was true in the United States—see Wittner 1997, 250–53), it had also very deliberatively developed into a horizontal, unhierarchical organization. Horizontal and collective decision making, in turn, has been a mainstay of feminist organizing. In fact, the revival of the feminist movement in the 1960s brought the WILPF to debate its relationship with feminism. In 1968, British member Margaret Tims was critical of the WILPF's attention to women's issues:

the two causes—of peace and freedom in the general sense and of women's freedom in the particular sense—are no longer synonymous and should be treated separately. By continuing to link them together, the WILPF is falling between two stools and being effective in neither cause.

The WILPF should therefore decide whether it is to concern itself specifically with women's freedom, or, as it is now called, the status of women, with a much greater emphasis on the needs of women in the under-developed countries; or whether it is to go on pursuing the general aims of peace and freedom, from a broadly political viewpoint. (Tim's Circular Letter, cited in Foster 1989, 55)

Tims' letter shows that the WILPF did not passively absorb or reproduce the ideological and policy changes that a reinvigorated international feminist movement brought about. Rather, its methodological commitment to skeptical scrutiny (Ackerly 2000, 10) made it possible for the WILPF to reflect on what kind of relation there was, if any, between women's freedom and the general aims of peace and freedom. This reflection manifested itself in the policy statements and initiatives of the 1970s.[7]

Many members of the WILPF at one time or another fulfilled the role of inside critic: from Helene Stähelin in 1946 in advocating caution against the nuclear energy and the possibilities of science, to Gertrud Woker and her Committee against Scientific Warfare, to Elise Boulding and Edith Ballantyne advocating increased contacts and cooperation among women's and peace organizations. The women of the French section were more insistent than others in bringing out economic arguments whenever they spoke about disarmament. For example, at the first International Congress after the war, French member Gabrielle Duchêne expressed her view that "true democracy" was diametrically opposed to an economic system dominated by the power of money (i.e., capitalism—La situation politique et le conditions de la Paix, G. Duchêne, 1946 Congress, SCPS microfilm, reel 141.2).

In the 1960s, the U.S. WILPF started more systematic contacts and exchanges with Soviet women that had profound impacts on the organization. Elise Boulding recalls one of those experiences in the following terms:

in 1961 the WILPF was invited to participate in hosting a group of Soviet women....And so we had a conference at Bryn Mawr...There may have been 8 or 10 of them, I'm not quite sure how many. And the equivalent number of WILPF members....Most of us were WILFP members but not all. And so that was an extraordinary occasion because we came to see the real heroism of these women who had all, you know, survived the war under great, great difficulties, and seen very, very much suffering. And they had violence, more than we in the United States. We hadn't really seen that kind of violence. We hadn't been overseas. And they spoke with such—they had such a strong sense of their role and what they had to do and their calling to build a peaceful society. And they were, and they were so open to listening. You know we were all learning from each other. But we were so impressed with their character, and who they were as people. And so that was an amazing experience...They were well dressed, and they carried themselves with an assurance that we didn't...more than ours, you know, and they had...were a highly developed society within society [talking about a later meeting with a Polish women's group]. (Interview with Elise Boulding, May 21, 2005)

Those meetings, as well as earlier meetings with Japanese women and the late 1960s and 1970s encounters with Vietnamese women, produced lasting changes in the WILPF. An African American WILPF delegate at a second conference with Soviet women in Moscow in 1964 (a conference focused on the search for common policies toward disarmament between Soviet and U.S. women) recalled "a vague feeling some American delegates received that the Soviet women were reluctant to speak in any way but generalities about their government's actions toward peace." However, instead of trying to convert Soviets to their way of thinking, the American peace delegates "tried to understand them"(Erna P. Harris, cited in Blackwell 2004, 174).

African American members' exchanges with Soviet women highlighted for them the connections they saw between racial relations in the United States and international tensions that contributed to a continued arms buildup:

At the Moscow Conference, we discussed disarmament ways to strengthen cooperation in the United Nations, and the German problem. But after a school was burned in Alabama, we talked about how the racial turmoil in the United States affects international tension. (Erna P. Harris, cited in Blackwell 2004, 174)

Increased participation in non-governmental organization meetings and increased involvement in joint activities with other organizations meant increased contacts with outside critics, especially people whose views would not otherwise be represented in the WILPF. And African American members from the U.S. section exerted an influence far beyond their marginal representation in the ranks of the WILPF (see Blackwell 2004, 165–94).

THE GENDERING OF LIBERAL MODERNITY AS AN INSPIRATION FOR CRITICAL RETHOUGHT ON DISARMAMENT

Many feminist scholars (Okin 1979; Pateman 1988; Di Stefano 1991; Elshtain 1992; Tickner 1992) have exposed the gendered construction of key elements of liberal modernity, among which are concepts central to liberal political thought and praxis. They argue that "[l]iberal political theory…extends a particular gendering experience into the norms of western society" (Sylvester 2002, 186). In other words, feminists claim that Western liberal political theory's values are inherently derived from the living experiences of men, not women. This has specific consequences for the content of key concepts in liberal political thought.

The idea of citizenship in liberal political thought is gendered insofar as it derives from contractual theory. Carol Pateman claims that Western theories of social contract depend on a "sexual contract" that solidified patriarchy and the subjection of women and other categories of people. She argues that the notion of contract itself implies the alienation of one's body and the erasure of the distinction between freedom and slavery. Paralleling Elshtain's (later) argument about sovereignty,[8] Pateman thus claims that the very thinking in terms of contract and free will inescapably bind one into "civil slavery" (Pateman 1988, 39–76). Moreover, the notions of consent and freedom underlying contractual theory are profoundly sexist because they ignore or hide the reality and multiplicity of ways in which consent is denied to women (Pateman 1979, 1988). But they also shape and delimit imagination, in that they don't allow us to think outside their very terms.

Nancy Hirschmann adds that in the liberal doctrines the notion of obligation is based on "voluntarist principles; that is, an obligation is a limitation on behavior, a requirement for action or nonaction, that the actor or nonactor has chosen or agreed to" (Hirschmann 1989, 1227). She argues that the liberal notion of "voluntary consent" harbors a masculine bias that denies the nonconsensual obligations that make up an important part of many women's lives and in fact denies them full participation in public life (Hirschmann 1989, 1229). Although these critiques question the roles and expectations of individuals within the nation-state, they can be equally valid in the international realm insofar as they highlight states' structural constraints to the expression of free will, and they question consent as the only legitimate source of obligation (Hirschman 1989).

Many feminists have also observed how modern concepts of reason, rationality, and science rely on masculinist assumptions and imagery grounded in (and justified and rationalized through) the domination of men over women (Keller 1982; Keller and Longino 1996; Merchant 1980; Harding 1986; Tickner 1992). Postmodern feminists and nonfeminists argue that liberal notions about science and rationality are based on a peculiarly modern need to find truths and certainties (Zalewski 2000, 35–36). In addition, for postmodern feminists the nexus power/knowledge is essential in understanding how Western science has been profoundly political, in the sense that political decisions have been an integral part of science praxis (see, for example, Zalewski 2000, 55–59). Post-war international relations practices and theories are infused with the modern "goals of scientific objectivity, emotional distance, and instrumentality," which are characteristics associated with, and defining of, masculinity (Hooper 2001, 13).

These theoretical developments can be seen in the evolution of the WILPF's discussions of, and motivations for their policy advocacy on the issue of disarmament and how it relates to international peace and security. As long as the women of the WILPF remained unquestioningly bound to the liberal internationalist tradition, they also reproduced the gendered assumptions of liberal political thought. In essence, between 1945 and 1975 the WILPF went through a shift from its entrenchment in liberal modern thought, with its underpinning notions of reactive autonomy (Sylvester 2002), logical rationality, and deliberative democracy, to more subversive, radical critiques of the international system.

Early WILPF policies on disarmament reflected a view of peace that loosely adhered to liberal modern ideology. The WILPF didn't arrive at this radical revision of its beliefs and policies suddenly in the 1970s. Rather, the change was the result of a three-decade-long process that favored the development of a feminist and loosely post-colonial critique of "the mutually constitutive projects characteristic of modernity—the making of states, science, militarism, and industrial capitalism" (Peterson 1992, 14).

This shift from liberal modernism to an understanding of gender subordination as both fundamental and structural has helped the WILPF, and can help theorists and practitioners more generally, understand both disarmament and the broader issues of human and international security. Through studying the changes in the WILPF's perspectives on disarmament, we can see the complexities and tensions of the relationship between women and peace and between global politics, global social relations, and global economics. Immediately after World War II, both the WILFP and the feminist movement more generally saw the arms race as a problem that could be solved in theory by science and in practice by law. In the meantime, the WILPF has come to recognize law and science as a part of a gender-biased structure of global politics, the deconstruction of which is key to the deconstruction of the arms race.

CONCLUSION: GENDER, WAR, MILITARISM, AND DEMOCRACY

The WILPF's current position on disarmament, recognizing that it is intricately linked to global political structures of gender subordination and militarism, is instructive for how to read and deal with what many have identified as the "coming arms race" (Evangelista and Reppy 2002). First, though women are not by nature more peaceful than men, women's peace movements have been able to secure a unique space in protesting arms race based on the intersection of gender and militarism in global politics. Second, an "arms race" cannot be seen as a problem divorced from war and militarism more generally; instead, it can be seen as a part of a larger gendered global political system that entrenches militarism. Third, the development of the WILPF's ideas on disarmament since World War II shows a growing understanding of the intersection of gender, militarism, and globalization. Finally, the states in the competitive arms races that were the subject of concern at the outset of this chapter will not be discouraged only by science and law, but by only by an approach that also critiques and reevaluates global political structure, perhaps on the basis of a feminist critique of liberal modern politics.

NOTES

1. Perhaps this is because women's peace groups' (perceived and actual) objection to war generally causes others to assume that reconstruction or disarmament fall outside their realms of interest or expertise. As my study of the WILPF demonstrates, however, this is a misperception, and women's organizations' general objection to war making and war fighting does not stop them from becoming familiar with specific preventive or reconstructive measures.

2. Ragaz did not conclude, however, that disarmament and the elimination of the war system would bring about "real peace": this could only be accomplished by guaranteeing political and civil rights and a collective right to self-determination (Discours d'Ouverture, Clara Ragaz, 1946 Congress, SCPC microfilm, reel 141.2, 17–18).

3. In Edith Ballantyne's words, "science and technology became the saviour [sic]" (Ballantyne's e-mail, September 24, 2006).

4. It is particularly interesting to notice here that Gertrude Baer referred to the WHO as "non-political" (Report of the Work of the WILPF with United Nations in Geneva, Gertrude Baer, IEC Meeting, 1955, Box 14 FD 3, SCPC, 7).

5. This was arguably more true for early antinuclear movements of the late 1940s and early 1950s. Cfr. Wittner (1993, 1997).

6. Gertrude Baer had suggested studying the utilization of solar energy as early as 1955 at the WHO (Foster 1989, 27).

7. The internal debate continued through the 1970s and 1980s, and the organization's relation with feminism remains indefinite to this day.

8. Jean Bethke Elshtain critiques the modern nation-state as embedded in sacrifical themes far from the feminist ethic of responsibility. She observes that the concept of sovereignty presupposes a gendered understanding of power as domination (Elshtain 1991, 150).

CHAPTER 13

When Is War Over? Women's Stories of Healing and Rebuilding after the War in El Salvador

Gwyn Kirk

On January 16, 1992, the government of El Salvador and the left-wing Frente Farabundo Martí para la Liberación Nacional (FMLN) signed Peace Accords to end 12 years of civil war. Women have made significant contributions to post-war reconstruction and healing of war-related violations and trauma. This chapter discusses some of their challenges and accomplishments, emphasizing the lengthy, multilayered processes involved in demilitarization, as suggested by the title question: When is war over?

Examining the historical circumstances that led to this war raises a second question: When did the war start? According to Conaway and Martínez (2004), the civil war in El Salvador was "the culmination of decades of economic marginalization, social segregation, political repression, failed land reform, and military control of the country" (11). A few aristocratic families controlled most of the nation's wealth and most people were desperately poor. This situation had roots in 300 years of colonization by Spain, followed by 200 years of U.S. political, economic, and military interventions. For decades, peasants and workers organized to change the gross inequalities that characterized the country. Their efforts met severe government repression, including assassinations of community leaders and armed attacks on protestors. In the 1970s, as government repression worsened, revolutionary organizations formed in rural and urban areas (Binford 2004; Wood 2004).

The government-backed assassination of Archbishop Oscar Romero in March 1980 and the massacre of funeral attendees provided the impetus for five revolutionary groups to join forces as the Democratic Revolution Front (FDR) with the FMLN as its military wing. The FMLN organized its first attack six months after Romero's assassination, and was supported by many noncombatants—peasants, workers, students, and members of faith-based communities. Government troops terrorized and massacred people in many communities suspected of harboring FMLN forces, especially in mountainous areas in the east and north of the country: Chalatenango, San Vicente, Suchitoto, and Morazán. Government forces pursued a scorched earth policy and destroyed forest cover, food supplies, and shelter through ground attacks, helicopter fire, and carpet bombing (Murray 1997; Thompson and Eade 2004). In a country of 6 million, an estimated 80,000 people were killed and 7,000 more "disappeared" (Ready, Stephen, and Cosgrove 2001, 184). Many were forced to abandon their homes and sources of livelihood. It was too dangerous to plant or tend crops; people could not care for their livestock or maintain their orchards. Half a million people were displaced internally; one million fled the country to refugee camps in Honduras, or to the United States (Conaway and Martínez 2004, 2).

Napalm, white phosphorus, and daisy-cutter bombs scarred people and the land, "some bombs leaving craters fifteen feet deep and as wide as a football field" (Whelan 1998, 35). The war exacerbated environmental destruction caused by decades of plantation agriculture that included deforestation, reduced soil fertility, and the use of hazardous pesticides, DDT among them (Faber 1993; Weinberg 1991).

IMPACTS OF THE WAR ON WOMEN

Women—especially young women—participated as FMLN combatants, making up an estimated 30 percent of the fighting force at the height of the war (Conaway and Martínez 2004, 2; Kampwirth 2002). Women were also *colaboradoras* who sustained communities and camps in FMLN-controlled zones, and *tenedoras*—supporters who lived in areas controlled by the FMLN.

Women were profoundly affected by the war as those responsible for generating household income, caring for children, and finding medical help, food, and shelter for their families. During the war, up to 51 percent of households were headed by women (Ready, Stephen, and Cosgrove 2001, 184–85). Reflecting on her experience, Cruz Rivas de Valladares, a member of La Florida Permaculture Community (La Libertad) said:

We experienced the cruelty of the war. We stumbled over corpses. We were in the middle of gunfire, also fire from rockets and planes. I was pregnant when I had to flee. I went to a camp in Honduras and had the baby there. I managed to come back and I looked for my husband who was with the guerillas. I lived in a refugee camp in San Salvador run by the Catholic Church. My husband is here now. For three years we had to live separately. I was responsible for our two daughters.[1]

Some women had to leave their children in the care of others or send them abroad for safety. Thousands of women were killed. Many thousands lost family members and suffered rape, abuse, and torture by government forces and death squads (Kampwirth 2002; Lorentzen 1998). A significant number of elderly people, especially women whose husbands and children were killed or who fled, were left without family support. Severe family disruption included high numbers of woman-headed households (29 percent) after the war (Conaway and Martínez 2004, 18).

Life in the refugee camps was hard, but some learned new skills and perspectives (MacDonald and Gatehouse 1994; McElhinny 2004; Thompson and Eade 2004). Miriam Chicas, who grew up in Perquín (Morazán), commented:

I was given work in health and they put my husband, Oscar, in charge of food distribution. Since this was our first experience of collective work, we were hesitant, but we adapted quickly…

When we came back to Perquín eight months later we had a very different vision. We began to work in community organizations. Oscar became a member of the community council and I started to work through the church. We women hadn't been very active outside of our homes, but we began to sense the need to do something. (quoted in Murray 1997, 16)

However Norma Stoltz Chinchilla (1997) identified "key ideological and cultural barriers" within armed revolutionary movements, including the FMLN, that limited women achieving greater equality:

- The lack of a gendered analysis of the revolutionary movement and the society it wanted to change, with a singular emphasis on class exploitation;
- The role of masculinist culture in the supposedly genderless vanguard party;
- The principle of self-sacrifice and obedience to authority; and
- A weak understanding of the importance of democracy and the role of civil society in the creation of a new society (Chinchilla 1997, 209–10).

THE 1992 PEACE ACCORDS

Military stalemate brought the government and the FMLN to negotiate a peace settlement, with the support of United Nations (UN) Secretary-General Javier Pérez de Cuéllar. This involved a series of negotiations and interim agreements over a two-year period that culminated in the signing of the Peace Accords at Chapultepec, Mexico, in January 1992 (Murray 1997, 21–23). The United Nations Observer Mission to El Salvador (ONUSAL) oversaw the disarmament, demobilization, and reintegration program and verified and monitored human rights violations committed during the war. The Peace Accords provided for downsizing of the military, demilitarization of the police force, legalization of the FMLN as a political party, commitment to the rule of law, and plans for reconstruction (Studemeister 2001).

Under the Land Transfer Program (*Programa de Transferencia de Tierras*, or PTT) ex-combatants on both sides could claim land for resettlement, as well as some noncombatants who had been affected by the conflict. About 22 percent of rural households received land under the PTT, a process fraught with delays, administrative problems, and discrimination against women—especially in the early stages (Reed 2005, 6). Ultimately, 35 percent of PTT beneficiaries were women, up from 11 percent during the land distribution program started in the 1980s, largely as a counterinsurgency measure (Gómez et al. 2002, 22). People struggled hard for these small plots but much of this land was not suitable for subsistence farming. Moreover, most recipients needed more technical training and financial assistance to be successful farmers. Some soon gave up farming and joined the ranks of overseas workers who send home monthly remittances, as discussed later.

Neoliberal economic imperatives mean that post-war agreements typically focus on getting business running again and do not address root causes of conflict or make provision for meaningful reconciliation or reparations (Lipschutz 1998). This was also the case in El Salvador, where the conservative Nationalist Republican Alliance party (ARENA), elected in 1989, sought to stimulate the post-war economy by opening new export markets and encouraging foreign investment. It implemented structural adjustment policies, including the privatization of banks and some public services. Macroeconomic policy favored the financial sector and the *maquila* factories surrounding San Salvador, rather than addressing the needs of communities trying to recover from the war or the thousand of dispossessed people who were attempting to survive in the informal economy.

Women from both the FMLN and the government participated in all phases of the negotiations. Ana Guadalupe Martinez, a high-ranking FMLN official, noted that her involvement was "not as a woman, but as the representative of a powerful armed group" (quoted in Conaway and Martínez 2004, 13). These authors report that, with hindsight, "many female FMLN fighters regret their lack of gender awareness during the peace process" (Conaway and Martínez 2004, 3). Nevertheless, they underline the importance of women's presence in the negotiations, which led to the inclusion of "*tenedores*—noncombatant FMLN supporters, and internally displaced people in conflict-affected areas" (2), as beneficiaries of reintegration packages, including people like Cruz Rivas de Valladares, quoted earlier. This inclusion of noncombatant women was highly unusual; peace agreements generally focus only on combatants, who, typically, are men.

The return to domestic life after the war was a difficult transition for some women combatants who were expected to return to traditional domestic roles; to support their husbands, brothers, and sons; and to help them resettle and gain recognition for their part in the war (Chinchilla 1997; Kampwirth 2002). Women combatants were not always respected for the part they played in the war, nor were they recognized for their new skills or capable leadership.

HEALING AND REBUILDING IN THE
AFTERMATH OF WAR

A growing literature has established the complex nature of the inter-related psychological, economic, political, legal, and spiritual processes involved in healing and rebuilding after the upheavals, atrocities, and trauma of war (e.g., Barsalou 2005; Cane 2002; Fletcher and Weinstein 2002; Simonovic 2004; Stover and Weinstein 2004). At the micro level, healing and rebuilding include personal healing from physical and emotional wounds, reestablishing trust in others, searching for the truth of what happened, and witnessing other people's testimony. It means using personal and family resources—skills, time, money, care, persistence, and imagination—to create new homes and livelihoods. At the community/ meso level, it includes repairing damaged buildings, revitalizing land, planting trees, enhancing water systems, providing health care, and fostering community renewal through art, music, video, or radio shows. It involves creating public memorials to heroes and martyrs and visioning new ways of living. At the institutional/macro level, healing and rebuilding means upholding the rule of law and international human rights standards; holding governments accountable for commitments contained in peace agreements; and supporting candidates for local and national office who will facilitate healing and rebuilding from war, including the adoption of national budget priorities that support sustainable development.

Memory, History, and Truth Telling

The ONUSAL set up a Truth Commission that heard testimony of war crimes and human rights abuses (Lagström 2005). The Truth Commission report condemned FMLN violence but estimated that government forces and death squads committed 85 percent of violent deaths (UN Security Council 1993, 43). The Commission admonished the government to set up a legal process to deal with those who had committed war crimes, including high-ranking government and military officials. Instead, the government pushed an amnesty law through the Legislative Assembly on March 20, 1993, five days after the Truth Commission report was published (Rubin 2004; Whitfield 2001). This law shielded war criminals from possible legal action, and successive presidents have refused to reopen this issue. Survivors, witnesses, journalists, and historians have pieced together information, establishing the truth of what happened at specific locations by listening to personal testimonies, exhuming gravesites, and detailing lists of people killed or missing (see, e.g., Danner 1994). Many people are calling for the repeal of the amnesty, "seen by activists and United Nations experts as the biggest hurdle to achieving respect for human rights" in El Salvador (Gutierrez 2007a).

Another ONUSAL recommendation was that the government set up a national memorial to those who were "disappeared" or killed by state forces as a form of "moral reparations," but the government ignored this (Amnesty International 2003). Instead, a coalition of nongovernmental organizations (NGOs) sponsored the construction of the Monument a la Memoria y La Verdad (Monument to Memory and Truth) in Cuscatlán Park, San Salvador, and dedicated in 2003. This long wall of black granite is inscribed with the names of more than 25,000 children, women, and men, along with the text: "A space for hope, to continue to dream and to build a society that is more just, humane and equitable." Many small towns in former war zones commissioned artists to paint murals and create memorials to honor those who were killed. The School of Art, established in 2005 by Claudia Bernardi and others in Perquín (Morazán), has sponsored murals.[2] Also, through the school, young people interviewed their elders to learn about community history before, during, and after the war (Bernardi 2006). The practice of commemorating violent deaths, like the assassination of Archbishop Romero on March 24, 1980, provides another continuing forum for mourning, remembrance, and experience of community and solidarity.

Healing Self, Family, and Community

During the war, many people lived in constant fear and anxiety. In the aftermath, women cared for traumatized family members, some of whom had sustained disabling injuries. This included people who had been arrested and tortured, and those who had witnessed or committed acts of violence. At the community level, women sought to console others who lost relatives through detention or combat. They cared for children who had experienced the horrors of war, sometimes the violent death of their parents. Community organizations, church groups, and feminist projects have provided a range of psychological, spiritual, and practical help. Staff of the Capacitar Wellness Center (Suchitoto), for example, teach holistic healing practices to community members, including body work, Tai chi, and ritual. They work with families affected by the war, domestic violence, and daily violence in the streets (Cane 2002).[3]

Women challenged police and military officials as they searched for relatives among the estimated 7,000 people disappeared by government forces. The COMADRES (Committee of Mothers and Relatives of Political Prisoners, Disappeared, and Assassinated Persons of El Salvador), formed in 1977, mainly comprised poor women whose husbands or children had been kidnapped or killed by death squads and government troops.[4] Over the years, this organization developed from a group of concerned relatives to a broader political movement committed to human rights (Bejarano 2002; Schirmer 1993). In 1983, the Marianella Garcia Villas Committee of Relatives of Victims of Human Rights Violations (CODEFAM) took up this issue also. Guadalupe Mejía Delgado, director of CODEFAM, went to barracks and prisons, and is credited with rescuing more than 1,500 people from arbitrary detention. Along with members of COMADRES, she continues to accuse the state "of hiding behind the veil of an amnesty law to avoid answering the question that the families of the missing ones always ask: Where are they?" (1000 Women for the Nobel Peace Prize 2005, 554).

Government forces abducted infants and young children from families living in the war zones. Some of these children were raised in orphanages or by military families in El Salvador; hundreds of others were adopted in North America and Europe. The Asociación Pro-Búsqueda de Niñas y Niños Desaparecidos (Organization for Disappeared Children) has worked closely with the University of California Human Rights Center at Berkeley to locate these children, who are now young adults. These organizations help to reunite families and seek to hold the government accountable for this wartime policy. Years later, when pressed by community organizers to apologize to families for abducting young children, a government official would say only "Sorry the children were misplaced."[5]

Rebuilding: Sustainable Communities

Displaced people demanded the right to return to their towns and villages while the war still raged, a courageous and defiant step that began to restrict the scope of military incursions (MacDonald and Gatehouse 1994; McElhinney 2004; Wood 2004). Others moved onto unoccupied land. Community members and NGOs took the lead in much post-war reconstruction at local level, sometimes with help from solidarity organizations outside El Salvador.[6] The Christian Committee of the Displaced (CRIPDES), with young single women in leadership roles, helped organize people to return to their homes (Thompson and Eade 2004). At the national level, support from international organizations was integral to the reconstruction process. This included UN agencies, donor governments (e.g., Canada, the European Union, Japan, and the United States), and international organizations ranging from the World Bank to Oxfam, which provided resources on a short-term basis.

Legacies of the war have included political polarization between the ARENA-controlled government and people in areas that supported the FMLN. In conversation, Rosa Cándida, mayor of Las Vueltas (Chalatenango), said that because her town is an FMLN stronghold, government support was weak. Their challenge is to continue to rebuild despite limited resources.

We have a small fund from central government, which we prioritize according to the greatest needs. This year we are improving the clinic and the school. We want to have a high school here. For the clinic we are getting some help from an international NGO. We need funds for roads and infrastructure. Part of the budget this year will go towards these costs. We also have a water project to improve the water system. We want a better solid waste treatment facility. We have a center for children with disabilities but need to expand it. The high school and solid waste are priorities but we don't have all the resources yet, so we are doing it bit by bit.[7]

María Esperanza Ortega, a member of the Association of War Victims of El Salvador and a founding member of the Coordination of Communities and Repopulation (CCR)[8] described the impetus for starting this organization based in Chalatenango:

From 1980–84 people had to leave their homes…even pregnant women and children had to leave this region. If you live far from your home place it's very difficult. People wanted to return. We demanded to be protected when we returned to our land. We saw it necessary to organize ourselves to carry out our struggle. I was one of the founders of the first Board of CCR on June 19, 1988 at the National University in San Salvador. This is how the dialogue and negotiation regarding the Peace Accords started. After the signing of the Peace Accords we started to work on development and formed women's groups, groups for healthcare, youth affairs, education, and so on.[9]

The CCR began working in 5 communities and now works with 100. It created the Foundation for the Cooperation and Community Development of El Salvador (CORDES), a major NGO, which provides technical support for small-scale farming, coffee production, and home gardens. CORDES supports coffee farmers (men) who have formed processing cooperatives for roasting (mainly done by women). Their roasted coffee brings a good price on the local market ($2.25 per pound). A goal is to have their plots certified as organic and to sell to fair-trade buyers in North America at higher prices.

The CCR also teaches people about health care, first aid, and physical therapy. This includes their community radio show: "How to Care for Ourselves in Our Own Homes." A board member reported:

We can recognize and use medicinal plants. Health care is poor in El Salvador and hospitals are very bad. There's a hospital in Chalatenango. Patients have to bring their own syringe and antiseptics because the hospital does not have them. We have a lot of experienced health workers because of the war. We want to build a small clinic here with independent doctors.[10]

In the same region, people from San José Las Flores returned to their bombed village in 1986. Nowadays, they own 200 cattle, which are raised collectively. They have rebuilt all the buildings in the village and have planted thousands of trees on the steep hillsides to reforest the area. Women run several co-ops: poultry, dairy, weaving, sewing, a bakery, a pharmacy, a restaurant, and a store. Also, the community has organized blockades to obstruct a Canadian mining company that has a concession from the Salvadoran government to explore mining operations in the area.

South of San Salvador, La Libertad is a department of displaced people. A community of 26 families—140 people, 70 percent of them under age

18—live at Comunidad de Permacultura La Florida, near Santa Tecla, on land acquired through the PTT. They have a well, a maize mill, and a small clinic. Permaculture gardening was introduced under the auspices of the Christian Base Communities network (CEBES). People grow vegetables; they cultivate bananas, avocados, jackfruit, papayas, and some coffee. Cruz Rivas de Valladares and her family live here.

We came here in 1986. We came with our bare hands, no belongings, nothing. We slept on the floor. There were rats. It was very difficult. When we came here this land was empty. Now we plant and harvest here. We've built our lives here. We grow maize, tomatoes, and beans. We have a little shop...very small income. I worked as a domestic worker for a year in the city. I came home when I had a day off. It's a better way of life these days, peaceful, but economically it's hard.[11]

The emphasis in these examples is on developing sustainable communities to provide everyday safety and security for all residents, autonomy over economic decisions, and meaningful opportunities for young people. These are far wider goals than those of income-generating projects. Marta Benavides, minister and community organizer, commented:

People drawn to income-generation projects are go-getters, focused on individual benefits rather than contributing to something bigger that can benefit the wider community. Those projects don't last long without a sustainable community as a base.[12]

Women's Organizing

As these examples show, women are leaders in local municipalities, community organizations, co-ops, and NGOs. Women are involved in projects that focus on arts and culture, like the School of Art in Perquín that was mentioned earlier. Other examples include the Ecological House, a community resource in Nahuizalco (Sonsonate), an area with a high proportion of indigenous people, and the Center for Education for a Culture of Peace and Folk Art Museum (Santa Ana), a free museum open to the public, focusing on visions of an ecologically sound society, what Marta Benavides calls "the work of the 23rd century."[13]

In the late 1980s and early 1990s a range of women's organizations formed to respond to ways the war and the 1986 earthquake affected women's lives and responsibilities. Some, like La Asociación de Mujeres por la Dignidad y la Vida (Women for Dignity and Life) and El Instituto de Investigación, Capacitación y Desarrollo de la Mujer (IMU) were explicitly feminist, and gave voice to women's subordination as *women,* not only as members of exploited classes (Stephen 1997). Such organizations sought to address the gaps and limitations in the post-war reintegration and reconstruction process. They sponsored women's self-development and post-war reconstruction, including education, skills exchanges, a radio network, child care projects, clinics, a bakery, job-related training for women, and small loans programs. They also provided training opportunities that prepared women to move into local and national leadership roles.

Labor unions have also organized women's committees, although some feminists have chosen to organize outside unions, as their perspectives do not fit with a class analysis that excludes gender (Mendez 2002). With the expansion of the *maquila* industry in the 1990s, women started organizing to improve the lives and working conditions of garment assembly workers. Constrained by global economic realities, they are circumspect in their demands of both government and factory owners for fear of losing jobs that Salvadoran women need.

BEYOND THE PEACE ACCORDS

The Peace Accords provided a crucial starting point for demilitarization, and the cease-fire agreement has held. Despite delays, the government reduced the military and reorganized the police force; the FMLN has reconstituted itself as a political party. Nearly 20 years later, however, El Salvador is still deeply affected by the war, and there is ample evidence of the nation's legacy of authoritarian rule and corruption in the judiciary and the police force (Cañas and Dada 1999; Popkin 2000; Thompson 1998; Wood 2005).

Demilitarization and Everyday Security

Physical security is still a fundamental issue for many people. The continued availability of small arms has fueled post-war crime rates, including armed robberies, kidnappings, and murders. Bars on windows and doors are commonplace; many people are reluctant to walk in the street after dark. Armed security men guard shopping malls, drug stores, and ice-cream parlors. In 1995, the office of the attorney general reported more homicides per day than during the war (Conaway and Martínez 2004, 18), and the homicide rate—one of the highest in the world—has continued to rise (DeCesare 2009).

Democratization and Civil and Political Rights

At national level the FMLN has gained ground in elections as the second major party, and controls many small municipalities. The ARENA party held onto the presidency for 20 years, from 1989 to 2009, when FMLN candidate Mauricio Funes was elected with 51 percent of the vote, promising to address social and economic equalities. However, ARENA still retains control of the Legislative Assembly through alliances with smaller parties. International election monitors reported many irregularities in the 2004 elections. In addition, Bush administration officials gave explicit warning that an FMLN victory could jeopardize temporary protected status for Salvadoran workers in the United States (Rubin 2004).[14] Also in 2009, ARENA campaign ads included this threat but FMLN supporters and Salvadoran migrants in the United States organized to counter it (Gonzalez 2009).

The ARENA government had pushed through controversial legislation like the amnesty law and the U.S.-Central America Free Trade Agreement (CAFTA) (Stop CAFTA Coalition 2006, 8). The National Assembly passed the Special Law Against Acts of Terrorism and Organized Crime in 2006, modeled on the U.S. PATRIOT Act. Ostensibly introduced to control gang violence, this seemed unlikely, as there was no program to protect witnesses. The law provided for prison terms of up to 60 years and has been applied to gang members, street vendors, and protestors. In 2007, for example, police used nightsticks, tear gas, and rubber bullets against demonstrators protesting the privatization of water distribution, and accused them of acts of terrorism (B. Carpenter 2007; Damon 2007; Gutiérrez 2007b). Funes has vowed to introduce some economic policies that address root causes of poverty and rehabilitation plans to reduce youth involvement in street gangs and crimes of violence (DeCesare 2009).

Economic Reconstruction

Economic reconstruction has been slow and uneven, and there has been little improvement in the nation's persistent inequality. In 2006, 31 percent of the population lived below the national poverty line, and the levels were higher in rural areas (*CIA World Fact Book* 2008). El Salvador took the dollar as its currency in 2001, so it no longer controls its monetary policy, and CAFTA will open up the country to further exploitation by U.S.-based companies. The war of bullets may be over, but a prolonged economic war continues.

An estimated 2.5 million Salvadorans live abroad, primarily in the United States. They send monthly remittances (*remesas*) to relatives back home, estimated at $3.8 billion in 2008, though these amounts dropped by some 10 percent in 2009 as a result of the global recession and U.S. job losses.[15] A third of the rural population relies on these payments—$140 per month on average—which make up 67 percent of El Salvador's foreign exchange, compared to the *maquila* sector (16 percent) and agro-exports (6 percent) (Rosa 2004). For those who receive them, these funds represent 40–60 percent of household income (Kandel et al. 2006, 98). Some families are able to use remittances to make home improvements, invest in small farming or business projects, and help their children stay in school (IFAD 2006; Sanchez 2006). More often, the money is spent on fast food, powdered coffee, diapers, over-the-counter medications, and other consumer items. The dozen or so wealthy families who dominated the plantation-style coffee and sugar production in the past, once the nation's main income earners, have diversified their investments and now also own shopping malls. Companies like Coca Cola, Pizza Hut, Subway, McDonald's, KFC, Wendy's, and Mister Donut are flourishing in El Salvador. They siphon the remittances back to the United States.

Researchers point to internal and external difficulties facing community reconstruction efforts as time goes by. Irina Silber (2004) emphasized some women's disengagement from community organizing in Chalatenango, citing individual exhaustion and disillusionment, growing inequalities among people, and many failed projects, which all attest to the difficulties of creating change. Vincent McElhinney (2004) noted growing bitterness among residents of Ciudad Segundo Montes, a community built with high hopes for economic justice that faces a "diminishing capacity to meet the needs of all its residents" (161).

High expectations for equality and justice, compounded by inexperience and individual shortcomings, are partly responsible for these problems. In addition, political and economic policies of the ARENA government and global economic trends have undermined and vitiated community efforts. The election of President Funes is a significant step in the right direction, though his decisions will be constrained by the ARENA-dominated National Assembly and the mandates of neoliberal economics. There is also the possibility of making new alliances with left-leaning Latin American governments, which may lead to fruitful partnerships in regional trade, energy, and health care (Burridge 2009).

It will require enormous systemic change, including a greater concern for women's rights, to create sustainable livelihoods, greater economic equality, adequate community services, and environmental security: that is, to actualize the promise of the Peace Accords and end the war.

NOTES

1. Personal interview with Cruz Rivas de Valladares, la Florida (La Libertad), March 19, 2007. Interpreter: Juan Rojas.

2. See the Walls of Hope Web site at http://wallsofhope.org/en/page/2/?q=rufina.

3. See the Capacitar International Web site at http://www.capacitar.org/commun/stories/elsalvador.html.

4. See, e.g., http://www.speaktruth.org/defend/profiles/profile_31.asp.

5. Jesse Dyer Stewart, US-El Salvador Sister Cities Co-coordinator, personal communication, March 19, 2007. Emphasis added.

6. See the US-El Salvador Sister Cities Program Web site at http://elsalvadorsolidarity.org/joomla/index.php?option=com_content&task=view&id=37&Itemid = 45.

7. Personal interview with Rosa Cándida, Las Vueltas, March 19, 2007. Interpreter: Jesse Dyer Stewart.

8. Now known as the Chalatenango Coordinating Committee for Development.

9. María Esperanza Ortega, Chalatenango, March 19, 2007. Interpreter: Jesse Dyer Stewart. During the war Esperanza Ortega organized 200 civilians on the

run from government troops. She lost three of her eight children: "Two died as combatants and one girl died of hunger" (1000 Women for the Nobel Peace Prize 2005, 126).

10. Comments made by a CCR board member, in personal interview with author, Chalatenango, March 19, 2007. Interpreter: Jesse Dyer Stewart.

11. Personal interview with Cruz Rivas de Valladares, La Florida (La Libertad), March 17, 2007. Interpreter: Juan Rojas.

12. Personal interview with Marta Benavides, Caracas, Venezuela, January 26, 2006.

13. Personal interview with Marta Benavides, Santa Ana, El Salvador, March 23, 2007.

14. Strong ties with the United States enabled the Salvadoran government to negotiate temporary protected status for some overseas workers in the United States after a devastating earthquake wiped out homes, farms, and jobs in El Salvador in 2001.

15. See http://www.state.gov/r/pa/ei/bgn/2033.htm#econ.

CHAPTER 14

Using Gender to Consider Post-Conflict Forgiveness

Sigal Ben-Porath

From the interpersonal to the international level, the acknowledgment of past wrongs and the request for and offering of forgiveness support the flourishing of human relations. In recent years, moral philosophy has regained an interest in debating the epistemological and ethical aspects of forgiveness.[1] Similarly, the field of moral education is engaged in a vivid debate over the concept of forgiveness and its educational consequences,[2] following its initial introduction into the field by multicultural scholars and educators who were seeking ways to overcome past wrongs and work toward the establishment of a just common society. Possibly prompted by a renewed interest in war and ethnic conflict, scholars have been debating various types of forgiveness and modes of teaching them in schools. Many perspectives in these scholarly and pragmatic discussions agree that an important part of the civic conditions for forgiveness can be attained in schools.

This chapter considers forgiveness in the context of overcoming social and international conflict (and not solely interpersonal conflict). It considers the issue of forgiveness through gendered lenses, looking for the unique contributions women's experiences and feminist philosophies have to offer the question. In this context it is suggested that the focus in most existing philosophical and educational literature on giving forgiveness should be augmented by attention to the side seeking forgiveness. In addition, a model of forgiveness geared toward creating a baseline for post-conflict reconciliation should give a proper place to claims of justice. An appropriate account of such claims of justice would incorporate not only principled notions of justice but also relational and care-based understandings of justice.

FORGIVENESS

Contemporary educational and moral literature offers three basic models of forgiveness. Well-known and most radical among them is the one offered by Jacques Derrida. Much like educational and other literature on the issue, it relies heavily on religious traditions: "As enigmatic as the concept of forgiveness remains," Derrida writes, "it is the case that the scene, the figure, the language which one tries to adapt to it belong to a religious heritage (let's call it Abrahamic, in order to bring together Judaism, the Christianities, and the Islams)" (Derrida 2001, 28). Derrida suggests that forgiveness is an act that is entirely at the hands, and heart, of the victim and is given unconditionally and without expectation of return. Forgiving the unforgivable is the only true act of forgiveness, for "If one is only prepared to forgive what appears forgivable, what the church calls 'venial sin,' then the very idea of forgiveness would disappear" (Derrida 2001, 32). Thus, forgiveness at its purest form cannot entail any expectations of restitution, repentance, or compensation. This is a very religious—more specifically, a very Christian—notion of forgiveness, based on a leap of faith as its true expression. It corresponds with earlier discussions, most notably Hannah Arendt's, of forgiveness as a singular and unworldly act, which is strictly intimate and relates (to use Emmanuel Levinas's notion) to the "face" of the other (Arendt 1998, 212–23). A moving manifestation of this form of unconditional forgiveness, generated solely by the emotions and beliefs of the victim rather than the actions of the sinner or wrongdoer, was seen in the 1981 trial of Henry Hays, a member of the Ku Klux Klan who was found guilty of lynching a black teenage boy. Before his verdict was read in the courtroom, he turned to the victim's mother and asked if she could ever forgive him. Quietly, she replied "I have already forgiven you."[3]

This model of forgiveness, albeit noble, bears little relevance beyond the religious and interpersonal context. Intergroup and international relations seem to require steps beyond a leap of faith and the declaration of forgiveness to establish peaceful relations between former adversaries. Hence, despite the moral appeal of this model, many authors acknowledge that other models should be considered for political and educational purposes. Derrida himself states that this pure form of forgiveness does not relate to the political process of reconciliation. Consequently, many discussions of forgiveness part with the Derrida model in establishing some link between justice and forgiveness. Restitution, and the restoration of justice, can be a prelude to a formal act of forgiveness. Forgiveness, if it is to be politicized, cannot be summarized as unworldly (as Derrida suggests) or entirely intimate (as Arendt suggest, echoing Levinas). The demand to do justice, by punishing the offender or compensating the victim, can be presented by the victim as a precondition to granting her forgiveness, which thus turns into a sociopolitical act. More broadly, the acknowledgment of injustice in past relations or actions is a necessary condition for ensuring that they do not occur again after forgiveness is granted. This link between justice and forgiveness is evident in other two widely debated models of forgiveness, the "strict model" and the "relaxed model."

The strict view of forgiveness presupposes the wrongdoer's repentance and/or just punishment, and proclaims the granting of forgiveness the victim's moral or religious duty. If the offender repents the wrong he did (with or without being punished, by God or man) and asks for forgiveness, its granting ideally ensues promptly. In a position spurred by the strict model, Smith (1997) argues that forgiveness is not a virtue but rather a moral duty of the victim, which is directly derivative of a claim of justice. Hence, for justice to be served the victim must forgive the offender when the appropriate conditions are fulfilled, otherwise he becomes a wrong-doer, an obstacle to justice (Smith 1997). This view is more political and carries further acknowledgment of the relational aspects of overcoming conflict. However, it is rightly criticized as too formal or rigid, requiring the victim to grant forgiveness as if it were her obligation; in this way it may turn the act of forgiveness from a moral commitment to an aspect of an exchange economy. Although this model is more readily translatable into social relations and interchanges among formerly adversarial groups, its rigidity may provide little direction to parties working to structure rela-tionship in the aftermath of conflict.

The Derrida model and the strict view are thus unsatisfactory as direc-tions for political and educational approaches for the reconstruction of relationship after group or national conflict. Situating forgiveness as a moral duty of the harmed side(s) does little to support the process of over-coming a feeling of hatred or shame and to provide a narrow, preliminary path toward post-conflict institution of just relations.

The relaxed view is sometimes described as the "no problem" model of forgiveness (White 2002). This is the model most commonly used in edu-cational settings, in particular in the education of young children. Under this model, children should learn to forgive easily and with no demand for punishment or compensations for harms done to them. We should teach children to forgive because "it is a matter, on the one side, of encourag-ing a willingness to apologize and make amends (if possible) combined, on the other, with a generous acceptance of people who have caused one hurt" (White 2002, 64). It is a version of the strict model, but forgiveness here is not precisely a duty; it is more of a social nicety. One's obligation to forgive is not a moral requirement but rather a social imperative or expec-tation, deriving from norms of politeness. White claims that this approach to forgiveness is a "generous-spirited attitude between equals" that is "well-suited to a liberal democratic multi-ethnic society" (White 2002, 62). However, equality between the two sides is not always expressed in group conflict, and merely assuming it for the sake of constituting a for-giving attitude does not establish equality in a multicultural society or in the context of conflict. Placing this model in the context of social politeness renders it irrelevant even to serious crimes, but White suggests that in the case of serious crimes or harms, the two sides need not live together, and hence the problem of forgiveness does not arise. This claim could be erroneous even in the context of interpersonal relations involving an offender and a victim—domestic violence comes to mind—and is similarly inaccurate in some cases of group conflict, as Papastephanou demonstrates:

In most [communal conflict] cases, and especially where these involve dislocation, or the legitimation of dislocations, or demographic alterations and other crimes of war, a parting of the ways is impossible as well as morally unacceptable. It is also unacceptable because it may presuppose the false essentialist claim that some ethnic groups cannot live together peacefully. . . . In such contexts, the idea that a relaxed notion of forgiveness is useful to the relations of communities involved in longstanding conflicts has very limited relevance. (Papastephanou 2003, 516)

In addition, this relaxed model of forgiveness as a social nicety is embedded in Western, English-speaking social norms, and thus it can hardly be translatable to other contexts and cultures.[4] It is hardly acceptable even from a religious Christian perspective,[5] and in cultures that view forgiveness as an abandonment of that part that was wronged in one's past, forgiveness can be understood as demeaning to the victim (or to wronged family members) and in no way as an offhanded nicety. Moreover, these models are stripped of historical context, rendering the educational efforts out of touch with the historical and social specificities of the communities in which they are practiced. If we teach that one must always work on one's internal ability to grant forgiveness, mainly in the hardest of circumstances when one suffered the worst harms, we place the burden of reconciliation solely or mainly on the victim, in addition to replicating the power relations that made her victim. In addition, such an educational approach may inadvertently teach lack of liability to potential offenders— they can sense that they are a priori forgiven, without any demand for punishment or reparation.

All three models—the unconditional, the strict, and the relaxed—are focused on the victim; in other words, they put a lot of emphasis, following Western religious traditions, on the moral requirement to forgive. The morality they endorse is based on the perspective of the victim, her entitlements and her duties. The educational approach they endorse is focused on teaching students to consider their commitments and their possible responses to instances of harm done to them. A change of perspective can be useful for the purposes of expansive education, as is suggested in the next section.

For the purpose of teaching forgiveness in the context of intergroup and international conflict, two variations on the previously described models are required. First, the model should give attention not only to the perspective of the forgiving side but also to the side seeking forgiveness. Gender-based observations of the interpersonal and international arenas have recognized that the two are relationally autonomous (Sylvester 2002), and that the process of forgiveness cannot happen in one without affecting and being affected by the other. Second, the model that would best serve the educational needs on the road toward peace is one that gives a proper place to claims of justice while maintaining an ethic of care.

LEARNING TO BE FORGIVEN

A public acknowledgment of past wrongs done by one's group to another, accompanied by an appropriate apology—an acceptance of moral responsibility—can open the door for more peaceful relations among former rivals. Some contemporary authors go as far as asserting that a public acknowledgment of violence, oppression, or atrocities accompanied by an appropriate apology can establish the sole basis necessary for the evasion of war.[6]

Certain political actors manifested a similar sentiment by apologizing for historical wrongs done by the nations they represent to other nations and minority groups.[7] The sentiment expressed in public apologies frames the model that is most relevant for the purpose of constituting just relations in a post-conflict context. It is an alternative to the three models described earlier, in that it is focused not on the duty of the victim to forgive but on the responsibility of the offender to seek forgiveness. In this it parts from the Abrahamic traditions and turns our moral and educational attention to the offender. One author claims that it is dangerous "to focus so much on the duty to forgive," particularly in an educational setting, because of the risk of encouraging an egocentric perspective that "no matter what we do or how we deal with it" forgiveness would be granted (Papastephanou 2003). Learning to demand forgiveness stands the risk of feeding unequal power relations rather than overcoming them. Overcoming anger and blame would more readily occur not through obliged forgiveness but rather through a sincere acknowledgment of wrongs and a common strife to establish the grounds for peaceful relations. It is important to stress that in most conflicts there is rarely one side that is victimized and another that independently perpetrates wrongdoing. A historical reading of most intergroup conflicts may find an "original sin"[8] that many—though not all—would acknowledge. But in the process of long-term conflict, war, or oppression, representatives of both sides can usually be found guilty of perpetrating some harm. In most cases both sides have grievances that would justifiably be described as worthy of considering and amending (Adorno 1986).[9] Striving to acknowledge wrongdoing and requesting forgiveness is a key component of building or renewing post-conflict relationships. Expanding awareness to differing historical perspectives that do not necessary depict their own group as a victim, but rather point to a more morally complex view of both history and morality, could support the construction of intergroup relationship without abandoning group affiliations.

This is even more obvious when one looks at the process of forgiveness through gendered lenses, as Nancy Hirschmann (1989) reminds us that human choice is *always* relational and never takes place in a vacuum. Hirschmann tells us that we should see decisions as made by actors with independent identity, but without a full range of choice or perfect knowledge (2004).

The history curriculum is typically an educational site where forms of recognition, acknowledgment, and forgiveness can be negotiated and expressed. Learning to regard the group one identifies with as blameworthy from some other group's perspective can be a sobering educational exercise. More often than not schools focus on "us" as a morally blameless entity. The pressures of subgroups who suffer past or present injustices are a possible force that may change the curriculum into a more inclusive and reflective one. In the history curriculum in American schools, the representation of blacks and Native Americans and the complex history of injustice they suffered is gradually made possible through the pressure of groups within the academic and sociopolitical arenas. Learning to acknowledge the complex relations among social groups can thus generate the first steps in the social process of forgiveness. The same can happen in the context of international conflict when rival groups learn to acknowledge the historical complexities through which their relations were formed. For this to happen, the educational system needs to rise above what Adorno (1986) calls "national vanity" or "narcissistic nationalism" and to consider the national group in which it operates as part of a complex relational international order in which no one is perfectly just.

JUST FORGIVENESS

Beyond changing the model of forgiveness to include the perspective of seeking forgiveness, it is important to consider the role justice plays in the facilitation of forgiveness. A proper response to claims of justice must not waive them, but it must also refrain from a strict economic formation of justice (such as "an eye for an eye") as a precondition for forgiveness. For the purpose of peace building and preserving democratic attitudes, relinquishing the demand for justice as the relaxed or no problem model expects cannot suffice. Even the Truth and Reconciliation Commission (TRC) in South Africa, which can be depicted as the closest in spirit to the requirement of the two latter models described earlier, does not abandon its demands for justice. While it provides formal forgiveness in exchange to confession and repentance, it incorporates this process into a political structure that provides peace and justice as a promise for both sides. The equality and just relations that are the political framework in which the

TRC operated in South Africa, for example, provide a justice-based back-drop to the forgiveness process that took place through the TRC. Although this is not a legal form of justice, as personal legal procedures were relinquished for the purpose of achieving truth and reconciliation, it is still a necessary background of political justice. More broadly, justice has a role in the political process of forgiveness, and it is important to locate forgiveness within this framework of just relations between former rivals.

A pertinent approach to forgiveness should take into account claims of historical and even personal injustice, and respond to them in an environment receptive to forgiveness. This does not mean that all claims can indeed be answered in their fullest, but it does mean that they should be sincerely acknowledged. Forgiveness must presuppose justice, at least in a loose sense of the mutual acknowledgment of wrongs and the mutual understanding that these wrongs are not to be repeated. In reflecting on the guilt of one's own group, one learns to seek forgiveness "for the culpability that remains after excuses, justifications, restitution and repentant reforms have been made and accepted—a culpability that warrants our continuing to be resented" (Cheshire 1992). Thus, as in the public education display of the South African TRC, it is more productive to express justice by acknowledging past wrongs in an effort to bring about reconciliation than to pursue justice in its retaliatory form. Still, a challenge to the power relations that generated the conflict and injustice is a minimal condition for forgiveness that presupposes justice.

In the context of group conflict this challenge to power relations is ideally expressed in a discussion of forgiveness that is based on publicly accessible declarations and expressions of seeking and granting forgiveness. Absent the access to emotional aspects of forgiveness that is fundamental to the interpersonal context, intergroup forgiveness has to be presented in public forms, education being principal among the nondeclaratory ones. The declarative spectrum of forgiveness includes representatives and leaders publicly asking for or granting forgiveness for past wrongs (acknowledging them is the basis for this act). It also includes moments that can serve as public epiphanies, such as the celebratory signing of a peace treaty (in the case of international conflict) or a cordial meeting between leaders of adversary sides. Beyond such public declarations, teaching about the other side and learning to see history and current affairs from the other's perspective is a crucial, ongoing method of generating appropriate conditions for acknowledging the other's perspective, accepting blame, and enabling forgiveness. Hence, the inclusion of various perspectives of history in the public education system serves the purpose of overcoming the dehumanization of the other side. In addition, it serves the purpose of inducing forgiveness by publicly acknowledging the harm one's side caused the other and the (at least partial or subjective) justifiability of the other's claims. This is by no means a simple demand, as the debate on patriotic education exemplifies. In wartime there is a growing demand to teach a narrow form of patriotic history and to incorporate triumphalist patriotism into the curriculum. But it is crucial to remember that the construction of a common memory, or at least compatible (rather than adversary) forms of communal memories, has an important role for the preservation of democratic attitudes and for the establishment of a basis for a common peaceful future. Thus, reversing and expanding the teaching of patriotic histories, and revising and expanding collective memory, is a fundamental role of public education and a crucial aspect of seeking forgiveness.

Some cultures are apprehensive of the idea of forgiveness, as it may seem disrespectful to the sacrifices and suffering of past times. By seeking forgiveness for their group's wrongdoing they might inadvertently be indicating a dismissal of the cause for which others in the group, forbears or even themselves have been struggling. How can the remembrance of past wrongs be reconciled with the seeking of forgiveness and the possibility of forgiveness? Margalit claims that one has an obligation to oneself to overcome painful memories in order to restore one's own well-being. He states that that "successful forgiveness is not forgetting the wrong done but rather overcoming the resentment that accompanies it" (Margalit 2002, 208; Cheshire 1992). For Margalit (2002) the claim of forgiveness is not from the agent who seeks forgiveness but rather from the victim herself. Considering the well-being of the offender and the well-being of the victim brings forth the fact that it is clearly in the interest of both to reach a state of forgiveness. In the interpersonal context, although it is sometimes easier to define who serves in which role, this state is hard to achieve for various psychological reasons, including an urge to revenge, a perception of the harm as irreversible, and a lack of trust, which leads to a disbelief in the wrongdoer's apology or repentance.[10] All of these aspects exist in the intergroup context as well, but they are more accessible and potentially amendable, at least in their public manifestations. Apologies, restitutions, and the restoration of justice can be made available upon a political decision. Their acceptance, accordingly, can symbolize forgiveness and support reconciliation even when some individuals may take longer to feel and express such forgiveness.

How can an ethics of care provide the framework for thinking about post-conflict justice in a way that can be incorporated into this view of forgiveness? This question becomes more pressing in the context of a protracted conflict, like the "war on terror," which has no clear temporal and geographical boundaries and no well-defined aims that the public can debate and agree upon. Many feminist scholars have suggested a framework of care as a basis for forgiveness and reconstruction (see, e.g., Robinson 1999; Sjoberg 2006a). Still, Joan Tronto (1993) suggests that care is only viable as a political ideal in a pluralistic liberal democracy, where the needs of the citizens stand at the center of the political process (see also Engster 2004). This suggestion is reminiscent of the argument that the relaxed model of forgiveness is dependent on a background of values, such as respect and equality, that is mostly characteristic of liberal democracies. If the background of liberal democracy is essential for flourishing caring relations as a political guideline and a public backdrop to forgiveness, what place does it have in the postbellum realm as a guiding principal for reciprocal forgiveness and reconciliation?

The morality of group action, much like its caring nature, is a loose appreciation of the sum of actions that are taken in the name of the group. In a similar way, the caring relations among groups can be considered through an interpretation of the actions taken by one group toward the other and vice versa. Power relations need to be taken into account in care relations in a similar way to their consideration in other types of moral relations.

The details of care relations can be developed in the private domain—among family members, in mentoring relations, in the health care professions, and so on. Care is grounded in those practices of human life that are reflective of our dependency on one another. The content of care can also be, and has been, developed more generally to offer guidelines for communal and other larger-scale ethical relations. Although care ethics is not meant to provide structured principles for ethical conduct, it can still offer guidelines for what would be considered ethical forms of relations among individuals, groups, and nations. The care-based feminist perspective complements existing visions of justice, which usually fail to acknowledge personal needs, relations, and preferences. The common focus on justice by political actors and theorists has often been critically described as relating to male more than to female perspectives. It relates to principles more than to persons, and to abstract political concepts (such as "security") rather than to more humane visions that often arise from women's experiences and feminist theories (such as human security). The reliance on care ethics in international relations coincides with existing perspectives of leading contemporary International Relations and political science scholars, who both describe and advocate for a stronger international community, one that can augment or trump national sovereignty in various cases (Feinstein and Slaughter 2004). The ethics and politics of care could serve as guidelines for such a system of international relations. As part of the construction of relation after conflict, and even during conflict when the possibility of the end of war is kept in mind, the ethics of care can lead to a more complex understanding of wrongdoing and suffering wrongs; of the need to consider the other's perspective, even if perceived as mistaken (or malicious); and the importance of seeking and granting forgiveness for the generation and maintenance of post-conflict relations.

Care ethics incorporates a number of evaluative tools to examine the means and ends of post-war practice and conduct, and thus offers a productive approach to forgiveness as it can be requested and given in a post-war context. Tronto (1993) argues that care is not just a disposition or attitude but a practice with certain distinctive features, including attentiveness, responsibility, competence, and responsiveness. Care ethics does not ask only *why* I should care and who I should care for, but also *how* I should care about other persons and about principles. Considering reciprocal forms of relationship, both inside a given society and in the international domain, requires attention to the mutual responsibilities individuals and societies have toward each other, and their ability to take responsibility for actions they have taken in the past. The acknowledgment of past wrongs and the seeking of forgiveness as a public display of position and intention can prove to be a key part of the reconstruction of relations after conflict.

What type of responsibilities do we have to those with whom we forge a relationship, and what happens when these relationships, as in the case of war and post-war conduct, are not based on care but rather on conflicting interests? For care theories to inform post-war conduct, including public processes of forgiveness, attention must be given to a variety of group and individual needs—the needs and preferences of those individuals who are emerging from the circumstances of war, and who are likely to require support in finding shelter, food, and other basic human needs, as well as to social and political needs and preferences on both sides. An ethics of care is constructed as always contextual and particularistic. It prefers personal attention to individuals in context over principles and abstract, universalist guidelines. Developing a response based on an ethics of care would require attention to the particularities of the relational context, to the details of the particular participants, and to the developing needs of a changing society (Bowden 1997). The emergence of new perspectives in a post-war context should be accepted as indications of crisis and change and should be supported as much as needed by the international community, which should refrain from imposing premature independence (as expressed by a lack of relational support).

Finally, "The perspective of care requires that conflict be worked out without damage to the continuing relationships" (Tronto 1987, 658). In some ways even the realities of war, and the pragmatic discussion of these realities, contain an understanding and an appreciation of at least the instrumental value of relational consideration (if not their intrinsic or ethical value). If care and relationality are not consulted to provide a framework within which principles of justice are developed and applied, universalism at best, or realism in most cases, will reign. If care, with its guidelines and evaluative tools, is brought in to augment justice in framing the post-war processes of healing, forgiveness, and emerging new relations, many of the pitfalls of post-war conduct could be avoided.

A post-conflict ethics of forgiveness that incorporates both justice and care can prove to be a promising alternative to the mainstream models of forgiveness. It can augment them with the perspectives not only of the victim but also of the perpetrator (and with the understanding that in most cases both sides can be depicted as either of those and must acknowledge their wrongdoing). The introduction of care ethics into the structure of post-war relations and a justice-based forgiveness is based on an acknowledgment of national global interdependence and its implications not only to economic realities but also, as importantly, to post-conflict relationship.

To publicly offer an acknowledgment of the other side's perspective and to wrongs done, and to seek forgiveness for these wrongs as a step in the process of instituting justice and care into post-war relations, is a significant part of educating for democracy and peace in the context of conflict. The educational system, along with political representatives and leaders, must share the burden of preparing the grounds for seeking forgiveness and facilitating its acceptance as a way to overcome animosities and institute more just and peaceful relations among former enemies.

NOTES

1. Some of the prominent examples are Hampton and Murphy (1988), Margalit (2002), Minow (2002), Brison (2002), and Haber (1991).

2. See most recently the debate in *the Journal of Philosophy of Education,* including White (2002), Barnes (2002), and Papastephanou (2003).

3. Michael Donald, a black teenager in Mobile, Alabama, was abducted, tortured, and killed in a Ku Klux Klan plot. A lawsuit brought by his mother, Beulah Mae Donald, later resulted in a landmark judgment that bankrupted one Klan organization and significantly influenced the membership and actions of others. See case number 84–0725, USDC Southern District of Alabama.

4. For a competing model of forgiveness that represents the incompatibility of a relaxed model to the Jewish and Israeli context see Margalit (2002). I thank Nicole Behnam, a graduate student and educational activist, for a discussion on the irrelevance of a relaxed model of forgiveness in the context of the Balkan wars and certain African cultures, such as the one in Sierra Leone, which view forgiveness differently from the Abrahamic traditions.

5. See a critique of the concept of "cheap grace" as a degradation of the Christian view on forgiveness in Bonhoeffer (2000).

6. Michael Ignatieff (1997) makes this claim in the context of the Balkan wars.

7. See President George W. Bush's apology in Senegal (MSNBC.com 2003). The Canadian government has been pondering similar acts in regard to various discriminations performed by the government in the past. A similar act of formal request for forgiveness was made by Prime Minister Ehud Barak of Israel to the Sephardic Jewish community for decades-long discrimination against them by governmental institutions.

8. A concept that, itself, has been the subject of much gender-based critique, including Suchocki (1994) and Spero (1996).

9. There are clear exceptions to this claim—slavery and Nazism are ready examples—but in most cases both sides can be identified as guilty of at least some wrongdoing, and thus the expectation from all to consider their contribution to past or present conflicts is relevant in most contexts.

10. Austin Sarat (2002) reminds us that reflecting on the universality of death may help transcend the urge to revenge hateful crimes and be able to separate death from dessert.

PART V

Texts and Contexts for Gender, War, and Militarism

CHAPTER 15

Feminism, Nationalism, and Globalism: Representations of Bosnian "War Babies" in the Western Print Media, 1991–2006

R. Charli Carpenter

> No one knew her name when she arrived. The staff at the hospital where she was abandoned at birth christened her "Emina." A temporary name, for an anonymous, unloved baby whose future is uncertain....To the nurses, she is just another tragic victim of the unspeakable Bosnian rape camps....Her mother could not bear the shame of that birth....She is 16, a Muslim schoolgirl from eastern Bosnia, made pregnant after being raped repeatedly by Serbian soldiers....When her daughter was born she told doctors to take it away....Meanwhile, in the same maternity ward where Emina lies this morning, happy fathers are arriving with flowers for their wives and newly born children. These are children born of love—while in the next cot is Emina, a child born of inhumanity.
>
> —Kim Willsher, "Born of Inhumanity," January 1993

I first became aware of the situation of Bosnia's war babies after reading the news article excerpted at the beginning of the chapter. Three messages jumped out at me from that piece: (1) children are being horribly affected by war and by war rape, (2) all this is happening in Bosnia for reasons and at a scale that is unprecedented, and (3) something should be done.

First, that article, like much similar reporting, constructs the rapes in Bosnia as *ethnic*, essentializing the identities of the perpetrators and of the babies: we hear of "Muslim schoolgirls" raped by "Serbian soldiers" to produce "Serbian" children. Second is the emphasis on *women* as victims of childbirth. "Rape has become a weapon of this war," the article states. The victims "cannot bear the shame" of giving birth to babies they cannot possibly love. Third, the babies themselves are described in the most hopeless terms, designed to underscore the barbarity of a country that could produce and then abandon such "tragic victims": this discourse figured in calls for humanitarian intervention but also fed into essentialist stereotypes of Bosnia as patriarchal, uncivilized, and incomprehensible to Western Europe.[1] The article thus situates the babies as hapless victims of a diabolical plan, one unleashed through women's victimization, one resulting from the barbarity of age-old ethnic hatreds, and one soluble only by the intervention of good-hearted outsiders.

This chapter explores the role of the global print media in calling attention to children born of wartime rape in Bosnia, and it examines media frames to understand why the agenda-setting function attempted by a number of journalists has *not* resulted in the emergence of "children born of rape" as a category of concern on the international agenda.[2]

On the one hand, the global media has been front and center in highlighting the presence and plight of war babies in different locations around the globe. Numerous reports of "rape babies" in war zones from Rwanda to East Timor to Sudan have appeared in the press over the past 10 years and continue to be a regular feature of atrocity reporting from hot spots around the world (Powell 2001; Wax 2004; Polgreen 2005). In Bosnia, in particular, there was no shortage of stories in the global press about the mass rapes, the pregnancies, and the babies abandoned in orphanages (Williams 1993; Horvath 1993; Jordan 1995; Drakulic 1993; Toomey 2003; Becirbasic and Secic 2002; Jahn 2005). As Linda Grant (1993) wrote, in early 1993 "the media was desperate for rape babies...rape in Bosnia was the hottest story of the year."

Yet in the 1990s, this public visibility did not translate into international pressure from human rights organizations or into state policies that would offset the types of harms to which children born of war rape are frequently subject. Domestic agenda-setting theory, often imported into studies of international human rights politics, posits an important relationship between media coverage, public awareness, and the policy agenda (McCombs and Shaw 1972; Dearing and Rogers 1996). Although in theory journalists do not tell the public what to think, they do tell people what to think *about* (Cohen 1963, 13). The CNN effect is often cited as a causal factor in provoking international attention to human rights abuses in certain countries, and press coverage is understood to be vital to the emergence of specific issues on the global agenda, leading then United Nations Secretary General Boutros Boutrous-Ghali to allegedly remark, "CNN is the sixteenth member of the Security Council" (Minear, Scott, and Weiss 1996).[3] If true, this agenda-setting failure would seem to be a puzzle.

Yet, as this chapter demonstrates, this is so only if we assume that the purpose behind reporting on "rape babies" in Bosnia was to put the babies' *human rights* on the global agenda. Instead, my analysis of these news articles suggests that the narratives were largely designed to play a different role, one that constructed the war rapes through discourse at the intersection of nationalism, feminism, and humanitarianism, rather than through a child-rights lens, and that functioned predominantly to construct violence in the Balkans as simultaneously horrific and distant from the "civilized," industrialized West.

I situate the global print media as an institution within the system of transnational players in conflict-affected regions. I then survey and critique the role sometimes played by journalists in constructing new human rights claims on the basis of reporting from war zones. Journalists adopt different strategies in conflict zones with different motivations; at times, the frames they choose can work at cross-purposes. Next, I analyze the specific frames used to describe children born of war rape in Bosnia and demonstrate how these frames fed into the three dominant constructions of human rights in the war, to the exclusion of attention to the specific needs of the babies themselves.

THE GLOBAL MEDIA AS A PLAYER IN CONFLICT ZONES

After the early post–Cold War interventions in Somalia and northern Iraq, a literature on the "CNN effect" emerged to posit a direct influence of the media on state foreign policy making as it relates to human rights crises; other scholarship has made a broader claim that the media influence public opinion, which then influences foreign policy (Carruthers 2000). Moving from the impact on states to the impact on human rights nongovernmental organizations (NGOs) and the global advocacy agenda, a variety of literature dealing with transnational advocacy networks suggests that the media salience of issues or emergencies is an important factor in their likelihood of being reported by the human rights sector (Dale 1993; Bob 2005). That the global media enable and promote attention to specific human rights issues is also suggested by comments in focus groups I conducted for this project: as one participant put it, "When reports come out and the public gets outraged by it, that is what drives change."

Moreover, *how* donor publics are encouraged to imagine a conflict can be as important as *which* conflict they are asked to consider or *what* information about that conflict is described (Dearing and Rogers 1996, 75). With respect to Bosnia, Gregory Kent (2006, 254–59) has argued that the British media distorted understandings of the conflict in several ways, including framing it as a civil war (when it was highly internationalized), failing to invoke the term "genocide" early on, essentializing the ethnic identities of participants in the conflict, and describing the conflict as "fighting" between "warring factions" rather than siege warfare against largely defenseless civilians. These constructs, Kent argues, inhibited decisive action by outsiders and shifted the focus away from Britain's responsibility as a bystander to what he interprets as genocide.

Yet research on the media's role in human rights agenda-setting posits a number of contradictory effects.[4] Ron and colleagues (2005) have found that advocacy networks also use the media to set their own agenda. The CNN effect has been critiqued on analytical and empirical grounds (Caliendo, Gibney, and Payne 1999): the Bosnian conflict has been described as "the best illustration of the absence of an automatic link between media images of suffering and decisive intervention to alleviate it" (Carruthers 2000). Piers Robinson (2000) has argued that the media's agenda-setting effect on foreign policy matters only when policy elites are uncertain as to a policy agenda; otherwise, they are likelier to reflect that agenda than actively construct it.

A number of scholars are in fact skeptical about the media's agenda-setting role altogether, suggesting that instead, powerful states use the media to "manufacture consent" for their preferred policies (Chomsky 1988). Caliendo and colleagues (2000) have pointed out that the volume of human rights reporting often correlates less to the nature of the abuses in a given country and more to great power interests. At a minimum, by choosing whether to publicize alleged atrocities, journalists play gatekeeper to global public opinion and can serve as a propaganda conduit for warring groups (Bickler et al. 2004).

THE WESTERN MEDIA AND BOSNIAN "RAPE BABIES"

The crusade for attention to mass rape in Bosnia is often said to have been kicked off by journalist Roy Gutman's story "Mass Rape: Muslims Recall Serb Attacks," which appeared in *Newsday* on August 23, 1992 (P. Stanley 1999, 76; Hansen 2001, 55; Skjaelsbaek 2006, 374); but earlier articles situating forced pregnancy and rape as deliberate strategies of the war appeared in the Western press as early as August 8, 1992 (Costello 1992). Later that fall, the Bosnian government issued a statistic indicating that 50,000 Muslim women had been raped; the European Community followed this up in December with an estimate of 20,000. These numbers, coupled with the graphic stories of many victims, were enough to mobilize considerable attention toward the situation of Bosnian and Croatian women, and by early 1993, a spate of rape stories had exploded across the Western media.

Rape reporting served as a catalyst to reframe women's rights as human rights and helped spark a successful transnational campaign against gender-based violence (Keck and Sikkink 1998). In telling the Western public to think about gender-based violence, the media helped set the stage for the UN to articulate mass rape as a threat to international peace and security, and it gave legal activists leverage to address sexual violence in the subsequent international tribunals.

Yet the Western media has been severely criticized for its role in human-rights reporting during and after the war, particularly around the sensitive issue of sexual violence. One set of critiques centered on the questionable sources some journalists drew upon in publicizing reports of rape. According to Rose Lindsey, stories of rape were derived in large part from "spin doctors from the predominantly Muslim Bosnia-Herzegovinian government who were 'selling' the rape stories to western media organizations" (Lindsey 2002). These led, among other things, to widely inflated estimates of the number of rape-related pregnancies and births and to a media narrative suggesting that thousands of Bosnian babies would soon be available for international adoption (P. Stanley 1999).

Feminist women's NGOs working with rape survivors in the former Yugoslavia also actively attempted to interface with the world press to draw attention to the rapes as crimes against women, although they competed not only with the government but also with nationalist women's organizations who framed the atrocities through an ethnic, rather than a gender, lens. The earlier problem for women's organizations was that rape was marginalized in accounts of atrocity, but once the story did break the issue became the type of reporting.

To a large extent, the Western media was uncritical of the distinction between different types of rape frames or how different women's organizations with different agendas constituted very different types of source for rape stories. Thus, reporting drew criticism from some women's organizations that accused reporters of "sensationalism" and critiqued their generally unreflective and simplistic portrayal of rape (Andric-Ruzicic 2003).

The most salient criticisms I heard when asking civil society actors about rape reporting after the war centered not on media representations but on the way in which reporters interfaced with survivors in the field. Journalists who sought firsthand testimonies rather than relying on the government or women's NGOs approached survivors directly in collective centers and hospitals, often showing little sensitivity for their respondents' emotional needs. The emblematic example is a reporter walking into a refugee camp and calling out, "Anyone here been raped and speak English?" (Grant 1993, 10). Any woman responding to such a question risked exposing herself to those around her.

To deal with the many requests for access to their clients, and to address the general lack of professional standards among war reporters, some local women's organizations developed strict guidelines of their own to govern their role as gatekeepers between the media and the women under their care. According to a representative of Medica Zenica, a German-funded organization founded to fulfill the need during the war for emergency reproductive health care, the first thing the organization does when receiving a request from a journalist is to "type their name into Google" and attempt to establish whether the journalist has expertise in the area of gender-based violence.

is reporting good/accurate?

how helpful can this really be?

In undertaking this array of activities, organizations such as Medica Zenica aim to protect female survivors while also securing their own organizational goals. Their expertise and ready supply of potential interviewees positions them as coveted access points for reporters interested in obtaining an interview with a raped woman. Medica Zenica has situated itself to make the most of this role, disseminating principles among local and foreign reporters much as it works to train local police on gender issues.[5]

I was told in interviews with Medica Zenica and similar organizations that the ideal type of rape survivor sought by journalists during the war was "preferably someone who had had a baby born of rape" during this period. Duska Andric-Ruzicic writes of reporters' requests for information from Medica Zenica, "I cannot recall a single contact with any journalists in the last seven years that did not contain a request along the lines of 'Could you get me an interview with a woman who was a victim of war rape, who was impregnated and had the child?'" (Andric-Ruzicic 2003, 108). Children themselves were rarely old enough to be interviewed, though in 1996 *Newsweek* reporter Stacy Sullivan managed to quote three-year-old Alen Muhic regarding some apparent teasing he experienced on the block, when children would call him Serb names (Sullivan 1996). More typically the testimony about the babies came from the mother, nurses or psychiatrists, and sometimes sympathetic individuals in the community.

In an analysis of the coverage of "rape babies" in the broadsheet press, Penny Stanley critiques representations of mass rape in the broadsheet press but argues that the media had "a decisive role in making the subject of rape visible" (P. Stanley 1999, 75). She suggests that the storyline about "rape babies" in particular appealed to many readers and publishers, especially when linked to the possibility of domestic gains for Western adoptive couples, because it constituted a "positive outcome" of the war: babies of rape was "one war issue that might have immediate practical consequences [for British or US parents], and would possibly not be halted by complex political bureaucracy" (P. Stanley 1999, 92).

Yet if babies born of rape were so salient in war reporting from Bosnia, both in their own right and in the context of rape reporting, and if coverage of rape as a whole catalyzed the human-rights community to address sexual violence as a crime, how can one explain the relative inattention to the babies by the community of organizations engaged in child protection during the war? In the sections that follow, I suggest that it might be erroneous to consider this an agenda-setting failure, insofar as the general thrust of the reporting was not in fact to construct claims that the babies' rights per se be protected. Rather, the babies functioned in these narratives as signifiers of atrocity against women, against cultural groups, and against the civilized international order.

Constructing Ethnic Divisions: Nationalism

Reports of forced pregnancy in Bosnia were first and foremost stories of ethnic crimes. Early on, the conflict was portrayed as resulting from hostility between discrete cultural groups, and cast as a war not among different armed factions with specific politico-economic agendas but as a war between Serbs, Croats, and Muslims as entire peoples (Banks and Murray 1999; Keen 1999).

Early on in the war, the Western media adopted the moniker "ethnic cleansing," in use by the perpetrators of the worst atrocities and a throwback to Nazi notions of racial purity, to describe the forced displacement of civilians (Kent 2006, 149);[6] and the term "ethnic" to describe the cultural/religious/political divisions in Bosnia was in widespread usage by August 1992.

As many authors have argued, this was a gross oversimplification of the conflict, which had its origins largely in ethnic scaremongering by nationalist leaders throughout the former Yugoslavia. Until the onset of the war, social cleavages were rarely articulated along religious or cultural lines but rather political or rural/urban divides (Bringa 1995). Significant portions of violent conflict during the war took place not across ethnic communities but within them as different factions contended for control over the leadership.[7]

Yet reporting of rape and forced pregnancy largely followed the ethnic hatreds script, casting the atrocities in ethnic terms corresponding to dominant Western understandings of who was to blame in the conflict. Such a narrative is at least somewhat misleading. Gender-based violence during the war certainly had an ethnic component, and in fact constituted a means to construct ethnic boundaries, but the media coverage of these dynamics scarcely captured this complexity. For example, women were also assaulted from within their own ethnic groups during the war. Feminists in the region documented the rise in domestic violence within each "ethnic" community at the onset of the conflict. Politically active women, especially those who opposed the war, were at risk.

Individuals in mixed marriages were also particularly vulnerable to sexual violence from within their family or families' "ethnic" group, but the rape of women in mixed marriages occurred according to a very different "ethnic" logic than that suggested by the media. Croat soldiers were reported to have raped Croatian women married to Bosniac men to punish the women for marrying outside the group; or to have raped Serb or Bosniac women married to Croatian men to punish their husbands for marrying outside the community (Morokvasic-Müller 2004).[8]

By contrast, narratives of babies as carriers of ethnicity across groups reinforced the notion that ethnic groups in Bosnia were clearly demarcated according to kinship, which, as suggested by the high rates of intermarriage before and during the war, was in fact hardly the case (Hansen

2001). Perpetuating and reconstituting this myth reduced the space for individuals committed to a fluid, multiethnic understanding of Bosnian identity. Nonetheless, as Rodgers argues, "Focus on the ethnic identity of the foetus...was common" (Rodgers 1998).

A critical reading of these broadsheet press narratives suggests that rather than promoting an understanding of children's rights and how to secure them, stories of "Bosnian rape babies" helped to construct and naturalize the very racialized understandings of the conflict and of kinship that would make securing their rights most difficult. Whereas ethnic homogeneity was a myth of sorts before and at the onset of the war, during the course of the war individuals in Bosnia increasingly came to identify with the ethnicities articulated in the local and global press. Framing the conflict as essentially "ethnic" in character and essentializing the babies as packages in which ethnic messages are communicated between discrete, homogenous warring groups helped construct the conflict environment as one in which liminality is inherently problematic—surely the worst possible environment in which to secure protection for children who are viewed as embodying "ethnic" multiplicity.

Constructing Women as War's Victims

A second representation of babies conceived through wartime rape in Bosnia centered on the negative impact these pregnancies presumably had on their mothers and tied into the argument not about child rights but about women's rights. A number of scholars have traced the burgeoning awareness of violence against women as a global phenomenon, now a salient issue in international society, to widespread outrage over reports of mass rape in Bosnia (Joachim 1998, 156).

Contrary to interview data collected by some feminist researchers during and after the war, dominant media accounts stressed the essential helplessness and victimhood of women. The Bosnian Muslim rape victim came to symbolize not just the plight of civilian women in war but also the insecurity of women per se at the hands of men and male-dominated security institutions (Slapsak 2001; Zarkov 1997).

The assumption that rape survivors are essentially devastated by their experience, or the equation of women's war experience with the vulnerability to rape flies in the face of women's agency during the war in a number of respects, and it imposes an unduly uniform understanding of the range of gender interpretations open to women and men within Bosnian society. First of all, not all Bosnian women remained in the civilian sector during the war: female military units formed on all sides in the conflict, and women and girls played important roles as snipers (Kaufman and Williams 2004, 426). Some took part in atrocities carried out in the many detention centers throughout the country.[9] Other women were active in civil society organizations, some opposing the war and creating cross-ethnic linkages, others in support of specific nationalist agendas.

More specifically, it negates the range of coping skills and strategies exhibited by rape survivors in Bosnia. Inger Skjaelsbaek's interviews with rape survivors after the war contradict the assumption that rape survivors were uniformly rejected by their male relatives because they were seen as damaged goods. To some extent, Skjaelsbaek found that survivors were able to use the ethnic dimension of their experience as a source of solidarity with their male relatives, who may also have been victims of war crimes; and a number of the women she interviewed had been able to maintained trusting, honest, supporting relationships with male partners after the rape (Skjaelsbaek 2006).

But the dominant media story was one of "weeping women," cast out by a shamed patriarchal society, and the existence of "rape babies" was viewed as the worst possible sequel for a wartime rape survivor, despite the wide variety of responses women exhibited toward these pregnancies. In many of these articles, the babies are situated not as human beings but as exemplars of their mothers' plight: "Nine months ago Kata gave birth to Stipo, the product of her nightmare, and began a forced existence apart from the friends and neighbours she had known" or "[Melisa's] baby is the repulsive product of repeated rapes by Serbian soldiers when they invaded last April" (Skjaelsbaek 2006).

Such constructions are inconsistent with a child rights view of this issue. The babies born of rape are described as part of the problem afflicting their mothers; hate toward the babies is assumed and naturalized; threats of infanticide or abandonment are whitewashed or treated as an ordinary and inevitable outcome of "ethnic cleansing." While the Bosnian rapes signaled a watershed in international understanding of women's human rights in armed conflict, these reports did little to connect the children's rights movement to the issue of wartime gender-based violence.

Constructing the Balkan "Other": Neo-Imperial Humanitarianism

According to several media framing studies of war coverage, a dominant misconception created and reflected by the media was the idea that the people of the Balkans had been at each other's throat since time immemorial (Kent 2006; Auerbach and Bloch-Elkon 2005). This view was popularized by journalist Robert Kaplan's (1994) monograph *Balkan Ghosts* and was reflected in elite Western discourse and written accounts of the war alike. In 1993, the *New York Times* described Bosnia-Herzegovina as "a vast and perilous ethnic morass that innocent outsiders enter at their peril" (Whitney 1993).

Constructions of both forced pregnancy itself and the reaction of victimized communities to an influx of "rape babies" played a role in creating the impression that Bosnia-Herzegovina was a land beyond the pale, apart from civilized Europe. As Hansen has written, "Constructing 'the Balkans' as a place where this happens implies therefore that the western 'we' is different because 'we' do not subscribe to this practice" (Hansen 2001, 61). Indeed as Hansen writes, the idea of (male) ethnic aggression and (female) victimization underlay both arguments for and against intervention in Bosnia and cut across depictions of all ethnic groups in the conflict. Men of both Serb and Bosniac "ethnic" communities were described in unsympathetic terms in these reports. Serbian soldiers were described as "bearded," "filthy," "covered with blood," "drunken," "brutal," and "feral." At the same time, men of the Bosniac community were implicitly situated as unsympathetic patriarchs who would turn away from their abused sisters, wives, and daughters and from their children.

Labels for the babies both reported and popularized by the press conveyed the impression that all sides in the conflict were behaving badly. The rapists are demonized for their "barbarous" policy of mass rape when babies were described as "children of hate," "products of barbarism," or "born of inhumanity." The rape victims' communities are also condemned implicitly for "abandoning unwanted children" or allowing them to languish "unloved" in orphanages simply because they "represent a shame to society." Invoking the "tragedy" of babies conceived through rape and then abandoned by local ethnic patriarchies figured ambiguously in calls for intervention and in the fatalism that nothing constructive was possible in Bosnia: that child's existence reminds the world of the human tragedy that is still Bosnia—a tragedy that, despite the efforts of the United Nations, we are still powerless to end (Barton 1994).

Banks and Murray discuss the contradictions inherent in the emergence of the term "ethnic" as a modifier for depictions of the war in Bosnia:

On the one hand, the Bosnian Muslims were Muslims—if of an apparently rather secular sort—and therefore would normally be placed in a "feared other" category. On the other hand, they were also clearly the underdogs, the victims of "ethnic cleansing," not its perpetrators. (Banks and Murray 1999, 154)

Media narratives of rape babies framed Bosnian society as rural, patriarchal, and primitive: it was these assumptions about characteristics of the victim group, as much as about the genocidal logic of the perpetrators, that rendered explicable to a Western audience the abandonment of babies and rejection of their mothers (B. Allen 1996, 89).

According to Robinson, stereotypes helped to construct a notion of Bosnia as both in the heart of Europe and culturally foreign and backward, a frame that helped Western European bystanders both indulge their sense of moral concern while remaining detached from the conflict as a European war. The view that Europeans were "just like us" was "juxtaposed ... with the notion that Bosnia was part of an ongoing Balkan nightmare which had frequently erupted into chaotic, ethnic violence and any involvement should be kept to a minimum or better still avoided at all costs" (B. Robinson 2004, 379).

Such frames obfuscated practical measures for securing these children's rights: the protection of the babies became embedded in an intervention narrative that called on Western states to "pluck" unloved children from the savagery of the Balkans to the safety of Western couples' waiting arms.

Thus, this narrative figured in calls for intervention, but it also fed into British efforts to appear to provide "assistance" while refusing political and military solutions to the war itself. Non-Balkan countries, in this case Britain, are charged with "plucking" war babies from their fate in a "barbarous" country where "long-buried hatreds have been dragged to the surface."

By contrast, relatively little coverage was given to grassroots efforts to counteract the stigma against the babies, the courage and coping skills of women who embraced their children, or the fact that many rape survivors dealt with their trauma by taking up arms as snipers, rather than by wasting away as outcasts. The imagery also constructs the children themselves as objects of pity, rather than subjects with rights the state is mandated to protect.

On the hunt for the worst story possible, reporters tended to put the saddest possible spin on what was usually a mixed bag of facts. Not only did such simplistic rhetoric draw attention away from questions of children as rights-bearers, but it perhaps helped invoke a backlash within Yugoslav society about the possibility of foreign involvement in the protection of these children in those cases where local adoptive families were unavailable.[10] For example, asked about international adoption by a reporter in 1993, Jelena Brasja, director of the Roman Catholic charity Caritas in Zagreb, was quoted as saying defensively, "We have a centuries-old culture here and we can manage to bring up these children...we are not savages" (Effertson 1993).

A Child-Rights Frame?

Both the transnational Muslim community and the Bosnian government made arguments opposing the idea of exporting "Muslim" babies to be raised in the West (Gledhill 1993). According to some, the rationale behind keeping abandoned babies in situ was the hope that their birth mothers might later be persuaded to raise them, despite the fact that in some cases mothers who had been urged to raise their babies after attempting to surrender them had ended up killing their children (Williams 1993).

Such arguments were reported on but seldom followed up on by the international press. The responsibility of the newly recognized states in the region to fulfill their obligations under the Convention on the Rights of the Child and make such decisions based on the best interests of the child did not figure prominently in these stories.

Articles with passages referencing the "babies-best interests" centered on three issues: (1) whether women should be permitted to abort their fetuses, given that Pope John Paul II came out in February 1993 as saying that the women should care for "these beings" inside them; (2) whether the babies' best interests were served by keeping them in the country, where they might suffer stigma; and (3) whether, in the case of foreign adoptions, it was ethical to streamline the process, insofar as it could result in improper vetting of prospective parents.

It is important to note, however, that these are expressed as moral or political dilemmas, not questions of child rights per se. The Convention on the Rights of the Child is not invoked. The term "best interests of the child," while implicit in these passages, is not used in these articles. Experts on child rights are not interviewed as sources.

After the war, we begin to see a more sophisticated kind of narrative, more nuanced, less sensationalist, one that treats the complexity of the child rights dimension as it is interconnected to the status of the women who gave birth to the babies. Some articles pay closer attention to the agency of survivors, diverging from the standard ethnicized script of the earlier wartime period. Toomey's (2003) article pays close attention not just to women who preferred to abandon their children but also to a survivor who chose to raise her daughter, emphasizing the best practices by Medica Zenica that assisted this family, and attempting to capture "the complex relationship with her child."

Interviews with the authors of these articles also suggest a more human rights–focused approach. This is reflected both in the complexity of the articles themselves and in the reporters' narratives about the rationale behind their project and their hopes for how the coverage might elicit change.

Additionally, these writers clearly took care to "do no harm" through the fact-finding process: several of them refused, for example, to share information on their sources with me when asked, out of concern for their respondents' anonymity. Two Danish journalists researching this topic in the summer of 2005 described the lengths they took to avoid retraumatizing informants: focusing not "on the past and the awful details of the rapes," but on describing the families' present situation; they consulted in advance with experts on torture counseling in their own country on "how to do an interview [just in case] we got in touch with either women or children—what should we avoid talking about, what danger signals should we look for and so on." An ethical responsibility toward their informants is also suggested by the efforts these reporters made to give back to the affected communities: many articles in this period concluded

Importance of the rights of the children

with opportunities for readers to send donations to specific families or civil society organizations.

Perhaps it is a different type of journalist who gravitates toward stories about marginalized populations in the aftermath of war, rather than in the heat of a conflict. But there are also far fewer such stories after the war, when as Toomey (2003) laments, "the plight of these women is no longer a fashionable cause."

CONCLUSION

This chapter has argued that three sets of tropes—one emphasizing women's victimization, one essentializing ethnicity, and one positioning Bosnia as beyond the civilized West, sometimes in combination—have characterized the vast majority of print media coverage of mass rape and rape babies in the former Yugoslavia. An examination of that media demonstrated how rare suggestions for protecting the babies themselves as rights-bearers were in this coverage, and how when they arose they very often took the grandiose and sensationalist form described as "airlifting" babies out or exporting them to "loving British couples" for adoption, rather than pressuring the Bosnian government to ensure their protection through formal means consistent with the Convention on the Rights of the Child. By discounting local governments' capacity to exercise their responsibilities under international law, the media drew attention away from these responsibilities and foreclosed human rights organizations' attention to the issue as a human rights concern.

At the same time, coverage of children born of war and their mothers exhibited the potential, to elicit transformative change and even galvanize local and international attention to the problems faced by children and women in post-conflict zones. Perhaps simplistic narratives are the most that can be expected: as Smillie and Minear (2004) point out, "the media are not a humanitarian instrument as such...there is only so much disaster news that the media can and will handle at one time."

The particular frames used have drawn attention away from the specific child rights questions at issue in these cases. These three narratives became embedded in international human rights institutions in such a way as to preclude attention to children born of war as subjects of human rights concern. They affected the international tribunal system and the developments in humanitarian law in response to mass rape and forced pregnancy. They affected the operational practices of humanitarian organizations in the field during the war, and then of local and international civil society organizations in Bosnia during the post-war period. Perhaps they also function to deflect attention away from the specific needs of these children and to pose structural constraints to agenda setting in this area. In that sense, how an issue is framed may indeed mute the agenda-setting effects of the quantity of coverage.

NOTES

1. Despite the fact that "Emina," the child in the article, had been adopted by a Croatian couple by the time the piece went to press, the baby is described as "anonymous, unloved," "forsaken," " and defined in terms of her biological origins, as "born of horror," "born of inhumanity"; the possibility of securing a future for such children in Bosnia is discounted, their "only hope" to be "airlifted to safety...[this] policy is the only sure chance these children have of survival."

2. This gap in the human rights agenda is explored more systematically in Charli Carpenter (2007).

3. Minear, Scott, and Weiss (1996) quoting Sylvana Foa, Boutrous-Ghali's spokesperson.

4. For an excellent overview of the literature and a critique of its incoherence see Gilboa (2005).

5. Correspondingly, Medica Zenica receives publicity through news articles quoting its staff and describing its work, and some more recent reports have concluded with injunctions for readers to provide donations to support the organization.

6. On the origins of the term "ethnic cleansing" see Kent (2006, 149).

7. For example, Bosniac Fikret Abdic led 25,000 Muslim refugees in an uprising against Alija Izetbegovic's government between 1994 and 1995. See Lischer (2005).

8. Children resulting from such "boundary-enforcing" rapes would not necessarily have been constructed as "of the enemy" in the sense that the media narrative suggested.

9. A female camp attendant involved in detentions of Bosniacs was described by a survivor in an interview: "She said she was from the 'White Eagles' and that things were going to change for us. The girl told us to take down the babies' pants to see if they had been circumcised. The men started talking about making us pregnant. That night the rapes began." See Fisk (1993).

10. For example, Stacy Sullivan followed up in 1996 and discovered nine orphans conceived in rape in one orphanage. Toomey reported that 13-year-old "Samira," remained institutionalized as late as 2004.

CHAPTER 16

Gendering the Empire's Soldiers: Gender Ideologies, the U.S. Military, and the "War on Terror"

Laura Sjoberg

More than a decade ago, Cynthia Enloe wrote about idealized notions of masculinity and femininity employed in the U.S. military that served to define the public face of the military as an organization (Enloe 1993). Jean Elshtain described these tropes as "just warrior" and "beautiful soul" (Elshtain 1983). Just warriors are men of valor, protecting their homes, families, and homelands through warfare justly pursued (Elshtain1983). Beautiful souls are pure, naïve women who need protection and whose needs motivate men's wars (Elshtain 1983). In the age of the "war on terror," these idealized notions of gender persist both within the U.S. military and in media coverage of it and its members. This chapter observes the continued presence and contemporary evolution of gendered ideologies in the narratives of idealized military masculinities and femininities.

This chapter explores the constructed gender roles in "hero" narratives about individual members of the U.S. military in the "war on terror" stylized by military press releases and the outlets that reported the stories. It reviews the stories the military tells and the public consumes of standouts like Pat Tillman, Jessica Lynch, Chris Carter, and Paul Ray Smith. This analysis produces two results: first, tropes of militarized masculinity and femininity pervade the military; second, the stories crafted for public consumption are, like the empire they serve, hypergendered. The chapter concludes by arguing that the legitimation and valorization of both the empire and its war making are reliant on these institutionalized ideologies of gender, which adapt to change over time and combine to present the empire as at once just (feminine) and all-powerful (masculine). It shows how these tropes are crucial to understand how gender ideologies shape the U.S. "war on terror" and the national identity more generally.

THE "STARS" OF THE "WAR ON TERROR"

Pat Tillman

Pat Tillman was an ex-NFL player who quit his job with the Arizona Cardinals to enlist, then was killed in the line of duty (MSNBC.com 2004). Tillman was characterized as a "role model of courage and patriotism" who "made the ultimate sacrifice in the war on terror" (MSNBC.com 2004). He was said to have "walked away from a career in football to a greater calling" (MSNBC.com 2004). Tillman was characterized as the patriotic example of "sacrifice, selflessness, and service" (Sportsillus-trated.com 2003) He was described as "an American original, a maverick who burned with intensity" (Coll 2004, A1). Tillman's loyalty, patriotism, and self-sacrifice were highlighted in the stories about him after his death and characterized him as a war hero who had died in battle protecting his country, loyal to the bitter end. Ann Coulter called him "virtuous, pure and masculine like only an American male can be" (Zirin 2005, 16).

It took almost five months for the U.S. military to admit that Tillman was killed by friendly fire, not by the enemy in protecting the United States. It took almost an additional year for the army and the media to acknowledge that Tillman's understanding of the war was less than perfectly support-ive. In fact, Tillman's family characterized him as "a fiercely independent thinker who enlisted, fought and died in service to his country yet was critical of President Bush and opposed the war in Iraq" and as someone who was an avid reader of Noam Chomsky and other leftist authors (Zirin 2005, 16). Dave Zirin describes the stylized narrative of Tillman's life and death as a result of the U.S. military's need to sell soldiers' masculinities (Zirin 2005, 16). He explains:

Tillman's transition from one-dimensional caricature to critically thinking human being is a long time coming. The fact is that in death he was far more useful to the armchair warriors than he had ever been in life. When the Pro Bowler joined the Army Rangers, the Pentagon brass needed a loofah to wipe their drool: He was white, handsome, and played in the NFL. For a chicken-hawk Administration led by a President who loves the affectations of machismo but runs from protesting military moms, the testosterone cocktail was impossible to resist. (Zirin 2005, 16)

Tillman's family accuses the government of covering up the real way he died in order to manipulate his story for media consumption ideal-izing his masculinity. His mother, Mary, argues that "They wanted to use him for their purposes. . . . They needed something that looked good, and it was appalling that they would use him like that" (Zirin 2005, 16). The story that would look good would characterize a good-looking, virile, and promising young man voluntarily taking upon his shoulders the responsibility to protect his country and its women and children, and making the ultimate sacrifice with bravery and purpose that would inspire others to fight—a story of the heroic masculinity of the male soldier.

Jessica Lynch

If strong, virile men fight wars, they do so to preserve the honor of pure, innocent women. In ancient times, those women were the actual prizes of war (e.g., Helen of Troy) who sat at the sidelines or safely "back home" being protected by the war effort without having to experience the horrors of fighting or see the carnage left from battle. Even though women are now members of the U.S. military who serve in most positions that men do, that image of the woman as *casus belli* remains. The stylized narratives of Jessica Lynch demonstrate the remnants of the beautiful soul image of women, even as they become soldiers.

Only a few days into the United States' invasion of Iraq, the story of Private Jessica Lynch was all over every news source in the United States. Lynch was widely believed to be the first American prisoner of war to be taken by the Iraqi military, even though four other prisoners were taken at the same time. The 19-year-old girl ostensibly went down fighting, was injured in battle, and was tortured in captivity (Kampfner 2003). The military's story is of a daring rescue. A battle was created for diversion and gunfire erupted in a hospital. Lynch was just a country girl who became a hero and a household name (Kampfner 2003).

Lynch was characterized as brave beyond her femininity (fighting) but limited by it (needing an elaborate, public rescue). Certainly, the portrayals of Lynch appear far from the traditional understanding of women as nonparticipants who need protection. Jessica Lynch was a *soldier* and a fighter. She was captured fighting, was brave through interrogation, and endured torture and rape, so the story says.

Still, a number of similarities between the portrayal of Jessica Lynch and the traditional just war understanding of "beautiful souls" are evident. That Lynch fought was described as remarkable, even though it would be expected of most soldiers. Women soldiers do not fight. Lynch, like many reservists, was said to have "joined the army to see the world" (Bragg 2003). Her choice, then, was not to fight, or to go to war, but to be a tourist. Instead, she was a *girl* who wanted some adventure and just happened to end up in an army supply tank with a gun in the desert in Iraq. Lynch was also *fought for* instead of fighting in much of the story—she was helpless, a captive in an Iraqi hospital. The soldiers needed to save her. She was so helpless that she needed to be rescued before the four other prisoners captured along with her. In fact, her rescue was so intricate that it required *faking* a battle. The most publicized rescue mission in military history followed. Of course, Lynch had to be saved—*war is about protecting innocent women*. She needed to be saved not just because she could be tortured but also because her being a woman meant she was vulnerable to sexual violence. Iraqis could not get away with inflicting sexual violence on American women. Lynch was at once presented as a glorified war hero and an innocent woman—a "beautiful soul" who could not escape the mold, even though she carried a gun and wore a uniform.

As if this story about Lynch were not gendered enough, it turns out that most of the story was a contrivance, presented by the U.S. military. As John Kampfner documents, the coverage of the Jessica Lynch story was a feat of news management by the Pentagon (Kampfner 2003, A1). In fact, Lynch had not gone down fighting—her gun had malfunctioned (Bragg 2003). She had not been shot at; she was injured in an automobile accident before the Iraqi ambush (Bragg 2003). Unlike those captured with her, Iraqi troops took Lynch to a hospital and treated her injuries (Kampfner 2003, A1). She was assigned one of only two nurses in the hospital (Kampfner 2003, A1). The Iraqi military abandoned the hospital, leaving Lynch there with the medical staff (Bragg 2003). She has no memory or evidence of rape; instead, a nurse sang to her and talked about her boyfriend (Kampfner 2003, A1). The medical staff at the hospital attempted a rescue of their own, putting Lynch into an ambulance sent to a U.S. checkpoint (Kampfner 2003, A1). The U.S. military, unaware of the ambulance's contents, fired on it. The next day, U.S. troops entered an unguarded hospital and recovered Lynch (Bragg 2003). The rescue was filmed; though no violence is ever shown, it is implied in the edited tape.

Lynch herself objects to this portrayal of her rescue. She characterizes herself as just another soldier and then just another prisoner of war (Bragg 2003). Lynch calls the elaborate rescue attempt unnecessary, and complains about being used as a symbol of American gender roles (Bragg 2003). The portrayals of Lynch as a woman of extraordinary bravery, as a victim of Iraqi cruelty and sexual violence, and as an innocent woman in need of saving were all stories constructed by the U.S. military and the media that published their press releases to achieve an idealized image of the militarized woman.[1]

Chris Carter *American Sniper*

If the stylized narrative of Pat Tillman valorizes his courageous death, and the public narratives of Jessica Lynch emphasize her need to be rescued, Chris Carter was a star of the war in Iraq because he both survived and rescued. Chris Carter, an Army captain, led a unit that had an embedded media contingent early in the war in Iraq. He was often quoted in new articles in the days before the invasion about the status of the preparations

(Tomlinson 2003). Carter became a celebrity when he rescued an elderly woman from a battle site just days into the war. As Jeordan Legon explains, "the elderly woman got stuck in a haze of smoke and bullets" and was shot as "she tried to cross a bridge south of Baghdad" (Legon 2003). In response, "Chris Carter did not hesitate. He ordered his Bradley armored vehicle onto the bridge while he and two men followed on foot . . . then the 31-year-old company commander pointed his M-16 rifle and provided cover for his men to carry the wounded woman to the safety of an ambulance" (Legon 2003).

This daring rescue, itself above and beyond the call of duty, was apparently only the start of a standout day for the soldier who would come to serve as America's model. As Chris Tomlinson relates, "by the end of this day, the Army would fight street to street, capture and kill scores of Saddam Hussein's troops, blow up a ruling party headquarters, and destroy heaps of ammunition and mortars" (Tomlinson 2003). Though there is little hard evidence to back up this claim, a number of news stories attribute the day's military successes to Carter as well. According to Legon, "Carter's unit . . . took control of the bridge and the whole town, Hindiya, within a matter of hours" (Legon 2003). In fact, "Carter's troops also destroyed tons of ammunition and weapons found at the area's Baath Party Headquarters" (Legon 2003).

The combination of Carter's alleged heroics and his sense of humor got Carter attention, and "a constant stream of reports filed by the Associated Press turned Carter into a semi-battlefield celebrity—a combination of deadly fighting machine, insightful commentator, and quipster" (Legon 2003). Among Carter's famous quips were sexual jokes about having taken over "Saddam's Love Shack" and jokes about the use of weapons and the progress of the war (Legon 2003). Stylized narratives about Carter characterized him as a symbol of the new, "tough but tender" idealized American masculinity—fierce, deadly, and efficient, but willing to risk his life to save a helpless, innocent woman in a time of need (Niva 1998). In this role, daily reports about Carter came to serve as the "ideal-type" of a soldier in Iraq, both to other soldiers and to readers. As an article in the *Chicago Sun-Times* recounts,

With the closing credits rolling on the war with Iraq, news junkie Kim Shepherd is going to miss her favorite battlefield celebrity. He's not a flak jacket-wearing correspondent, a tireless anchor, or a retired general-turned analyst. He's a soldier, and he's been the Forrest Gump of the War. Capt. Chris Carter seems to be the omnipresent soldier and quipper of Operation Freedom. (Roeper 2003, 11)

Stylized narratives about Carter, then, were characterizations of what today's U.S. soldier should be—still virile, strong, and self-sacrificing but also closely connected to the (women) civilians who remain the *casus belli* for men's wars.

Paul Ray Smith

If the idealized American man is one who protects innocent civilians, is patriotic in times of war, and is brave in battle, his protection is not only offered to civilians but also to *his* civilians—to his wife and children "back home." Paul Ray Smith "died while helping ward off 100 or more Iraqi soldiers from his band of about 16 combat engineers outside of Saddam International Airport . . . Smith was shot in the head and killed" (Leary 2004).

Stories of the death of Paul Ray Smith were followed by stories about how devoted Smith had been to his family, and how military men protect and love their families. In the military's online summary of Smith's life (featuring him as a medal of honor recipient), it is explained that, "when anyone would ask what he wanted to do as an adult, he always said, 'I want to be a Soldier, get married, and have kids' " (U.S. Army 2005). During the ceremony where Smith was awarded the medal of honor, President George W. Bush pointed out that "we thank his family for the father, husband, and son and brother who can never be replaced," emphasizing the soldier as a member of the family (U.S. Army. 2005).

In addition to the Medal of Honor ceremony, Smith was honored by the nationally televised dedication of a Tampa, Florida, area post office in his name. At this dedication, the family Smith left behind was key to the ceremony. The *St. Petersburg Times* reported that "Sgt. 1st Class Paul Ray Smith's memory is preserved in the plaque and photograph at the post office on Mile Stretch drive, not far from where Birgit and their children live" (Leary 2004). The *St. Petersburg Times* also published the army's characterization of Smith as the ideal military man: husband, soldier, and protector:

We can remember a husband who cherished his wife. We can praise a father who loved his children. We can recall a soldier who cared for his men. And we can celebrate the life and legacy of a man who gave the last full measure of devotion to his country. (Leary 2004)

Other news reports also juxtaposed Smith's loyalty to his family and his bravery in battle. The *USA Today* story reporting the awarding of the Medal of Honor begins with "Sgt. 1st Class Paul Ray Smith of Tampa left his wife and two children to go to the war in Iraq" (Sharp 2005). The *Washington Post* explained that "in Paul Ray Smith, the military has singled out an inspirational role model for a war that has not gone as well as its architects once expected" (Baker 2005, A01). This is important because, "after so many deaths to mourn and fewer recent clear-cut victories, the commemoration of Smith's actions seemed to serve as a morale boost for the armed forces in the 25th month of a war whose end is not yet in sight" (Baker 2005, A01).

THE GENDERED IDEAL-TYPES OF SOLDIERS
IN THE U.S. MILITARY

These stories of the heroes of the "war on terror" betray gendered tropes that still dominate a U.S. military that has begun to "allow" women into most positions in its fighting forces. The ideal-type roles prescribed for men are reminiscent of the citizen-warrior expectations from ancient times and more recent characterizations of militarized masculinity, while the roles prescribed for women replicate traditional perceptions of women as innocent and defenseless, on the sidelines of conflict.

Cynthia Enloe explains that "militarized forms of manliness" not only pervade the militaries of modern states, but shape both military and state identity (Enloe 1993, 25). The ideal type in a given society is used by soldiers and citizens to "construct hierarchies of militarized masculinity among themselves" (Enloe 1993, 56). Enloe is not arguing that the same gender norms dominate and define citizenship in every state around the world. Instead, she explains that "variations in militarized masculinity may deserve more of our attention," especially because "particular variations do not only spring from diverse cultural groundings; they may also be dictated by historically significant militarisms" (Enloe 1993, 73).

Like militarized masculinity, militarized femininity is a concept that changes with the historical and cultural grounding of militarism. Militarized femininity is a militarism that relies on control of the bounds of femininity and the behavior of (individual and all) women within the confines of those bounds (Enloe 1993, 174). Like militarized masculinity, militarized femininity is culturally and temporally specific, but it relies generally on the construction of hierarchies on the basis of assumed membership in a gender-based group. In other words, though the specific prescriptions for men's and women's behavior changes over time and place, ideal types of militarized masculinity and femininity can be seen as barometers for the military and strategic culture of a state in global politics. The remaining work of this chapter, then, is to ask how the notions of militarized masculinity and femininity in these four hero narratives reflect and reproduce the military and strategic culture of the United States during the "war on terror."

GENDERED NARRATIVES IN SERVICE
OF GENDERED EMPIRE

The current militarized masculinities and femininities in the United States are demonstrated in the hero narratives of Pat Tillman, Jessica Lynch, Chris Carter, and Paul Ray Smith. Across these stories, the ideal militarized man is strong in battle but willing to die for the cause of the "war on terror," unquestioningly loyal to the cause, indefatigably upbeat about the war generally and his participation specifically, irrevocably committed to

protecting both the people "back home" generally and his family specifically, and committed to the ethical treatment of the helpless wherever he
might find them. In other words, although at some points in U.S. history
the idealized militarized masculinity has been the "just warrior" (Elshtain
1983), and at others, it has been "superman" (Enloe 1993, 71), the current
militarized masculinity requires both of American soldiers.

The rising breadth and importance of standards for militarized masculinity can be described as "hypergendered" expectations.[2] As Meghana
Nayak explains, "hypermasculinity is the sensationalistic endorsement of
elements of masculinity, such as rigid gender roles, vengeful and militarized reactions, and obsession with order, power, and control" and
is salient when agents' masculinities "feel threatened or undermined,
thereby needing to inflate, exaggerate, or otherwise distort their traditional masculinity" (Nayak 2006, 43).

If militarized femininity has also changed, it has changed to become
something of a paradoxical relationship: women have come to be expected
to participate in the military, national defense, and war efforts,[3] but their
participation has come to be understood as passive, feminine, and even
demure.[4]

The combination of a hypermasculine image of male soldiers and the
preservation of traditional images of women as civilians, even as they join
the military, are symptomatic of a hypergendered empire in the United
States. As Enloe argues, militarized masculinities and femininities represent and reproduce the genderings of the states they reside in. The hypermasculinity of the current militarized masculinity shows the intense focus
on power and virility in the United States today, while the emphasis on
traditional femininity shows the need to appear (tender and) just.

As Zillah Eisenstein argues, "gender differentiation will be mobilized
for war AND peace" in the age of Bush, and the American empire will
be focused on manliness (Eisenstein 2004). In this empire, war is carried
out for the dual purposes of security and to transform and control populations (Duffield 2002, 1049–71; Hardt and Negri 2001, 2004). If, in this age
of empire, militarized ideal-types of gender reflect the character of empire
and gender differentiation will be employed in service of the empire's
goals, each hero narrative reviewed here can tell us something about the
dimensions of the (hypergendered) American empire.

The story of Tillman can tell us of the United States' attachment to undying faith and interest in projecting mightiness. Though, by most accounts,
we now understand that Tillman was actually an active citizen, who inter-
acted with, questioned, and analyzed the policies of the U.S. government,
the original stories that the military put out about Tillman emphasized
his "loyalty" and "patriotism" at a time when there was precious little of
that going around, and prized unquestioning faith (MSNBC.com 2004).
Additionally, the stories of Tillman specialized in linking these virtues to
the "affectations of machismo" that came from Tillman's NFL career and

were part of a "testosterone cocktail" projected by the Bush Administration, which projected a special sort of mightiness reserved only for empire (Zirin 2005, 16).

If the story of Tillman tells us of the attachment that the (hypergendered) American empire has to undying faith, the story of Lynch tells us about an empire that perceives itself as having a softer side. Pictures and stories of the pretty, blonde teenager who was at once a war hero and a helpless captive portrayed the United States as a just actor in the face of those unjust actors (e.g., Iraqis) who would commit the ultimate crime of torturing a (white) woman. The story about Lynch was one about an empire that was brave but just, fierce but vulnerable, and willing to defend any attacks on its vulnerability. Defending Lynch from defiled Iraqis occurred with many of the same storylines and plot elements that defending New York after 9/11 had, on a smaller scale. After the Lynch story, the American empire is not only mighty and masculine but also *right* in its own right.

If the story of Tillman tells of an empire that is mighty, and the story of Lynch tells of an empire that is right, then the story of Chris Carter tells of an empire that is to be liked and respected. Chris Carter's story tells of an empire that is benevolent (sometimes, even, saving the enemy) but potent (conquering when it sees fit), that is personable and likable (even joking on the battlefield) but successful (at achieving military and strategic dominance). Like Carter, the story implies that the American empire is down to earth, friendly, and compassionate—but able to get down to business at the drop of a hat.

The story of Smith defines the meaning of honor in empire. According to the stories, to Smith, soldiering and fathering were essential, and intertwined, parts of citizenship.[5] What it means to be honorable in the empire, then, is to be intimately attached to those citizens you are responsible for (i.e., your wife and children) but still willing to die for the cause of the empire (i.e., in battle).

Through these four examples of idealized militarized gender roles, we see an American empire that would like to be viewed as commanding unconditional loyalty, that is mighty, fair and just, likable, potent, and honorable. These traits are projected through hypergendered ideal-types, often unrepresentative either of the people they are told of *or* the empire they represent. In a time of uncertainty and the struggle of the "war on terror," these idealized images form the basis for the United States' (military) identity, both as it prosecutes an uncertain battle and as it ventures into the 21st century.

NOTES

1. These constructions are all the more problematic in the face of the irony that the story told about Jessica Lynch was not true of her, but much more substantially resembled the plight of another American woman soldier. Shoshana Johnson was

a member of Jessica Lynch's company, and one of the four other prisoners of war the Iraqi military captured that day. She was an African American single mother of two. Unlike Jessica Lynch, she did go down fighting. Unlike Jessica Lynch, Johnson was injured in battle—she was shot in both ankles. Johnson was kept in a prison guarded by the Iraqi military. And unlike Jessica Lynch, Shoshana Johnson's story is all but unknown. William Douglas wonders if Shoshana Johnson's relative obscurity is because she did not have the right face to serve as the heroine for a new militarized femininity. See Douglas (2003). See also Johnson (2010), a memoir released between the writing and publication of this chapter.

2. My thinking on this has been heavily influence by the work of Jennifer Heeg Maruska, including Heeg Maruska (2010).

3. See, for example, that every reference in the *Congressional Record* to the soldiers fighting in the "war on terror" is to "the men and women" fighting, or "the men and women" who have lost their lives, putting them on an equal playing field without recognizing that the military and its fighting forces in the "war on terror" remain close to 85 percent male.

4. For example, the stories of Jessica Lynch, which emphasize that she was a "tourist" and wanted to be a "schoolteacher," even though she had a uniform and a gun, and the outright rejection of the femininity of Lynndie England, Sabrina Harmon, and Megan Ambuhl, who participated in the prisoner abuse at Abu Ghraib (see, for a longer explanation, Sjoberg and Gentry [2007]).

5. See the army Web site, http://www.army.mil/medalofhonor/smith/pro file/index.html.

CHAPTER 17

Fireman Fetishes and *Drag King Dreams:* Queer Responses to September 11

Deborah Cohler

On October 12, 2001, columnist Peggy Noonan published an homage to "manly men" in the *Wall Street Journal,* participating in a widespread American cultural fetishization of a certain kind of white, American masculinity. "We are experiencing a new respect for old-fashioned masculinity," she writes:

a new respect for physical courage, for strength, for the willingness to use both for the good of others.... You didn't have to be a fireman to be one of the manly men of Sept. 11. Those businessmen of Flight 93...who didn't live by their hands or their backs but who found out what was happening to their country, [they] said goodbye to the people they loved, snapped the cell phone[s] shut and said, "Let's roll." Those were tough men, the ones who forced that plane down in Pennsylvania. They were tough, brave, guys. (Noonan 2001)

Noonan contrasts these handsome and handy working-class heroes not only to professional American men (the "Dockers generation" according to Maureen Dowd 2001), but to grieving white American women, oppressed "fledging feminists of Afghanistan," and "terrorist" Arab men. This post-9/11 mass cultural celebration of virile, physical masculinity is framed through the logic of nationalist heteronormativity in mainstream media outlets such as the *Wall Street Journal,* the *New York Times,* and *Esquire* magazine.[1] In addition to reconstructing laboring men as American heterosexual heroes, however, the revival of "old-fashioned" masculinity also participated in structuring queer responses to 9/11. What are the ways in which 9/11 has transformed representations of queer genders and sexualities? How do representations of female and male masculinities, gay sex, and gay identities shape the discourses of war, fear, and nationalist identity on what I have previously termed the U.S. "homefront" (Cohler 2006)? What are the ramifications of heroic white masculinity for the erasure of the post-9/11 violences and disappearances of men of color in the United States? And how might post-9/11 representations of homosexuality help us to understand the consequences of 9/11 for studies of gender, war, and media more widely?

Representations of sexuality, sexual identity, and queer communities in LGBTQ media can illustrate two vectors of LGBTQ cultural productions after September 11, 2001.[2] Some responses sought to produce LGBTQ communities as part of an antiwar, antiracist American communities and coalitions. Others argued for the inclusion of LGBTQ people as "Americans" united with all other Americans in their grief and outrage following the attacks. By focusing on constructions of white masculinity in a range of LGBTQ cultural responses to 9/11, we can read the central role of nationalism in the production of both oppositional and communitarian responses to 9/11 from queer communities.

Sexuality was both invisible and omnipresent in public responses to 9/11. On San Francisco's Castro Street, a shrine appeared in memory of Mark Bingham, a white, gay passenger on United Airlines Flight 93. In New York City, amid signs seeking information on missing relatives and friends (N. Miller 2003), posters captioned "The Empire Strikes Back" depicted Osama bin Laden being sodomized by the Empire State Building (Puar and Rai 2002). On the "700 Club" Christian television program, the Rev. Jerry Falwell blamed "the pagans, and the abortionists, and the feminists, and the gays and the lesbians" for the attacks ("Falwell Apologizes" 2007). Public responses to 9/11, seemingly disconnected from such "private" concerns as sexuality, were in fact infused with sexual meanings and sexual resonances.

In U.S. mass media coverage of 9/11 and its aftermath, discourses of American exceptionalism, depoliticized multiculturalism, and Western modernity shared the stage with insistent heteronormativity. Inderpal Grewal has noted that "within popular culture, multiculturalism's work was to show that 'we are all Americans' after all: multiculturalism, in a moment of crisis, could call for the American nationalism" (Grewal 2005, 213). Such nationalism was almost always predicated on implicit heterosexuality. After 9/11, as media coverage slowly shifted from mourning (the deaths of those killed on that day) to blame (blaming the specific hijackers, or all Muslims, or people who "look Muslim," or the Bush administration, or abortionists), to revenge (the drive for counterattack that facilitated the war on Afghanistan), to nationalist aggression dependent on binary ideologies of religion, modernity, and gender. Resistance to these master narratives was present, but usually via discourses of home-front heteronormativity. The fierce maternal pacifism of Cindy Sheehan, for example, produces an oppositional response to war through the symbolism of maternal citizenship.[3] This chapter considers a selection of LGBTQ responses to and in U.S. mass culture after 9/11 examining the place of gay Americans in a heteronormative homeland.

LGBTQ pundits participated in the broad representational confusion in the autumn of 2001. As others have documented, a multicultural nationalist monoculture presided over alarming and immediate violences against Arab and South Asian American men and women,[4] while unmarked, usually white American "women" were classified as mourners, victims, mothers, and then—shortly after the U.S. invasions of Afghanistan and Iraq—as soldiers (Cohler 2006). Gay media makers struggled for "appropriate" responses to 9/11, and many created images and texts that located "gay Americans" within a broader American dialogue. The functions of sexuality and gender identities in these LGBTQ responses illustrate constructions of citizenship through narratives of homonormative nationalism.

Lesbian serial cartoonist Alison Bechdel's biweekly "Dykes to Watch Out For" both embeds her characters within American responses to 9/11 and seeks to establish possibilities for such responses that exceed or defy narratives of a unified American public seeking revenge, war, or binary constructions of "us" and "them." A cartoon entitled "Real World" published October 3, 2001, depicts its cast of "dykes" performing daily tasks on September 11 such as carrying groceries, getting ready for work, and caring for aging parents or young children, all while watching televisions news reports, praying for peace, comforting students, and passing vandalized mosques with fighter jets flying overhead. This wordless cartoon (particularly notable from an artist notoriously and delightfully verbose) presents its LGBTQ characters as part of a broader America responding to an indescribable horror (thus, the wordless cartoon) through the media (newspapers, televisions, or computers appear in 6 of the 11 panels), with community engagement, and through family retrenchment. In one sequence, African American Jezanna fights with her father over posting an American flag on their door: she supplements his patriotic flag with a peace sign. In other panels, same-sex partners snuggle while watching the news or reading the newspaper. Bechdel's "Real World" serves to bear witness to the first day of the "homefront": its cast of characters reflect leftist and liberal responses of protest (one character carries a protest sign out of her cooperative house while her housemates are "visualizing" peace on the living room floor) and organizing, alongside acts of witness that draw the cartoon characters into a broader American moment of imagined community (Anderson 1983). Though sex itself is absent in the cartoon, queer community identities become modalities of Americanness through domestication.

In "Real World's" most ambiguous panel, two white characters—lesbian and occasional drag king Lois and transman Jerry—walk in front of a mosque with broken windows. In the background, a police officer takes notes while military jets fly overhead. In the foreground, Lois and Jerry are carrying a sack of groceries. It is unclear if they are bringing aid to the mosque or if they just happen to be walking by, observing or oblivious to the hate crime. This panel, the only one that depicts Islam or Muslims, is foregrounded by white queer masculinity. Lois and Jerry form a visual frame around Islam in America that is also bounded by a police car and military fighter jets. From a dramatically different thematic, ideological, and stylistic perspective, yet alongside Noonan's fetishistic invocations, Bechdel's cartoon frames Muslims in the United States through their relations to white masculinity.

Dan Savage's September 20, 2001, "Savage Love" column entitled "My Dumb Job" also engages questions of queer masculinity and reflects on the national moment of imagined community via media engagement, but he positions homosexuality quite differently than Bechdel (Savage 2001). Whereas Bechdel does not comment explicitly on sexual identity or sex acts, but embeds LGBTQ people as part of shared grief and, importantly, public, pacifist responses to the attacks, Savage explicitly scolds his readers for "thinking about their sex lives at a time like this!"

Savage's sex advice column, written Wednesday September 12, 2001, contains letters sent to Savage within hours of the attacks. For much of the column, Savage disciplines these writers for having had sex on their minds on 9/11. In response to the lead letter in the column, signed "Normal Straight Male," he writes, "You sent me your e-mail...less than 35 minutes after the south tower of the World Trade Center collapsed...Thousands of people in New York City, Washington DC, and Pennsylvania had died or were dying horrifying deaths, and all you could think about were gay men who liked to *fist*? What the hell is wrong with you?" Another letter sent the same day complains that recent "Savage Love" columns (about AIDS education) were "boring." Savage responds, "I'm guessing that since you managed to be bored...on Tuesday September 11,...you didn't know anyone who was flying...that day. Lucky you." Savage claims his right to be an angry "queen" in juxtaposition to his correspondents, whose interest in sex acts he deems improper on 9/11. His gay identity is a proper vehicle for his rage at both the "suicidal Islamic radicals, their heads stuffed with absurdities" and the sanctimonious Christian commentators calling for prayer on television (whom he calls "Jesus' employees"). For Savage, like Bechdel, LGBTQ Americans experience collective grief; yet unlike Bechdel, Savage models not familial and civic engagement but instead participates in the imagined national community by publicly shaming those who circumvent metanarratives of grief and a "world changed" in their situationally inappropriate interest in sex. Yet despite his disavowal of all things sexual on 9/11, he ends his column with this call for (sexualized) revenge:

Let's catch every bastard who had anything to do with the attacks....Once the towers are up [again], let's drag the bastards to the top by their balls, set their asses on fire, and toss them over the side.

In a column that begins by disciplining his correspondent "Normal Straight Male" for homophobic interest in gay male sex on September 11, Savage ends with a similarly violently sexualized representation of (Muslim) men's genitals that frighteningly anticipates the sexual torture at Abu Ghraib prison a few years later and simultaneously reclaims the American history of lynching. Whereas Savage claims that sex has no place on September 11, sex and sexualized language infuse this column. In his disavowal, Savage channels sexuality as a modality for American, gay, masculine rage, thus illustrating profound connections of sexuality and violence to languages of nationalism.

Lesbian columnist Norah Vincent also eroticizes nationalist masculinity in *The Advocate* (a national gay lifestyle magazine). In her essay, "In Praise of Machismo," she declares: "everyone is getting off on this post-terrorism man thing, it seems, except us dykes. Or at least that's what I thought until I caught myself ogling a [male] construction worker the other day" (Vincent 2002). Vincent inserts lesbian desire squarely in to heteronormative, post-9/11 home-front culture: "After September 11, everyone was talking about masculinity, mostly because any heterosexual woman who hadn't previously fetishized firemen now felt compelled to do so, if only out of gratitude." Here, as in Savage's column, erotic desire is present in LGBTQ community commentary through its disavowal—Vincent says she feels grateful, not sexually aroused. Norah Vincent performs a rhetorical contortion to position her own desire for the firemen as asexual, and as a consequence, her fireman fetish is both heteronormative and still homosexual: "the friendly fireman embodies all these things unthreateningly, and that is why we like and even desire him." Unlike the threatening terrorists, firemen can be admired as "a work of art [of] masculine beauty" from an allegedly safe distance. Vincent filters her desire through both her desire *for* a fireman (or construction worker) and her desire to emulate him. This is a queer desire indeed, but one produced through heteronormativity, nationalism, and masculinity.

Masculinity also plays a key role in cultural narratives of United Airlines Flight 93. The flight bound for San Francisco crashed in rural Pennsylvania after its passengers and crew apparently thwarted the hijackers' attempts to make the aircraft the fourth weapon of the attack. Scores of newspaper and magazine articles, books, and films have valorized and eulogized the flight's passengers, and have analyzed and mythologized the significantly unknowable events that took place midflight. Much of this mythology centers on the heroic self-sacrifice of a group of men (almost all the narratives assume that the heroes were the male passengers) who physically overcame the hijackers.[5] Among the eulogies and mythologies, the representations of gay male first-class passenger Mark Bingham present narratives of gay citizenship and heroic masculinity.

Mark Bingham has been memorialized by the gay community through numerous media representations and community accolades. *The Advocate* magazine named him "Person of the Year" for 2001, the gay rugby

league of which he was a founding member named their annual tourna-
ment in his honor, Melissa Etheridge produced a pop song in his honor,
and gay male composer Robert Seely dedicated a choral composition to
him written for the 2002 Gay Games in Chicago. Bingham's name was
invoked in the U.S. Congress when it passed domestic partner legislation
for the District of Columbia.[6] Republican senator John McCain delivered
Bingham's eulogy (Barrett 2002, 92–94). *Advocate* staff writer Jon Barrett's
(2001) cover story on Bingham, and his subsequent book *Hero of Flight 93:
Mark Bingham* (Barrett 2002) must mediate potentially conflicting narrative
trajectories of Bingham as an "American hero" and a "gay role model."
Barrett's rhetoric skillfully positions Bingham as simultaneously entirely,
normatively masculine and also an "authentic" gay man. Barrett asks if
Mark Bingham was a "gay hero, or a hero who was gay?" (Barrett 2002, 7).
In Barrett's biography, the answer is both.

Barrett's account of Bingham's life constructs Mark Bingham as a quintessential American man. Bingham's childhood poverty living with his
single mother, his charismatic rise to fortune, his athleticism, and his gre-
garious personality all contribute to an All-American story of success. His
working-class origins place him beside Noonan and Vincent's fetishized
firemen and construction workers; and his frat-boy social life at UC Berkeley, his reported distaste for effeminate gay men, and his ambivalence
toward aspects of the "gay scene" further locate him within normative
American masculinity rather than gay difference or marginalization. Yet
simultaneously, the terms through which Barrett describes Bingham's
sexual identity place the young hero within an alternative genealogy of
American homosexuality: in the tradition of Walt Whitman, Bingham is a
hypermasculine, not an effeminate, gay man. And his masculine comrade-
love sets the stage for Bingham's heroic acts and his valorization both
among and apart from the married fathers turned heroes on Flight 93.

Barrett positions Bingham as essentially gay and essentially masculine.
Bingham's involvement in the gay male "bear community" and in rugby
are presented as evidence of his masculine, all-Americanness. Barrett
defines "a bear" as "a gay man who is attracted to a beard and perhaps a
little weight....But at the same time being a bear can...represent an idealized friendship between gay men" (68). Homosexuality is narrated as a
site of masculine identification and desire. Rugby also signifies aggressive
masculinity. Mark Bingham's position on his rugby team was a forward,
"the bigger, more aggressive players who are responsible for directing
the forward plays of the game...rugby is a battle of will" (43). Barrett
foreshadows Bingham's assumed role as a leader of the revolt on Flight
93, ascribing to him characteristics of fearlessness, leadership, and brute
strength.

Hero of Flight 93 also constructs a vision of a multicultural America that
includes Bingham's white gay masculinity as a crucial element. A narrative
of benign multiculturalism introduces homosexuality in the biography's

narrative. Barrett constructs Bingham's Chi Psi college fraternity as a locus of tolerance. "[I]t was the diversity of those members [of Chi Psi] that really set the Lodge apart. 'When most people think fraternity,' [one of Bingham's fraternity brothers recounts to Barrett] 'they think of a bunch of guys who are 6-foot-tall, white, and wearing athletic gear. But we had 5-foot-4 Filipino guys, Hispanic guys, black guys and white guys'" (55). Barrett then positions Bingham as a piece of the fraternity's diversity, "A 6-foot-4 white guy who played on an athletic team, Mark had his own way of contributing to the diversity of the house" (55). Here, white, gay masculinity becomes a critical element of American multiculturalism. Barrett implies that Mark Bingham is an American hero in part because he was gay, and a gay hero because he embodied normative masculinity: he "loved sports and wasn't the least bit interested in dressing or acting in an effeminate manner" (55).

Barrett's biography presents Mark Bingham both as a gay hero and as a "hero who just happened to be gay." The author crafts a narrative of depoliticized American diversity through Bingham's youthful masculinity and apparent distaste for certain aspects of urban gay culture (and his embrace of others); this sentimental biography of "a man who fought back on September 11" skillfully places Bingham within both the dominant story of American heroics *and* within liberal LGBT narratives of gay Americans. The linchpin holding together the heteronormative and the homonormative is a certain presentation of white masculinity that can encompass gay men and can hail women from Maureen Dowd to Norah Vincent.

A very different rendering of white masculinity after 9/11 can be found in Leslie Feinberg's 2006 novel, *Drag King Dreams*. *Drag King Dreams* presents solidarity among gendered, sexual, and national outsiders as both the consequence of and the antidote to conservative and neoliberal formations of citizenship. The production of queer and transgender masculine identities in the context of wartime culture depends, in this novel, on structures of national belonging or abjection as much as on debates over gender and sexuality. White queer masculine subjectivities turn on solidarity with men of color but also simultaneously through plots that necessitate the disappearances of South Asian and Arab American men.

Drag King Dreams charts the post-9/11 life of its first-person narrator and gender indeterminate protagonist, Max.[7] Max transforms from an individual defensive street fighter to a participant in collective activist struggle; hir journey through the novel is one of increasing political action and increasing solidarity with hir Muslim neighbors. *Drag King Dreams* weaves together street violence and state violence against queers, transpeople, Arabs, South Asians, undocumented residents, and war resisters. Feinberg invites readers to understand violence against queers as parallel and intersecting with long American histories of racial violence and newer iterations of state-sponsored and home-front hostilities, detainments, and discipline.[8] Through this narrative argument for solidarity, the gendered constructions of Feinberg's characters are produced as much through their relationships to a post-9/11 state as they are through other more familiar discourses of gender, such as gay liberation or transsexual identity.

Feinberg refashions the meaning of Manhattan as a post-9/11 "ground zero": for *Drag King Dreams*, September 11 marks both rupture and continuity for sexual, gendered, and racial outsiders in the United States. Feinberg makes clear that the novel's economically marginal and gender-queer characters had been struggling well before the autumn of 2001. Yet the post-9/11 police state in New York City brings about new regimes of power and heightens the consequences of existing ones.

The most direct link between queer masculinity and post-9/11 state repression in the novel is represented in the arrest of Thor, an FTM (female-to-male) antiwar activist. Thor is arrested for a gender transgression—for using the "wrong" bathroom—at a protest against the detention of Muslim men after 9/11. "He left the protest at the detention center alone to go to the bathroom. The cops followed him and busted him in the john" (201). Not only is Thor's arrest a vivid reminder of the continual cultural and state violence against trans people, but the arrest for gender transgression occurs at a protest in support of disappeared Muslim men. As Thor's supporters from a rainbow of political and cultural communities amass outside the police station where he is held, the chant comes from the crowd, "Stop the War! Free Thor!" For Feinberg's novel, both Muslim men and transmen should have the ability to function freely in civil society, but both Muslim men and transmen are denied that right. *Drag King Dreams* insists that queer rights are workers' rights, are immigrant rights, as are the rights for safety from racial, sexual, or gendered violence. Unlike his Muslim comrades who remain incarcerated, Thor is released from jail because of the savvy negotiations of his civil rights lawyer and the massive crowd of supporters who demand his release outside the police station. The novel constructs a clear binary system of oppressed and oppressor: resistance must come through collective struggle, even though such resistance may produce violence (such as Thor's beating at the hands of the police). Thor's arrest registers his threat to the state both as an antiwar activist and as a genderqueer. "Stop the War and Free Thor!" produces Thor's masculine transgender subjectivity through conditions of cultural injustice and his individual gender transition.

The novel's protagonist, Max, is a Jewish "old school butch" whose gender identity is fundamentally masculine, but who (like the novelist hirself) is not a transsexual. Jewish Max models a form of Semitic alliance with hir Muslim neighbors, Mohammed and Hatem, and performs hir queer masculinity through masculine "cousinly" solidarity with heterosexual and normatively gendered Muslim men. Max's gender is a point of difference between hirself and hir Muslim neighbors, but it is also a point of narrative connection.

Mohammad leans forward and says to Heshie, "You are always welcome at my store. Anytime. Your friend here, she...he is like my own family."

Mohammad looks chagrined at having stumbled on my pronoun. I am taken aback. What am I surprised about? That he knows I'm queer? Who doesn't?...Mohammad places his hand on my elbow,..."We are cousins."...I will never be a stranger in Egypt. (266)

Whether discussing politics, drinking coffee together, or confronting neighborhood injustices, Mohammad and Max are drawn together homosocially through a common, if tricky, shared masculinity (there are no female Muslim characters in this novel) and through their shared biblical histories. As Mohammad confers kinship upon Max, their shared vulnerable masculinities become a powerful ingredient for cross-cultural, cross-racial, and cross-religious alliance.

Feinberg's protagonist also seeks alliances with a group of *hijra* whom ze encounters in Manhattan before 9/11. Yet this alliance is both seductive and troubled. Max not only forges alliances with his Middle Eastern neighbors and genderqueer comrades, but ze also seeks connections among differently gendered people across history and culture in the shared geography of lower Manhattan. In an early section of the novel, Max recalls the previous year when ze stumbled into a Navratri celebration in "Little India":

I wanted so much to step into this circle, to become part of it, but this was not my dance.

I watched women dancing differently than men; some old women dancing differently than some young. . . .

And then I noticed one person who did not dance like the women or the men....I saw another person, dressed in a flowing sari not unlike those worn by women standing nearby, who I would have guessed was born male-bodied.

I wanted to create a path across the street...but what would I say? In what language? What made me feel connected to them?...There's so much I don't know. Are they sacred in their culture, while I am profane in mine?...Once, long ago we were all honored. Perhaps now what we share is the almost forgotten memory of ancient songs. (32–33)

Feinberg's text presents awareness of cultural difference and a desire for a transcultural and transhistorical connection among differently gendered people. On the one hand, Max is aware that "this was not my dance" and that ze does not have any unmediated claim to kinship with the *hijra* whom ze sees at the celebration. On the other hand, the narrative does forge a connection between genderqueer Max and the *hijra*: they share "memory of ancient songs" from which they have both emerged as others within their respective cultures. Unlike Mohammed's historical assertion that he and Max are "cousins," Max's unspoken affinity with the unnamed *hijra* serves not to forge a history of resistance, or to enable direct homosocial connections, but to produce a mythic common origin for differently gendered people across history and culture.

Although the novel invites alliances between U.S.-born LGBTQ people and men of Arab and South Asian descent who are getting caught in the post-9/11 "dragnet" (175) of state repression, genderqueer identity does not automatically produce oppositional subjects in the novel. Feinberg undercuts any automatic alliances among genderqueers through the minor characters. "Weasel"—another FTM character committed to performing white masculinity—functions as an example of class warfare within the ranks of transmen and genderqueers. When Max refuses to listen to Weasel's racist joke, Weasel counters, "I don't know why you have it in for me, bro. What I'd ever do to you? We're all in this together. We're up against The Man." Feinberg refuses a politics of identification based solely on gender or sexual orientation as Max replies, "You're a trust fund baby from Connecticut. Your family owns half this island. You *are* The Man...I'm not your brother....Get the hell out of my sight" (267–68). Weasel's class status and his racism—as he leaves the bar he shouts "You'll be sorry, you Jew bastard!" (269)—place him outside the sphere of solidarity and opposition. Though Feinberg's novel relies on narratives of transcultural and transhistorical connections among differently gendered people, and though the novel explicitly calls for coalition and solidarity, the figure of Weasel illustrates the limits of what can appear to be an all-inclusive politics: characters who work to understand cultural difference are embraced; racism and class privilege stand outside the circle of mutual support and cross-community connection.

The novel concludes in a jail cell: Max and hir friends have been arrested following the massive antiwar, anti-detention protest. As the incarcerated comrades plot collective struggle in their jail cell, they are each called out by prison guards. Each of Feinberg's genderqueer characters is hailed by their given name—a discursive gendered violence that will either usher in or stand in for police brutality. The novel ends with an ambivalent tone of hope and triumph—though a heterosexual Muslim ally, Hatem, remains incarcerated; another friend, Netaji, a Hindu cabdriver, has been deported; and Max's chosen family continues to face state violence, Max has found hir way back to collective struggle and away from individual alienation.

Gender identities are produced in direct opposition to the repressive state apparatus in this final scene. The reader knows Thor both is and is not "Carol Finster," Ruby both is and is not "Tyrone Lanier," and Max both is and is not "Maxine Rabinowitz" as the characters are called from the collective jail cell by their legal names (300–302). Here state violence *is* gendered violence. *Drag King Dreams* produces trans and queer identities in explicit opposition to the state, but the novel just as surely produces such identities through engagement with state power and home-front nationalism. Max's masculine gender identity is produced not just through hir erotic communications with the "old school femme" he meets online, but just as forcefully through hir desire for transcultural connection to the *hijra* in Little India and through his masculine bonding across religious lines with hir Semitic "cousins" Mohammed and Hatem. Home-front nationalism, both its repressive effects and its representational politics, delineate Feinberg's production of queer masculinities as a struggle of the abject against the powerful: the work of "the people who don't have papers, don't have passbooks" (224) to reside in national or gendered safety, against the police, the government, and the "trust-fund babies from Connecticut" who support them.

Feinberg's novel works to produce collective struggle as the necessary response to oppressive state and ideological violence. Feinberg's Max must negotiate hir gender and sexual identity in *Drag King Dreams*, but this negotiation is conducted through Max's relation to a national culture and a state apparatus hostile not only to gender and sexual transgression but in the midst of nationalist, racial, and geopolitical violence. Max comes into hir own subjectivity through solidarity and histories that align Jews with Muslims, transmen with drag queens and gay men, and activists with street fighters. Gender identity and sexual identity are produced through solidarity and resistance to state power in this home-front novel. Without the backdrop of war and the omnipresence of state repression, Max would remain in sexual and gendered isolation, in "no man's land" rather than in struggle and solidarity.

Queer responses to the cultural moment of 9/11 reflect broader cultural changes and continuities. While some LGBTQ pundits sought refuge in narratives of national belonging, others, such as novelist Leslie Feinberg, strove to produce a queer subject through resistance to state power and though solidarity among gendered, national, and sexual outsiders. On the one hand, articles in *The Advocate* do not differ much from those in the *New York Times:* nationalist boundaries are shored up, racial and gendered politics function in the service of state interests, and resistance to metanarrative of a national family become unthinkable or abject. To assume that LGBTQ speakers stand outside of the effects of national culture is to be naive at best. On the other hand, such texts illustrate the ways in which even explicitly countercultural or oppositional texts are dependent on the narratives they might seek to undermine. By examining a suite of LGBTQ textual responses to post-9/11 American national culture, I hope to suggest ways in which sexual and gender identities both constitute heteronormative national culture and the ways in which nationalist culture delineates even oppositional sexual and gendered identities and communities. Through this understanding, the ideological consequences of subcultural images of "inclusion" or "diversity" as well as broader civic debates over "gays in the military" or the representational power of sexualized images from Abu Ghraib can be seen as parts of ongoing contests over power, identity, and national belonging.

NOTES

1. As well as Noonan and Dowd, see Patricia Leigh Brown (2001).

2. Terminology indicating sexual desires and sexual orientations carries a range of meanings. For the purposes of this chapter, I try to follow the terms of the authors under discussion when sensible. When writing in my own voice, I use the (somewhat bulky, but descriptive) acronym "LGBTQ" to indicate a coalition of lesbian, gay, bisexual, transgender/transsexual, and queer concerns. "Queer" generally indicates an oppositional stance (which may or may not encompass transgender/transexual issues), as opposed to the more assimilationist or mainstream "gay" or "gay and lesbian." These usages are partial and contingent.

3. See, for example, the title of Sheehan's book: *Not One More Mother's Child* (2005).

4. See chapter Five, "Transnational America: Race and Gender after 9/11," Grewal (2005).

5. Another component of the gendered story concerns the flight attendants (coded female) who boiled water to pour on the hijackers.

6. On September 26, 2001, Representative Bill Delahunt (D-MA) said to those opposing the legislation, "One of the four passengers who appear to have thwarted the hijackers of United Flight 93 was a gay man, a 31-year old rugby star from San Francisco named Mark Bingham. Her was a hero...and [is] this how we thank him for his heroism" (Clymer 2001).

7. Feinberg, and other advocates of gender pluralism and transgender visibility, uses the pronouns "ze" and "hir" in lieu of she/he or him/her for individuals whose gender does not fall into the categories male or female. I am following Feinberg's own usage for hirself and for the characters in *Drag King Dreams*, some of whom are referred to as he or she, and others as ze. However, in the first-person narrative of the novel, the protagonist, Max, is never referred to by a third-person pronoun—my use of "ze" for Max is my own best guess.

8. For a critique of racial/sexual analogies, see Halley (2000).

Conclusion: The Interrelationship between Gender, War, and Militarism

Laura Sjoberg and Sandra Via

The wealth and diversity of the theoretical and empirical contributions of each chapter in this collection on gender, war, and militarism cannot possibly be covered succinctly in one conclusory chapter. The contributions to this volume tell us about the struggle for post-conflict reintegration for girls associated with the fighting forces in Sierra Leone alongside the gendered nature of neoliberal globalization that beget such companies as Blackwater as the militaries of the future. Each author summarizes what her individual studies tell us about gender, war, and militarism; perhaps our efforts in the conclusion are best spent exploring what the chapters in this book tell us together.

Here, we argue that the sum of these chapters is more than the parts. These chapters offer unique, in-depth looks at many situations surrounding gender, war, and militarism, but their diversity says as much as their depth. Viewed together, these explorations show gender, war, and militarism as conceptually and interdependent, empirically international, intrinsically intersectional, and in need of academically interdisciplinary analysis.

THE CONCEPTUAL INTERDEPENDENCE OF GENDER, WAR, AND MILITARISM

In the introduction, we promised that the feminist approaches in this volume would look at two interconnected issues in the complex matrix of gender, war, and militarism: the impacts of war and militarism on people (especially but not limited to women) and the gendered construction of war and militarism, linked to systems of power and inequality based on race, class, nation, and so on.

A number of the chapters in this volume looked at the effects of militarism on women. Gwyn Kirk reports that women were profoundly dispropor- tionately affected by the war in El Salvador. She describes the tribulations of women who, as heads of 51 percent of Salvadoran households, struggled to make ends meet as their homes often sat in the middle of territory being contested by gunfire. Kirk explains that many women "suffered rape, abuse, and torture by government forces and death squads." As Kirk describes, however, the overwhelming impact of the conflict on women's daily lives did not end with the cease-fire and the end of the event of the war. Instead, asking "when did the war end?" Kirk explores the gender-specific chal- lenges of rebuilding political organization and social life in El Salvador.

Susan Shepler's chapter also shows gender-based impacts of war and militarism. She explains that, "by some estimates, girls make up a third of the population of children abducted by rebel groups in Sierra Leone." Although Shepler does not focus on girls' gender-specific experiences *as* captives,[1] she explores girls' gender-specific challenges in reintegration to their societies after they had been freed by their military captors. As She- pler explains, women and girls are often an expressed priority in United Nations documentation about the reconstruction programs, but in real- ity, "as the girl combatants moved into the interim care centers and the reintegration phase, there was a lack of attention to the need for separate and gender-specific services for girls." Shepler notes that, while "the prob- lems of war-affected girls are [often] different from the problems of war- affected boys, and yet reintegration programs tend to be one-size-fits all, to the detriment of girls."

In addition to studying the disproportionate impacts of war and milita- rism on women, the chapters in this book explore the gendered construc- tion of war and militarism. Laura Sjoberg's chapter uses four well-known hero stories of U.S. soldiers in the "war on terror" to read the gendered desires and self-identifications of the American empire as "command- ing unconditional loyalty, that is, mighty, fair and just, likable, potent, and honorable." She demonstrates that these traits are projected through hypergendered ideal typical stories that are often unrepresentative of the people they are told of or the empire they represent. Still, these stories show that gender is key to American discourses of militaristic honor, with- out which the empire would be left without a justification for its wars.

Denise Horn's chapter also looks at how American militarism is tied to gendered images of American citizens. Noting that "the process of nation- alistic support is inextricably linked with the process of militarization, and women play an integral role within this process," Horn looks at the U.S. military's gender-based expectations of soldiers, their wives, and their families as part of a system to procure soldier loyalty. Horn points out a clear link between national interest and family readiness in U.S. military discourses, which imply that the entire system of militarism (or, in the military's terms, "national security") is dependent on the cooperation of women on the "homefront." Horn's study identifies the military family as a site of the intersection of gender, war, and militarism as well as foreign policy and welfare policy—and shows the intricate links between the "homefront" and the "warfront" where gender roles support and construct military loyalty and, therefore, military success.

Sandra Via's chapter focuses on the links between globalization, hegemonic masculinity, and militarism. Complicating feminist analyses that critique the public/private dichotomy in social and political life, Via frames the rise of private military corporations (PMCs) as a victory for the private sector over the public sector, which has not benefited women, who are traditionally associated with the private sector, but instead has masculinized the private sector while feminizing and disempowering the public sector. This shift, Via contends, is producing a new militarized masculinity in the era of PMCs—that of a hypermasculinized private army. This private army, in competition with the public army, which now allows women and gays and does women's work (peacekeeping), shows that gender is not only an essential component of militarism but also a contested space *within* militarism.

The chapters in this volume together show that gender constructs war and militarism, which in turn construct gender—the concepts are interdependent, inseparable, and mutually constitutive. Militarism constitutes women and men's individual lives, which constitute militarism as a gendered concept, cycled through and affected by changes in wars and changes in gender relations but ultimately resilient.[2]

THE INTERNATIONAL NATURE OF GENDER, WAR, AND MILITARISM

Cynthia Enloe (1989) famously taught us that "the personal is international, and the international is personal." If anything, the chapters in this volume highlight that point. Denise Horn and Laura Sjoberg's chapters demonstrate that individual identities are not only sometimes appropriated to fuel a war effort, but control and appropriation of individual women and men's lives through gendered narratives is often a linchpin of war making. Charli Carpenter's chapter shows that even babies, as yet incapable of communicating for themselves, can become the site of highly contested political struggle at the international level.

We learn from these chapters that absolutely distinguishing between the personal, national, and international level of war and militarism lacks conceptual and empirical rigor at best. Sandra Via's chapter links states, substate corporate actors, and individuals to the global (gendered) militaristic culture, and Stephanie Anderson's chapter demonstrates that individual identity, national identity, and international identity can be interwoven.

Still, though it would be an error to say that gender, war, and militarism are related only or mostly at one level of analysis or another, it is also important to note that the chapters here also demonstrate that the personal, national, and international are not just one big conceptual blur. After all, almost every chapter in this collection shows the importance of nationalist fervor in linking gender and militarism. In addition, two chapters in particular show that competitive relations *between states* are gendered and affect individual and national constructions of ideal-typical gendered identity.

Stephanie Anderson's chapter demonstrates the international nature of the links between gender, war, and militarism as it explains the European Union's (EU) militarization as a reaction to gendered perceptions of its relationship with the United States. She explains that "the EU, with its focus on economics, cooperation, and communication, has appeared helpless on the world stage where force was needed. As a result, the EU is depicted as the woman in its relationship with the United States." This (perceived or actual) feminization of the EU, Anderson contends, has provided an inspiration for the militarization of the EU in the form of the European Security and Defense Policy. She argues that the EU is trying to look tough and project an image in line with idealized militarized masculinities in competition with the United States.

Charli Carpenter's chapter shows a different angle of the international nature of the relationship between gender, war, and militarism. She explains that stories of Bosnian war babies "played a role in creating the impression that Bosnia-Herzegovina was a land beyond the pale, apart from civilized Europe" in a discourse she identifies as neo-imperial humanitarianism. She demonstrates that the gendered narratives about war babies in Bosnia in the global print media were in service of outsiders' desire to consume the conflict in a certain way, where "stereotypes helped to construct a notion of Bosnia as both in the heart of Europe and culturally foreign and backward, a frame that helped Western European bystanders both indulge their sense of moral concern while remaining detached from the conflict as a European war." Here, inter-European relations were inscribed on and transcribed by babies' bodies.

In short, the combination of the chapters in this volume demonstrates that we cannot look at individuals, states, and interstate relations as separable levels of analysis where any one is seen as having an advantage in explaining the relationships between gender, war, and militarism. In fact, it is impossible to see these levels as anything but interdependent—the personal is national is international, and vice versa. Still, it is important to note that these chapters also show that it is not just individuals, substate groups, and states that are entrenched in gendered militarism but also interstate relations and the international system itself, which do not disappear because we analyze the other parts of the global political story at the same time.

AN INTERSECTIONAL VIEW OF GENDER, WAR, AND MILITARISM

If these chapters together teach us anything, it is that gender, war, and militarism, though conceptually interdependent, do not exist in a vacuum. Instead, as we argued briefly in the introduction, they are related in a world where there are also racial, national, cultural, religious, and class dynamics that infiltrate and affect global politics from everyday lives to international structures.

Ronni Alexander demonstrates the intersection between cultural governance, indigenization, gender, and militarization in the Bougainville crisis, explaining that "the pyramid of colonization privileged white over non-white, male over female, and some ethnicities over others, generally ensuring white men secure a spot on the top and relegating indigenous women to the bottom." Alexander effectively links gender hierarchy to other hierarchies among Pacific Island societies and argues that militarism is a permissive and necessary condition of these hierarchical social relations.

Tami Jacoby tells a different story about the relationship between identities in Israeli society. She explains the tension around Israeli women's "right to fight" in terms of identity struggles about gender and nationalism. As Jacoby observes, some Israeli women see the right to fight as a women's rights issue, but others see the right to abstain from fighting as a feminist issue. Complicating the matter further are those women who desire the right to fight not for gender equality but for service to the cause of Israeli nationalism, in discursive competition with those women who see it as a feminist imperative not to become involved in the (gendered) Israeli nationalistic project.

A third picture of the intersection between gender, war, and militarism and other political identities can be found in the description of rape in the ethnocidal conflicts in the Nuba Mountains and Darfur provided by Sondra Hale. Hale's description shows a complicated intersection of gendered and raced stereotypes at many levels of these conflicts. On the surface level, Hale demonstrates that an oversimplified and media-sensationalized story of the Sudanese civil war as a conflict between "Arabs" and "Africans" at once misrepresents the conflict and gives belligerents unifying identities to deploy. Hale demonstrates that these and deeper, more complicated ethnic tensions are constantly inscribed on women's bodies through the perpetration of genocidal rape—where a rape is a marker of cultural difference, a (physical and symbolic) erasure of cultural difference, and part of a campaign of cultural destruction. If each rape holds those meanings, the rapes as a collective carry both culturally destructive and gender subordinating messages that are at once distinct and inseparable.

Spike Peterson's theoretical approach helps us see the linkages between race, class, gender, culture, war, and militarism. Peterson argues that the subordinated are cast as feminine, devalorizing "not only the empirical gender category of women, but also sexually, racially, culturally, and economically marginalized men." The feminization of those marginalized in global politics, Peterson tells us, "produces even as it obscures vast inequalities of power, authority, and resource distribution." In war and militarism, she describes intersectionality appearing in othering narratives about the enemies of European imperialism and in the techno-war paradigm of the contemporary U.S. military. Peterson argues that it is not only gender, race, and culture that intersect to help us find feminization in global politics but also masculinism, militarism, and imperialism.

The empirical and theoretical accounts of gender, war, and militarism overlying race, culture, religion, economics, nationalism, and other forces of social power in global politics suggest two conclusions about intersectionality. First, a gender lens looking at war and militarism finds not only gender but also the intersection of gender with these other identities in personal and global politics. Second, if we see these intersections not as paths crossing coincidentally in the wind, but instead as structural factors in global social and political life, we see the conceptual interdependence of gender, war, and militarism broadens to include other, distinguishable but inseparable, sites of domination and subordination in global politics on the basis of identity.

THE INTERDISCIPLINARY STUDY OF GENDER, WAR, AND MILITARISM

Coming to this project as political scientists, we as editors were initially interested in the political dimensions of the relationship between gender, war, and militarism. The lesson we have taken away from the contributions to this volume is the value-add of interdisciplinary approaches to questions previously considered disciplinary, like the question of gender, war, and militarism.[3]

The cultural studies approach Deborah Cohler uses to discuss how different U.S. gay media grappled with and shaped the discursive shifts in U.S. mass culture after 9/11 provides a unique view of the solidification of a heteronormative American national family as a monolithic unit through the mourning, blame, and revenge stages of the reaction to the September 2001 terrorist attacks. By analyzing queer interactions with the hetero culture of an America that queer citizens were at once inside and outside, Cohler gives substantial insights not only into her own empirical material on gay cultural responses but also into the material presented in the other chapters in the volume. Cohler's analysis demonstrates the partial, hybrid, tense, and fragile fault lines of cultural inclusion and exclusion, and how so many of those fault lines hold or break on the basis of gender-based perceptions. This complex view of cultural construction can be used to read many of the empirical situations presented in other areas of the book.

Sigal Ben-Porath's philosophical approach shows another contribution of interdisciplinary analysis. Rather than starting at the women involved in war and militarism, like many political scientists or anthropologists, she asks what philosophical insights can tell us about the relationship between gender, war, and militarism at the conceptual level, and what that in turn can tell us about forgiveness in international conflict. Her chapter no less addresses the themes of this volume because it approaches them from a philosophical perspective; instead, it helps us see that many of the questions the authors of this volume ask can be seen as bidirectional. In the introduction to this volume, we frame gender as a set of characteristics expected of people based on their perceived membership in sex classes. We were implying that the assumed naturalness of those values needed to be questioned, critiqued, and revised. Sigal Ben-Porath's chapter, however, addresses similar issues from a different direction, asking what forgiveness between international actors would look like if it involved more values that have been traditionally associated with femininity (and therefore discredited) in international politics. This volume barely scratches the surface of that theme, but it would be an excellent point of departure for future research—what would an approach to questions of war and militarism look like that explicitly prized values traditionally associated with femininity?

The rich interdisciplinary contributions of these chapters are also visible when we look at the approaches to wartime rape in the chapters by Sondra Hale (an anthropologist) and Liz Kelly (a sociologist also considering issues of law and legal studies). Sondra Hale's account of genocidal rape in the Sudanese civil war provides evidence from years of field research and intricate ethnographic observation to argue that these rapes are more than genocide and more than gender subordination—they are a complex, symbolic intersectional oppression on the basis of race and culture. Liz Kelly's account of sexual violence as a continuum provides a wide sampling of statistical and narrative evidence of sexual violence across cultures, contexts, and conflicts to argue that it is legally and conceptually better not to distinguish between (normal) rape and wartime rape if we hope to redress gender subordination. In conversation, the two approaches describe sexual violence and war and peace as continua, rather than distinct and separable concepts, while noting the crucial role culture plays in inscribing gender in conflict and the intersectional nature of gender subordination and sexual violence. They provide different evidence, different methods, and different analytical frameworks that together tell us more than one perspective could hope to.

Even feminist approaches from different academic disciplines ask different questions of the relationship between gender, war, and militarism, and use different methods to address those questions. These different scholarly languages, however, are anything but a liability. Instead, after putting together this collection of chapters, we are convinced that interdisciplinary conversation is not only useful for analyzing the concepts that this volume addresses but essential to produce the most rigorous analysis of global politics that we can. Hayward Alker (1996) once called international studies an "inter-discipline," to us, these chapters prove that if he was not correct, he should have been. The analyses in this collection are richer for seeing gender, war, and militarism through political science, economics, philosophy, law, anthropology, sociology, and cultural studies than they would be if they spoke a single disciplinary language.

GENDER, WAR, AND MILITARISM: FEMINIST PERSPECTIVES LOOK FORWARD

As wars change and gender relations change, the gendered discourses and practices of wars and militarisms change as well. It is important for those of us who self-identify as feminist scholars to be vigilant in watching the changes in gendered warfare, rather than, like some, assuming that advances like women's participation in sexual violence in war mean that women now face war and militarism on an equal playing field with men. If the chapters in this book tell us anything, they tell us that nothing could be further from the truth almost a decade into the 21st century. Instead, gender is still a linchpin of war justification, a key concept in nationalism, a central target in genocide, and a crucially neglected factor in postwar reconstruction and reconciliation. Women are still fighting for equal participation in wars with gendered structures and gendered impacts. Although some women are soldiers, most women are civilians who suffer physically, economically, socially, and psychologically from war making and war fighting. Further, even women who fight in wars sometimes do so at great risk to themselves (Hillman 2009), or perhaps against their will.[4] Though people who theorize about and advocate for the advancement of women in and the degendering of structures of global politics have much to celebrate, it is crucial to remember that at the intersection of gender, war, and militarism we find not just vestiges of gender discrimination but pervasive feminization on the basis of gender, race, class, nationality, religion, and other "otherings" in global politics.

NOTES

1. See MacKenzie (2009).

2. Borrowing a page from the realist textbook, perhaps we could propose that the conceptual interdependence of gender, war, and militarism is pervasive in the face of changes *within* the system of gender subordination in international politics because the system itself actually has not changed.

3. Which, before this project, Laura Sjoberg (at least) would have identified as the problem of gender and international security or gender and global security in the disciplinary terms of the international relations and security studies subdisciplines of political science.

4. See chapter 7, "Post-war Trajectories for Girls Associated with Fighting Forces in Sierra Leone," by Susan Shepler.

References

Abdalla, A., S. Hussein, and S. Shepler. 2002. "Human Rights in Sierra Leone." *A Research Report to Search for Common Ground.* Washington, D.C.: Search for Common Ground.

Abdullah, I. 2002. "Youth Culture and Rebellion: Understanding Sierra Leone's Wasted Decade." *Critical Arts* 16 (2): 19–37.

Abdullah, I., Y. Bangura, C. Blake, L. Gberie, L. Johnson, K. Kallon, S. Kemokai, P. K. Muana, I. Rashid, and A. Zack-Williams. 1997. "Lumpen Youth Culture and Political Violence: Sierra Leoneans Debate the RUF and the Civil War." *Africa Development* 22 (3/4): 171–216.

Ackerly, Brooke A. 2000. *Political Theory and Feminist Social Criticism.* Contemporary Political Theory. Cambridge: Cambridge University Press.

Addis, Elisabetta, Valeria E. Russo, and Loranza Sebesta. 1994. *Women Soldiers: Images and Realities.* New York: St. Martin's Press.

Adorno, Theodor W. 1986. "What Does Coming to Terms with the Past Mean?" trans. Timothy Bahti and Geoffrey Hartman. *Bitburg in Moral and Political Perspective*, ed. Geoffrey Hartman. Bloomington: Indiana University Press.

African Rights. 1995. *Facing Genocide: The Nuba of Sudan.* New York: African Rights.

Aidi, Hishaam D. 2005. "Slavery, Genocide and the Politics of Outrage: Understanding the New Racial Olympics," *Middle East Report* 234: 40–56.

Albano, Sondra. 1994. "Military Recognition of Family Concerns: Revolutionary War to 1993." *Armed Forces and Society* (Winter): 283–302.

Alexander, Michael, and Timothy Garden. 2001. "The Arithmetic of Defence Policy." *International Affairs* 77 (3): 509–29.

Alison, Miranda. 2009. *Women and Political Violence: Female Combatants in Ethno-National Conflict.* London: Routledge.

Alker, Hayward. 1996. *Rediscoveries and Reformulations.* Cambridge: Cambridge University Press.

Allen, Amy. 2008. *The Politics of Our Selves: Power, Autonomy, and Gender in Contemporary Critical Theory.* New York: Columbia University Press.

Allen, Beverly. 1996. *Rape Warfare: The Hidden Genocide in Bosnia-Herzegovina.* Minneapolis: University of Minnesota Press.

Allen, David. 2003. "Okinawans Join Global Anti-War Protests." *Stars and Stripes* (January 19). Available at: http://www.stripes.com/article.asp?section=123&article=12589. Accessed 29 April 2010.

Alt, Betty Sowers, and Bonnie Domrose Stone. 1991. *Campfollowing: A History of the Military Wife.* New York: Praeger Publishing.

Alvarez, Lizette, and Deborah Sontag. 2008. "When Strains on Military Families become Deadly." *New York Times* (February 15).

"America's Deputy Sheriff." 2003. *The Financial Times* (June 21): 6.

Amnesty International. 1999. *Sri Lanka: Torture in Custody.* Available at: www.amnestyusa.org/countries/sri_lanka/reports.do. Accessed 14 May 2010.

Amnesty International. 2003. *Monument to Memory and Truth.* Available at: http://translate.google.com/translate?hl=en&sl=es&u=http://web.amnesty.org/library/index/. Accessed 14 October 2007.

Amnesty International. 2004. "Darfur: Rape as a Weapon of War: Sexual Violence and Its Consequences." *Al Index: AFR 54/076/2004:* 9. Available at: http://www.amnesty.org/en/library/asset/AFR54/076/2004/en/f66115ea-d5b4–11dd-bb24–1fb85fe8fa05/afr540762004en.pdf. Accessed 24 April 2007.

Amnesty International. 2005. *Sexual Assault Research.* London: Amnesty International.

Anderson, Benedict. 1983. *Imagined Communities: Reflections of the Origin and Spread of Nationalism.* New York: Verso.

Andric-Ruzicic, Duska. 2003. "War Rape and the Political Manipulation of Survivors." In *Feminists Under Fire: Exchanges Across War Zones,* ed. Wenona Giles, Malathi de Alwis, Edith Klein, Kuluka Siva, and Maja Korac. Toronto: Between the Lines Press.

"Anglos Spearhead Anti-Mordechai Demo." 2001. *Haaretz special for the on-line edition* (May 11). Available at: http://www2.haaretz.co.il/special/mordechai-e/a/363653.asp. Accessed 13 May 2002.

Anonymous. 2005. *A Woman in Berlin: Diary 20 April 1945 to 22 June 1945.* London: Virago.

Arendt, Hannah. 1998. *The Human Condition.* Chicago: University of Chicago Press.

Auerbach, Yehudith and Yaeli Bloch-Elkon. 2005. "Media Framing and Foreign Policy: The Elite Press vis-a-vis US Policy in Bosnia." In *Journal of Peace Research,* 42 (1): 83–99.

Bah, K. A. 1997. *Rural Women and Girls in the War in Sierra Leone.* Occasional Paper. London: Conciliation Resources.

Bahr, Egon. 2002. "Europa muss erwachsen werden." *Die Welt* (April 6).

Baker, Peter. 2005. "Soldier Killed in Iraq Gets Medal of Honor." *Washington Post* (April 5): A01.

Baldi, G., and M. MacKenzie. 2007. "Silent Identities: Children Born of War in Sierra Leone." In *Born of War: Protecting Children of Sexual Violence Survivors in Conflict Zones,* ed. R. C. Carpenter, 78–93. Bloomfield, Conn.: Kumarian Press.

Banks, Marcus, and Monica Wolfe Murray. 1999. "Ethnicity and Reports of the 1992–1995 Bosnian Conflict." In *The Media of Conflict,* ed.Tim Allen and Jean Seaton. London: Zed Books.

Barnes, L. P. 2002. "Forgiveness, the Moral Law and Education: A Reply to Patricia White." *Journal of Philosophy of Education* 36: 519–34.

Barrett, John. 2002. *Hero of Flight 93: Mark Bingham.* Los Angeles: Advocate Books.

Barroso, José Manuel. 2005. Speaking Notes at the Press Conference, "European Parliament: Europe 2010: A Partnership for European renewal. Prosperity, Solidarity and Security" at the European Parliament, 17.30, Brussels, January 26, SPEECH/05/44.

Barsalou, Judy. 2005. *Trauma and Transitional Justice in Divided Societies.* Special report no. 135. Washington, D.C.: United States Institute for Peace.

Barton, Clara. 1898. *The Red Cross in Peace and War.* Washington, D.C.: American Historical Press.

Barton, Fiona. 1994. "The Bosnia Rape Baby Who Puts the World to Shame." *Mail on Sunday, London* (May 1): 16.

Bastick, Megan, Karin Grimm, and Rahel Kunz. 2007. *Sexual Violence in Armed Conflict: Global Overview and Implications for the Security Sector.* Geneva: Geneva Centre for the Democratic Control of Armed Forces.

BBC News. 2005. "US Troops to Remain in Europe" (February 23). Available at: http://news.bbc.co.uk/2/hi/americas/4292269.stm. Accessed 14 April 2010.

BBC News. 2008a. "Putin Vows 'Arms Race' Response" (February 8). Available at: http://news.bbc.co.uk/2/hi/7234817.stm. Accessed 29 April 2010.

BBC News. 2008b. "Australia Fears Arms Race" (September 10). Available at: http://news.bbc.co.uk/1/hi/world/asia-pacific/7607575.stm.

Bechdel, Alison. 2003. *Dykes and Sundry Other Carbon-Based Life-Forms to Watch Out For.* Los Angeles: Alyson Publications.

Bechdel, Alison. 2006. *Fun Home: A Family Tragicomic.* New York: Houghton Mifflin.

Becirbasic, Belma, and Dzenana Secic. 2002. *Invisible Casualties of War.* London: Institute for War and Peace Reporting. Available at: http://www.iwpr.net/index.pl?archive/bcr3/bcr3_200211_383_4_eng.txt. Accessed 18 July 2006.

Beck, Birgit. 2002. "Rape: The Military Trials of Sexual Crimes Committed by Soldiers in the Wehrmach, 1939–1944." In *Home/Front: The Military, War and Gender in 20th Century Germany,* ed. Karen Hagerman and Stefanie Schuler-Springorum. New York: Berg.

Bedont, Barbara, and Katherine Hall-Martinez. 1999. "Ending Impunity for Gender Crimes under the International Criminal Court." *Brown Journal of World Affairs* 65.

Beevor, Antony. 2002. *The Fall of Berlin 1945.* New York: Penguin.

Bejarano, Cynthia. 2002. "Las Super Madres De Latino America: Transforming Motherhood by Challenging Violence in Mexico, Argentina, and El Salvador." *Frontiers: A Journal of Women's Studies* 23: 126–50.

Bernardi, Claudia. 2006. "School of Art and Open Studio, Perquin, El Salvador." Available at: http://www.sancarlosfoundation.org/index.asp?Type=B_EV&SEC={F84650A5-8B15-4013-B95D-8387E27E1DF3}&DE=.

Berstein, Richard. 2005. "Europe Is Still Europe." *New York Times* (June 7). Available at: http://www.nytimes.com/2005/06/07/international/europe/07europe.html. Accessed 15 April 2010.

Bevacqua, M. 2000. *Rape on the Public Agenda: Feminism and the Politics of Sexual Assault.* Boston, Mass.: Northeastern University Press.

Beyer, Lisa. 2001. "War on Harassment: Israel Cracks Down on Sexual Harassment within its Army." *Time Europe* (July 3): 25.

Bickler, Colin, Anthony Borden, Yigal Chazan, Alan Davis, Stephen Jukes, John MacLeod, Andrew Stroehlein, Stacy Sullivan, John Vultee, and John West.

2004. *Reporting for Change: A Handbook for Local Journalists in Crisis Areas.* Washington, D.C.: Institute of War and Peace Reporting.

Binford, Leigh. 2004. "Peasants, Catechists, Revolutionaries: Organic Intellectuals in the Salvadorean Revolution, 1980–1992." In *Landscapes of Struggle: Politics, Society, and Community in El Salvador,* ed. Aldo Lauria-Santiago and Leigh Binford, 105–25. Pittsburgh, Pa.: University of Pittsburgh Press.

Blackwater Worldwide. 2008. "2008 Training Course Catalog." *Blackwater Worldwide.* Available at: http://www.blackwaterusa.com/images/pdf/Course%20cat.pdf. Accessed 28 May 2008.

Blackwell, Joyce. 2004. *No Peace without Freedom: Race and the Women's International League for Peace and Freedom, 1915–1975.* Carbondale: Southern Illinois University Press.

Blanchard, Eric M. 2003. "Gender, International Relations, and the Development of Feminist Security Theory." *Signs* 28 (4): 1289–1312.

Bledsoe, C. 1990. "School Fees and the Marriage Process for Mende Girls in Sierra Leone." In *Beyond the Second Sex: New Directions in the Anthropology of Gender,* ed. P. R. Sanday and R. G. Goodenough. Philadelphia: University of Pennsylvania Press.

Bob, Clifford. 2005. *The Marketing of Rebellion: Insurgents, the Media and International Activism.* Cambridge: Cambridge University Press.

Bonhoeffer, Dietrich. 2000. *Discipleship,* volume 4, ed. John Godsey and Geffrey B. Kelly, trans. Barbara Green and Reinhard Krauss. Minneapolis, Minn.: Fortress Press. (Previously published as *The Cost of Discipleship*)

Bowden, Peta. 1997. *Caring: Gender-Sensitive Ethics.* New York: Routledge.

Bragg, Richard. 2003. *I Am A Soldier Too: The Jessica Lynch Story.* New York: Alfred P. Knopf.

Brah, Avtar, and Ann Phoenix. 2004. "Ain't I a Woman? Revisiting Intersectionality." *Journal of International Women's Studies* 5 (3): 75–86.

Bringa, Tone. 1995. *Being Muslim the Bosnian Way: Identity and Community in a Central Bosnian Village.* Princeton, N.J.: Princeton University Press.

Brison, Susan. 2002. *Aftermath and The Remaking of a Self.* Princeton, N.J.: Princeton University Press.

Brittain, Melisa. 2006. "Benevolent Invaders, Heroic Victims and Depraved Villains: White Femininity in Media Coverage of the Invasion of Iraq." In *(En)gendering the War on Terror: War Stories and Camouflaged Politics,* ed. K. Hunt and K. Rygiel, 73–96. Burlington, Vt.: Ashgate.

Broder, John M., and James Risen. 2007. "Blackwater Tops Firms in Iraq in Shooting Rate." *New York Times* (September 27).

Brooks, A. 2005. *The Disarmament, Demobilisation, and Reintegration of Children Associated with the Fighting Forces: Lessons Learned in Sierra Leone 1998–2002.* Dakar, Senegal: Imprimerie Graphi Plus.

Brooks, Stephan, and William Wohlforth. 2005. "Hard Times for Soft Balancing." *International Security* 30 (1): 72–108.

Brown, Melissa T. 2001. "Bring Me Peacekeepers? Military Recruitment and the Cultural Construction of Soldiering." Paper presented at the International Studies Association Conference, Chicago, Illinois.

Brown, Melissa T. 2006. "A Woman in the Army Is Still a Woman: Recruitment of Women into an All-Volunteer Force." Paper Presented at the Annual Meeting of the International Studies Association, San Diego, California.

Brown, Patricia Leigh. 2001. "Heavy Lifting Required: The Return of Manly Men." *New York Times* (October 28, sec. Week in Review): 5.

Brown, Sarah. 1988. "Feminism, International Theory, and International Relations of Gender Inequality." *Millennium: Journal of International Studies* 17 (3): 461–75.

Brown, Wendy. 1992. "Finding the Man in the State." *Feminist Studies* 18 (1): 7–34.

Brown, Wendy. 1997. "The Impossibility of Women's Studies." *differences* 9 (3): 79–101.

Brownmiller, S. 1975. *Against Our Will: Men, Women and Rape.* Harmondsworth, UK: Penguin.

Brubaker, Rogers, and David D. Laitin. 1998. "Ethnic and Nationalist Violence." *Annual Review of Sociology* 24: 423–52.

Burds, Jeffrey. 2009. "Sexual Violence in Europe in World War II, 1939–1945." *Politics and Society* 37: 35–73

Burguieres, M. K. 1990. "Feminist Approaches to Peace: Another Step for Peace Studies." *Millennium* 19 (1): 1–18.

Burman, E. 1994. "Innocents Abroad: Western Fantasies of Childhood and the Iconography of Emergencies." *Disasters* 18 (3): 238–53.

Burridge, Danny. 2009. *El Salvador: Promises, Perils and Reality* (North American Congress on Latin America) (June 16). Accessed at: https://nacla.org/node/5892.

"'Bush's New Poodle' Sarkozy 'to Conquer America's Heart.'" 2007. *Daily Mail.* Available at: http://www.dailymail.co.uk/news/article-492209/Bushs-new-poodle-Sarkozy-conquer-Americas-heart.html. Accessed 14 April 2010.

Bussey, Gertrude Karman, and Margaret Tims. 1965. *Women's International League for Peace and Freedom, 1915–1965: A Record of Fifty Years' Work.* New York: Allen & Unwin.

Butler, Christopher, Tali Gluch, and Neil Mitchell. 2007. "Security Forces and Sexual Violence: A Cross-National Analysis of a Principal—Agent Argument." *Journal of Peace Research* 44 (6): 669–87.

Butler, Judith. 1993. *Bodies that Matter.* New York: Routledge.

Butler, Judith. 2004. *Undoing Gender.* New York: Routledge.

Caliendo, Stephen, Mark Gibney, and Angela Payne. 1999. "All the News That's Fit to Print? *New York Times* Coverage of Human Rights Violations." *Harvard Journal of International Press Politics* 4 (4): 48–69.

Cañas, Antonio, and Héctor Dada. 1999. "Political Tranistion and Institutionalization in El Salvador." In *Comparative Peace Processes in Latin America,* ed. Cynthia J. Arnson, 69–95. Washington, D.C.: Woodrow Wilson Center Press.

Cane, Patricia Mathes. 2002. *Trauma Healing and Transformation.* Santa Cruz, Calif.: Apacitar International.

Carpenter, Bill. 2007. "CISPES Protest at SF Consulate of El Salvador." San Francisco: Independent Media Center. Available at: http://www.indybay.org/newsitems/2007/10/10/18453235.php. Accessed 30 July 2008.

Carpenter, R. Charli. 2006. "Recognizing Gender-Based Violence Against Civilian Men and Boys in Conflict Situations." *Security Dialogue* 37 (1): 83–103.

Carpenter, R. Charli. 2007. "Setting the Advocacy Agenda: Theorizing Issue Emergence and Non-Emergence in Transnational Advocacy Networks." *International Studies Quarterly* 51 (1): 99–120.

Carruthers, Susan L. 2000. *The Media at War: Communication and Conflict in the Twentieth Century.* London: MacMillan.

Center for Defense Information. 2004. "The EU Security Strategy and Relations with the United States." Luncheon briefing by Tomas Valasek, Director, CDI

Brussels Center for Strategic and International Studies, Washington, DC, February 10. Available at: http://www.cdi.org/friendlyversion/printver sion.cfm?documentID=2071. Accessed 15 May 2007.

Chang, Iris. 1997. *The Rape of Nanking: The Forgotten Holocaust of World War II.* New York: Penguin.

"Charlemagne: A Woman's Place?" 2008. *Economist* 31 (May): 57.

Chatterjee, Partha. 1989. "Colonialism, Nationalism and Colonised Women: The Contest in India." *American Ethnologist* 16 (4): 622–33.

Cheshire, Calhoun. 1992. "Changing One's Heart." *Ethics* 103: 76–96.

Chin, Christine. 1998. *In Service and Servitude: Foreign Female Domestic Workers and the Malaysian "Modernity" Project.* New York: Columbia University Press.

Chinchilla, Norma Stoltz. 1997. "Nationalism, Feminism, and Revolution in Central America." In *Feminist Nationalism,* ed. Lois A. West, 201–19. New York: Routledge.

Chodorow, Nancy. 1978. *The Reproduction of Mothering.* Berkeley: University of California Press.

Chomsky, Noam. 1988. *Manufacturing Consent.* London: Pantheon.

CIA World Factbook. 2008. "El Salvador." Available at: https://www.cia.gov/ library/publications/the-world-factbook/geos/es.html. Accessed 29 April 2010.

Clark, Graham. 2007. "President's Private Warriors." *The Courier Mail* (September 29): M18.

Clymer, Adam. 2001. "House Approves D.C.'s Law on Rights of Domestic Partners." *New York Times* (September 26).

Cockburn, Cynthia. 1998. *The Space between Us: Negotiating Gender and National Identities in Conflict.* London: Zed Books.

Cockburn, Cynthia. 2007. *From Where We Stand: War, Women's Activism and Feminist Analysis.* London: Zed Books.

Cohen, Bernard. 1963. *The Press and Foreign Policy.* Princeton, N.J.: Princeton University Press.

Cohen, Dara Kay. 2007. "Explaining Sexual Violence During Civil War: Evidence from Sierra Leone (1991–2002)." Working Paper. Abstract available at: http://www.stanford.edu/~dkcohen/research.html. Accessed 28 April 2010.

Cohen, Eliot A., Michael Eisenstat, and A. J. Bacevich. 1998. "Israel's Revolution in Military Affairs." *Survival* 40 (1): 48–67.

Cohler, Deborah. 2006. "Keeping the Home Front Burning: Renegotiating Gender and Sexual Identity in U.S. Mass Media after September 11." *Feminist Media Studies* 6 (3): 245–61.

Cohn, Carol. 1987 "Sex and Death in the Rational World of Defense Intellectuals." *Signs* 12 (4): 687–718.

Cohn, Carol. 2000. "How Can She Claim Equal Rights When She Doesn't Have to Do as Many Push-ups as I Do?" *Men and Masculinities* 3 (2): 131–51.

Colman, Penny. 1998. *Rosie the Riveter: Women Working on the Home Front in World War II.* New York: Crown Publishers.

Conaway, Camille Pampell, and Salomé Martínez. 2004. *Adding Value: Women's Contributions to Reintegration and Reconstruction in El Salvador.* Washington, D.C.: Women Waging Peace.

Conciliation Resources. 1997. "Gender and Conflict in Sierra Leone." Available at: http://www.c-r.org/resources/occasional-papers/gender-conflict-sierra-leone.php. Accessed 29 April 2010.

Connell, N., and C. Wilson. 1974. *Rape: The First Sourcebook for Women*. New York: New American Library.

Connell, R. W. 1987. *Gender and Power: Society, the Person, and Sexual Politics*. Stanford, Calif.: Stanford University Press.

Connell, R. W. 1990. "The State, Gender and Sexual Politics: Theory and Appraisal." *Theory and Society* 19 (5): 507–44.

Connell, R. W. 1995. *Masculinities*. Berkley: University of California Press.

Connell, Raewyn. 2006. "Northern Theory: The Political Geography of General Social Theory." *Theory & Society* 35 (2): 237–64.

Costello, D. 1992. "Girl Tells of Mass Rapes in Bosnia" *QNP* (August 8).

Coulter, C. 2006. "Being a Bush Wife: Women's Lives through War and Peace in Northern Sierra Leone." PhD diss. in cultural anthropology and ethnology. Uppsala University, Uppsala, Sweden.

Coulter, C. 2008. "Female Fighters in the Sierra Leone War: Challenging the Assumptions?" *Feminist Review* 88: 54–73.

Cowburn, Malcolm, and Lena Dominelli. 2001. "Masking Hegemonic Masculinity: Reconstructing the Paedophile as the Dangerous Stranger." *British Journal of Social Work* 31: 399–415.

Cox, Robert. 1986. "Social Forces, States, and World Orders: Beyond International Relations Theory." In *Neorealism and its Critics*, ed. Robert O. Keohane. New York: Columbia University Press.

Coy, M., Horvath, M., & Kelly, L. 2007. *It's Just Like Going to the Supermarket: Men Talk about Buying Sex in East London*. London: Child and Woman Abuse Studies Unit.

Cuomo, Chris J. 1996. "War Is not Just an Event: Reflections on the Significance of Everyday Violence." *Hypatia* 11 (4): 30–45.

Dale, Stephens. 1996. *McLuhan's Children: The Greenpeace Message and the Media*. Toronto: Between the Lines.

Damon, Chris. 2007. "Salvadoran Activists Targeted with US-style repression." *Peacework* 34 (378): 18–19.

Danner, Mark. 1994. *The Massacre at El Mozote: A Parable of the Cold War*. New York: Vintage.

Dearing, James W., and Everett M. Rogers. 1996. *Agenda Setting (Communication Concepts)*. Thousand Oaks, Calif.: Sage Publications.

DeCesare, Donna. 2009. *Salvadoran Gangs: Brutal Legacies and a Desperate Hope* (North American Congress on Latin America) (November 23). Accessed at: https://nacla.org/node/6260.

Denov, M., and C. Gervais. 2007. "Negotiating (In) Security: Agency, Resistance, and Resourcefulness among Girls Formerly Associated with Sierra Leone's Revolutionary United Front." *Signs: Journal of Women in Culture and Society* 32 (4): 885–910.

Derrida, Jacques. 2001. *On Cosmopolitanism and Forgiveness*. London: Routledge.

Development Studies Network. 2005. Women, Gender and Development in the Pacific Papers. Available at: http://devnet.anu.edu.au/GenderPacific/index.html. Accessed 9 February 2008.

Dewitte, Lieven. 1998. "1st Female F-16 Pilot Graduates from IAF Course." *F16.net* (December 28). Available at: http://www.f-16.net/news_article103.html. Accessed 9 December 2009.

Di Stefano, Christine. 1991. *Configurations of Masculinity: A Feminist Perspective on Modern Political Theory.* Ithaca, N.Y.: Cornell University Press.

Douglas, William. 2003. "A Case of Race? One POW Acclaimed and Another Ignored." *Seattle Times* (November 29).

Dowd, Maureen. 2001. "Liberties, Hunks and Brutes." *New York Times* (November 28).

Downie, Andrew. 2008. "Is Latin America Heading for an Arms Race?" *Christian Science Monitor,* January 16. Available at: http://www.csmonitor.com/World/Americas/2008/0116/p07s01-woam.html. Accessed 29 April 2010.

Drakulic, Slavenka. 1993. "Women Hide Behind a Wall of Silence." *The Nation* (March 1).

Drakulic, Slavenka. 2008. "Rape as a Weapon of War" (June 26). Available at: www.iht.com/articles/2008/06/26/opinion/eddrakulic.php. Accessed 18 February 2009.

Duchene, F. 1972. "Europe's Role in World Peace." In *Europe Tomorrow: Sixteen Europeans Look Ahead,* ed. R. Mayne, 32–47. London: Fontana.

Duffield, Mark. 2002. "Social Reconstruction and the Radicalization of Development: Aid as Relation of Global Liberal Governance." *Development and Change* 33: 1049–71.

Eckert, Amy. 2009. *Outsourcing War.* Unpublished book manuscript.

Effertson, Laura. 1993. "Children of Rape: The War Produces a New Generation of Victims." *Maclean's* (May 24).

Eisenstein, Zillah R. 2004. *Against Empire: Feminisms, Racisms, and the West.* London: Zed Books.

Eisenstein, Zillah R. 2007. *Sexual Decoys: Gender, Race and War in Imperial Democracy.* London: Zed Press.

Elshtain, Jean Bethke. *Women and War* New York: Basic Books.

Elshtain, Jean Bethke. 1983. "On Beautiful Souls, Just Warriors, and Feminist Consciousness." In *Women and Men's Wars,* ed. Judith Stiehm. Oxford: Pergamon Press.

Elshtain, Jean Bethke. 1991. "Sovereignty, Identity, Sacrifice." *Millennium: Journal of International Studies* 20 (3): 395–406.

Elshtain, Jean Bethke. 1992. "Sovereignty, Identity, Sacrifice." In *Gendered States: Feminist (Re)Visions of International Relations Theory,* ed. V. Spike Peterson, 141–54. Boulder, Colo.: Lynne Rienner Publishers.

Engster, Daniel. 2004. "Care Ethics and Natural Law Theory: Toward an Institutional Political Theory of Caring." *The Journal of Politics* 66 (1): 113–35.

Enloe, Cynthia. 1983. *Does Khaki Become You? The Militarisation of Women's Lives.* London: Pluto Press.

Enloe, Cynthia. 1989. *Bananas, Beaches and Bases: Making Feminist Sense of International Politics.* Berkeley: University of California Press.

Enloe, Cynthia. 1990. "Women and Children: Making Feminist Sense of the Persian Gulf War." *Village Voice* 25 (9).

Enloe, Cynthia. 1993. *The Morning After: Sexual Politics at the End of the Cold War.* Berkeley: University of California Press.

Enloe, Cynthia. 2000. *Maneuvers: The International Politics of Militarizing Women's Lives.* Berkeley: University of California Press.

Enloe, Cynthia. 2004. *The Curious Feminist—Searching for Women in a New Age of Empire*. Berkeley: University of California Press.

Enloe, Cynthia. 2005. "What if Patriarchy Is 'the Big Picture'? An Afterword." In *Gender, Conflict and Peacekeeping*, ed. Dyan Mazurana, Angela Raven-Roberts, and Jane Parpart, 280–83. New York: Rowman & Littlefield.

Enloe, Cynthia. 2007. *Globalization and Militarism: Feminists Make the Link*. Lanham, Md.: Rowman & Littlefield.

de l'Estang, François Bujon. 1996. "France, Europe and the Transatlantic Partnership San Diego State University, April 18th, 1996." Available at: http://www.ambafrance-us.org/news/statmnts/1996/statem2.asp. Accessed 14 April 2010.

de l'Estang, François Bujon. 1998. "The French-German Relations, Europe and the Transatlantic Partnership." Presented at the Joint Conference with the French and German Ambassadors University of Berkeley, February 26, and University of Stanford, February 27. Available at: http://www.ambafrance-us.org/news/statmnts/1998/buj2702.asp. Accessed 14 April 2010.

Estrich, S. 1987. *Real Rape: How the Legal System Victimizes Women Who Say No*. Cambridge, Mass.: Harvard University Press.

Evangelista, Matthew, and Judith Reppy. 2002. *The United States and Asian Security*. Peace Studies Program Occasional Paper #26. Available at: http://government.arts.cornell.edu/assets/faculty/docs/evangelista/United%20States%20and%20Asian%20Security.pdf. Accessed 29 April 2010.

Eyre, Dana P., and Mark C. Suchman. 1996. "Status, Norms, and the Proliferation of Conventional Weapons: An Institutional Theory Approach." In *The Culture of National Security*, ed. Peter J. Katzenstein, 79–113. New York: Columbia University Press.

Faber, Daniel. 1993. *Environment under Fire: Imperialism and the Ecological Crisis in Central America*. New York: Monthly Review Press.

"Falwell Apologizes to Gays, Feminists, Lesbians." 2001. *CNN* (September 14). Available at: http://archives.cnn.com/2001/US/09/14/Falwell.apology. Accessed 7 October 2007.

Fanthorpe, R. 2001. "Neither Citizen nor Subject? 'Lumpen' Agency and the Legacy of Native Administration in Sierra Leone." *African Affairs* 100: 363–86.

Feinberg, Leslie. 2006. *Drag King Dreams*. New York: Carroll & Graf Publishers.

Feinstein, Lee, and Anne-Marie Slaughter. 2004. "A Duty to Prevent." *Foreign Affairs* 83 (1): 136–50.

Ferme, M. 1998. "The Violence of Numbers: Consensus, Competition, and the Negotiation of Disputes in Sierra Leone." *Cahiers d'Études Africaines* 38 (2): 150–52.

Fernandes, Leela. 1997. *Producing Workers: The Politics of Gender, Class, and Culture in the Calcutta Jute Mills*. Philadelphia: University of Pennsylvania Press.

Fernandes, Leela. 2000. "Rethinking Globalization: Gender and the Nation in India." In *Feminist Locations: Global/Local/Theory/Practice in the Twenty-First Century*, ed. Marianne de Koven. New Brunswick, N.J.: Rutgers University Press.

"50% See Blair as Bush's Lapdog." 2002. *The Guardian* (November 14). Available at: http://www.guardian.co.uk/politics/2002/nov/14/foreignpolicy.uk1. Accessed 14 April 2010.

Finnemore, Martha. 1996. *National Interests in International Society*. Ithaca, N.Y.: Cornell University Press.

Fischer, Joschka. 2000. Federal Minister for Foreign Affairs, speech at the 36th Munich Conference on Security Policy, February 5. Available at: http://www.auswaertiges-amt.de/diplo/en/Infoservice/Presse/Reden/Archiv/2000/000205-36thMunichConference.html. Accessed 16 September 2005.

Fisk, Robert. 1993. "Bosnia War Crimes: The Rapes Went on Day and Night." *The Independent* (February 8).

Fithen, C., and P. Richards. 2005. "Making War, Crafting Peace: Militia Solidarities & Demobilization in Sierra Leone." In *No Peace, No War: An Anthropology of Contemporary Armed Conflicts*, ed. P. Richards and James Currey, 117–36. Athens: Ohio University Press.

Fletcher, L. 2007. "Turning Interahamwe: Individual and Community Choices in the Rwandan Genocide." *Journal of Genocide Research* 9 (1): 25–48.

Fletcher, Laurel E., and Harvey M. Weinstein. 2002. "Violence and Social Repair: Rethinking the Contribution of Justice to Reconciliation." *Human Rights Quarterly* 24 (3): 573–639.

Foster, C. 1989. *Women for all Seasons: The Story of the Women's International League for Peace and Freedom.* Athens: University of Georgia Press.

Freeman, Carla. 2001. "Is Local: Global as Feminine: Masculine? Rethinking the Gender of Globalization." *Signs: Journal of Women in Culture and Society* 26 (4): 1007–37.

French Foreign Ministry Web site. 2002. Cited in the British American Security Information Council. "A Long Way from Consensus: Threat Perceptions in European NATO and the Future of Missile Defense." Presentation by Dr. Ian Davis (Executive Director, BASIC) to the Conference on Transatlantic Missile Defence, sponsored by the George C. Marshall European Center for Security Studies, in cooperation with Office of Secretary of Defense for International Security Policy, Garmisch-Partenkirchen, Germany, April 5–7, 2004. Available at: http://www.basicint.org/nuclear/NMD/marshall.htm. Accessed 14 April 2010.

Friedman, Jonathan C. 2002. *Speaking the Unspeakable: Essays on Sexuality, Gender, and Holocaust Survivor Memory.* Lanham, Md.: University Press of America.

The Future Strategic Context for Defence. 2001. London: Ministry of Defence.

Garasu, Lorraine, and Volker Boge. 2004. "Papua New Guinea: A Success Story of Postconflict Peacebuilding in Bougainville." In *Searching for Peace in Asia Pacific: An Overview of Conflict Prevention and Peacebuilding Activities*, ed. Annelies Heijmans, Nicola Simmonds, and Hans Van de Veen. Boulder, Colo.: Lynne Rienner Publishers.

Garasu, Sister Lorraine. 2002. "The Role of Women in Promoting Peace and Reconciliation." *Accord: An International Review of Peace Initiatives* 12 (Special Issue: Weaving Consensus: The Papua New Guinea–Bougainville Peace Process). Available at: http://www.c-r.org/our-work/accord/png-bougainville/women-peace-reconciliation.php. Accessed 12 December 2007.

Gardam, Judith. 1993. "Gender and Non-combatant Immunity." *Transnational Law and Contemporary Problems* 3: 345–70.

Gavey, N. 2005. *Just Sex? The Cultural Scaffolding of Rape.* London: Routledge.

"Gay Soldier Fled to 'Come to Terms with Sexuality.'" 2001. *The Telegraph* (May 2). Available at: http://www.telegraph.co.uk/news/uknews/1328752/Gay-soldier-fled-to-come-to-terms-with-sexuality.html. Accessed 8 December 2009.

"Gender Skirmishes in the IDF." 2001. *The Jerusalem Post Internet Edition* (August 6). Available at: http://www.highbeam.com/doc/1P1-46111620.html. Accessed 28 April 2010.

Gertjejanssen, Wendy Jo. 2004. "Victims, Heroes, Survivors: Sexual Violence on the Eastern Front During World War II." PhD diss., University of Minnesota.

Gibson-Graham, J. K. 1994. " 'Stuffed If I Know!': Reflections on Post-modern Feminist Social Research." *Gender, Place, and Culture* 1 (2): 205–24.

Gilboa, Eytan. 2005. "The CNN Effect: The Search for a Communication Theory of IR." *Political Communication* 22: 27–44.

Gilligan, Carol. 1982. *In a Different Voice: Psychological Theory and Women's Development.* Cambridge, Mass.: Harvard University Press.

Gimenez, Martha E. 2001. "Marxism, and Class, Gender, and Race: Rethinking the Triology." *Race, Gender & Class* 8 (2): 23–33.

Gledhill, Ruth. 1993. "Muslims Give Adoption Warning." *London Times* (January 5).

Global Security. 2005. "Revolutionary United Front (RUF)." Available at: http://www.globalsecurity.org/military/world/para/ruf.htm. Accessed 8 December 2008.

Glueck, Keith. 2001. "Marines Hold Family Readiness Conference" (July 13). Available at: http://fhp.osd.mil/news/jul01/news_71301_001.shtml. Accessed 19 March 2008.

Gnesotto, Nicole. 2004. "Introduction—ESDP: Results and Prospects." *EU Security and Defence Policy* 12: 27–31.

Goldenberg, Suzanne. 2001. "Two Steps Forward, One Back for Israel's Women." *Guardian Unlimited: World Dispatch* (March 23).

Goldstein, Joshua S. 2001. *War and Gender: How Gender Shapes the War System and Vice Versa,* Cambridge: Cambridge University Press.

Gómez, Ileana, Nelson Cuellar, Susan Kandel, and Herman Rosa. 2002. *Rural Poverty and the Environment in El Salvador: Lessons for Sustainable Livelihoods.* San Salvador: PRISMA.

Gordon, Margaret, and Stephanie Riger. 1991. *The Female Fear: The Social Cost of Rape.* Urbana: University of Illinois Press.

Gottschall, Jonathan. 2004. "Explaining Wartime Rape." *Journal of Sex Research* 41 (2): 129–36.

Gowans, Tammy. 2007. "The Sad Truth behind the Stigma of Being a Military Wife" (March 27). Available at: http://www.associatedcontent.com/article/184046/the_sad_truth_behind_the_stigma_of.html?page=3. Accessed 10 March 2008.

Grant, Linda. 1993. "Anyone Here Been Raped and Speak English?" *The Guardian* (August 2).

Grant, Rebecca. 1991. "The Sources of Gender Bias in International Relations Theory." In *Gender and International Relations,* ed. Rebecca Grant and Kathleen Newlands. Indianapolis: Indiana University Press.

Gray, John. 1992. *Men Are from Mars, Women Are from Venus: A Practical Guide for Improving Communication and Getting What You Want in Your Relationships.* New York: HarperCollins.

Gray, William P. 1945. "World Battlefronts: Women's War." *Time* (May 7).

Greer, Germaine. 1971. *The Female Eunuch.* London: Paladin.

Grewal, Inderpal. 2005. *Transnational America: Feminisms, Diasporas, Neoliberalisms.* Durham, N.C.: Duke University Press.

Gutiérrez, Raúl. 2007a. "Amnesty Law Biggest Obstacle to Human Rights, Say Activists." *Inter Press Service* (March 26).

Gutiérrez, Raúl. 2007b. "El Salvador: Spectre of War Looms after 25 Years of Peace." *Inter Press Service* (July 29).

Gutman, Roy. 1992. "Mass Rape: Muslims Recall Serb Attacks." *Newsday* (August 23).

Haber, Joram Graf. 1991. *Forgiveness*. Lanham, Md.: Rowman & Littlefield.

Hagan, John, Wenona Rymond-Richmond, and Patricia Parker. 2005. "The Criminology of Genocide: The Death and Rape of Darfur." *Criminology* 43 (3): 525–62.

Hakena, Helen. 2005. "Papua New Guinea: Women in Armed Conflict." In *Gender Mainstreaming in Conflict Transformation: A Thousand Dialogues*, ed. Rawwida Baksh-Sodeen, 160–70. London: Commonwealth Secretariat.

Hale, Sondra. Forthcoming. "By Any Other Name: Gender and Genocide—Women of Darfur and the Nuba Mountains." In *Sudan's Killing Fields: Perspectives on Genocide*, ed. Laura Beny, Sondra Hale, and Lako Tongun. Ann Arbor: University of Michigan Press.

Halley, Janet E. 2000. " 'Like Race' Arguments." In *What's Left of Theory? New Works on the Politics of Literary Theory*, ed. Judith Butler, John Guillory, and Kendall Thomas. New York: Routledge.

van Ham, Peter. 2004. "Europe Gets Real: The New Security Strategy Shows the EU's Geopolitical Maturity." American Institute for Contemporary German Studies at Johns Hopkins. Available at: http://www.aicgs.org/analysis/c/vanham.aspx. Accessed 17 June 2009.

Hamner, J., and S. Saunders. 1984. *Well-Founded Fear: A Community Study of Violence to Women*. London: Hutchinson.

Hampton, Jean, and Jeffrie Murphy. 1988. *Forgiveness and Mercy*. New York: Cambridge University Press.

Hansen, Lene. 2001. "Gender, Nation, Rape: Bosnia and the Construction of Security." *International Feminist Journal of Politics* 3 (1): 55–75.

Harding, Gareth. 2003. "Analysis: EU Talks Tough, Goes Global." *United Press International* (June 17).

Harding, Sandra. 1986. *The Science Question in Feminism*. Ithaca, N.Y.: Cornell University Press.

Hardt, Michael, and Antonio Negri. 2001. *Empire*. Cambridge, Mass.: Harvard University Press.

Hardt, Michael, and Antonio Negri. 2004. *Multitude: War and Democracy in the Age of Empire*. New York: Penguin.

Harrison, Deborah, and Lucie Laliberté. 1997. "Gender, the Military, and Military Family Support." In *Wives and Warriors: Women and the Military in the United States and Canada*, ed. Laurie Weinstein and Christie White. Westport, Conn.: Greenwood.

Harvey, David. 2005. *A Brief History of Neoliberalism*. New York: Oxford University Press.

Havini, Marilyn Taleo. 2004. "Women in Community during the Blockade." In *As Mothers of the Land: The Birth of the Bougainville Women for Peace and Freedom*, ed. Josephine Tankunani Sirivi and Marilyn Taleo Havini, 70–84. London: Pandanus.

Hayden, Robert. 2000. "Rape and Rape Avoidance in Ethno-national Conflicts: Sexual Violence in Liminalized States." *American Anthropologist* 102 (1): 27–42.

Hedgpeth, Dana. 2009. "Blackwater Sheds Name, Shits Focus." *Washington Post* (February 14). Available at: http://www.washingtonpost.com/wp-dyn/content/article/2009/02/13/AR2009021303149.html. Accessed 9 December 2009.

Heeg Maruska, Jennifer. 2010. "When Are States Hypermasculine?" In *Gender and International Security: Feminist Perspectives,* ed. Laura Sjoberg. New York: Routledge.

Heijmans, Annelies, Nicola Simmonds, and Hans van de Veen, eds. 2004. *Searching for Peace in Asia Pacific: An Overview of Conflict Prevention and Peacebuilding Activities.* Boulder, Colo.: Lynne Reinner Publishers.

Higate, Paul. 2009. "Private Military Security Companies and the Problem of Men and Masculinities." Paper Prepared for the First European Conference on Politics and Gender, January 21–23, Queen's University, Belfast.

Hill, Chrisopher. 1990. *European Foreign Policy: Power Bloc, Civilian Power—or Flop?* San Francisco, Calif.: Westview Press.

Hillman, Elizabeth L. 2009. "Front and Center: Sexual Violence in U. S. Military Law." *Politics and Society* 37 (1): 101–29.

Hirschmann, Nancy J. 1989. "Freedom, Recognition and Obligation: A Feminist Approach to Political Theory." *The American Political Science Review* 83 (4): 1227–1444.

Hirschmann, Nancy J. 2004. *The Subject of Liberty: Toward a Feminist Theory of Freedom.* Princeton, N.J.: Princeton University Press.

HM Crown Prosecution Service Inspectorate and HM Inspectorate of Constabulary. 2007. *Without Consent: A Report on the Joint Review of the Investigation and Prosecution of Rape Offences.* London: HMCPSI.

Hooper, Charlotte. 1998. "Masculinist Practices and Gender Politics: The Operation of Multiple Masculinities in International Relations." In *The "Man" Question in International Relations,* ed. Marysia Zalewski and Jane Parpart. Boulder, Colo.: Westview Press.

Hooper, Charlotte. 2001. *Manly States: Masculinities, International Relations, and Gender Politics.* New York: Columbia University Press.

Horrigan, Christopher. 1992. "The Combat Exclusion Rule and Equal Protection." *Santa Clara Law Review* 32: 229–64.

Horvath, Danielle. 1993. "Children of the Rapes." *World Press Review* (June).

Human Rights Watch. 1996. *Shattered Lives: Sexual Violence during the Rwandan Genocide and Its Aftermath.* New York: Human Rights Watch.

Human Rights Watch. 2003. "We'll Kill You if You Cry." *Sexual Violence in the Sierra Leone Conflict* 15 (1A). New York: Human Rights Watch.

Human Rights Watch. 2004. *Living in Fear: Child Soldiers and the Tamil Tigers in Sri Lanka* 16 (13C). New York: Human Rights Watch.

Hunt, Krista. 2002. "The Strategic Co-optation of Women's Rights: Discourse in the 'War on Terrorism.'" *International Feminist Journal of Politics* 4 (1): 116–21.

Hunt, Krista, and Kim Rygiel. 2006a. "(En)Gendered War Stories and Camouflaged Politics." In *(En)gendering the War on Terror: War Stories and Camouflaged Politics,* ed. K. Hunt and K. Rygiel, 1–24. Burlington, Vt.: Ashgate.

Hunt, Krista, and Kim Rygiel, eds. 2006b. *(En)gendering the War on Terror: War Stories and Camouflaged Politics.* Burlington, Vt.: Ashgate.

Huston, Nancy. 1983. "Tales of War and Tears of Women." In *Women and Men's Wars,* ed. Judith Stiehm. Oxford: Pergamon Press.

IFAD. 2006. "IFAD, EC and CGAP Launch New Initiative to Promote Remittance Services for Poor Rural People." (Release number IFAD/41/06) Available at: http://www.ifad.org/media/press/2006/41.htm.

Ignatieff, Michael. 1997. *The Warrior's Honour: Ethnic War and the Modern Conscience.* New York: Penguin.

Inter-Parliamentary Union. 2005a. "Women in Politics: 1945–2005." Available at: http://www.ipu.org/PDF/publications/wmn45–05_en.pdf. Accessed 21 October 2008.

Inter-Parliamentary Union. 2005b. "Women's Suffrage: A World Chronology of the Recognition of Women's Rights to Vote and to Stand for Election." Available at: http://www.ipu.org/wmn-e/suffrage.htm. Accessed 14 April 2010.

Inter Press Service News Agency Web site. 2006. "Fijian Deaths in Iraq Revive Mercenaries' Issue" (December 6). Available at: http://ipsnews.net/print. asp?idnews=33580. Accessed 27 December 2007.

"Irish Troops to Serve under EU Flag." 2000. *The Irish Time* (March 4).

Islam, Shada. 2003. "The EU's First-Ever Security Doctrine." Yale Center for the Study of Globalization. Available at: http://yaleglobal.yale.edu/display. article?id=2023. Accessed 5 November 2007.

Israeli Government Press Office. 2004. "Women in Israeli Combat Units." *The Jewish Week* (January 2).

Jacoby, Tami Amanda. 2005. *Women in Zones of Conflict: Power and Resistance in Israel.* Montreal: McGill-Queen's University Press.

Jahn, George. 2005. "More Than a Decade Later, Bosnian Children Born of War Rape Start Asking Questions." Associate Press Newswire, February 20. Available at: http://www.encyclopedia.com/doc/1P1-108930646.html. Accessed 30 April 2010.

Jeffords, Susan. 1989. *The Remasculinization of America: Gender and the Vietnam War.* Bloomington: Indiana University Press.

Jeffreys, Sheila. 2007. "Double Jeopardy: Women, the US Military and the War in Iraq." *Women's Studies International Forum* 30: 16–25.

Jervis, Robert. 1976. *Perception and Misperception in International Politics.* Princeton, N.J.: Princeton University Press.

Joachim, Jutta. 1998. "Shaping the Human Rights Agenda: The Case of Violence against Women." In *Gender Politics in Global Governance,* ed. Mary Meyer and Elisabeth Prugl, 142–60. Lanham, Md.: Rowman & Littlefield Publishers.

Johnson, D. H. 2003. *The Root Causes of Sudan's Civil Wars.* Bloomington: Indiana University Press.

Johnson, Holly. 1996. *Dangerous Domains: Violence Against Women in Canada.* Scarborough: Nelson Canada.

Johnson, Shoshana, with M. L. Doyle. 2010. *I'm Still Standing.* New York: Simon and Schuster.

Jordan, Michael. 1995. "A Murky Future Lies ahead for Bosnia's Children of Rape Byline." *Miami Herald* (July 1).

Junor, Beth, and Katrina Howse. 1995. *Greenham Common Women's Peace Camp: A History of Non-Violent Resistance.* New York: Working Press.

Kagan, Robert. 2002. "Power and Weakness." *Policy Review* 113: 5–23.

Kaldor, Mary. 2006. *New and Old Wars: Organized Violence in a Global Era,* 2nd ed. London: Polity Press.

Kampfner, John. 2003. "The Truth about Jessica." *The Guardian* (May 15): A1.

Kampwith, Karen. 2002. *Women and Guerilla Movements: Nicaragua, El Salvador, Chiapas, Cuba.* University Park: Pennsylvania State University Press.

Kandel, Susan, and Herman Rosa, with Ileana Gómez, Margarita García, Leopoldo Dimas, and Nelson Cuéllar. 2006. "El Salvador." In *Escaping Poverty's Grasp: The Environmental Foundations of Poverty Reduction,* ed. David Reed, 94–119. London: Earthscan.

Kaplan, Laura Duhan. 1994. "Woman as Caretaker: An Archetype That Supports Partriarchal Militarism." *Hypatia, Special Issue: Feminism and Peace* 9 (2): 123–32.

Kaplan, Robert D. 1994. *Balkan Ghosts: A Journey through History.* London: Vintage.

Kaufman, Joyce, and Kristen Williams. 2004. "Who Belongs? Women, Marriage, and Citizenship." *International Feminist Journal of Politics* 6 (3): 416–35.

Keck, Margaret, and Kathryn Sikkink. 1998. *Activists Beyond Borders: Advocacy Networks in International Politics.* Ithaca, N.Y.: Cornell University Press.

Keen, David. 1999. "Who's It Between? 'Ethnic War' and Rational Violence." In *The Media of Conflict: War Reporting and Representations of Ethnic Violence,* ed. Tim Allen and Jean Seaton, 81–101. London: Zed Books.

Keen, David. 2003. "Greedy Elites, Dwindling Resources, Alienated Youths: The Anatomy of Protracted Violence in Sierra Leone." *Internationale Politik und Gesellschaft* 10 (2): 67–94.

Keen, David. 2005. *Conflict and Collusion in Sierra Leone.* Oxford: James Currey.

Keller, Evelyn Fox. 1982. "Feminism and Science." *Signs, Feminist Theory* 7 (3): 589–602

Keller, Evelyn Fox, and Helen E. Longino. 1996. *Feminism and Science.* Oxford: Oxford University Press.

Kelly, Liz. 1987. *Surviving Sexual Violence.* Cambridge, UK: Polity Press.

Kelly, Liz. 1996. "Weasel Words: Pedophiles and the Cycle of Abuse." *Trouble and Strife* 33: 44–49.

Kelly, Liz. 2002. *A Research Review on the Reporting, Investigation and Prosecution of Rape Cases.* London: Her Majesty's Crown Prosecution Service Inspectorate.

Kelly, Liz. 2005. *How Violence Is Constitutive of Women's Inequality and the Implications for Equalities Work.* The Equality and Diversity Forum Seminar, November, London. Child and Woman Abuse Studies Unit, London Metropolitan University.

Kelly, Liz, Shelia Burton, and Linda Regan. 1996. "Beyond Victim or Survivor: Sexual Violence, Identity and Feminist Fheory and Fractice." In *Sexualizing the Social: Power and the Organization of Sexuality,* ed. Lisa Adkins and Vicky Merchant, 77–101. London: Macmillan.

Kelly, Liz, Jo Lovett, and Linda Regan. 2005. *A Gap or a Chasm: Attrition in Reported Rape Cases?* London: Home Office.

Kelly, Liz, and Linda Regan. 2001. *Rape: The Forgotten Issue? A European Attrition and Networking Study.* London: Child and Woman Abuse Studies Unit.

Kelly, Liz, Jennifer Temkin, and Susan Griffiths. 2006. *Section 41: An Evaluation of New Legislation Limiting Sexual History Evidence in Rape Trial.* Available at: www.homeoffice.gov.uk/rds/pdfs06/rdsolr2006.pdf. Accessed 14 May 2010.

Kent, Gregory. 2006. "Organized Diaspora Networks and Homeland Peacebuilding: The Bosnian World Diaspora Network as a Potential Development Actor." *Conflict, Security, and Development* 6 (3): 449–69.

Keohane, Robert. 1989. "International Relations Theory: Contributions of a Feminist Standpoint." *Millennium* 18 (2): 245–53.

King, Ynestra. 1989. "If I Can't Dance in Your Revolution, I'm Not Coming." In *Rocking the Ship of State*, ed. Ynestra King and Adrienne Harris. Boulder, Colo.: Westview Press.

Kinsella, Helen. 2005. "Securing the Civilian: Sex and Gender in the Laws of War." In *Power and Global Governance*, ed. Michael Barnett and Raymond Duvall, 249–72. Cambridge: Cambridge University Press.

Kirk, Lisbeth. 2004. "Europe Must Defend Itself, Says Military Chief." *EUObserver. com* (January 19).

Klinger, Cornelia and Gudrun-Axeli Knapp, eds. 2008. *Constellations of Inequality* [Über-Kreuzungen: Fremdheit, Ungleichheit, Differenz]. Munster: Verlag Westfalisches Dampfboot.

Knapp, Gudrun-Axeli. 2005. "Race, Class, Gender: Reclaiming Baggage in Fast Travelling Theories." *European Journal of Women's Studies* 12 (3): 249–65.

Kornblum, Lori S. 1984. "Women Warriors in a Men's World: The Combat Exclusion." *Law and Inequality* 2: 351–444.

Kronsell, Annica. 2005. "Gendered Practices in Institutions of Hegemonic Masculinities: Reflections from Feminist Standpoint Theory." *International Feminist Journal of Politics* 7 (2): 280–98.

Kronsell, Annica. 2008. "The Organization of Europe's New Security and Defense: Looking at the 'Battlegroups' through a Feminist Lens." Presented at the 49th ISA Annual Convention in San Francisco, California.

Kubosova, Lucia. 2007. "Sarkozy Brings in EU Troops to Celebrate Bastille Day." *EU Observer* (July 16).

Küchler, Teresa. 2008. "Margot Wallstrom Fed up with EU 'Reign of Old Men.'" *EU Observer* (February 8).

Kupchan, Charles. 2002. "The End of the West." *The Atlantic Monthly*, November. Available at: http://www.cfr.org/publication.php?id=5101.

Kuper, Leo. 1981. *Genocide: Its Political Use in the Twentieth Century*. New Haven, Conn.: Yale University Press.

Lagström, Christine. 2005. "The Disappeared Children of El Salvador—A Field Study of Truth, Justice and Reparation." Master's thesis, University of Lund, Faculty of Law. Available at: http://www.jur.lu.se/Internet/Bib lioteket/Examensarbeten.nsf/0/6B7721A7AE6206F5C12570200056C859/ $File/xsmall.pdf?OpenElement. Accessed 18 October 2007.

Lamb, S. 1999. *New Versions of Victim: Feminists Struggle with the Concept*. New York: New York University Press.

Leander, Anna. 2005. "The Market for Force and Public Security: The Destabilizing Consequences of Private Military Companies." *Journal of Peace Research* 42 (5): 605–22.

Leary, Alex. 2004. "Singular Honor for Fallen War Hero." *St. Petersburg Times* (October 30).

Legon, Jeordan. 2003. "Soldier Risks Life to Rescue Civilian Caught in Crossfire." *CNN.com*, Heroes of the War. Available at: http://www.cnn.com/SPECIALS/2003/iraq/heroes/carter.html. Accessed 1 August 2007.

Lehr, Doreen Drewry. 1999. "Military Wives: Breaking the Silence." In *Gender Camouflage: Women and the U.S. Military*, ed. Francine D'Amico and Laurie Weinstein, 117–42. New York: New York University Press.

Leigh, David. 2004. "Who Commands the Private Soldiers? Allegations of Abuse Have Raised Wider Questions about the Role—and Accountability—of Civilian Contractors." *The Guardian* (May 17).

Levinson, David. 1998. *Ethnic Groups Worldwide: A Ready Reference Handbook.* New York: Greenwood.

Lindsey, Rose. 2002. "From Atrocity to Data: Historiographies of Rape in Former Yugoslavia and the Gendering of Genocide." *Patterns of Prejudice* 36 (4): 59–78.

Lipschutz, Ronnie D. 1998. "Beyond the Neoliberal Peace: From Conflict Resolution to Social Reconciliation." *Social Justice* 25 (4): 5–19.

Lischer, Sarah Kenyon. 2005. *Dangerous Sanctuaries: Refugee Camps, Civil War and the Dilemmas of Humanitarian Aid.* Ithaca, N.Y.: Cornell University Press.

Livermore, Rebecca. 2007. "How to Get the Most out of Being a Military Spouse" (April 13). Available at: http://www.associatedcontent.com/article/202972/how_to_get_the_most_out_of_being_a.html. Accessed 10 March 2008.

Lorentzen, Lois A. 1998. "Women's Prison Resistance: *Testimonios* from El Salvador." In *The Women and War Reader,* ed. Lois A. Lorentzen and Jennifer Turpin, 192–202. New York: New York University Press.

Lorentzen, Lois Ann, and Jennifer Turpin, eds. 1998. *The Women and War Reader.* New York: New York University Press.

Luciak, Ilja. 2001. *After the Revolution: Gender and Democracy in El Salvador, Nicaragua, and Guatemala.* Baltimore, Md.: Johns Hopkins University Press.

MacDonald, Mandy, and Mike Gatehouse. 1994. *In the Mountains of Morazán: Portrait of a Returned Refugee Rommunity in El Salvador.* New York: Monthly Review Press.

Macintyre, Martha. 2000. "Violence and Peacemaking in Papua New Guinea: A Realistic Assessment of the Social and Cultural Issues at Grassroots Level." *Development Bulletin* 53: 34–37.

MacKenzie, Megan. 2009. "Securitization and Desecuritization: Female Soldiers and the Reconstruction Women in Post-Conflict Sierra Leone." *Security Studies* 18 (2): 241–61.

Mackey, Robert. 2009. "Taliban Blame 'Blackwater' for Pakistan Bombings." *New York Times* (November 17). Available at: http://thelede.blogs.nytimes.com/2009/11/17/taliban-blames-blackwater-for-pakistan-bombings/. Accessed 9 December 2009.

MacKinnon, Catherine. 1993. *Only Words.* Cambridge, Mass.: Harvard University Press.

MacKinnon, Catherine. 1994. "Rape, Genocide, and Women's Human Rights." *Harvard Women's Law Journal* 17: 5–16.

MacKinnon, Catherine. 2001. *Sex Equality.* New York: Foundation Press.

MacKinnon, Catherine. 2006. *Are Women Human? And Other International Dialogues.* Cambridge, Mass.: Harvard University Press.

Mamdani, Mahmood. 2007. "The Politics of Naming: Genocide, Civil War, Insurgency." *London Review of Books* 29 (5): 5–8.

Manners, Ian. 2006. "Normative Power Europe Reconsidered: Beyond the Crossroads." *Journal of European Public Policy* 13 (2):189.

Mansaray, Binta. 2000. "Women Against Weapons: A Leading Role for Women in Disarmament." In *Bound to Cooperate: Conflict, Peace and People in Sierra Leone,* ed. Anatole Ayissi and Robert-Edward Poulton. Geneva, Switzerland: United Nations Institute for Disarmament Research.

Margalit, Avishai. 2002. *The Ethics of Memory*. Cambridge, Mass.: Harvard University Press.

"Marines Hold Family Readiness Conference." 2002. (July 13). Available at: http://fhp.osd.mil/news/jul01/news_71301_001.shtml. Accessed 19 March 2008.

Marsh, Mendy, and Jeanne Ward. 2006. "Sexual Violence against Women and Girls in War and Its Aftermath: Realities, Responses, and Required Resources." A Briefing Paper prepared for the Symposium on Sexual Violence in Conflict and Beyond, June 21–23, Brussells, Belgium. Available at: http://www.humanitarianreform.org/humanitarianreform/Portals/1/cluster%20approach%20page/clusters%20pages/Gender/Gender%20Toolkit/x-%20SV%20Against%20Women%20-%20UNFPA%20Briefing.pdf. Accessed 9 December 2009.

Mazurana, Dyan, Susan McKay, Khristopher Carlson, and Janel Kasper. 2002. "Girls in Fighting Forces and Groups: Their Recruitment, Participation, Demobilization, and Reintegration." *Peace and Conflict: Journal of Peace Psychology* 8 (2): 97–123.

Mazurana, Dyan, Angela Raven-Roberts, and Jane Parpart, eds. 2005. *Gender, Conflict, and Peacekeeping*. New York: Rowman & Littlefield Publishers.

Mazzetti, Mark, and James Risen. 2009. "Fine and Inquiry Possible or Blackwater Successor." *New York Times* (November 18). Available at: http://www.nytimes.com/2009/11/19/world/middleeast/19blackwater.html?_r=1. Accessed 9 December 2009.

McCall, Leslie. 2004. "The Complexity of Intersectionality." *Signs* 30 (3): 1771–1800.

McClintock, Anne. 1995. *Imperial Leather: Race, Gender and Sexuality in the Colonial Contest*. New York: Routledge.

McColgan, Aileen. 1996. *The Case for Taking the Date Out of Rape*. London: Pandora.

McCombs, Maxwell E., and Donald L. Shaw. 1972. "The Agenda-Setting Function of Mass Media." *The Public Opinion Quarterly* 36 (2): 176–87.

McCullough, Ed. 2005. "Summit May Favor Tackling Causes of Terrorism Over Military Response." *Associated Press* (March 7). Available at: http://www.commondreams.org/headlines05/0307–04.htm. Accessed 8 January 2006.

McDonald, Sharon. 1988. "Drawing the Lines: Gender, Peace, and War." In *Images of Women in Peace and War*, ed. Sharon McDonald, Pat Holden, and Shirley Ardener. Madison: University of Wisconsin Press.

McElhinny, Victor J. 2004. "Between Clientelism and Radical Democracy: The Case of Ciudad Segundo Montes." In *Landscapes of Struggle: Politics, Society, and Community in El Salvador*, ed. Aldo Lauria-Santiago and Leigh Binford, 147–65. Pittsburgh, Pa.: University of Pittsburgh Press.

McFerran, Ann. 2007. "Life after Death for Africa's Child Soldiers." *The Independent* (April 7). Available at: http://www.independent.co.uk/news/world/africa/life-after-death-for-africas-child-soldiers-446360.html. Accessed 9 December 2009.

McKay, Susan. 2006. "Girlhoods Stolen: The Plight of Girl Soldiers During and After Armed Conflict." In *A World Turned Upside Down: Social Ecological Approaches to Children in War Zones*, ed. Neil Boothby, Alison Strang, and Michael Wessells, 89–110. Bloomfield, Conn.: Kumarian Press.

McKay, Susan, and Dyan Mazurana. 2004. *Where Are the Girls? Girls in Fighting Forces in Northern Uganda, Sierra Leone and Mozambique: Their Lives Dur-*

ing and After War. Montreal: International Centre for Human Rights and Democracy.

McLean, Renwick. 2005. "Muslim Nations Skip Meeting With Europe." *The New York Times* (November 28): A9.

Mendez, Jennifer Bickham. 2002. "Creating Alternatives from a Gender Perspective: Transnational Organizing for *Maquila* Workers' Rights in Central America." In *Women's Global Activism: Linking Local Struggles and Transnational Politics,* ed. Nancy A. Naples and Manisha Desai, 121–41. New York: Routledge.

Merchant, Carolyn. 1980. *The Death of Nature: Women, Ecology, and the Scientific Revolution.* San Francisco: Harper & Row.

Merle, Renae. 2006. "Storm-Wracked Parish Considers Hired Guns: Contractors in Louisiana Would Make Arrests, Carry Weapons." *Washington Post* (March 14): A01.

Mikanagi, Yumiko. 2004. "Okinawa: Women, Bases and US-Japan Relations." *International Relations of the Asia-Pacific* 4 (1): 97–111.

Miller, Laura L. 1998. "Feminism and the Exclusion of Army Women from Combat." *Gender Issues* 16 (3): 33–64.

Miller, Nancy K. 2003. " 'Portraits of Grief': Telling Details and the Testimony of Trauma." *differences* 14 (3): 112–35.

Minear, Larry, Colin Scott, and Thomas Weiss. 1996. *The News Media, Civil War and Humanitarian Action.* Boulder, Colo.: Lynne Reinner Publishers.

Minow, Martha. 2002. *Breaking the Cycles of Hatred: Memory, Law and Repair.* Princeton, N.J.: Princeton University Press.

Mitchell, Neil, and Tali Gluch. 2004. "The Principals and Agents of Political Violence and the Strategic and Private Benefits of Rape." Paper presented at the annual meeting of the American Political Science Association, Chicago.

Moon, Katharine. 1998. *Sex Among Allies: Militarized Prostitution in U.S.–South Korea Relations.* New York: Columbia University Press.

Morokvasic-Müller, Mirjana. 2004. "From Pillars of Yugoslavism to Targets of Violence: Interethnic Marraiges in the Former Yugoslavia and Thereafter." In *Sites of Violence: Gender and Conflict Zones,* ed. Wenona Giles and Jennifer Hyndman. Berkeley: University of California Press.

Morris, Benny. 2004. *The Birth of the Palestinian Problem Revisited,* 2nd ed. Cambridge: Cambridge University Press.

Morris, Madeline. 1996. "By Force of Arms: Rape, War, and Military Culture." *Duke Law Journal* 45 (4): 651–781.

Motro, Helen Schary. 2000. "Indicting Inappropriate Behaviour: Israeli Law Counters Sexist Culture, Gets Tough on Sexual Harassment." *The Jewish Journal of Greater Los Angeles* (April 21).

MSNBC.com. 2003. "Speaking in Senegal Today, President Bush Acknowledged That America Was Wrong for Her Involvement in the Slave Trade." Available at: http://www.msnbc.com/news/936376.asp?cp1=1. Accessed 27 July 2003.

MSNBC.com. 2004. "Ex-NFL Star Tillman Makes Ultimate Sacrifice" (April 26). Available at: www.msnbc.msn.com/id/4815441/. Accessed 24 March 2007.

Mueller, John E. 1970. "Presidential Popularity from Truman to Johnson." *American Political Science Review* 64: 18–33.

Mueller, John E. 1973. *War, Presidents, and Public Opinion.* New York: Wiley.

Murphy, Craig. 1996. "Seeing Women, Recognizing Gender, Recasting International Relations." *International Organization* 50 (3): 513–38.

Murray, Kevin. 1997. *El Salvador: Peace on Trial.* Oxford: Oxfam UK and Ireland.

Naimark, Norman M. 1995. "Soviet Soldiers, German Women, and the Problem of Rape." In *The Russians in Germany: A History of the Soviet Zone of Occupation, 1945–1949.* Cambridge, Mass.: The Belknap Press of Harvard University Press.

National Forum for Human Rights. 2001. *National Forum for Human Rights Annual Report 2001: Sierra Leone.* Freetown, Sierra Leone: National Forum for Human Rights.

NATO Web site. 2005. "NATO-Russia Compendium of Financial and Economic Data Relating to Defence: Defence Expenditures of NRC Countries (1980–2004)." Press release. June 9–10. Available at: http://www.nato.int/docu/pr/2005/p050609e.htm. Accessed 14 April 2010.

Nayak, Meghana. 2006. "Orientalism and 'Saving' U.S. State Identity after 9/11." *International Feminist Journal of Politics* 8 (1): 42–61.

Nayak, Meghana, and Jennifer Suchland. 2006. "Gender Violence and Hegemonic Projects." *International Feminist Journal of Politics* 8 (4): 467–85.

Niarchos, Catherine N. 1995. "Women, War, and Rape: Challenges Facing the International Tribunal for the Former Yugoslavia." *Human Rights Quarterly* 17 (4): 649–90.

Niva, Steve. 1998. "Tough and Tender: New World Order Masculinity and the Gulf War." In *The "Man Question" in International Relations,* ed. Jane Parpart and Marysia Zalewski. Boudler, Colo.: Westview Press.

Noonan, Peggy. 2001. "Welcome Back, Duke." *Wall Street Journal* (October 12). Available at: http://www.peggynoonan.com. Accessed January 2005.

Nussbaum, Martha. 2000. *Women and Human Development: The Capabilities Approach.* New York: Cambridge University Press.

Nye, Joseph S. 2004. *Soft Power: the Means to Success in World Politics.* New York: Public Affairs.

O'Callaghan, Mary-Louise. 2002. "The Origins of the Conflict." In *Conciliation Resources.* Available at: http://www.c-r.org/our-work/accord/png-bougainville/origins-conflict.php. Accessed 18 December 2007.

O'Hanlon, Michael, Steven Everts, Laurence Freedman, Francois Heisbourg, Charles Grant and Daniel Keohane. 2004. "The American Way of War: The Lessons for Europe." In *A European Way of War,* ed. Steven Everts et al., 41–42. London: Centre for European Reform.

Okin, Susan Moller. 1979. *Women in Western Political Thought.* Princeton, N.J.: Princeton University Press.

Olujic, Maria B. 1998. "Embodiment of Terror: Gendered Violence in Peacetime and Wartime in Croatia and Bosnia-Herzegovina." *Medical Anthropology Quarterly* 12 (1): 31–50.

"1000 Women for the Nobel Peace Prize." 2005. *1000 Peace Women across the Globe.* Zurich, Switzerland: Scalo Press.

Otunno, Olara A. 1998. "Protection of Children Affected by Armed Conflict." Report by the Special Representative of the Secretary General for Children and Armed Conflict. New York: United Nations.

Papandoniou, Ioannis. 2003. "Greek Defense Minister Says PASOK Cannot Take Election Victory for Granted [*sic*] [in Greek]" *Athens Ependhitis* (June): 16.

Papastephanou, Marianna. 2003. "Forgiving and Requesting Forgiveness." *Journal of Philosophy of Education* 37 (3): 503–24.

Pape, Robert. 2005. "Soft Balancing Against the United States." *International Security* 30 (1): 7–45.

Pateman, Carole. 1979. *The Problem of Political Obligation: A Critical Analysis of Liberal Theory.* Chichester: Wiley.

Pateman, Carole. 1988. *The Sexual Contract.* Stanford, Calif.: Stanford University Press.

Patkin, Terri Toles. 2004. "Explosive Baggage: Female Palestinian Suicide Bombers and the Rhetoric of Emotion." *Women and Language* 27 (2).

Patten, Chris. 2004. "Europe and America—Has the Transatlantic Relationship Run Out of Road?" Speech by The Rt Hon, External Relations Commissioner, Lady Margret Hall, Oxford, 13 February. Available at: SPEECH/04/77, http://europa.eu/rapid/pressReleasesAction.do?reference=SPEECH/04/77&format=HTML&aged=0&language=FR&guiLanguage=en. Accessed 1 August 2007.

Paul, T. V. 2005. "Soft Balancing in the Age of U.S. Primacy." *International Security* 30 (1): 46–71.

Peterson, V. Spike, ed. 1992. *Gendered States: Feminist (Re)Visions of International Relations Theory.* Boulder, Colo.: Lynne Rienner Publishers.

Peterson, V. Spike. 1999. "Sexing Political Identity/Nationalism as Heterosexism." *International Feminist Journal of Politics* 1 (1): 21–52.

Peterson, V. Spike. 2003. *A Critical Rewriting of Global Political Economy: Integrating Reproductive, Productive, and Virtual Economies.* London: Routledge.

Peterson, V. Spike. 2005. "Power, Privilege and Feminist Theory/Practice." *Politics & Gender* 1 (2): 350–58.

Peterson, V. Spike, and Anne Sisson Runyan. 1999. *Global Gender Issues: Dilemmas in World Politics.* Boulder, Colo.: Westview Press.

Pettman, Jan Jindy. 1996. *Worlding Women: A Feminist International Politics.* London: Routledge.

Phoenix, Ann, and Pamela Pattynama, eds. 2006. "Special Issue: Intersectionality." *European Journal of Women's Studies* 13 (3).

Plaut, Martin. 2003. "A Brief Sojourn with Mr. Solana." BBC Worldservice Radio Interview and News Report (July 19). Available at: http://www.consilium.europa.eu/uedocs/cmsUpload/Martin%20Plaut%20-%20report.pdf. Accessed 29 April 2010.

Polgreen, Lydia. 2005. "Darfur's Babies of Rape Are on Trial from Birth." *New York Times* (February 11). Available at: http://faculty.arts.ubc.ca/job/360/data/darfurrape.pdf. Accessed 29 April 2010.

Popkin, Margaret. 2000. *Peace Without Justice: Obstacles to Building the Rule of Law in El Salvador.* Pennsylvania: Pennsylvania State University.

Powell, Siam. 2001. "East Timor's Children of the Enemy." *The Weekend Australian* (March 10).

Prince-Gibson, Eetta. 2001. "Religious Leaders Attack IDF on the Gender Battlefield." *Jewish Bulletin News of Northern California* (March 16). Available at: http://www.jewishsf.com/bk010316/iidfwomen.shtml. Accessed 14 May 2010.

Prizel, Ilya. 1998. *National Identity and Foreign Policy: Nationalism and Leadership in Poland, Russia, and Ukraine.* Cambridge: Cambridge University Press.

Prusher, Ilene R. 1998. "Can a Glass Ceiling be Olive Drab?" *Christian Science Monitor* (May 13).

Puar, Jasbir K., and Amit S. Rai. 2002. "Monster, Terrorist, Fag: The War on Terrorism and the Production of Docile Patriots." *Social Text* 20 (3): 117–48.

Raghavan, Sudarsan, Joshua Partlow, and Karen DeYoung. 2007. "Blackwater Faulted In Military Reports From Shooting Scene." *Washington Post* (October 3): A01.

Ready, K., L. Stephen, and S. Cosgrove. 2001. "Women's Organizations in El Salvador: History, Accomplishments, and International Support." In *Women and Civil War: Impact, Organizations, and Action*, ed. Krishna Kumar, 183–204. Boulder, Colo.: Lynne Rienner Publishers.

Reardon, Betty. 1985. *Sexism and the War System*. New York: Teacher's College Press.

Reardon, Betty. 1993. *Women and Peace: Feminist Visions of Global Security*. Albany: State University of New York Press.

Reed, David. 2005. *Changing the Political Economy of Poverty and Ecological Disruption*. Washington, D.C.: World Wide Fund, Macroeconomics Program Office.

Regan, Linda, and Liz Kelly. 2003. *Rape: Still a Forgotten Issue*. London: Child & Woman Abuse Studies Unit/Rape Crisis Network Europe.

Rehn, Elisabeth, and Ellen Johnson Sirleaf. 2002. *Women, War, Peace: The Independent Experts' Assessment of the Impact of Armed Conflict on Women and Women's Role in Peace-building*. New York: United Nations Development Fund for Women (UNIFEM).

Richards, Paul. 1995. "Rebellion in Liberia and Sierra Leone: A Crisis of Youth?" In *Conflict in Africa*, ed. Oliver Furley, 134–70. London: Tauris.

Richards, Paul. 1996. *Fighting for the Rain Forest: War, Youth, and Resources in Sierra Leone*. Oxford, UK: James Currey.

Richardson, Diane. 2000. *Rethinking Sexuality*. London: Sage.

Ridberg, Maia. 2001. "She's in the Navy Now." *The Jerusalem Post* (June 8). Available at: http://jpost.com/Editions/2001/06/10/Features/Features.27850.html. Accessed 18 June 2006.

Risman, B. 2005. "Gender as Social Structure: Theory Wrestling with Activism." *Gender and Society* 18 (4): 429–50.

Robinson, Bridget. 2004. "Putting Bosnia in its Place: Critical Geopolitics and the Representation of Bosnia in the British Print Media." *Geopolitics* 9 (2): 379.

Robinson, Fiona. 1999. *Globalizing Care: Ethics, Feminist Theory and International Relations*. Boulder, Colo.: Westview Press.

Robinson, Piers. 2000. "The Policy-Media Interaction Model: Measuring Media Power During Humanitarian Crisis." *Journal of Peace Research* 37 (5): 613–33.

Rodgers, Jane. 1998. "Bosnia, Gender and the Ethics of Intervention in Civil Wars." *Civil Wars* 1 (1): 103–16.

Roeper, Richard. 2003. "Soldier's Known for Making the News, in a Good Way." *Chicago Sun-Times* (April 23): 11.

Ron, James, Howard Ramos, and Kathleen Rodgers. 2005. "Transnational Information Politics: NGO Human Rights Reporting, 1986–2000." *International Studies Quarterly* 49: 557–87.

Rosa, Herman. 2004. *Economic Integration and the Environment in El Salvador*. San Salvador: PRISMA.

de Rose, François. 2000. "A European Pillar in the Alliance?" *NATO at Fifty*. The Eisenhower Institute, Gettysburg College. Available at: http://www.eisenhower institute.org/themes/past_themes/nato/perspectives/deRose.dot. Accessed 19 February 2007.

Rubin, E. Sasley. 2002. "Gen X." *The New Republic* (April 15).

Rubin, Joe. 2004. "El Salvador: Payback." *Public Broadcasting Services* (October). Available at: http://www.pbs.org/frontlineworld/elections/elsalvador/. Accessed 14 July 2008.

Ruddick, Sara. 1989. *Maternal Thinking: Towards a Politics of Peace*. New York: Houghton-Miffin.

Russell, D. E. H. 1984. *Sexual Exploitation: Rape, Child Sexual Abuse, and Workplace Harassment*. Thousand Oaks, Calif.: Sage Publications.

Rynning, Sten. 2003a. "Why Not NATO? Military Planning in the European Union." *Journal of Strategic Studies* 26 (March 1): 53–72.

Rynning, Sten. 2003b. "Coming of Age? The European Union's Security and Defence Policy." Odense: Chapter of Certified Fraud Examiners Working Chapter No. 10.

Said, Edward. 1979. *Orientalism*. New York: Vintage Books.

Said, Edward. 1993. *Culture and Imperialism*. New York: Knopf.

Saito Takao, et al. 2007. *Anataha Senso de Shinemasuka* [Will you be killed in action in the future?]. NHK Shuppan, 230.

Sanchez, Marcela. 2006. "Putting Remittances to Work." *Washington Post* (December 9). Accessed at: http://www.washingtonpost.com/wp-dyn/content/article/2006/12/08/AR2006120801304.html.

Sarat, Austin. 2002. "When Memory Speaks: Remembrance and Revenge in Unforgiven." In *Breaking the Cycles of Hatred: Memory, Law and Repair*, ed. Martha Minow. Princeton, N.J.: Princeton University Press.

Sasson-Levy, Orna. 2003. "Feminism and Military Gender Practices: Israeli Women Soldiers in 'Masculine' Roles." *Sociological Inquiry* 73 (3): 440–65.

Savage, Dan. 2001. "Savage Love: My Dumb Job." *The Stranger* (September 20). Available at: www.thestranger.com/archive/savage.html. Accessed January 2005.

Save the Children UK. 2002. "Extensive Abuse of West African Refugee Children Reported." London: Save the Children.

Save the Children UK. 2005. *Forgotten Casualties of War: Girls in Armed Conflict*. London: Save the Children.

Scahill, Jeremy. 2005. "Blackwater Down." *The Nation* (October 10).

Scahill, Jeremy. 2007. "A Very Private War." *The Guardian* (August 1). Available at: http://www.globalpolicy.org/component/content/article/168/36004. html. Accessed 9 December 2009.

Scharioth, Klaus. 2005. "The New Security Challenges and Europe's International Role." *German Federal Foreign Office Website* (January 20). Available at: http://www.auswaertiges-amt.de/www/en/ausgabe_archiv?archiv_id=6807. Accessed 25 March 2006.

Schirmer, Jennifer. 1993. "The Seeking of Truth and the Gendering of Consciousness: The CoMadres of El Salvador and CONAVIGUA widows of Guatemala." In *"Viva": Women and Popular Protest in Latin America*, ed. Sarah A. Radcliffe and Sally Westwod. New York: Routledge.

Schulhofer, Stephen. 1998. *Unwanted Sex: The Culture of Intimidation and the Failure of Law.* Cambridge, Mass.: Harvard University Press.

Sciolino, Elaine. 2005. "Europe Is Divided and Wary About the US." *New York Times* (February 20): 6.

Scott, Catherine V. 1995. *Gender and Development: Rethinking Modernization and Dependency Theory.* Boulder, Colo.: Lynne Rienner.

Scott, Joan. 1987. "Gender: A Useful Category for Historical Analysis." In *Gender and the Politics of History,* ed. Joan Wallach Scott. New York: Columbia University Press.

Segal, Mady Wechsler. 1999. "Military Culture and Military Families." In *Beyond Zero Tolerance: Discrimination in Military Culture,* ed. Mary Fainsod Katzenstein and Judith Reppy. Lanham, Md.: Rowman & Littlefield.

Sharlach, Lisa. 1999. "Gender and Genocide in Rwanda: Women as Agents and Objects of Genocide." *Journal of Genocide Research* 1 (3): 387–99.

Sharp, Deborah. 2005. "Valor in Iraq Earns Medal of Honor." *USA Today* (March 30).

Sheehan, Cindy. 2005. *Not One More Mother's Child.* Kihei, Hawaii: Koa Books.

Sheehy, Elizabeth. 1996. "From Women's Duty to Resist to Men's Duty to Ask: How Far Have We Come." *Canadian Women's Studies* 20 (3): 98–104.

Shepler, Susan. 2002. "Les Filles-Soldats: Trajectoires d'après-guerre en Sierra Leone." *Politique Africaine* 88: 49–62.

Shepler, Susan. 2005. "Conflicted Childhoods: Fighting Over Child Soldiers in Sierra Leone." PhD diss. Berkeley, University of California. Available at: http://proquest.umi.com/pqdlink?Ver=1&Exp=11–28–2014&FMT=7&DID=982818511&RQT=309&attempt=1&cfc=1. Accessed 28 April 2010.

Shuman, Ellis. 2001a. "In the IDF, It's Combat Girls Vs. Yeshiva Guys." *Dateline* (August 20). Available at: http://israeliculture.about.com/library/weekly/aa082001a.htm. Accessed 18 April 2005.

Shuman, Ellis. 2001b. "Israel's First Female Combat Pilot." *Dateline* (June 25).

Sierra Leone. 1991. *The Constitution of Sierra Leone, 1991.* Act No. 6 of 1991.

Sierra Leone Truth and Reconciliation Commission. 2004. *Sierra Leone Truth and Reconciliation Report.* Freetown. Available at: http://trcsierraleone.org/drwebsite/publish/index.shtml. Accessed 19 May 2009.

Silber, Irina Carlotta. 2004. "Not Revolutionary Enough? Community Rebuilding in Postwar Chalatenango." In *Landscapes of Struggle: Politics, Society, and Community in El Salvador,* ed. Aldo Lauria-Santiago and Leigh Binford, 166–86. Pittsburgh, Pa.: University of Pittsburgh Press.

Simonovic, Ivan. 2004. "Attitudes and Types of Reaction Toward Past War Crimes and Human Rights Abuses." *Yale Journal of International Law* 29 (2): 343–62.

Sion, Liora. 2006. "Too Sweet and Innocent for War"?: Dutch Peacekeepers and the Use of Violence." *Armed Forces & Society* 32 (3): 454–74.

Sirivi, Josephone Tankunani, and Marilyn Taleo Havini, eds. 2004. *. . . as Mothers of the Land: The Birth of the Bougainville Women for Peace and Freedom.* Canberra, Australia: Pandanus Books.

Sivakumaran, Sandesh. 2007. "Sexual Violence Against Men in Armed Conflict." *The European Journal of International Law* 18 (2): 253–76.

Sjoberg, Laura. 2006a. *Gender, Justice, and the Wars in Iraq.* Boulder, Colo.: Rowman & Littlefield.

Sjoberg, Laura. 2006b. "The Gendered Realities of the Immunity Principle: Why Gender Analysis Needs Feminism." *International Studies Quarterly* 50 (4): 889–910.

Sjoberg, Laura. 2007. "Agency, Militarized Femininity, and Enemy Others." *International Feminist Journal of Politics* 9 (1): 82–101.

Sjoberg, Laura. 2009. "Introduction to *Security Studies*: Feminist Contributions." *Security Studies* 18 (2): 183–213.

Sjoberg, Laura, and Caron Gentry. 2007. *Mothers, Monsters, Whores: Women's Violence in Global Politics*. London: Zed Books.

Skapoulli, Elena. 2004. "Gender Codes at Odds and the Linguistic Construction of a Hybrid Identity." *Journal of Language, Identity, and Education* 3 (4): 245–60.

Skjaelsbaek, Inger. 2001. "Sexual Violence and War: Mapping Out a Complex Relationship." *European Journal of International Relations* 7 (2): 211–37.

Skjaelsbaek, Inger. 2006. "Victim and Survivor: Narrated Social Identities of Women Who Experienced Rape During the War in Bosnia-Herzegovina." *Feminism and Psychology* 16 (4): 374.

Slapsak, Svetlana. 2001. "The Use of Women and the Role of Women in the Yugoslav War." In *Gender, Peace and Conflict*, ed. Inger Skjelsbaek and Dan Smith. London: Sage.

Sloan, Stanley, and Heiko Borchert. 2003. "Europe, U.S. Must Rebalance Soft, Hard Power." *Defense News* (September 8–15).

Smillie, Ian, and Larry Minear. 2004. *The Charity of Nations*. Bloomfield, Conn.: Kumarian Press.

Smith, Dorothy. 1987. *The Everyday World as Problematic: A Feminist Sociology*. Toronto: University of Toronto Press.

Smith, Tara. 1997. "Tolerance and Forgiveness: Virtues or Vices?" *Journal of Applied Philosophy* 14 (1): 31–41.

Solana, Javier. 2000. "Where Does the EU Stand on Common Foreign and Security Policy?" presented at the Forschungsinstitut Der Deutschen Gesellschaft Fuer Auswaertige Politik, Berlin, November 14. Available at: http://www.consilium.europa.eu/cms3_applications/applications/solana/details.asp?cmsid=246&BID=107&DocID=63975&insite=1. Accessed 9 August 2008.

Solana, Javier. 2007. "Identity and Foreign Policy," *ESDP Newsletter* (January): 9

Spero, M. H. 1996. "Original Sin, the Symbolization of Desire, and the Development of the Mind: A Psychoanalytic Gloss on the Garden of Eden." *Psychoanalysis and Contemporary Thought* 19: 499–562.

Spivak, Gayatri Chakravorty. 1987. *In Other Worlds: Essays in Cultural Politics*. London: Methuen.

Spohn, Cassia, and Horney, Julie. 1996. "The Impact of Rape Law Reform on the Processing of Simple and Aggravated Rape Cases." *Journal of Criminal Law and Criminology* 86 (3): 861–84.

SportsIllustrated.com. 2003. "Tillman Killed in Afghanistan: Former Cardinals Safety Walked Away from NFL to Join Army Rangers" (April 23). Available at: sportsillustrated.cnn.com/204/football/nfl/04/23/tillman.killed/. Accessed 24 March 2007.

Stabile, Carol A., and Deepa Kumar. 2005. "Unveiling Imperialism: Media, Gender, and the War in Afghanistan." *Media, Culture, and Society* 27 (5): 765–82.

Stanley, Alessandra. 1991. "War in the Gulf: Home Front; War's Ribbons Are Yellow with Meaning of Many Hues." *New York Times* (February 3). Available at: http://www.nytimes.com/1991/02/03/us/war-in-the-gulf-home-front-war-s-ribbons-are-yellow-with-meaning-of-many-hues.html. Accessed 12 December 2009.

Stanley, Penny. 1999. "Reporting of Mass Rape in the Balkans: Plus Ca Change, Plus C'est Meme Chose? From Bosnia to Kosovo." *Civil Wars* 2 (2): 74–110.

Steans, Jill. 1998. *Gender and International Relations: An Introduction.* New Brunswick, N.J.: Rutgers University Press.

Stephen, Lynn. 1997. *Women and Social Movements in Latin America: Power from Below.* Austin: University of Texas Press.

Stiehm, Judith. 1982. "The Protected, the Protector, the Defender." *Signs* 5 (3): 367–76.

Stiehm, Judith, ed. 1983. *Women and Men's Wars.* Oxford: Pergamon Press.

Stiehm, Judith. 1989. *Arms and the Enlisted Woman.* Philadelphia, Pa.: Temple University Press.

Stoler, Ann Laura. 1991. "Carnal Knowledge and Imperial Power." In *Gender at the Crossroads,* ed. Micaela di Leonardo, 51–101. Berkeley: University of California Press.

Stoller, Silvia, and Nielsen, Camilla. 2005. "Asymmetrical Genders: Phenomenological Reflections on Sexual Difference." *Hypatia* 20 (2): 7–26.

Stone, Bonnie, and Betty Alt. 1990. *Uncle Sam's Brides: The World of Military Wives.* New York: Walker and Co.

Stop CAFTA Coalition. 2006. *Monitoring Report: DR-CAFTA in Year One.* Available at: http://www.cispes.org/cafta/CAFTA_Monitoring_sept12.pdf. Accessed 18 October 2007.

Stover, Eric, and Harvey Weinstein, eds. 2004. *My Neighbor, My Enemy: Justice and Community in the Aftermath of Mass Atrocity.* Cambridge: Cambridge University Press.

Studemeister, Margarita. 2001. *El Salvador: Implementation of the Peace Accords.* Washington, D.C.: U.S. Institute of Peace.

Suchocki, Marjorie H. 1994. "The Idea of God in Feminist Philosophy." *Hypatia* 9 (4): 57–68.

Sullivan, Stacy. 1996. "Born Under a Bad Sign." *Newsweek* (September 23).

Sylvester, Christine. 2002. *Feminist International Relations: An Unfinished Journey.* Cambridge: Cambridge University Press.

Tagliabue, John. 2003. "Blair Reassures U.S. on European Defense." *International Herald Tribune* (October 18): 3.

Taylor, Louise. 2003. "'We'll Kill You If You Cry': Sexual Violence in the Sierra Leone Conflict." New York: Human Rights Watch. Available at: http://hrw.org/reports/2003/sierraleone/sierleon0103.pdf. Accessed 14 May 2010.

Temkin, Jennifer. 2000. "Prosecuting and Defending Rape: Perspectives from the Bar." *Journal of Law and Society* 27 (2): 219–34.

Temkin, Jennifer. 2002. *Rape and the Legal Process.* Oxford: Oxford University Press.

Terry, Jennifer. 2006. UCLA Lecture given in Los Angeles, on "Governmentality, Sentimentality, and Imperial Erotics in 'Extreme Cinema Verite'" (May 22).

Thomas, Pamela. 2005. "The Pacific: Gender Issues in Conflict and Peacemaking." In *Gender Mainstreaming in Conflict Transformation: Building Sustainable Peace,* ed. Rawwida Baksh-Sodeen. London: Commonwealth Secretariat.

Thompson, Martha. 1998. "Transition in El Salvador: A Multi-Layered Process." In *From Conflict to Peace in a Changing World: Social Reconstruction in Times of Transition,* ed. Deborah Eade, 88–94. Oxford: Oxfam.

Thompson, Martha, and Deborah Eade. 2004. "Women and War: Protection Through empowerment in El Salvador." In *Development, Women, and War: Feminist Perspectives,* ed. Haleh Afshar and Deborah Eade, 220–37. Oxford: Oxfam.

Tickner, J. Ann. 1992. *Gender in International Relations: Feminist Perspectives on Achieving Global Security.* New York: Columbia.

Tickner, J. Ann. 1999. "Why Women Can't Run the World: International Politics According to Francis Fukuyama." *International Studies Review* 1 (3): 3–11.

Tickner, J. Ann. 2001. *Gendering World Politics: Issues and Approaches in the Post–Cold War Era.* New York: Columbia University Press.

Tickner, J. Ann., and Sjoberg, Laura. 2006. "Feminism." In *International Relations Theories,* ed. T. Dunne, M. Kurki, and S. Smith. Oxford: Oxford University Press.

Tilly, Charles. 2004. *Social Movements, 1768–2004.* London: Paradigm Publishers.

Tomlinson, Chris. 2003. "Battling for a Bridge and a Town, U.S. Troops Risk their Lives to Rescue an Elderly Woman." *San Diego Union-Tribune* (March 31).

Toomey, Christine. 2003. "Cradle of Inhumanity." *Sunday Times* (November 9). Available at: http://www.timesonline.co.uk/tol/comment/columnists/christine_toomey/article668528.ece. Accessed 4 March 2008.

Tran, Mark. 2009. "Blackwater Bosses Approved Bribes after Guards Killed Iraqis, Paper Claims." *The Guardian* (November 11). Available at: http://www.guardian.co.uk/world/2009/nov/11/blackwater-denies-iraq-killings-claims. Accessed 9 December 2009.

Treaty of European Union (1993), Title I:B.

Tronto, Joan. 1987. "Beyond Gender Difference to a Theory of Car." *Signs: Journal of Women in Culture and Society* 12 (4): 644–63.

Tronto, Joan. 1993. *Moral Boundaries: A Political Argument for an Ethic of Care.* New York: Routledge.

Truth Commission for El Salvador. 1993. *From Madness to Hope: The 12 Year War in El Salvador.* Report of the Truth Commission for El Salvador. Reprinted in The United Nations and El Salvador, 1990–1995. The United Nations Blue Books Series, vol. IV. New York: United Nations.

Truth and Reconciliation Commission of Sierra Leone. 2004. "Volume 3b: Chapter 3: Women and the Armed Conflict." *The Final Report of the Truth & Reconciliation Commission of Sierra Leone.* Available at: http://www.trcsierraleone.org/drwebsite/publish/index.shtml. Accessed 14 May 2010.

"UE/Defence: Progress Expected in Military Capabilities Field." 2005. *Europe* (May 2005): 4.

United Nations Children's Fund (UNICEF). 1997. *Cape Town Principles and Best Practices.* Symposium on the Prevention of Recruitment of Children into the Armed Forces and on Demobilization and Social Reintegration of Child Soldiers in Africa, Cape Town, South Africa. Available at: http://www.unicef.org/emerg/files/Cape_Town_Principles(1).pdf.

United Nations Division for the Advancement of Women. 2007. "Convention on the Elimination of All Forms of Discrimination against Women." Available at: http://www.un.org/womenwatch/daw/cedaw/states.htm. Accessed 13 April 2010.

United Nations Educational, Scientific and Cultural Organization (UNESCO) Institute for Statistics. 2000. "Economic Activity Rate by Sex, 13 Age Groups, 1950–2010 (ILO estimates/projections)" [code 4270]. Available at: http://data.un.org/Data.aspx?q=Economic+activity+rate+by+sex%2c+13+age+groups&d=ILO&f=srID%3a4270. Accessed 10 September 2009.

United Nations Educational, Scientific and Cultural Organization (UNESCO) Institute for Statistics Institute for Statistics. 2009a. "Literacy Rates, Aged 15–24, by Sex, Per Cent (United Nations Educational, Scientific and Cultural Organization Institute for Statistics /MDG)" [code 29999]. Available at: http://data.un.org/Data.aspx?q=Literacy+rates+15–24&d=SOWC&f=inID%3a10. Accessed 10 September 2009.

United Nations Educational, Scientific and Cultural Organization (UNESCO) Institute for Statistics. 2009b. "Women in Parliamentary Seats, Per Cent (IPU/MDG)" [code 1020]. Available at: http://data.un.org/Data.aspx?q=Women+in+parliamentary+seats&d=GenderStat&f=inID%3a125. Accessed 10 September 2009.

United Nations High Commissioner for Refugees. 2001. *Prevention and Response to Sexual and Gender-Based Violence in Refugee Situations: Inter-agency Lessons Learned Conference Proceedings. 27–29 March 2001*. Geneva: United Nations High Commissioner for Refugees.

United Nations Security Council. 1993. *From Madness to Hope: the 12-year war in El Salvador: Report of the Commission on the Truth for El Salvador*. Annex. S/25500 (1993): 187–92.

United Nations Security Council. 1994. *Final Report of the Commission of Experts Established Pursuant to Security Council Resolution 780, (1992)*. UN Doc. S/1994/674.

United Nations Statistics Division. 1999. Topics 2.7, 3.8, 4.4, 5.1, and 6.1. United Nations Women's Indicators and Statistics Database (Wistat), version 4. Available at: http://www.library.mcgill.ca/edrs/data/other/WISTAT/Wistat.html. Accessed 14 April 2010.

U.S. Army. 2005. "Sargent First Class Paul Ray Smith." Purple Heart Summary. Available at: http://www.army.mil/medalofhonor/smith/profile/index.html. Accessed 30 April 2010.

U.S. Department of State. 2010. "Background Note: El Salvador." Available at: http://www.state.gov/r/pa/ei/bgn/2033.htm. Accessed 29 April 2010.

Utas, M. 2005. "Agency of Victims: Young Women in the Liberian Civil War." In *Makers & Breakers: Children & Youth in Postcolonial Africa*, ed. A. Honwana and F. de Boeck, 53–80. Trenton, N.J.: Africa World Press.

Vickers, Jeanne. 1993. *Women and War*. London: Zed Books.

Victor, Barbara. 2003. *An Army of Roses: Inside the World of Palestinian Women Suicide Bombers*. New York: Rodale Press.

Vincent, Norah. 2002. "In Praise of Machismo." *The Advocate* (June 11): 72.

de Waal, Alex, 2004a. "Counter-Insurgency on the Cheap." *London Review of Books* (August 5).

de Waal, Alex. 2004b. "Tragedy in Darfur." *Boston Review* (October–November).

Waever, Ole. 1995. "Identity, Integration and Security: Solving the Sovereignty Puzzle in EU Studies." *Journal of International Affairs* 48 (2): 46–86.

Walker, Clive, and Dave Whyte. 2005. "Contracting Out War?: Private Military Companies, Law and Regulation." *International and Comparative Law Quarterly* 54: 651–89.

Walters, Valerie E. L., and Gwen Mason. 1994. *Women in Top Management in Africa: The Sierra Leone Case*. African Association for Public Administration and Management (AAPAM). Available at: http://unpan1.un.org/intradoc/groups/public/documents/AAPAM/UNPAN026475.pdf. Accessed 14 April 2010.

Ward, Jeanne. 2002. *If Not Now, When? Addressing Gender-Based Violence in Refugee, Internally Displaced and Post-conflict Settings. A Global Overview.* Reproductive Health for Refugees Consortium. Available at: http://www.rhrc.org/resources/gbv/ifnotnow.html. Accessed 8 November 2006.

Warren, Karen J., and Duane L. Cady. 1994. "Feminism and Peace: Seeing Connections." Special Issue: Feminism and Peace. *Hypatia* 9 (2): 4–20.

Wax, Emily. 2004. "Rwandans Struggle to Love Children of Hate." *Washington Post* (March 29).

Weinberg, Bill. 1991. *War on the Land: Ecology and Politics in Central America.* Atlantic Highlands, N.J.: Zed Books.

Weinberger, Sharon. 2007. "Facing Backlash, Blackwater Has a New Business Pitch: Peacekeeping." *Wired.* Available at: http://www.wired.com/politics/security/news/2007/12/blackwater. Accessed 27 May 2008.

Weinstein, Laurie, and Christie C. White, eds. 1997. *Wives and Warriors.* Westport, Conn.: Bergin & Garvey.

Whelan, Tensie. 1998. "A Tree Falls in Central America: The Growth of Environmentalism." *The Amicus Journal* 10 (4): 28–38.

White, Patricia. 2002. "What Should We Teach Children about Forgiveness?" *Journal of Philosophy of Education* 36 (1): 57–67.

The White House. 2006. "Progress and the Work Ahead in Iraq." *The White House, Office of the Press Secretary, Fact Sheet* (January 10).

Whitfield, Teresa. 2001. "The UN's Role in Peace-building in El Salvador." In *El Salvador: Implementation of the Peace Accords,* ed. Margarita Studemeister, 33–40. Washington, D.C.: United States Institute of Peace.

Whitney, Craig. 1993. "Peacemaking's Limit." *New York Times* (May 21).

Whitworth, Sandra. 2004. *Men, Militarism, and UN Peacekeeping: A Gendered Analysis.* Boulder, Colo.: Lynne Rienner Publishers.

Willemse, Karin. 2005. "Darfur in War: The Politicization of Ethnic Identities?" *International Institute for the Study of Islam in the Modern World Review* 15: 14–15.

Williams, Carol. 1993. "Bosnia's Orphans of Rape: Innocent Legacy of Hatred." *L.A. Times* (July 24).

Williams, Joyce, and Karen Holmes. 1981. *The Second Assault: Rape and Public Attitudes.* Westport, Conn.: Greenwood Press.

Willsher, Kim. 1993. "The Baby Born of Inhumanity." *QNP* (January 12).

Wilson, Jamie. 2005. "Mercenaries Guard Homes of the Rich in New Orleans." *The Guardian.* Available at: http://www.guardian.co.uk/world/2005/sep/12/hurricanekatrina.usa/print. Accessed 28 May 2008.

Wittner, Lawrence S. 1993. *One World Or None: A History of the World Nuclear Disarmament Movement through 1953.* Stanford Nuclear Age Series. Stanford, Calif.: Stanford University Press.

Wittner, Lawrence S. 1997. *Resisting the Bomb: A History of the World Nuclear Disarmament Movement, 1945–1970.* Stanford Nuclear Age Series. Stanford, Calif.: Stanford University Press.

"Women Plan Tennis to Aid War Relief." 1918. *New York Times* (April 21). Available at: http://query.nytimes.com/gst/abstract.html?res=9507E4DC1F3FE433A25752C2A9629C946996D6CF. Accessed 9 December 2009.

Wood, Elisabeth J. 2005. "Challenges to Political Democracy in El Salvador." In *The Third Wave of Democratization in Latin America: Advances and Setbacks,* ed. Frances Hagopian and Scott P. Mainwaring, 179–201. New York: Cambridge University Press.

Wood, Elisabeth J. 2004. "Civil War and Reconstruction: The Repopulation of Tenancingo." In *Landscapes of Struggle: Politics, Society, and Community in El Salvador,* ed. Aldo Lauria-Santiago and Leigh Binford, 126–46. Pittsburgh, Pa.: University of Pittsburgh Press.

Wood, Elisabeth Jean. 2006. "Variation in Sexual Violence During War." *Politics and Society* 34 (3): 307–41.

Wood, Elisabeth Jean. 2008. "Sexual Violence during War: Toward an Understanding of Variation." In *Order, Conflict, and Violence,* ed. Stathis Kalyvas, Ian Shapiro, and Tarek Masoud, 321–51. Cambridge: Cambridge University Press.

Wood, Elisabeth Jean. 2009. "Armed Groups and Sexual Violence: When is Wartime Rape Rare?" *Politics and Society* 37: 131–61.

Young, Iris Marion. 2003. "The Logic of Masculinist Protection: Reflections on the Current Security State." *Signs* 29 (1): 1–25.

Young, Iris Marion. 2005. "The Logic of Masculinist Protection: Reflections on the Current Security State." In *Women and Citizenship,* ed. Marilyn Friedman. New York: Oxford University Press.

Yuval-Davis, Nira. 1997. *Gender & Nation.* London: Sage.

Zalewski, Marysia. 1995. "Well, What is the Feminist Perspective on Bosnia?" *International Affairs* 71 (2): 339–56.

Zalewski, Marysia. 1996. "'All These Theories Yet the Bodies Keep Piling Up': Theorists, Theories, and Theorizing." In *International Relations: Positivism and Beyond,* ed. Steve Smith, Ken Booth, and Marysia Zalewski. Cambridge: Cambridge University Press.

Zalewski, Marysia, and Jane Parpart, eds. 1998. *The "Man" Question in International Relations.* Boulder, Colo.: Westview Press.

Zalewski, Marysia. 2000. *Feminism After Postmodernism: Theorising through Practice.* London: Routledge.

Zarkov, Dubravka. 1997. "War Rapes in Bosnia: On Masculinity, Femininity and the Power of Rape Victim Identity." *Tijschrift voor Criminologie* 39 (2): 140–51.

Zine, Jasmin. 2006. "Between Orientalism and Fundamentalism: Muslim Women and Feminist Engagement." In *(En)gendering the War on Terror: War Stories and Camouflaged Politics,* ed. Krista Hunt and Kim Rygiel, 27–49. Burlington, Vt.: Ashgate.

Zirin, Dave. 2005. "Pat Tillman, Our Hero." *The Nation* (October 6). Available at: http://www.thenation.com/doc/20051024/zirin. Accessed 30 April 2010.

Index

About the Editors and Contributors

EDITORS

Laura Sjoberg is an Assistant Professor of Political Science at the University of Florida. She received her PhD from the University of Southern California and her JD from Boston College Law School. Her research is in the area of gender and international security, focusing on analysis of war making and war fighting. Sjoberg's first book, *Gender, Justice, and the Wars in Iraq* (2006), presents a feminist reformulation of just war theory and an application of that reformulated theory to the wars in Iraq since the end of the Cold War. She is also author (with Caron Gentry) of *Mothers, Monsters, and Whores: Women's Violence in Global Politics* (2007). Her work has been published in *International Studies Quarterly, International Relations, International Studies Review, Politics and Gender,* and other journals.

Sandra Via is a PhD candidate in the Planning, Governance, and Globalization program at Virginia Polytechnic Institute and State University. She holds a master's degree in political science from Virginia Tech. She has worked on the question of the impact of neoliberal ideology on higher education and on the relationship between universities and communities in furthering economic development policy in Southside Virginia. She is currently completing her dissertation, which is a study of the ways expected gender roles influence the public reception and effectiveness of celebrity activists.

CONTRIBUTORS

Ronni Alexander received her PhD in International Relations from Sophia University. She is Professor in the Faculty of Law and the Graduate School of International Cooperation Studies at Kobe University. Her research covers a broad range of subjects in international relations and peace research. In particular, she is focusing on three areas. One, a relatively recent interest, is peace education. This is primarily in the context of Popoki's Peace Project, a peace education initiative she began last year, which involves both research and implementation. It is based on her DVD, "Popoki's Peace Message," and *Popoki's Peace Book*. The second area is the "endogenous security" of the Pacific Island countries, focusing on such topics as implications of the coups in Fiji for women, violence against women, sex work, and HIV/AIDS. The third area involves the broader issues of gender, peace, and violence, looking at such questions as the role of gender and sexuality in the building of peace and the ways states, gender, and sexuality interrelate.

Stephanie Anderson is Associate Professor of Political Science at the University of Wyoming. She holds a PhD from the University of Cambridge (UK) and an MSc from the London School of Economics. Her research focus is on the European Union as an international actor, international relations, and security issues. She is author of *Crafting the EU Security Policy: In the Pursuit of a European Identity* (2008). Her work has also appeared in several journals, including *Armed Forces and Society, Current Politics and the Economics of Europe,* and *European Foreign Affairs Review.*

Sigal Ben-Porath received her PhD in political philosophy from Tel-Aviv University in 2000. Subsequently, she was a postdoctoral fellow at Princeton University's Center for Human Values. She moved to the University of Pennsylvania in 2003 to become a special assistant to the president, as well as a research associate at the Graduate School of Education, where she is currently an assistant professor. She teaches courses on the philosophy of educational policy, theories of justice, and ethics in practice. Her research focuses on the intersection between political philosophy and education, with an emphasis on issues of democratic citizenship, justice, and education. She has published articles on the regulation of intimacy, civic education in wartime, post-war care ethics, and just relations between adults and children. Her first book *Citizenship under Fire: Democratic Education in Times of Conflict* was published in 2006. Her most recent book, *Tough Choices: Structured Paternalism and the Landscape of Choice,* was published in 2010.

R. Charli Carpenter holds a PhD from the University of Oregon and is currently Assistant Professor of Political Science at the University of Massachusetts. Her research and teaching interests include international norms and identities, gender and violence, war crimes, comparative geno-cide studies, and humanitarian action. She is the author of *Innocent Women and Children: Gender, Norms and the Protection of Civilians* (2006). Carpenter's current research focuses on the human rights network, investigating why certain issues, but not others, end up on the international agenda. She is particularly interested in the human rights of children born as a result of wartime rape and has edited a collection of essays on this topic entitled *Born of War: Protecting Children of Sexual Violence Survivors in Conflict Zones* (2007). Her current book project centers on the social construction of children's human rights during the war in the former Yugoslavia.

Deborah Cohler is Associate Professor of Women and Gender Studies at San Francisco State University. She researches the intersections of lesbian subjectivity, nationalism, and gender identity in early twentieth-century England as well as the transnational production of queer identities in the early twenty-first century. She is particularly interested in the effects of wartime nationalist discourses on constructions of sexuality and gender and has published articles on the rise of lesbian identity on the British "homefront" in World War I (*Journal of the History of Sexuality*) and the gendered and sexual landscape of post-9/11 U.S. mass culture (*Feminist Media Studies*). Her book, *Queer Inversions: Gender Deviance, Female Sexuality, and Nationalism* (2010), was recently published.

Catia Cecilia Confortini holds a PhD from the School of International Relations of the University of Southern California and teaches in the Peace and Conflict Studies Program at Wellesley College. Her dissertation, entitled *Imaginative Identification: Feminist Critical Methodology in the Women's International League for Peace and Freedom, 1945–1975*, received the Peace and Justice Studies Association's Award for Best Dissertation of 2009. Her research focuses on feminist approaches to peace studies and the contributions of feminist peace activism to the theory and practice of peace. Her work has appeared in *Peace and Change,* the *International Feminist Journal of Politics, International Politics,* the *International Studies Encyclopedia,* and *Peace and Freedom,* the magazine of the U.S. Section of the Women's International League for Peace and Freedom (WILPF). She is a member of the Los Angeles Board of WILPF.

Cynthia Enloe is Research Professor of International Development and Women's Studies at Clark University. Her research and teaching explore feminist ways of making sense of women in globalized factories, war, militarism, and international politics. Among her books are *Bananas, Beaches and Bases* (2000), *Maneuvers: The International Politics of Militarizing Women's Lives* (2000), *The Curious Feminist: Women in a New Age of Empire*

(2004), and *Globalization and Militarism: Feminists Make the Link* (2007). In recent years, Enloe has been invited to lecture and give special seminars on feminism, militarization, and globalization in Japan, Korea, Turkey, Canada, Britain, and numerous colleges across the United States. She has written for *Ms. Magazine* and *Village Voice* and has appeared on National Public Radio and the BBC. She serves on the editorial boards of several scholarly journals, including *Signs* and the *International Feminist Journal of Politics*.

Megan Gerecke received her master's degree in political science at McGill University. Her research interests include comparative social policy, gender, conflict, and inequality. She has served as a research officer with the International Labour Organization's International Institute for Labour Studies and the McGill Institute for Health and Social Policy. She coauthored *The Work Equity Canada Index* (2008), *Employment-oriented Crisis Responses: Lessons from Argentina and the Republic of Korea* (2009), and "Social Security Spending in Times of Crisis" in *Global Social Policy* (forthcoming).

Sondra Hale is Professor of Anthropology and Women's Studies at the University of California, Los Angeles (UCLA). She has published *Gender Politics in Sudan: Islamism, Socialism, and the State* (1996) and many articles and book chapters on the topics of international gender studies; gender and social movements; women, war, conflict, and genocide; gender and citizenship; exile studies; and cultural studies. Her regional interests are in the Middle East and Africa. She is the coeditor of *The Journal of Middle East Women's Studies* and is currently coediting *Sudan's Killing Fields: Perspectives on Genocide*, under contract with the University of Michigan Press. Her work in progress is on gender and perpetual-conflict situations and political organizing in exile. Hale is an activist who was a founder of Feminists in Support of Palestinian Women and is the founder and coordinator of the Darfur Task Force. Hale's activism also includes various antiwar/anti-occupation activities (Iraq, Palestine, Lebanon). In addition to various teaching awards, Hale was given the Fair and Open Academic Environment Award from the Academic Senate of UCLA and has received awards from the National Science Foundation, the American Association of University Women, the National Endowment for the Humanities, and others.

Denise M. Horn is an Assistant Professor of International Affairs and Political Science at Northeastern University, Boston, where she spearheaded the development of a peer-to-peer training program in grassroots activism and advocacy, conducting local trainings in Boston and international trainings in South Africa, Brazil, and Thailand. She is now developing Northeastern's Global Corps Practicum, which had its inaugural launch in India in fall 2009, and will continue in Thailand this summer. Her book, *Women, Civil Society and the Geopolitics of Democratization* (2010), explores the gendered implications of democracy promotion for U.S. geopolitical strategy and global stability.

Tami Amanda Jacoby is Associate Professor of Political Studies and Acting Director of the Centre for Defence and Security Studies at the University of Manitoba, Winnipeg, Canada. She has published numerous articles on the Arab-Israeli conflict, women's movements in the Middle East, terrorism, and Canadian foreign policy. She is the author of *Bridging the Barrier: Israeli Unilateral Disengagement* (2007) and *Women in Zones of Conflict: Power and Resistance in Israel* (2005) and is coeditor of *Redefining Security in the Middle East* (2002).

Liz Kelly holds a PhD in Sociology and is Professor of Sexualised Violence at London Metropolitan University, where she is also director of the Child and Woman Abuse Studies Unit. She has been active in the field of violence against women and children for almost 30 years. She has published more than 70 book chapters and journal articles and is the author of *Surviving Sexual Violence* (1988), which established the concept of a "continuum of violence." She has just completed a project looking at trafficking of persons for labor and sexual exploitation in Central Asia. In 2000, Kelly was awarded a CBE (Commander of the Order of the British Empire) in the New Year's Honours List for "services combating violence against women and children," and in January 2005, she was appointed to the Board of Commissioners of the Women's National Commission.

Gwyn Kirk is a scholar-activist concerned with gender, race, and environmental justice in the service of genuine security, peacemaking, and creating a sustainable world. Her current research focuses on organizing efforts to promote cleanup and healing from environmental contamination caused by war and preparations for war. Kirk holds a PhD in political sociology from the London School of Economics. She is the coeditor of *Women's Lives: Multicultural Perspectives,* 4th edition (2007), a book that is used in women's studies classes and by feminist activists. She has written widely on ecofeminism, militarism, and women's peace organizing. She is a founding member of the International Women's Network Against Militarism, which links scholars and activists dealing with negative effects of U.S. military bases, budgets, and operations on local communities in the Asia-Pacific region and the United States. She is a member of the Women's International League for Peace and Freedom, San Francisco.

V. Spike Peterson is Professor in the School of Government and Public Policy at the University of Arizona, with courtesy appointments in the Department of Gender and Women's Studies, the Center for Latin American Studies, and International Studies. Her research interests include feminist international relations theory, global political economy, and critical post-structuralist and feminist theorizing. In 2003 she published *A Critical Rewriting of Global Political Economy: Integrating Reproductive, Productive and Virtual Economies* (2003), which introduced alternative analytics for examining intersections of ethnicity/race, class, gender, and national hierarchies in the context of today's globalizing—and polarizing—dynamics. She recently published, with Anne Sisson Runyan, *Global Gender Issues in the New Millennium* (2010). Her current research investigates informalization, global householding, and "coping, combat, and criminal economies" in conflict zones.

Susan Shepler is an Assistant Professor of International Peace and Conflict Resolution at American University. She received her PhD from the University of California, Berkeley, for research on the reintegration of former child soldiers and changing models of childhood and youth in postwar Sierra Leone. She has published articles on performance and child rights, the special concerns of girl child soldiers, transnational child fosterage in West Africa, and education and politics in Sierra Leone.

Elisabeth Jean Wood is Professor of Political Science at Yale University and Professor of the Santa Fe Institute. In her research on civil wars—patterns of political violence, the logic of collective action, the conditions for robust negotiated settlements—she draws on ethnographic field research; formal modeling; and analysis of macroeconomic, human rights violations, and other data. Her research currently focuses on patterns of sexual violence during war. She is the author of *Forging Democracy from Below: Insurgent Transitions in South Africa and El Salvador* (2000) and *Insurgent Collective Action and Civil War in El Salvador* (2003).